Microsoft

Understanding
Microsoft®
Windows 2000
Distributed Services

David Chappell

Understanding Microsoft Windows 2000 Distributed Services

Published by **Microsoft Press**
A Division of Microsoft Corporation
One Microsoft Way
Redmond, Washington 98052-6399

Library of Congress Cataloging-in-Publication Data

Chappell, David (David Wayne)
   Understanding Microsoft Windows 2000 Distributed Services / David Chappell.
      p. cm.
   Includes index.
   ISBN 1-57231-687-X
      1. Microsoft Windows (Computer file)   2. Operating systems (Computers)   I. Title.

   QA76.76.O63 C454   2000
   005.4'4769--dc21

                                                                        99-462382

Printed and bound in the United States of America.

1 2 3 4 5 6 7 8 9   QMQM   5 4 3 2 1 0

Distributed in Canada by Penguin Books Canada Limited.

A CIP catalogue record for this book is available from the British Library.

Microsoft Press books are available through booksellers and distributors worldwide. For further information about international editions, contact your local Microsoft Corporation office or contact Microsoft Press International directly at fax (425) 936-7329. Visit our Web site at mspress.microsoft.com.

Acquisitions Editor: Eric Stroo
Project Editor: Alice Turner
Technical Editor: Jim Fuchs

Chapter 10

Web Application Services 369

Contents

Foreword

Programmers are from Mars.

Technical managers are from Venus.

David Chappell is one of the few people I know who is well-liked and respected on both planets.

I first met David on June 27, 1995 at the first USENIX Conference on Object Oriented Technologies (COOTS). He and I were the token COM speakers at an otherwise fairly researchy conference. Upon arrival, I saw that David was presenting a COM tutorial, as was I, which caused me great concern since I didn't want to give the same tutorial as another speaker. After sitting through his half-day discussion of IUnknown, proxy/stub architectures, monikers, and IDispatch, I couldn't imagine a more different tutorial than the one I was giving on the exact same topics. David miraculously made it through an entire half-day tutorial without writing or showing a single line of code. While literally hundreds of Microsoft program managers do that every day, David actually conveyed a lot of technical information and had great perspective due to his recent recovery from a bout with CORBA.

Coincidentally, at that conference both David and I consummated book contracts. Mine was for *Essential COM* with Addison Wesley. His was for *Understanding ActiveX and OLE* with Microsoft Press. Though we both started writing at approximately the same time, David finished at least a year earlier than I did. Upon publication, he sent me a copy of his book with a note stating, "See Don, not one line of code." I was blown away and realized the crown of "definitive COM book" had just been taken. To this day, I still recommend *Understanding ActiveX and OLE* as a great "first book" on COM for both programmers and the management staff they oversee.

Fortunately for book authors, technology evolves. Both *Essential COM* and *Understanding ActiveX and OLE* are woefully out of date, especially when one factors in the arrival of Windows 2000. While OXID resolution and IRemUnknown (two topics David nailed in *Understanding ActiveX and OLE*) are still with us, they have taken a back seat in importance relative to technologies such as IIS, OLE DB/ADO, MSMQ, and Active Directory. The pervasiveness of COM+ further obsoletes many previous discussions of COM and even MTS (a topic that post-dated *Understanding ActiveX and OLE*). While COM component DLLs are still the deployment unit of choice, a modern COM application relies on many distributed communication protocols, not just DCOM. For that reason, I think David's new book could not be more on target.

Don Box
http://www.develop.com/dbox
February 2000

Preface

Authors always write the book that they would themselves like to read. When I learn about a new area, I'm interested first in the big picture. What is the overall structure of the subject? What are its parts? How do those parts fit together? And to some degree, at least, how do those parts work? This book tries to answer those questions for the core Windows 2000 services that support distributed applications.

This book contains virtually no code and not one screen shot. Please don't read it expecting to learn how to implement a Windows DNA application or how to configure Active Directory or anything similarly concrete. Instead, read this book if you want to understand the architecture and concepts that underlie the Windows 2000 distributed environment. And although much of this book is about technologies that are appearing for the first time in this new release, my goal isn't really to focus on what's new. Instead, I've tried to present a coherent picture of Microsoft's enterprise application environment as it stands at a particular moment in time. The release of Windows 2000 provides a convenient checkpoint in a constantly changing sea of technologies, and I've used it to circumscribe exactly which topics I cover. With very few exceptions, if something isn't part of the first Windows 2000 release it's not described here.

Who This Book Is For

A large part of this book's intended audience is developers looking for a foundation in Microsoft's key Windows DNA technologies.

What's here tries to provide both a broad view and enough detail to be useful. Yet this book also includes sections on Active Directory, Kerberos, and public key technology, none of which is usually considered a developer topic. I'm convinced, however, that building distributed applications in the Windows 2000 world requires at least a basic knowledge of all three. Directory services and security services affect everybody, and developers are no exception. In fact, I hope that even administrators who never write a line of code will find these chapters useful as an introduction to the topics.

And speaking of people who don't write code, this book is also aimed at managers. My goal has been to explain each technology in enough detail to give technical managers a solid feeling for what it does and how it works, but not so much detail as to make them lose interest (most of the time, anyway). I also hope that reading this book will give managers some sense of the complex, multifaceted world in which their developers must live.

Finally, I hope that advanced undergraduate and beginning graduate students will find the material in this book useful. Windows 2000 provides one of the best examples we've yet seen of an integrated, coherent set of distributed services, making it an appealing pedagogical target. The impending ubiquity of those services should also make them appealing to students; some knowledge of what's actually used in the world is not a bad thing for new graduates to have.

How To Read This Book

This is not a book that must be read in strict sequence. Depending on what you already know and what you'd like to know, you can read any chapters that look interesting. Here's my advice:

- If you're new to this world or want to start with a broad overview, read Chapter 1.
- If you're interested in Windows 2000 directory and distributed security services, read Chapters 2 through 4

(ideally in that order). Later chapters reference this material, and you'll eventually want to know at least a good chunk of it, but the later chapters should still mostly make sense even if you skip the directory and security topics on your first pass.

- If you're primarily interested in more traditional developer topics, jump to Chapter 5. Each chapter after this assumes you've read the previous one, so unless you already know an area you should probably read these in order.

I'm a big believer in doing what interests you, and the margin notes in this book are meant to help you do that. If a section seems too detailed, I encourage you to read only the notes until you get to a topic that looks more interesting. You can always come back later and read the complete text if you need to.

Acknowledgments

This book is rooted in the seminars I've written and delivered on these topics over the last few years. I'd like to begin by thanking everybody who has listened to me talk about these subjects—you played a huge part in shaping this book.

I also had significant help from a large group of remarkable reviewers, all of whom took time away from their own pursuits to help me with mine. My sincere thanks to Rudolph Balaz, Bob Beauchemin, John Brezak, Mark Brown, Peter Brundrett, Ilan Caron, Charlie Chase, Behrooz Chitsaz, Andrew Cushman, Paul Darcy, Ted Demopoulos, Michael Dennis, Alan Dickman, Michael Emanuel, Bill Estrem, Trevor Freeman, Jocelyn Garner, Phil Garrett, David Gristwood, Michael Gross, Richard Harrington, Markus Horstmann, Peter Houston, Efim Hudis, Doron Juster, Mary Kirtland, Andreas Luther, Joe Maloney, Jim Moffitt, Eric Newcomer, David Platt, Adithya Raghunathan, Dave Reed, Patrick Questembert, and Roger Wolter. Yet despite all of this expert assistance, responsibility for any remaining errors lies solely with me.

I'm especially grateful to Don Box, both for insightful review comments and for contributing a foreword that made me realize how fast our world changes (as if I could forget).

I'd also like to thank the people I've worked with at Microsoft Press, including Eric Stroo, whose patience I tried many times; Jim Fuchs, this book's hard-working and wide-ranging technical editor; and Alice Turner, who is hands down my favorite of all the editors I've ever worked with.

Finally, I'd like to thank Michele Bahneman of Hudson, Wisconsin for a timely and much-appreciated batch of chocolate chip cookies, and especially Diana Catignani for all kinds of affectionate support throughout the final phases of this project.

David Chappell
www.chappellassoc.com
Minneapolis/San Francisco
February 2000

Chapter One

The Windows 2000 Distributed Environment

What's required to build an effective distributed environment? What does it take to transform a group of individual computers into a usable, manageable whole? Over the last twenty years or so, we in the computer industry have had plenty of experience with this problem, and perhaps the most important thing we've learned is that answering these questions is not simple. Distributed environments pose a number of difficult problems.

Creating an effective distributed environment isn't simple

First, a distributed environment requires some kind of distributed infrastructure, complete with the services needed to make that environment usable. How is information about the people, computers, and applications in the environment made available? How are the services and information a distributed environment provides made accessible to the right users, yet kept inaccessible to the wrong users? Second, a distributed environment should allow the creation of distributed applications. Doing this well requires solving yet another set of hard problems. For example, how should these diverse pieces of software communicate? How will they find one another? How can scalable applications be created, applications that support many simultaneous users, Web-based

Building a distributed environment requires solving a number of complex problems

and otherwise? Finally, an effective distributed environment implies the ability to manage a potentially large number of applications, computers, and users, spread around a building, a campus, or the entire world. Distributed management brings its own set of challenges that must be solved to create a workable environment.

Successfully creating an effective distributed environment requires using the right distributed services. Microsoft Windows 2000, the successor to Windows NT 4.0, includes the most powerful group of distributed services ever bundled with a mainstream operating system. While similar services have been available from various vendors (including Microsoft) for several years, the release of Windows 2000 marks the first time a complete set has been made a standard part of the system. Accordingly, deploying Windows 2000 in all but the simplest configurations requires using the distributed services it includes. The goal of this book is to help you understand what those services are, what they have to offer, and how they fit together.

Defining Distributed Services

What exactly is a distributed service? Answering this question requires thinking first about how networks are organized. Nearly all networks today use several protocols simultaneously, organizing them into layers as shown in Figure 1-1.[1] As the figure shows, the bottom layer contains various kinds of subnetworks, which are just ways to physically move bytes between machines. Example subnetworks include local area networks (LANs) such as Ethernet, wide area networks (WANs) such as frame relay networks, and various kinds of point-to-point connections such as T-1 and T-3 lines.

---

1. It's still common to use the seven-layer Open Systems Interconnection (OSI) model to illustrate network layers, but it shouldn't be—the model is more than twenty years old and hopelessly out of date. The layered structure shown here is a more useful description of how networks are built today.

Figure 1-1 *A typical network today organizes its protocols into layers.*

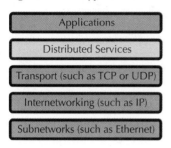

Most organizations use several different kinds of subnetworks, so the next layer in the stack houses a protocol capable of routing data across diverse subnetworks. This function is commonly called internetworking, and the most widely used choice for this protocol today is the Internet Protocol (IP). But IP, like most internetworking protocols, is unreliable—it might lose some of the data it's transferring. Accordingly, the transport layer protocol above it can add reliability, guaranteeing that whatever data is sent actually arrives at its destination. Not every application needs this reliability, though, so simpler transport layer protocols also exist that don't guarantee delivery. Today's most common choice for a reliable transport protocol is the Transmission Control Protocol (TCP), while the most popular choice for an unreliable transport protocol is the User Datagram Protocol (UDP).

IP, TCP, and UDP are today's most common middle-layer protocols

The protocols described so far collectively provide a way to move bytes, perhaps reliably, between machines connected to any kind of subnetwork. If you're a masochist, you can build a bare-bones distributed environment using only the services these protocols provide. For example, distributed applications can be built that access the transport protocol's services directly through an application programming interface (API) named *sockets*. In the Microsoft environment, this API is called *Windows Sockets* or, more often, just *Winsock*. Winsock-based applications can be simple and fast, and plenty of them exist.

Services can be built directly on a transport protocol such as TCP

Creating common
distributed services
makes more sense than
building directly on a
transport protocol

Yet creating an application directly on a transport protocol can be a little challenging—all the developer has to build on is a way to move bytes between machines. Trying to create a true distributed environment with only a basic byte transfer service to work with is nobody's idea of a good time. Instead, distributed services built on top of some transport protocol can underlie an application and provide an infrastructure for a distributed environment. Because distributed services are implemented between—that is, in the middle of—a distributed application and the transport layer, they're sometimes called *middleware*. Whatever they're called, however, a powerful set of distributed services helps immeasurably in building an effective distributed environment.

What should those distributed services be? Reasonable people can disagree on the answer, but it's sometimes useful to think of the essential distributed services as falling into two broad categories:

- *Infrastructure services*   This category includes directory services that make it easier to find resources in a distributed environment and security services that control access to information and services in that environment. One might easily argue that many other technologies also fall into this category, but to keep this book to a manageable length, I've chosen to focus on directory and security services.

- *Application support services*   The group of services in this category support building distributed applications using remote procedure calls (RPCs), message queuing, or Web-based access via the Hypertext Transfer Protocol (HTTP). This category also includes services that make it easier to build more scalable and correct distributed applications, such as services for performing transactions involving multiple databases.

Some of the distributed services in Windows 2000 have been part of earlier releases of Windows NT, while others are new with this most recent version. Whatever their genesis, these technologies as a group comprise a powerful, well-integrated set of services that offers a solid foundation for building a distributed computing environment.

Infrastructure Services

In any distributed environment, many services can be considered part of the infrastructure. A distributed file service that allows access to files on other machines is very nice to have, for instance, as is some way to submit work to remote printers. But because they're new in this release and because they solve critical problems, two infrastructure services are of paramount importance in Windows 2000: directory services and distributed security services.

Good directory and distributed security services are essential

Directory Services

By definition, a distributed environment has users, applications, and computers scattered about. To effectively use the environment's resources, each of these must be able to find the required resources when they're needed. One part of a distributed application, for example, might need to find another part running on a different system. Printers might be scattered in various places, yet still must be accessible to users of the environment. And each of those users should be able to log in from any of a number of workstations and still be presented with his or her own familiar environment, which requires finding information about each user's personal preferences.

Lots of information must be made accessible in a distributed environment

All of these things and more can be accomplished using a directory service. The most widely used directory service in data networks today is the Domain Name System (DNS), and Windows 2000 makes extensive use of DNS. But Windows 2000 also includes

Windows 2000 relies on both DNS and Active Directory

Active Directory, a wholly new directory service that implements the Lightweight Directory Access Protocol (LDAP). To see how DNS and Active Directory work together, it's useful to first take a look at how domains are organized in Windows 2000.

Users and computers are grouped into domains

Domains in Windows 2000   Like earlier versions of Windows NT, Windows 2000 allows grouping users and computers into *domains*. Using domains is not required, of course, and not all computers or users belong to a domain, but to fully use Windows 2000's distributed services, domains are all but obligatory. Figure 1-2 shows an example Windows 2000 domain installed at a fictitious financial services firm called QwickBank. Although a domain can mix Windows 2000 systems with computers running Windows 9x or older versions of Windows NT—a subject that's discussed in more detail in Chapter 2—this example assumes that the domain is purely Windows 2000.

Figure 1-2   *Workstations, member servers, and one or more domain controllers can be grouped into a domain.*

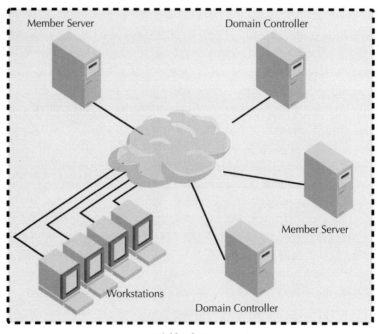

qwickbank.com

As Figure 1-2 shows, a domain can contain computers acting in various roles, including:

- *Workstations*   These systems act as clients, and in a pure Windows 2000 environment typically run Windows 2000 Professional.
- *Member servers*   These systems typically run some flavor of Windows 2000 Server, and might host various kinds of applications. A Web server, a database management system (DBMS) such as Oracle or Microsoft SQL Server, or some other kind of server application is likely to run on a member server.
- *Domain controllers*   Every domain must have at least one domain controller, and most will have two or more. A domain controller must run some version of Windows 2000 Server and, as described shortly, plays an important role in keeping a domain functioning.

There are no particular requirements about the physical location of the machines in a domain. The machines might all be in the same room, or they might be spread across several countries. Whatever its geographic boundaries, however, every domain must have a name. In earlier versions of Windows NT, domains were assigned NetBIOS names, simple character strings that could be essentially anything. In Windows 2000, however, every domain must be assigned a DNS name. For instance, since the domain in Figure 1-2 is deployed at a company named QwickBank, the domain is named qwickbank.com. Windows 2000 domains in a particular organization are likely to be assigned names that contain whatever DNS name has been allocated to that organization. And as is described in Chapter 2, Windows 2000 domains can be organized into trees and forests, allowing domains to be grouped together in useful ways.

Every Windows 2000 domain is assigned a DNS name

Active Directory   Like all directory services, Active Directory provides a database to store information about a domain, and provides protocols that let clients access and modify the information in that database. Every domain controller in a domain has a copy

Active Directory provides a replicated database accessible throughout a domain of the complete directory database for that domain, and changes made to any copy of that data are automatically replicated to all other copies. The information in that database is organized into a hierarchy, providing a natural way to construct names.

DNS is used to locate an appropriate Active Directory server

To locate a copy of the Active Directory database for a particular domain, a client uses DNS. DNS is a very widely deployed technology today, providing the backbone directory for the worldwide Internet and countless private networks. As shown in Figure 1-3, a client requests DNS to provide the location of a domain controller for a particular domain. The DNS server responds with the IP address of that machine, and the client can then contact it to access the desired information. (The client caches the domain controller's address, so a DNS lookup isn't required before every Active Directory access.)

Figure 1-3 *A client uses DNS to find the right domain controller.*

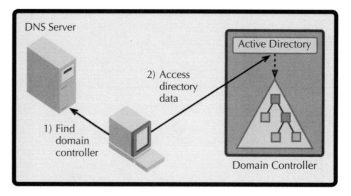

Active Directory and DNS are complementary

To get at the information in Active Directory, a client uses LDAP. LDAP is a multi-vendor standard defined by the Internet Engineering Task Force (IETF), and it's supported by virtually all major directory service vendors today. In many ways, LDAP is complementary to DNS. DNS is simple and fast, and it's an effective technology for straightforward tasks such as mapping machine names to individual machine addresses. In Windows 2000, these traditional functions are still performed by DNS—Active Directory doesn't change this. But DNS is not so good at providing fine-grained access to information in a directory database, which is where LDAP shines. The information Active Directory stores about people, printers, distributed applications, and more is actually accessed via LDAP; DNS is used only to find the right domain controller to look in.

Having a single directory service in a distributed environment is a very attractive goal. Given the profusion of competing technologies in this area, it's also been very hard to achieve. With the emergence of DNS and LDAP as multi-vendor standards, however, this long-sought goal is finally within reach. For a more detailed examination of DNS and Active Directory in Windows 2000, see Chapter 2.

Distributed Security Services

Having a good directory service can be a great boon—it makes life better for everybody who uses a distributed environment. Yet there are some potential users of that environment whose lives we'd like to make worse rather than better. Almost every Windows 2000 domain has the potential to attract attackers, people who'd like nothing better than to illicitly access, modify, or otherwise mess with the domain's information. As a result, it's critical that a domain's infrastructure include good distributed security services.

Good security services are essential

Distributed security comprises several different services. The most important of these are the following:

- *Authentication* Proves you are who you say you are. When you log in, for example, you're typically required to enter your password, a value that only you know. Since only you know this value, entering it correctly authenticates you.

- *Authorization* Determines what you're allowed to do. Once a server knows who you are, that is, once you've been authenticated, the next problem is to determine what operations you're allowed—authorized—to perform. Can you read this file? Modify that directory entry? Authorization is also sometimes known as *access control.*

- *Data integrity* Ensures that data isn't modified in transit. An attacker might read a packet from the wire, modify it, then send it on its way. If the receiver of that data can't tell that what it's getting isn't what was sent, problems can ensue. A data integrity service allows a receiver to detect modifications in the data it receives.

- *Data privacy* Ensures that data isn't read in transit. To accomplish this, the data is encrypted by the sender, then decrypted on the receiving system. This service is also sometimes referred to as *confidentiality*.

Encryption underlies many aspects of distributed security

Encryption is a fundamental security mechanism that underlies more than just data privacy, and it's a simple idea: it means transforming data into a form that can't be read until it has been decrypted. Encryption algorithms typically perform this transformation using a key, which is just a byte string of some length. The distributed security services in Windows 2000 make use of both *secret key* encryption, in which the same key is used for encryption and decryption, and *public key* encryption, where different keys are used for encryption and decryption.[2]

Windows 2000 supports several protocols for distributed technology

To provide distributed security services, security protocols are required. Windows 2000 has built-in support for three primary security protocols:

- *NTLM* The acronym stands for NT LAN Manager, which betrays this protocol's origins. The standard security protocol in earlier versions of Windows NT, NTLM is supported in Windows 2000 for backward compatibility.

- *Kerberos* The core security protocol in Windows 2000, Kerberos relies primarily on secret key encryption.

---

2. Secret key encryption is also called *private key, symmetric, single key,* or *shared secret* encryption, but I'll say secret key throughout this book. Similarly, public key encryption is also known as *asymmetric* encryption, but I'll continue to use public key.

- *Secure Sockets Layer (SSL)* The standard security protocol for the Internet, SSL can also be applied in other environments. SSL uses both public key and secret key encryption. A version of SSL has been standardized by the IETF under the name Transport Layer Security (TLS), and Windows 2000 supports both SSL and the newer TLS.

In a pure Windows 2000 domain, users rely on Kerberos to log in—NTLM is no longer needed. Yet many, perhaps even most, organizations will also use SSL to address some of their distributed security requirements. These two protocols are at the heart of distributed security in Windows 2000.

Kerberos Kerberos was created at the Massachusetts Institute of Technology in the early 1980s, and an open implementation of the protocol has been available for many years. Although Windows 2000 Kerberos doesn't use this code—it's a completely new implementation done by Microsoft—the fact that Kerberos has been in the public domain for so many years is one of its most attractive attributes. No one yet knows how to prove that a protocol is completely secure, so the best we can do is let security experts (and hackers) around the world examine and attack a protocol. Because it's been available for a relatively long time, Kerberos has attracted a good deal of this kind of attention. More important, it has withstood the attacks well enough to earn the trust of the security community. And like LDAP, Kerberos is defined today in a standard specified by the IETF.

> Kerberos is a trusted, well-understood technology

Kerberos typically uses secret key encryption to provide authentication, although a newer Kerberos option, one also supported in Windows 2000, adds the ability for a user to log in using public key technology as well. If the client requests it, Kerberos can also provide data integrity and data privacy, both of which always rely on secret key encryption. To provide these services, Kerberos must know various things about the users, computers, and applications

> Kerberos provides authentication, data integrity, and data privacy

in a particular domain. The Kerberos software therefore makes use of the Active Directory database, which means that the security and directory services in Windows 2000 are tightly integrated with one another.

Using Kerberos, a user can acquire a byte string called a *ticket*, then reliably identify herself by presenting this ticket to a server. As shown in Figure 1-4, a client contacts Kerberos's Key Distribution Center (KDC) running on a domain controller to acquire a ticket to a particular server application in that domain. The client then presents this ticket to that application, which can use it to authenticate the client.

Figure 1-4 *Kerberos allows users to acquire tickets, then present those tickets to prove their own identity.*

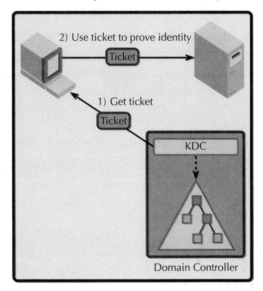

Although it's not shown in the figure, acquiring a ticket also involves securely acquiring encryption keys that can be used to provide data integrity and data privacy services between the client and the application. How this is accomplished and much more about Windows 2000 Kerberos is described in Chapter 3.

Public Key Technologies   Kerberos is a fine choice for a security service in a well-defined environment, such as a company or university. In the enormous, anonymous world of the public Internet, however, Kerberos is less appropriate. The SSL protocol, originally created by Netscape, is an effective alternative for this more diffuse, less structured environment.

Like Kerberos, SSL can provide authentication, data integrity, and data privacy. Also like Kerberos, SSL uses secret key encryption to provide data integrity and data privacy. Unlike Kerberos, however, SSL always relies on public key encryption for authentication. With public key technology, a user or server application that wishes to prove its identity can add a *digital signature* to a message. That client can than present the signed message along with a *certificate*, allowing the receiver to authenticate the sender. Figure 1-5 shows a greatly simplified version of how SSL allows a client to prove its identity to a server using a digital signature and certificate.

SSL can also provide authentication, data integrity, and data privacy

Figure 1-5   *SSL can use certificates and digital signatures for authentication.*

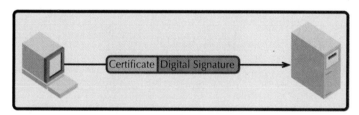

As Figure 1-5 shows, SSL doesn't explicitly rely on a shared server between client and server as does Kerberos. Instead, certificates are issued by organizations called *certification authorities,* and unlike tickets, which typically expire in only a few hours, certificates can remain valid for months or even years. The mechanisms required to issue, use, and manage certificates, sometimes referred to as a public key infrastructure (PKI), are not simple, and Windows 2000 includes a good deal of technology devoted to

SSL relies on public key technology, including certificates and certification authorities

addressing these issues. That technology, along with the basics of public key encryption and the SSL protocol, is described in Chapter 4.

Application Support Services

Distributed environments must support distributed applications

Directory services and security services are essential pieces of a distributed environment's infrastructure. Every time a user logs in to a pure Windows 2000 domain, for example, both Active Directory and Kerberos are used. But to a great degree, people build distributed computing environments to support distributed applications. Accordingly, services that support these applications are also critically important.

Windows 2000 includes several services for supporting distributed applications

The core directory and security services in Windows 2000 are brand new—they didn't exist in older versions of Windows NT. This is not the case for the application support services. While some entirely new technologies in this area have been added to Windows 2000, most of its services for supporting distributed applications are new versions of what was available in Windows NT 4. The most important of those services are the following:

- *The Component Object Model (COM) and Distributed COM (DCOM)* Provide basic component services, the foundation for building software from components.

- *Data access services* Provide APIs for accessing data, the most important of which is ActiveX Data Objects (ADO).

- *Distributed transaction services* Guarantee that operations involving multiple databases or other software can behave correctly by relying on the Distributed Transaction Coordinator (DTC).

- *COM+* Extends COM with more advanced component services, including transaction services, services for building more scalable applications, and others.

- *Message queuing services* Provide services for message-oriented communication using Microsoft Message Queuing (MSMQ).

- *Web services*   Provide services for building Web-accessible applications, including Active Server Pages (ASPs) supported by Internet Information Services (IIS).

Even though they're not completely new, these services will form the foundation for a large number of distributed applications. Understanding what they provide and how they fit together is essential for anyone planning to work in a Windows 2000 world.

Component Services: COM and DCOM

Modern software development makes extensive use of *objects*, which are encapsulated combinations of code and data. Different programming languages implement objects in similar but not identical ways. For example, C++, Java, and Microsoft Visual Basic all support objects, but each language has its own idiosyncratic view of what an object is and how it behaves. If all software were developed in only one of these languages, we could adopt its notion of an object universally, and everything would be fine. But for better or worse, the Windows 2000 world is a more diverse place than that. We often need to create software that can be used by other software regardless of the language either is written in. And given the near-universal acceptance of object technology today, we'd like to use objects to do it. What's needed is a standard approach to objects that's usable from any language.

Object technology is ubiquitous but heterogeneous

That is exactly what COM provides. By defining a common set of conventions for creating and using objects—conventions that can be applied in virtually any language—COM provides a standard way for any chunk of software to access services provided by any other chunk of software. Because it's so broadly applicable and so useful, COM is used in some way by most software created today for the Microsoft environment.

COM provides a standard way for software to provide services to other software

Like other kinds of objects, a COM object provides its services through *methods*, which are generally much like the procedures and functions of non-object-oriented languages. Methods are

COM objects implement interfaces that contain methods

grouped into *interfaces*, and a COM object can potentially implement several different interfaces. Figure 1-6 shows a COM object with two interfaces, IAccount and ITransfer. In this example, IAccount has three methods: Credit, which credits a deposit to a specific account; Debit, which subtracts money from an account; and GetBalance, which returns the balance in a particular account. ITransfer has only a single method, MoveMoney, which transfers money from one account to another. Every COM object is built to expose its services via interfaces, and clients always access those services solely by invoking an interface's methods.

Figure 1-6 *A COM object exposes its services through methods grouped into interfaces.*

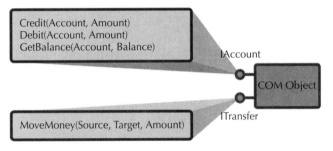

A COM object can run in the same process or in a different process than its client

Figure 1-7 illustrates another important fact about COM: whether a COM object is implemented in a dynamic link library (DLL) loaded into its client, in a separate process on the same machine as its client, or on some other machine entirely, it exposes its services in just the same way. In fact, a client need not be aware of which implementation is in use unless it cares to be—COM provides the necessary plumbing to hide the differences. Clients talk to objects in DLLs and objects in processes on the same machine using basic COM, but to communicate with an object running on another machine, more is required. For this, clients use DCOM.

Invoking a COM method is like calling a local or remote procedure

Invoking a method in a COM object is much like calling a procedure or a subroutine in a non-object-oriented language. Invoking a method in a remote COM object is likewise much like the conventional notion of a remote procedure call (RPC). The basic notion of RPC[3] is simple: take the familiar notion of a procedure call, then extend it across a network. A client making the call can behave much as if it were making an ordinary local call, but the procedure actually executes in some other process on another machine. To programmers accustomed to writing code that makes procedure calls—that is, to pretty much all programmers—this is a very familiar model.

Figure 1-7 *A COM object can look the same to its client no matter how it's implemented.*

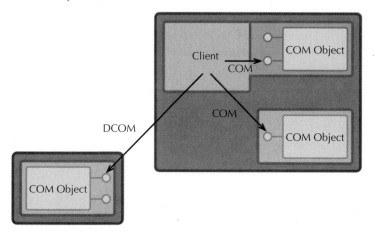

COM was first made available in 1993, and DCOM was added with the release of Windows NT 4 in 1996. In both of these incarnations, COM was entirely RPC-oriented. In the Windows 2000 release, however, COM also supports asynchronous (that is, non-blocking) communication. For a more detailed look at COM and DCOM, see Chapter 5.

---

3. The term RPC is arguably a little outdated today. Instead of calling procedures, modern programmers call methods in objects, and so the term *remote method invocation* is sometimes used. But the concept is much the same—little more than the terminology has changed.

Data Access Services

A large percentage of distributed applications access some kind of data. Most often, that data is stored in a DBMS. While each commercial DBMS typically provides its own API for applications to access the data it contains, it's also useful to have one common API that can be used for many different data sources.

Microsoft has defined several different interfaces for data access

Microsoft has made several attempts at providing that common interface. The oldest interface, and still the most widely supported, is an API named Open Database Connectivity (ODBC). ODBC is defined as a group of C function calls, and ODBC drivers are available today for most popular DBMS's. But with the advent of COM, APIs defined as C function calls became passé. Today, Microsoft defines most new APIs—for data access and other purposes—as a group of COM objects, with each object implementing an appropriate set of interfaces. The first COM-based, generic data access interface Microsoft produced was OLE Database, more often called just OLE DB. While OLE DB is very powerful, it's also a bit too complex for the average developer. Accordingly, Microsoft created yet another data access interface called ActiveX Data Objects (ADO).

ADO is the most commonly used data access interface for new applications today

As Figure 1-8 shows, an application can potentially use any of the three interfaces. ADO is always implemented on top of OLE DB, while OLE DB might or might not be implemented on ODBC. ADO can be used effectively from all kinds of programming languages, however, and it's the data access interface Microsoft most encourages developers writing new applications for Windows 2000 to use. The Windows 2000 data access interfaces are described in more detail in Chapter 6.[4]

---

4. It's not obvious what data access interfaces have to do with Windows 2000 distributed services. Why bother to mention them here at all? The answer is that describing how some other Windows 2000 distributed services work, especially the transaction services provided by COM+, requires knowing at least the basics of Microsoft's data access interface technologies.

Figure 1-8 *An application can use ADO, OLE DB, or ODBC to access data.*

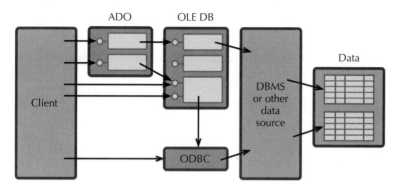

Distributed Transaction Services

Transactions play an important part in many distributed applications. A transaction can be viewed (in a slightly simple-minded way) as a group of operations, such as changes to one or more databases, that must commit or abort as a single unit. Either every operation in the transaction happens, or none of them do. For example, transferring money between two bank accounts requires incrementing one account balance and decrementing the other. If only one of these actions occurs, someone will be unhappy. Wrapping both operations in a transaction ensures that both events occur or neither one does.

Most DBMS's today support transactions, and so applications can sometimes meet their transactional requirements by relying on the underlying DBMS. (In fact, all three of Microsoft's data access interfaces allow applications to start and end DBMS-managed transactions). Yet it's not uncommon for the operations in a transaction to span multiple DBMS's. In this case, the transaction management functions of any one of the DBMS's involved typically won't be sufficient. Instead, some other service is required to make sure

Transactions are important for many kinds of applications

Some transactions must span multiple DBMS's

that the operations in this distributed transaction commit or abort as a group. In Windows 2000, a service named the Distributed Transaction Coordinator (DTC) is responsible for doing this.

DTC allows transactions to span multiple DBMS's on multiple machines

DTC allows applications to use transactions that span multiple machines and multiple DBMS's. DTC can be used with Microsoft's DBMS, SQL Server, and with DBMS products from other companies, such as Oracle, and IBM's DB2. Although DTC runs only on Microsoft operating systems, it can also ensure transactional behavior for DBMS's running on other systems, including UNIX and IBM mainframes. How DTC works is described in Chapter 7.

Component Services: COM+

COM+ is the next generation of COM technology

COM has become ubiquitous—it's used in some way by the great majority of software written for Microsoft operating systems today. Software technology is a dynamic thing, however, and Windows 2000 introduces the next iteration of COM-based technology. Known as COM+, this release doesn't change the fundamentals of COM—objects, interfaces, and methods remain much the same. Instead, COM+ brings several additions to this existing foundation.

Many aspects of COM+ are derived from the former MTS

An important subset of the technologies in COM+ is derived from those originally made available in the Microsoft Transaction Services (MTS). Although the "MTS" name is no longer used, the services it provided survive in Windows 2000 as part of COM+. Those services, including support for transactions, authorization based on a client's role, object state management, and more, are enhanced somewhat in COM+, but developers who already understand how MTS works will have no trouble grasping this part of COM.

COM+ also includes several other services, including the following:

- *Queued Components* Allows methods in COM objects to be invoked across MSMQ rather than using COM's traditional mechanisms.
- *COM+ Events* Allows objects to subscribe to events, then be notified when those events occur.
- *Miscellaneous other features* For example, object pooling, which allows caching instances of COM objects for later reuse.

The Windows 2000 release also supports a feature called Component Load Balancing (CLB). Originally part of COM+, it's available as a technology preview for Windows 2000. The code is fully functional, but the official CLB release is in another product, shipping shortly after Windows 2000. CLB allows COM objects to be created on the most available system in a defined cluster of machines, and so allows intelligently balancing an application's load across those systems.

Many (although not all) of COM+'s features are provided by an enhanced version of the standard COM runtime library, commonly referred to as just the COM runtime. Beginning with COM's initial release, this library has provided standard services used by virtually all COM objects. With COM+, services that were previously provided by MTS are now built into the COM runtime, and some new services are added. As shown in Figure 1-9, the COM runtime can interpose itself between clients and COM objects, intercepting all calls made on those objects. By getting in the middle of every client request made to an object,

COM+ provides many of its services through an enhanced version of the COM runtime library the COM runtime can automatically provide services such as transactions, authorization, and state management. The enhancements COM+ brings to COM are described in more detail in Chapter 8.

Figure 1-9 *An enhanced version of the COM runtime library, a key part of COM+, provides various services to COM objects.*

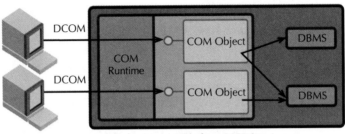

Windows 2000 Server

Message Queuing Services

Making a client wait for a response before going on can sometimes be a problem

For some kinds of distributed applications, the RPC style of communication provided by COM and DCOM is perfect. There are times, however, when RPC just won't do. For instance, with RPC each remote call blocks the client; the client can't perform other work until it receives a response from the server. In some cases, this can make the client seem very unresponsive, leading to unhappy users. Another limitation of RPC is that both the client and the server must be running at the same time—there's no way for the client to post a message that can be picked up by the server at some later time. While RPC is simple for developers to understand and use, it's also a little inflexible.

Message queuing allows a client to send a message, then proceed without waiting

For distributed applications that can't live within the constraints imposed by RPC, message queuing can be a good alternative. Although sometimes a little more complex than RPC, message queuing offers more flexibility. Now, a client need no longer wait for a response from its server—in fact, that server might not even be running at the time the client sends a request. Instead, applications communicate by sending messages to queues and receiving messages from queues.

First released in late 1997, MSMQ allows building distributed applications that communicate through queues. As shown in Figure 1-10, MSMQ allows an application to send a message to a queue.

Figure 1-10   *With MSMQ, the parts of a distributed application communicate by sending messages to and receiving messages from queues.*

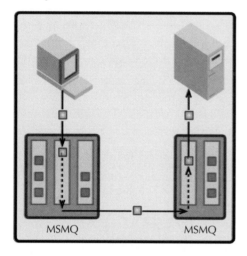

If necessary, MSMQ can then route that message to some other queue, from which it eventually is retrieved by another application. This application might send a message back to the sender, typically via a different queue. The sender isn't required to wait for a response, and might not even be running when the message is sent. With MSMQ, making a request and getting a response to that request are completely separate, unlike the lockstep call and response of RPC. MSMQ can be a powerful tool for many kinds of distributed applications, and it's described in Chapter 9.

MSMQ provides message queuing services

Web Services

Access from the Web has become essential

How many distributed applications will be built for Windows 2000 that don't have at least the option of a Web browser interface? The correct answer is a number very close to zero. Whether used on the public Internet or across an organization's intranet, applications today must be Web-accessible—users demand it.

IIS allows browsers to access files and applications

To meet that demand, Windows 2000 includes Internet Information Services (IIS). Like all Web servers, IIS allows its browser clients to request ordinary files containing HyperText Markup Language (HTML) tags; the clients request those files by means of Uniform Resource Locators (URLs). Also like other Web servers, IIS allows clients to pass it URLs that identify applications as well as files. As those applications execute, they dynamically generate HTML and other information which is then passed back to IIS and on to the browser that requested it.

As Figure 1-11 shows, there are many ways for IIS to produce the information sent back to the client.

Figure 1-11 *IIS provides several ways to generate the information it returns to browser clients, ranging from reading simple files to constructing complex applications that access databases.*

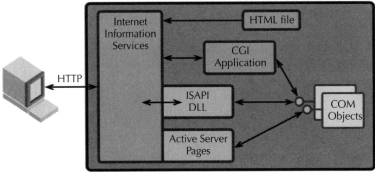

Windows 2000 Server

The simplest approach is for IIS to read HTML-tagged data from an ordinary file. It's also possible to run an application that dynamically generates that HTML, perhaps by first querying a database. IIS supports several different ways to create this kind of application, including:

- *The Common Gateway Interface (CGI)*   Allows creating applications that run as a separate process each time a new request is made.
- *The Internet Server API (ISAPI)*   Allows creating DLLs that are loaded on demand.
- *Active Server Pages (ASPs)*   A technology that allows developers to create programs—using relatively simple scripting languages such as Visual Basic Scripting Edition (more commonly called VBScript)—that are executed on the Web server. ASPs provide the best combination of power and ease of use, and so are the most common approach for building applications with IIS.

Applications that use any of these approaches can create and use COM objects, which gives the applications access to databases, other applications, and more. IIS is also integrated with COM+, allowing those applications to use the services it provides, including transactions and others.

IIS applications can use COM objects and COM+ services

Given the popularity of Web browser interfaces, the relative ease of building Web-based applications, and the demand for accessibility across public and private networks, many new distributed applications that in the past might have been built in some other way are today created using Web technology. The standard way to do that in Windows 2000 is by using IIS. How Web-based applications work with IIS is described in Chapter 10.

Managing Distributed Services

Like many other aspects of Windows 2000, distributed services must somehow be managed. The standard approach to creating Windows 2000 management tools is to build those tools as *Microsoft Management Console (MMC) snap-ins*. Although MMC

Management tools are created as MMC snap-ins

can also be used on other Microsoft operating systems, it's applied consistently throughout Windows 2000 as the approach for building management tools.

Multiple MMC snap-ins can be combined into an MMC console

An MMC snap-in is a COM component, and it must run under the control of an *MMC console*. A single console might contain one or more MMC snap-ins, each focused on a particular task, and different consoles can be created for different purposes. For example, one administrator might create a console that includes all of the snap-ins used to manage Active Directory, while another might regularly use a console that contains only the Component Services snap-in used to manage COM+ applications. Even though this isn't a hands-on guide to Windows 2000 administration, I'll mention snap-ins as appropriate throughout the rest of this book.

Using Windows 2000 Distributed Services

Real applications will use many of Windows 2000's distributed services together

The simplest way to get a sense of how the distributed services in Windows 2000 work together is to look at a couple of example applications. Both of the examples shown in this section address the same problem—a very simple distributed banking system deployed at the fictitious QwickBank corporation—and both rely at bottom on the simple banking COM object described earlier in this chapter. As shown in Figure 1-6 on page 16, this object has two interfaces: IAccount, with the methods Credit, Debit, and GetBalance; and ITransfer, containing the single method MoveMoney. Using these methods, a client of the object can manipulate account balances, check those balances, and move money between accounts. Since account balances are actually maintained as entries in one or more databases, the object uses the appropriate database to carry out each operation. And because some of the operations, such as that carried out by ITransfer's MoveMoney, might require atomic changes to two different databases, both example applications will make use of the transaction services provided by COM+ and DTC. (In fact, it's likely that the applications would also use other COM+ services, although no others are referenced in this simple scenario.) The end user acting as this object's client might be a bank teller handling requests from walk-in customers, or perhaps the customer himself, accessing his own account over the Internet. The following scenarios illustrate both of these possibilities.

An Example with a DCOM Client

The first scenario is shown in Figure 1-12. In this example, the client application—perhaps written in Visual Basic or C++—uses DCOM to access an instance of the banking object just described. To do this, however, the client must first use DCOM to create the object on the server machine. Transparently to the application, the client system uses Active Directory to find a machine on which it can create the object (step 1 in Figure 1-12).

A client can use Active Directory to determine where an object should be created

Figure 1-12 *A client can use DCOM to access business logic, relying on other services for a complete application.*

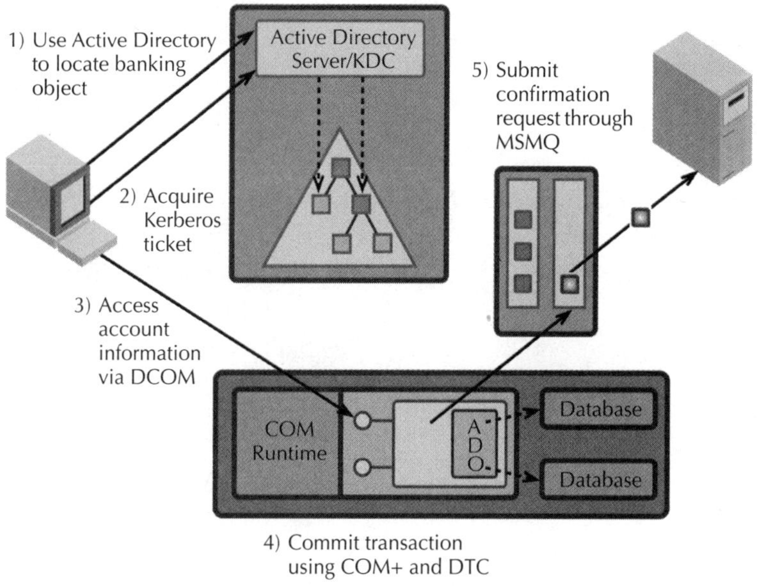

1) Use Active Directory to locate banking object

Active Directory Server/KDC

5) Submit confirmation request through MSMQ

2) Acquire Kerberos ticket

3) Access account information via DCOM

COM Runtime

A D O

Database

Database

4) Commit transaction using COM+ and DTC

Although it's not shown in Figure 1-12, the client might first contact a DNS server to find the right domain controller, but eventually, the client issues an LDAP query to that domain controller. Active Directory then returns the location of the server machine on which the banking object should be created.

Object creation might require getting a Kerberos ticket

But that server machine shouldn't allow just anybody to create and access its objects. Instead, this application uses Kerberos for distributed security, which requires the client machine to first acquire a ticket to the application from the KDC[5] (step 2 in Figure 1-12). Once this is done, the client's request to create the object can proceed, with the request relying on DCOM and COM+ to carry out the mechanics of the task.

Once an object is created, the client can invoke its methods

Once the client creates the object, the client can modify accounts by invoking the methods in IAccount and ITransfer (step 3 in Figure 1-12). Each client has its own instance of the banking object, and a single instance might even be used over and over to work with many different accounts. Each call to IAccount's Credit and Debit methods results in changes to the appropriate database to reflect the new account balance. And as shown in Figure 1-12, the object uses ADO to access those databases.

The COM runtime and DTC can guarantee transactional behavior

Some operations the client can perform might require a transaction spanning more than one database. For example, a client might call ITransfer's MoveMoney method, requesting that money be moved between accounts in two different databases. In this case, either both database operations—a subtraction and an addition—should happen, or neither one should. The COM runtime, relying ultimately on DTC, can ensure that this transactional behavior is correctly provided (step 4 in Figure 1-12).

---

5. The client probably also needs a ticket to access Active Directory, although this isn't shown in the figure.

Some operations might require more than just modifying the databases. It might be QwickBank's policy, for example, to send customers written confirmation for every transfer over $10,000. To do this, the banking object's MoveMoney method builds an MSMQ message and sends it to the correct queue (step 5 in Figure 1-12). Another application on some other system will eventually read this message from the queue and see that the written confirmation is printed and sent to the customer. It's even possible to make sending this message part of the same transaction in which the databases are updated. This guarantees that the message will be sent only if the transfer is successful.

Some requests might also be made through MSMQ

An Example with a Web Browser Client

Building a banking system with a DCOM client makes good sense if that system will be used only by tellers in the bank. Each teller's workstation can have a custom DCOM client installed, and the server machine can be accessed over the bank's internal network. But what happens when the bank's management decides to let customers access their own accounts over the Internet?

To make this possible, a Web-based interface must be added to this application. In Windows 2000, this turns out to not be all that difficult. The core functions provided by the banking object remain the same. All that's required is to change how the client accesses those functions. In fact, it's entirely possible to simultaneously use both DCOM and Web-based clients in the same application.

Web-based clients can access the same business object

Figure 1-13 shows how a Web-based version of this simple banking system might look. The client is now any Web browser— Netscape Navigator, Microsoft Internet Explorer, or something else—running on any operating system. This client accesses the banking object via a Web page, so the client must provide a URL for the page. URLs typically contain embedded DNS names, so

A Web browser can use DNS to locate the server and SSL to authenticate itself the client first contacts a DNS server to locate the machine this page is on (step 1 in Figure 1-13). Next, just as in the previous example, the client needs to prove its identity to the server that creates the banking object. Although it's possible to use Kerberos here, an Internet application is more likely to use SSL. Accordingly, authentication is accomplished using public key technology (step 2 in Figure 1-13).

Figure 1-13 *The same business logic as shown in Figure 1-12 can be accessed from a browser client.*

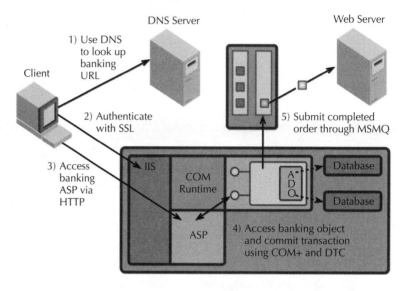

Methods in a COM object can be invoked from an ASP script

The customer can now begin working with his account. In the previous example, the user interface seen by a bank teller was entirely under the control of the client software's developer. Here, the client's user interface must be a Web page of some kind. That Web page might provide forms to fill in, boxes to check, and so on, all aimed at making it easy for customers to work with their accounts. However the user interface is done, customers eventually submit requests via HTTP to the Web server, which in this example is IIS (step 3 in Figure 1-13). A VBScript program in an ASP script loaded by IIS can pass each request to the banking object, invoking this object's methods as needed (step 4 in Figure 1-13). The code for this banking object can be exactly the same as in the previous example—all that changes is that the object's methods are now invoked by an ASP script rather than by a DCOM client. When the order is submitted, the object again relies on ADO to access the data, uses COM+ and DTC to commit the transaction, then sends off any required messages using MSMQ (step 5 in Figure 1-13).

Both of these examples solve the same problem, and the heart of the application—the COM object that allows clients to query and modify accounts—is the same in both cases. The two scenarios differ in how the client locates this object, how the application provides distributed security, and how client requests are passed across the network. In some cases, DCOM-based clients are the right solution, while in others, Web-based clients are better. For either situation, however, Windows 2000 provides a solid set of well-integrated services, making it easier to build flexible, secure distributed applications. However you look at it, these services represent a step forward for organizations using Microsoft operating systems.

Windows 2000 distributed services are a step forward

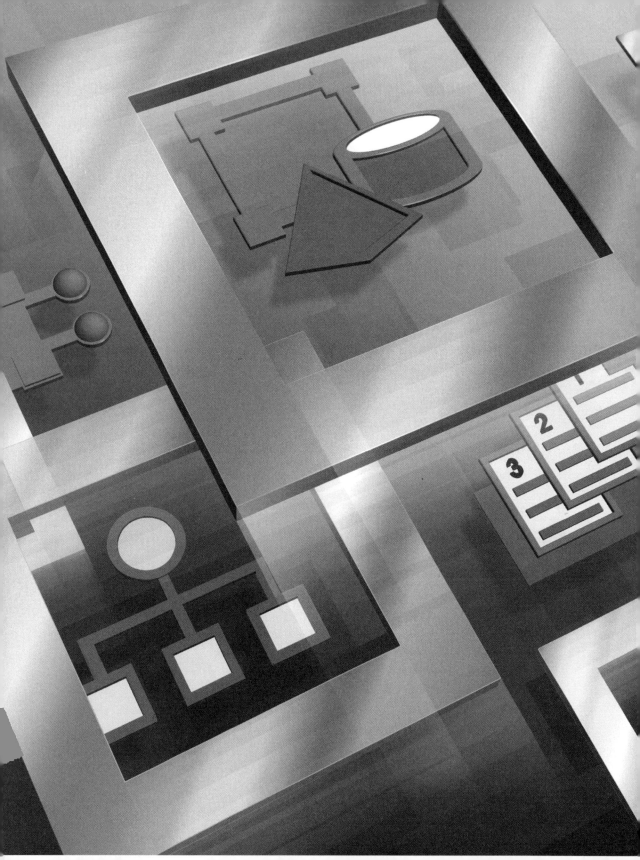

Chapter Two

Directory Services

Every distributed computing environment needs a place to store information about people, machines, and applications. When you log in to a computer, for example, it needs to find information about your account, such as your password. When you attempt to access some application—say, a distributed file service—somewhere on the network, your machine needs to locate the server that application is running on. When you send e-mail, it's convenient to have a way for the e-mail software to look up the address of the recipient.

It's possible to solve each of these problems separately. This is essentially what Microsoft Windows NT 4 does: the Security Accounts Manager (SAM) database stores information about your account; the Windows Internet Name Service (WINS) might be used to find an appropriate file server; and the Exchange directory service can map a person's name to a specific e-mail address. But using a different service to solve each of these very similar problems doesn't make much sense. The fundamental problem—finding information about something in the distributed environment—is the same in every case, so why not solve all of these problems in the same way?

Providing a single solution is the goal of Microsoft Windows 2000's Active Directory. Rather than require each distributed application to cobble together its own idiosyncratic solution, Active Directory provides a standard way for every application to store and retrieve

Distributed environments have lots of information that must be made accessible

It makes sense to provide one way to access information in a distributed environment

Active Directory provides a common place to store and locate information

information in a distributed Windows 2000 environment. Because it touches so many parts of the distributed environment, it's fair to say that Active Directory is the most important new technology in Windows 2000.

Defining Directory Services

Directory services all have two main components: a *database* that contains the information in the directory and *protocols* that allow the directory's users to access that information. Windows 2000 includes two different directory services—the Domain Name System (DNS) and Active Directory—and it's important to understand the role each one plays.[1]

DNS is an essential directory service today

DNS is by far the most popular directory service in data networks today. Since it's used to look up names such as stanford.edu or qwickbank.com, we all use DNS every time we access a Web page or send e-mail on the Internet. DNS is also widely deployed in most organizations' internal networks, since it's all but impossible to build an effective TCP/IP environment without it.

DNS doesn't address the whole problem

Like all directory services, DNS defines a database and a protocol that allows access to that database. And for what it was intended to do, DNS is a very good technology. Mapping names to machine addresses, for example, is one of its primary functions, and DNS performs it very well. Yet DNS alone isn't sufficient as a complete directory service. If all you want to do is look up the IP address of the machine named diana.qwickbank.com, DNS is great—it's fast and simple. If you'd like to search a directory database for a list of all users whose last name is "Smith", however, DNS is less effective. While DNS is an essential part of a modern distributed environment, it doesn't completely solve all of the directory problems that environment poses.

---

1. Windows 2000 also supports WINS, which maps NetBIOS names to IP addresses, for backward compatibility. A pure Windows 2000 environment might not require NetBIOS, however, depending on exactly which services are used. Without NetBIOS, WINS is no longer needed.

To address this, another standard directory technology has emerged. Called the Lightweight Directory Access Protocol (LDAP), it is derived from X.500, an earlier and much more complex directory technology. Controlled by the Internet Engineering Task Force (IETF), LDAP is supported today by virtually every major directory service vendor. This list includes Microsoft—Active Directory is an implementation of LDAP.

Active Directory implements LDAP

Unlike DNS, which is intended to allow access to relatively simple kinds of information, LDAP is explicitly designed for directories that store and access much more complex data. For the kind of global directory service that DNS provides, LDAP probably wouldn't be a great choice—it's too complicated. But for getting at diverse kinds of information in a more local environment, LDAP works well.

Ultimately, then, DNS and LDAP are complementary technologies. Given this, why not use them together? This is exactly what's done in Windows 2000. As described in Chapter 1, a client uses DNS to find a domain controller, and then uses Active Directory to access information about objects in the domain. By letting each directory service do what it does best, Windows 2000 builds on what already exists—a worldwide DNS infrastructure—while providing new services with LDAP.

Together, DNS and Active Directory provide a more complete solution

DNS in Windows 2000

Despite the advent of Active Directory, DNS continues to perform its usual functions in Windows 2000. Mapping DNS names to IP addresses, looking up Internet mail servers, and many other tasks are still done by DNS—Active Directory doesn't change this. But Windows 2000 nevertheless brings some changes to DNS. Understanding these changes requires knowing a little bit about how a DNS database is structured.

A DNS server traditionally maintains its information in a simple format called a *zone file*. Each zone file contains some number of *resource records*, each with a specific information type such as A (address) or MX (mail exchange). When a DNS client needs to find the IP address of the machine named diana.qwickbank.com, for example, that client requests the value of the A record containing that name. That A record also contains the IP address of diana.qwickbank.com, so the result of this query is the address of the desired machine. Similarly, looking up an e-mail address such as smith@qwickbank.com requires finding a machine that can accept mail for qwickbank.com. To do this, a DNS client requests MX records for the name qwickbank.com, and the values returned indicate where this mail should be sent.

Finding a Domain Controller

Using DNS to find a domain controller, as an Active Directory client does, requires taking advantage of a relatively new addition to DNS called SRV (service) records. Defined in Request for Comments (RFC) 2052, an SRV record allows a client to find a particular service, not just a machine. Each SRV record contains a name in the form *service.protocol.domain*, and also contains the name of a machine at which that service can be found.

For Active Directory, a client needs to find a machine that's providing LDAP service for a given Windows 2000 domain. This machine is, of course, a domain controller for that domain, and how the process works is shown in Figure 2-1. To find a domain controller for the Windows 2000 domain qwickbank.com, for instance, a client issues a DNS query for the SRV record containing the name ldap.tcp.qwickbank.com. This request is asking for a machine that provides the LDAP service, accessed using the protocol TCP (the only choice for LDAP), for the domain qwickbank. com. The result of this query is the name of a domain controller for the qwickbank.com domain, which in the example is dc1. qwickbank.com. The client next accesses the A record for this domain controller to learn its IP address, which in this case is

Also, client machines that are dynamically assigned IP addresses at boot time through the Dynamic Host Configuration Protocol (DHCP) can use Dynamic DNS to remotely add A records containing those addresses.

Handy as the ability to change DNS data from a remote system is, it introduces something else to worry about: security. How can a DNS server control which clients are allowed to modify the data it contains? In Windows 2000's DNS implementation, the client and server negotiate which protocol should be used to authenticate the client. Not too surprisingly, the default is Kerberos, the Windows 2000 core protocol for distributed security.

Storing DNS Data

ata can be stored
Active Directory
database

The information accessible through DNS is, of course, stored in the DNS database no matter how it gets there—through Dynamic DNS or by someone manually editing a file. Traditional DNS stores its records in ordinary files, the zone files mentioned earlier. But given that Windows 2000 includes a more general database used by Active Directory, why bother to maintain a separate storage mechanism for DNS? In Windows 2000, all DNS data can optionally be stored in the database maintained by Active Directory instead of in zone files. Although it's not mandatory, turning this option on can make life simpler for directory administrators, since they now need to be concerned with only a single directory database. Perhaps even more important, because both DNS and Active Directory replicate data, storing DNS data in the Active Directory database results in having only a single replication topology to maintain.

As shown in Figure 2-2, Windows 2000 DNS also supports the standard DNS replication protocols. This allows a Windows 2000 DNS server to replicate information with a vanilla DNS server running on, say, a UNIX system.

192.23.14.5, and then contacts that domain controller using LDAP. And to avoid doing this lookup every time an application on the client machine needs access to the Active Directory database, the address of the domain controller is cached on the client for future use.

Figure 2-1 ***DNS SRV records are used to locate domain controllers.***

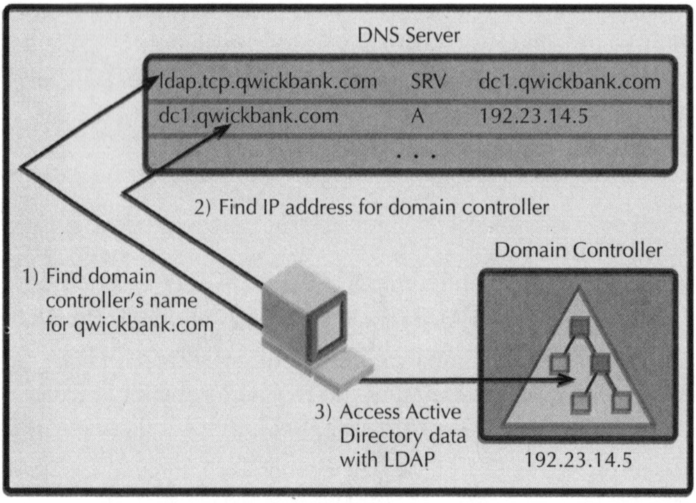

Dynamic DNS

SRV records aren't the only relatively recent addition to DNS exploited in Windows 2000. Windows 2000's DNS implementation also supports Dynamic DNS. Defined in RFC 2136, Dynamic DNS extends the DNS protocol to allow clients to modify the DNS database from a remote system. Prior to Windows 2000, making changes to a zone file typically required logging in to the machine on which that file was stored and editing the file manually. With Dynamic DNS, remote clients can change information stored in DNS using the DNS protocol itself.

Dynamic
clients to
mation rem

Letting clients modify DNS data is quite useful. For example, when a Windows 2000 domain controller boots it can automatically add an SRV record for itself to the appropriate DNS server.

Figure 2-2 *Even if its data is stored in the Active Directory database, Windows 2000 supports standard DNS replication.*

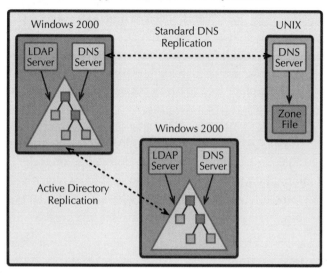

It's worth emphasizing that Active Directory doesn't require using the DNS implementation included with Windows 2000. All it requires is that whatever DNS server is deployed support SRV records. And although support for Dynamic DNS is nice to have, Active Directory will work fine without it. Life will be harder for administrators without Dynamic DNS—they'll need to manually maintain SRV records for domain controllers, for example—but it's not strictly required.

Understanding Active Directory

Active Directory is built entirely on LDAP. As is described later in this section, the LDAP standards don't define a complete solution, so there are a number of cases where technology beyond those standards is used. Still, Active Directory follows LDAP's dictates for naming, organizing, and accessing the data it stores. Accordingly, understanding Active Directory requires understanding LDAP.

Active Directory is based on LDAP

Active Directory implements both Version 2 of the LDAP protocol, defined in RFC 1777, and Version 3, defined in RFC 2251. Both documents define only how clients access a directory database. Yet even defining how clients access a directory requires specifying how those clients should name information stored in the directory. This, in turn, requires specifying the types of information that can be stored and how that information is structured. A description of how all of this is done follows.

First, though, a word of warning: because LDAP is derived from X.500, it uses that earlier standard's information definition techniques and information naming style. If they seem convoluted to you, and they probably will, blame it on X.500. Standards can be a mixed blessing.

Organizing Information

Active Directory entries are referred to as objects

Information stored in an LDAP database must be organized into a hierarchy. This hierarchy is built from some number of *object entries*, more commonly called just *objects.*[2] As shown in Figure 2-3, directory objects can be either *containers*, which have other objects beneath them, or *leaves*, which don't have other objects beneath them.

Each object is of some object class, which defines what attributes it can have

Every container and leaf object is of some *object class*, which determines what kind of *attributes* (also known as *properties*) that object can contain. The definition of an object class can specify both mandatory and optional attributes, so the types of information in objects of a given class might vary a bit. Whatever its class, though, every object is made up of attributes, and each attribute contains a type and one or more values of that type. As shown in Figure 2-4, an attribute can be single-valued or multivalued. A single-valued attribute might contain something like your name,

---

2. Don't confuse directory objects with COM objects, C++ objects, or any other kind of object. Objects in Active Directory aren't really objects in the conventional sense—they contain only data, not methods—but for better or worse, "object" has become the commonly used term.

while a multivalued attribute might contain a list of your telephone numbers. Each attribute is assigned a particular *object identifier*, which is a globally unique value assigned by some authority. Microsoft can allocate object identifiers, as can the national standards bodies of various countries. A tool in the Windows 2000 resource kit can also be used to create your own object identifiers.

Figure 2-3   *Each object in an LDAP database is either a container or a leaf.*

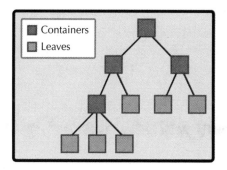

Figure 2-4   *Each object contains some number of attributes, which can be single-valued or multivalued.*

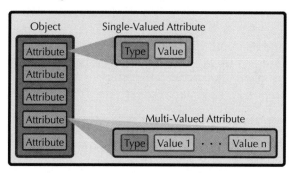

The set of rules that defines what kinds of data can be stored in a particular database and the allowed relationships among that data is known as a *schema*. The Active Directory schema is defined entirely as a group of object classes and attribute types. In fact, as is described later in this chapter, the definitions of the object classes and attribute types that make up the schema are

An Active Directory schema is a group of object classes and attribute types themselves stored in Active Directory, which makes those definitions relatively easy to browse. The schema can also be modified, allowing user organizations, software vendors, and others to add their own object classes and attribute types. This can be useful, but requires care—unfettered schema modification can create problems down the road. You'll particularly want to avoid adding redundant object classes and attribute types—a directory is supposed to reduce redundancy, not encourage it.

The standard schema that ships with Active Directory is not a simple thing; it defines a large number of object classes and attribute types. Getting a feel for what it includes isn't too hard, however. Following are some examples of the object classes defined by the Active Directory schema, and some of their attributes.

User contains information about a particular user in some domain. The attributes defined for the User class include:

- *Common-Name*   The user's name.
- *User-Principal-Name, or UPN*   The name used to log in to a Windows 2000 domain.
- *Address*   The user's mailing address.
- *Telephone-Number*   A list of this user's telephone numbers.
- *E-mail-Addresses*   A list of e-mail addresses for this user.

Computer contains information about a particular machine in a domain. Attributes for the Computer class include:

- *Common-Name*   The machine's name.
- *Operating-System*   For example, "Windows 2000".
- *Operating-System-Service-Pack*   For example, "SP2".
- *Machine-DNS-Name*   For example, "diana.qwickbank.com".
- *Machine-Role*   Workstation, server, or domain controller.

Print-Queue contains information about a printer. The Print-Queue class attributes include:

- *Printer-Name*   The display name of this printer.
- *Location*   Where the printer is physically located.
- *Print-Status*   The current print status of this printer.
- *Print-Language*   For example, "PostScript".

Organizational Unit, commonly called an *OU*. Objects of this class are containers used to logically organize an Active Directory domain in a way that makes administrative sense. OUs are important, as we will see later in this chapter, and their attributes include (among many more):

- *Organizational-Unit-Name*   The name of this OU.
- *Postal-Address*   The mailing address of this OU.
- *Telephone-Number*   One or more phone numbers for this OU.

Many, perhaps even most, OUs in Active Directory don't correspond to real organizations, and so they often don't have addresses or phone numbers. OUs usually model the way a particular directory hierarchy is managed rather than the actual structure of an organization.

Naming Information

LDAP defines only how clients access a directory database. Yet doing this apparently simple thing requires specifying how the information in that database is defined. It also requires specifying how the client should identify that information. In other words, LDAP defines how objects in the directory are named.

The information stored in a Windows 2000 domain directory database is organized into a hierarchy. Naming a particular object in the directory, then, requires specifying which domain that object is in and the object's name within that domain's hierarchy. DNS names are used to identify a domain, but to identify individual objects within a domain clients use LDAP naming.

LDAP names are hierarchical

Recall that each object contains some number of attributes. To name an object, one of those attributes is designated as the *relative distinguished name* (*RDN*) of that object. In an object of the class Organizational Unit, for example, the value of the attribute Organizational-Unit-Name is chosen as the object's RDN. In an object of the class User, the value of the Common-Name attribute can be chosen as the RDN.

A distinguished name uniquely identifies an object in the directory

RDNs must be unique in the level below a given container. In other words, the RDN of every object that appears immediately below another object must be different from the RDNs of its siblings. Given this fact, it's possible to uniquely name an object within a particular domain. All that's required is to concatenate an object's RDN together with the RDNs of all the objects above it in this domain's hierarchy, including the name of the domain itself. The result is called a *distinguished name*. Every object in every Active Directory domain has a distinguished name, and the quickest way to find a directory object (although not the only way, as we'll see) is to pass this name to an Active Directory server.

For example, Figure 2-5 shows a partial view of the naming structure for the Windows 2000 domain us.qwickbank.com. Below the root are two objects of the class Organizational Unit, each of which is assigned an RDN based on the value of its Organizational-Unit-Name attribute. This attribute type is abbreviated as OU, so the RDN of the object for QwickBank's Accounting department is OU=acct, while the RDN of the object for the Sales department is OU=sales.

Objects of the Organizational-Unit class are containers, so below these objects can appear other objects. In the domain shown in Figure 2-5, both the Accounting and Sales departments have their own computers and users, so each department has a container for each of these two categories. In this example, the RDNs for these objects are the same in both departments and both are OUs, but this isn't required. Below these containers are leaf objects of various classes, each assigned an RDN using an appropriate attribute from that object's class. The Sales department has users named Li, Smith, and Catignani, for example, each of whom has an object of the class User. The RDN for each of these objects again uses the attribute Common-Name, so the RDN of, say, Smith's object is CN=smith.

Figure 2-5 *Each domain contains a hierarchy of named objects.*

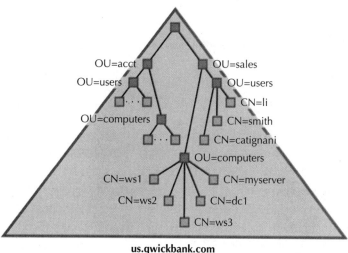

us.qwickbank.com

To identify Smith's unique object in this domain, a client must provide that object's distinguished name. As already described, forming this name is easy: you just concatenate the RDN of Smith's object with those of the container objects above it in the tree. The only challenging part of doing this is deciding what name to use for the domain itself, because domains are assigned DNS names rather than LDAP names. The solution Microsoft has chosen is the one defined in RFC 2247: to divide a DNS name into two or more attributes of the type Domain Component, abbreviated as DC. The domain us.qwickbank.com, for example, can be assigned the LDAP-style name DC=us, DC=qwickbank, DC=com.

A DNS name can be represented using LDAP-style naming

Given all this, the distinguished name for Smith's object in the Windows 2000 domain us.qwickbank.com is CN=smith, OU=users, OU=sales, DC=us, DC=qwickbank, DC=com. If you pass this name to an Active Directory client, it will turn the last three elements into the DNS name us.qwickbank.com, use this name to find a domain controller for that domain, and then pass the first three elements of the distinguished name to that domain controller. The LDAP server on that machine can then use the portion of the name it receives to locate Smith's object.

Variations on this naming scheme are also possible. For instance, Active Directory allows using LDAP URLs as defined in RFC 2255. An example of the LDAP URL form for the distinguished name just given is LDAP://CN=smith, OU=users, OU=receivables, DC=us, DC=qwickbank, DC=com.

Active Directory names can potentially be used on the Internet

One final point worth making is that because Windows 2000 domains have DNS names, Active Directory names can be used to uniquely identify objects on the Internet. For example, a distinguished name or LDAP URL might be used by an LDAP client in one organization to locate and access an object in some other organization's Active Directory database. For this to work, of course, appropriate administrative settings for security and other issues must be established. Once this is done, Active Directory names can be used globally.

Accessing Information

LDAP is defined as a set of operations, each with appropriate parameters

LDAP allows a client to connect to the directory, perform operations on the information stored in that directory's database, and then release the connection. Some of the operations defined by this protocol are:

- *Bind* Establishes a connection with an LDAP server.
- *Search* Returns one or more attribute values from one or more objects that meet specified criteria.

- *Modify*   Changes the values of one or more attributes in an object.
- *Delete*   Removes an existing object.
- *Add*   Adds a new object.
- *Unbind*   Releases a connection with an LDAP server.

When an application wishes to look up something in Active Directory, the LDAP client on that application's machine can begin by sending a Bind request to the Active Directory server (assuming that an appropriate domain controller has already been found). Next, the LDAP client issues a Search request. Each Search specifies several parameters, including:

To look up information, a client relies on an LDAP Search

- The name of the object at which the search should begin.
- The depth of the search: just this object, all objects in the level below this one, or the entire tree below this object.
- A filter that specifies which information to search for. (This filter is expressed as a group of one or more attribute values.)
- A list of attribute types whose values should be returned from objects that match the search.
- A maximum amount of time the search can take.

In the example shown in Figure 2-6, a client is requesting a search that applies to all objects in the entire subtree below the Sales OU. The search includes a filter indicating that only objects containing attributes of the type Common-Name with the value "Smith" match this search, and lists Address and Telephone-Number as the attributes whose values should be returned from each matching object. This search would return the address and telephone number of everybody named "Smith" in the specified OU. Once the search completes, the client might issue other operations, or it might send an Unbind request to release the connection with the LDAP server.

Figure 2-6   *An example LDAP Search request that specifies where to search, what criteria must be matched, and more.*

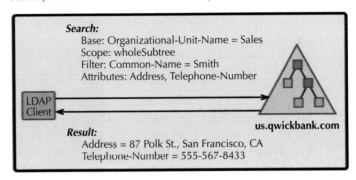

Search:
Base: Organizational-Unit-Name = Sales
Scope: wholeSubtree
Filter: Common-Name = Smith
Attributes: Address, Telephone-Number

LDAP Client

Result:
Address = 87 Polk St., San Francisco, CA
Telephone-Number = 555-567-8433

us.qwickbank.com

Controlling Access to Information

Active Directory typically uses Kerberos for authentication

Putting all kinds of information, including user accounts, in one database makes that database a tempting target for attackers. Active Directory therefore defines authentication and authorization mechanisms that protect the data it contains. For authentication, LDAP version 2 supports only simple passwords, but LDAP version 3 allows negotiating which authentication protocol should be used. Active Directory, of course, defaults to Kerberos.

Objects and attributes each have an ACL

Once a domain controller knows who it's talking to—that is, once its client has been authenticated—it then must determine what kind of access that client has to the objects in the directory. In other words, it must make an authorization decision. Active Directory uses standard Windows 2000 access control lists (ACLs) to accomplish this. An ACL is a list of authorized users and groups of users, and each object in an Active Directory database has a list assigned to it. When a client tries to access an object, Active Directory examines that object's ACL to determine whether the client's request should be granted. Active Directory also assigns an ACL to individual attributes in each object, allowing very fine-grained access control. And by default, newly created objects in the directory inherit the ACL from their parent object, so explicitly establishing permissions for every object isn't required. (This is a primary reason why a directory hierarchy should be designed to reflect how that directory is managed rather than the corporate structure of the organization.) While managing the ACLs for Active Directory objects and attributes can get tiresome for an administrator, they remain an essential aspect of an enterprise-class directory service.

Categorizing Information

To a large degree, Active Directory is just a standard LDAP server. But as we've already seen, LDAP defines only how clients access a directory, so the LDAP standards alone aren't enough to build an effective directory service. In Windows 2000, Active Directory includes a number of things that aren't defined by LDAP or any other multi-vendor standard. Among the most important of these is the way Active Directory categorizes stored data.

Active Directory subdivides the objects in its directory database[3] into three distinct types. As shown in Figure 2-7, every Active Directory domain has data in all three categories, which are as follows:

Each Active Directory database contains three types of data

- *Domain data*   Contains the domain's user data, such as OU, user, and computer objects. All of the objects shown in Figure 2-5 (on page 45) qualify as domain data, for example, and a typical user of Active Directory sees nothing else. To most users, Domain data is all that Active Directory contains.

- *Schema data*   Contains the schema for the domain— that is, the descriptions of the object classes and attribute types allowed for the objects.

---

3. The database management system used in Active Directory is the Extended Storage Engine (ESE), which is also used by Exchange and other Microsoft products.

- *Configuration data* Contains information about other domains with which the domain has relationships. As described later in this section, domains can be grouped into trees and forests, and so a list of all domains with which the domain has been grouped is kept here. This type of data also includes the locations of domain controllers in the related domains, information about security relationships with those other domains, and more.

Figure 2-7 *Every domain contains three types of data.*

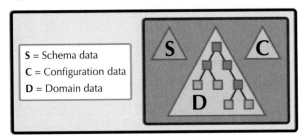

All three kinds of data are really nothing more than ordinary directory objects, the object classes and attribute types of which are limited to those specified in the Schema data. Still, the distinction among the three categories is important, as you will see shortly.

Finding Information: Indexes and the Global Catalog

If a client knows what domain an object is in, and knows the distinguished name of the object, then accessing it using LDAP is easy. But what if the client knows the domain to search, and knows one or more attributes of the desired object, but doesn't know that object's distinguished name? One option is to use LDAP to perform the kind of search shown earlier, specifying where in the tree the search should begin, what attribute values to search for, and more. Yet in a domain of any size, doing this kind of search runs the risk of being unacceptably slow, since it might need to examine a large number of objects.

Fast database searches are hardly a new problem, however. A well-known and efficient way to search a database for objects that contain attributes with specified values is to build an index for those attributes. As long as the attributes whose values you're searching for are in this index, finding the objects that contain them is quick and easy. To speed up searches, then, Active Directory automatically indexes a frequently-searched set of attribute types, and it allows an administrator to specify other attribute types that should be indexed. Once the indexes exist, searches for values of indexed types will be much faster, since now only the index is searched—there's no need for Active Directory to search an entire domain or sub-tree within a domain.

Attributes can be indexed to speed up searches

But here's an even harder problem: suppose a client knows nothing more than the attributes it wishes to search for. Not only does this ignorant client not know the distinguished name of the desired object, it doesn't even know which domain that object is in. Even if the attribute is indexed, a search of every domain in this client's purview could take an unreasonable amount of time.

To solve this problem, Active Directory provides a *global catalog (GC)*. The GC contains a replica of every object in each of a group of domains. But it's only a partial replica—the GC's copy of the object includes only a few of its attributes, those that are likely to be of global interest to clients using those domains. Microsoft defines various standard attributes that are always in the GC, and administrators can define attributes in the GC, too.

The global catalog allows searching for attributes in objects contained in one or more domains

Figure 2-8 shows how the GC works. Both domains in the figure, us.qwickbank.com and europe.qwickbank.com, share a single GC. If a client issues a query looking for an indexed attribute with the value "smith", for instance, the global catalog can be searched for that attribute value. Once it's been found in the GC, the search can directly access the object in the correct domain, because the GC contains the distinguished name of that object.

Figure 2-8 *A GC can index information in multiple domains.*

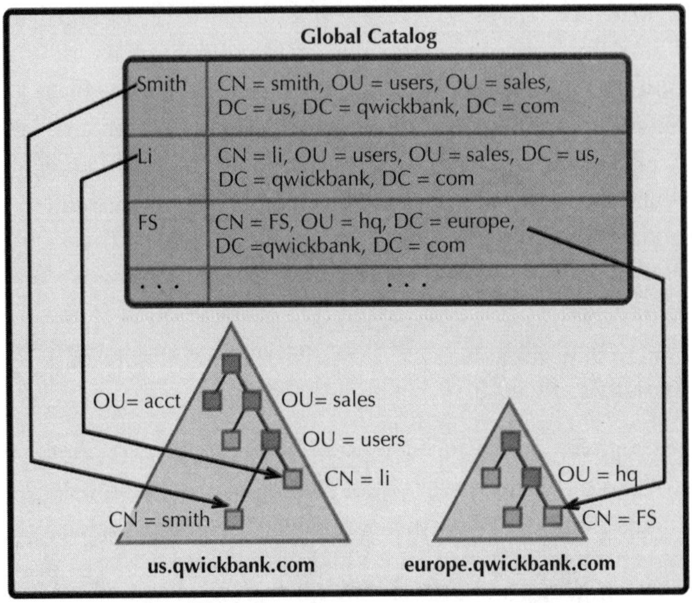

The information in the GC is stored on one or more domain controllers in the domains to which it applies—not every domain controller need have a copy. (A domain controller that contains a copy of this information is sometimes referred to as a *global catalog server.*) In fact, there is no separate database for the GC. Instead, its information is maintained in the same physical file that contains the rest of the Active Directory database.

Each object has an unchanging GUID assigned to it

Here's another interesting use of the GC: because every object has a distinguished name, you can always access a particular object if you know that name. But distinguished names can change, sometimes in ways beyond your control. Suppose, for example, that some administrator decides to change the name of an OU that's above the user object for Smith in the us.qwickbank.com domain. The distinguished name for Smith's object has now also changed, and any software that uses the old name will no longer be able to find Smith's object. But by using the GC there's always a reliable way to return to a specific object, even if its distinguished name has changed. This mechanism depends on the fact that every object in Active Directory is assigned a globally unique identifier (GUID) when it is created, a GUID that's stored in the object and never changed. Most important, this GUID is always indexed in the GC. To be guaranteed of returning to a given object, regardless of how that object's distinguished name might change, a client can acquire and hold on to the object's GUID. When the client looks up this GUID in the GC, it will always be sent to the desired object.

One more important use of the GC is during the login process. When you log in to a Windows 2000 domain, your user object in Active Directory must be found—it's where your password is kept, among other things. If every login required a search of the entire database in even one domain, happy Windows 2000 users would be hard to find. At the same time, if logging in required providing your distinguished name, you also would probably not be too pleased. Instead, in Windows 2000, logging in requires typing only a User Principal Name (UPN) identifying a user and a domain. For example, the user Smith might have the UPN smith@us.qwickbank.com (notice that UPNs can potentially be identical to a user's email address, which makes life simple). To find Smith's object given this UPN, the login process uses the GC. This allows you to efficiently log in not only from machines in your home domain, but from any machine in a domain that shares a GC with your home domain.[4]

Domain login relies on the GC

This raises a fairly obvious question about the GC that I haven't yet addressed: exactly which domains does a particular GC apply to? Having one worldwide GC apply to all Windows 2000 domains would be impractical and an enormous security risk, so that can't be the answer. Instead, domains whose objects can be searched from a single GC must be grouped into a domain tree or a forest, two concepts that are described next.

---

4. It's worth pointing out that UPNs must be unique within a set of domains that share a GC. Although two user objects with the RDN CN=smith can exist in different OUs in the us.qwickbank.com domain, for instance, only one of those users can be assigned the UPN smith@us.qwickbank.com.

Grouping Domains: Domain Trees and Forests

Domains grouped into a domain tree must have contiguous DNS names

If two or more Windows 2000 domains have contiguous DNS names, those domains can be grouped into a *domain tree*. In the example shown in Figure 2-9, qwickbank.com is the root domain for a domain tree containing the domains us.qwickbank.com, europe.qwickbank.com, and several more. The DNS name of each domain in a domain tree must end in the name of that domain's parent, allowing the domains as a whole to form a contiguous namespace.

Figure 2-9 *Domains with contiguous DNS names can be grouped into a domain tree.*

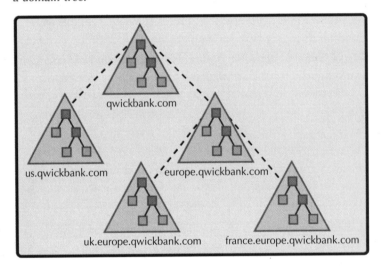

Domains in a domain tree all trust each other

Domain trees can be useful. For example, an LDAP search request made at the root of a domain tree and specifying a search of the entire tree will in fact search the entire domain tree. Domain trees also make managing distributed security easier, because every domain in a domain tree by default has a two-way trust relationship established with every other domain in that tree. These trust relationships are implemented by Kerberos, and how they work is described in more detail in Chapter 3.

But what if it's not feasible to group all of the domains in an organization into a domain tree? What if several domains need to be formed into a cohesive whole but still retain noncontiguous DNS names? In this case, those domains can be grouped into a *forest*. A forest is defined as a group of one or more domain trees, where each domain tree contains one or more domains.

Unlike a domain tree, a forest does not have one common root domain. Instead, as shown in Figure 2-10, the domains and domain trees that make up a forest can have any legal names. For example, suppose that the QwickBank Corporation were actually a wholly-owned subsidiary of Stanford University (unlikely, I know, but it's just an example). In this case, it might well make sense to join the domains of both organizations into a forest as shown in Figure 2-10.

Domains grouped into a forest need not have contiguous DNS names

Figure 2-10 *Domain and domain trees with non-contiguous DNS names can be grouped into a forest.*

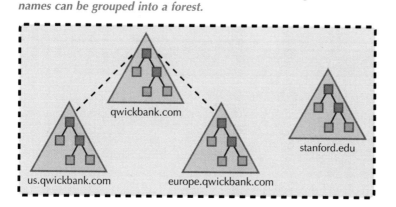

What does it really mean to group domains into a forest? How is a forest different from just a bunch of domains? Understanding the answers requires understanding what domain trees and forests really are, because both have more precise definitions than those given so far. Put more formally, then, a domain tree is a group of domains that share a common GC, have the same values for their

Domains grouped into a domain tree or forest must have a common schema

Configuration and Schema data (which means, among other things, that they have trust relationships among them as described in the next chapter), and whose names form a contiguous DNS namespace. A forest is very similar: it's a group of domains and/or domain trees that share a common GC and have the same values in their Configuration and Schema data (and so have trust relationships), but whose domain names do *not* necessarily form a contiguous namespace.

A more complete (and more abstract) diagram of a forest that contains a domain tree is shown in Figure 2-11. Note that while only two of the domains are grouped into a domain tree, all three domains share the same GC, and all three have the same Configuration and Schema data. Each domain has its own unique Domain data, however, containing information specific to each domain.

Figure 2-11 *Domains grouped into a domain tree or a forest have the same Configuration and Schema data, and share a common GC, but their Domain data is different.*

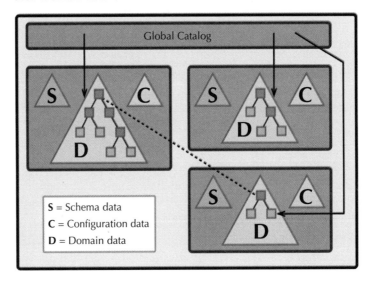

In practice, organizations should determine which domains will be in the same tree or forest when those domains are first created.

In the first release of Active Directory, at least, there's no standard way to join two independent domains, domain trees, or forests together. One reason for this limitation is the requirement that all domains in a domain tree or forest have a common schema, something that's difficult to achieve when already-existing domains are grouped together.

Replication

Having a common, widely used directory service is a great thing. But widespread use also makes that service indispensable; if the information it contains becomes unavailable, life gets hard for the people and applications in that distributed environment. Because of this, Active Directory allows *replication*: storing and synchronizing copies of the directory database on multiple domain controllers within a single domain. Replicating directory data increases availability of that data in case of system or network failures, and it can also improve performance by spreading client requests across more than one directory server.

Replication makes a directory service more available and more scalable

While it's officially possible for a domain to have only one domain controller, it's not an especially good idea; if this machine fails, all of the people and applications using that domain will feel it. In most cases, then, a domain will have two or more domain controllers, each of which has a complete copy of the Active Directory database for that domain. Any changes made by clients to Domain data in that database will be propagated to all replicas of the database on all domain controllers in that domain. Changes to Schema data and Configuration data, however, are not limited to a single domain. Instead, because this information must be kept consistent throughout a domain tree or forest, changes to the Schema or Configuration made in one domain are replicated to all domains in the same domain tree or, if one exists, the same forest.

A domain defines a replication boundary

Active Directory uses
multi-master replication

In Windows NT versions 4 and earlier, each domain contained one Primary Domain Controller (PDC) and zero or more Backup Domain Controllers (BDCs). In this world, any changes to the Windows NT directory database were made to the replica stored on the PDC, and then copied to the BDCs in that domain. Windows 2000 changes this structure. Rather than the single-master style of replication used previously, where only one domain controller held a read/write copy of the database, Active Directory uses multi-master replication. Now, a client can make changes to any copy of the Active Directory database on any domain controller, and those changes will automatically propagate to the directory databases maintained by all other domain controllers in that domain. In Windows 2000, the distinction between PDC and BDC goes away—a domain controller is a domain controller is a domain controller.[5]

Sites   Replication is a fine idea, one that improves performance and availability. But done naively, replication can have pathological side effects. For example, imagine a large Windows 2000 domain covering the entire United States. When an Active Directory client in New York City uses DNS to find a domain controller, that client should not be assigned to a server in San Francisco. Clients need to be able to access domain controllers that are in some sense nearby. Similarly, since most organizations have much more network bandwidth available in a single building than they do across the country, it usually makes sense to perform directory replication more frequently between a pair of domain controllers in the same New York office than between a domain controller in New York and another one in San Francisco. To make these kinds of rational behavior possible, Active Directory uses the concept of *sites.*

---

5. Well, almost. A few operations can only be performed on the domain controller that is designated as *operations master* for that operation. For example, modifying the schema requires contacting the domain controller that's assigned the role of operations master for schema modification. Also, as already mentioned, not every domain controller need have a copy of the GC database—which ones contain this information is determined administratively.

A site is just a specified group of IP subnets, defined by an administrator, that represents an area of the network where connectivity is fast and reliable. For example, a group of 10-Mbps Ethernets in the same building would be a good candidate for a site, while two Ethernets in different cities connected over a slow wide area network would not. Figure 2-12 illustrates this idea, showing two interconnected sites.

A group of IP subnets with good connectivity can be grouped into a site

Figure 2-12   *A site is a group of IP subnets with fast, reliable connectivity.*

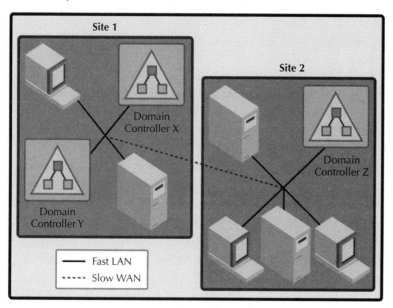

At first blush, you might expect that each site must be contained within a single domain. This turns out not to be true. Instead, there is no required correlation between the logical structure of Active Directory—domains, OUs, and so on—and the physical structure embodied in sites. A domain certainly can be subdivided into two or more sites, but it's also possible for a single site to span two or more domains. Sites are physical, domains are logical, and they can be combined in any way that makes sense for a particular organization.

Sites can cross domain boundaries

Defining sites intelligently is a key part of making Active Directory work well. Clients will automatically be assigned to a domain controller in the same site, if one exists, for example, so parceling domain controllers among sites is important. Also, the way replication is done within a single site is quite different from how it's accomplished between sites. The frequency of intra-site replication can't be changed—changes are replicated about every five minutes (although some changes are replicated immediately). Inter-site replication, on the other hand, can be scheduled by an administrator and typically happens less frequently. Because of this, sites are one of an administrator's best weapons in the battle against excessive replication traffic.

Minimizing replication traffic is important

Another important weapon in this battle is user education. Because Active Directory is accessible from anywhere in a domain, it's tempting to treat it as a general-purpose database, one capable of holding any kind of data. But while Active Directory does provide a generic service, it's optimized for mostly read-only operations on relatively small chunks of information. Users can certainly modify data stored in Active Directory, but they should not put in its database either information that changes frequently or very large information. The reason is simple: every change made to that database must be replicated across all copies of the data. Frequent updates to large amounts of information stored in an Active Directory database will result in excessive replication traffic. When deciding what should be stored in Active Directory, keep this fact in mind. Treating any directory service, including Active Directory, as if it were a general-purpose database won't lead to pleasant results. Especially in a large domain that's divided into several sites connected by slow links, taking pains to minimize replication traffic is an unquestionably good idea.

How Replication Works   LDAP defines how clients access a directory service but is silent about how directory servers talk to one another.[6] Accordingly, Microsoft has defined its own protocols to accomplish replication. As shown in Figure 2-13, an Active Directory client uses LDAP to modify the directory database in some domain controller, but Active Directory uses other protocols to replicate those changes. The primary choice is a Microsoft RPC-based protocol running over TCP/IP, although the Simple Mail Transfer Protocol (SMTP) can be used in some cases.

Protocols other than LDAP are used for replication

Figure 2-13   *Changes a client makes with LDAP are replicated using different protocols.*

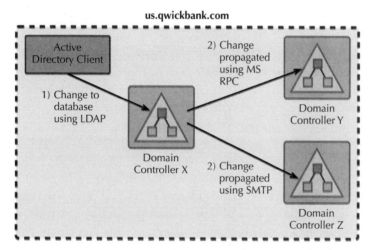

When a client uses LDAP to change an object in any replica of the Active Directory database, the domain controller that holds that replica will copy the new values to other domain controllers in that domain. Only the changed attributes are replicated, of

Every domain has a replication topology

---

6. This is true today, at least. The IETF is currently working on defining replication standards for LDAP-based directory services.

course—the entire database isn't copied. In a domain with only a few domain controllers, each domain controller can communicate its changes directly to all the others. In a domain with many domain controllers, however, the *replication topology* determines how changes are propagated. Every change eventually arrives at every domain controller in the domain, but a direct connection between each pair of domain controllers isn't required.

Intra-site replication should happen more frequently than inter-site replication

Active Directory automatically establishes and maintains a replication topology among domain controllers within a site, although administrators can customize it if they choose. And even though inter-site links are established manually by administrators, Active Directory still determines what replication connections exist. Also, replication traffic sent between sites is compressed, while intra-site traffic is not. Given that Active Directory's inter-site replication mechanisms are optimized for relatively infrequent replication over relatively slow links, taking the time to compress and then uncompress the transmitted information makes sense.

Regardless of how sites are used, however, multi-master replication is inherently more scalable than the single-master approach used in Windows NT 4; all changes are no longer required to go to a single domain controller. Multi-master replication is also more complex, however, and one obvious question arises: what happens when two different clients simultaneously change the same attribute in the same object in different replicas? Which change wins? The answer, as you might expect, is that the change made last is the one that eventually gets applied everywhere.

Each change to an attribute in some domain controller causes that system to increment its USN

Replication is important, and so it's worth taking a closer look at exactly how it's accomplished. Active Directory uses an integer counter called an Update Sequence Number (USN) instead of a timestamp to keep track of replication updates. Each domain controller maintains a USN that is incremented whenever a client changes an attribute in some object in that domain controller's replica, and the current USN is stored with the changed attribute.

Each domain controller also keeps track of the last USN it received from its replication partners. When it's time to replicate, a domain controller asks each partner for all changes with USNs higher than the last USN it received from the partner, and then applies those changes to the objects in its replica.

For example, imagine two domain controllers X and Y that are replication partners. As shown in Figure 2-14, suppose that domain controller X has received changes to attributes a, b, and c, and assigned each change an appropriate USN. Suppose, too, that the last USN X knows about from its partner Y is 113. Domain controller Y has changed attributes p and q, assigning each an appropriate USN, and the last USN it has received from X is 386.

Figure 2-14 *Domain controller X asks domain controller Y for all changes since the last USN X received from Y.*

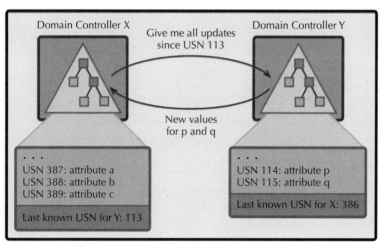

When it's time to replicate, X asks Y for all changes with USNs greater than 113, and Y responds by sending the changes to attributes p and q. Similarly, as shown in Figure 2-15, Y asks X for all changes with USNs greater than 386, and X sends back new values for attributes a, b, and c. The process is simple, and the result is that every domain controller gets only what it needs to bring its copy of the directory database up to date.

Figure 2-15 *Domain controller Y asks domain controller X for all changes since the last USN Y received from X.*

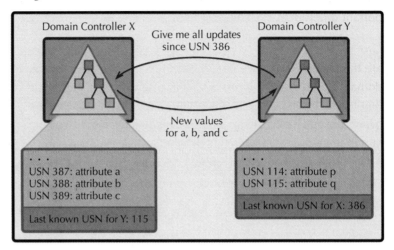

Groups

The idea of a group is straightforward: it's just a collection of users, computers, and/or other groups. And groups are important, too, because they're used in ACLs, Group Policy (described later in this chapter), and even for e-mail distribution lists. Yet in Windows 2000, groups are not an especially simple idea, and they're also a bit different than groups in Windows NT 4.

Windows 2000 defines two types of group and three group scopes

Windows 2000 defines two general categories of groups: *distribution groups* and *security groups*. Distribution groups are intended to be used for defining e-mail lists—they can't be used for access control—so a distribution group will never appear in an ACL. Security groups, however, are intended to be used for access control, and as described in the next section, they can also be used with Group Policy. Both kinds of groups have a specific scope, however, of which Windows 2000 defines three different types: *universal*, *global*, and *domain local*. For the most part, each of these three is defined with respect to one or more of the domains in a particular forest. Groups with any of these three scopes can contain users or other groups (although the exact rules for how different types of groups can be nested get complicated), but important differences exist among them.

Groups with universal scope, commonly called universal groups, are the simplest. A universal group can have members from any domain in a particular forest, and it can be used in any domain in that forest. In other words, universal groups are just what they sound like: groups that can be defined anywhere in a forest, contain members from anywhere in a forest, and can be used anywhere in that forest.

The obvious question to ask at this point is, why have any other kind of group? Since universal groups are simple and broadly applicable, why not always use them? If a forest is relatively small, and especially if it contains no slow links between sites or domains, universal groups might be all that's required. But using only universal groups in a large forest can lead to performance problems. The primary reason for this is that the list of members in a universal group is always kept in a forest's GC. This increases the size of the catalog and, more important, the amount of replication traffic that's generated when a universal group's membership is changed. In a large forest, using only universal groups is likely to result in a very large GC and a significant amount of replication traffic.

To avoid this performance hit, you might choose to define some groups as having only global scope. Like universal groups, these global groups can be used anywhere in the forest in which they're defined. They can, for example, appear in ACLs on any resource in any domain in that forest. But unlike universal groups, the members of a global group can be drawn only from a single domain in that forest. This makes them a little harder to use, since administrators can't arbitrarily add members to a global group without making sure those members belong to the domain in which that group is defined, but it also makes them more efficient. There is an entry for each global group in the GC, but unlike universal groups, that entry does not contain a list of that group's members. This makes the GC database smaller and reduces replication traffic.

Domain local groups can have members from any domain in a domain tree or forest, but be used in only one domain

The third option is groups with domain local scope. This kind of group, called a domain local group, is essentially the reverse of a global group. While a global group can have members from only one domain but be used in any domain in a forest, a domain local group can have members from any domain in a given forest, but can be used in only a single domain. For example, a domain local group can appear only in ACLs on resources in the domain for which that group is defined. Like global groups, their existence but not their membership is recorded in the GC for the forest in which they're defined. This means that using them reduces the GC's size and the amount of replication traffic that's generated, just like global groups do.

One final but important point to make about groups in Windows 2000 is that the rules for what kinds of groups can be used and exactly how they can be used vary depending on whether a domain is running in *native* mode, where all domain controllers (although not necessarily all workstations and member servers) are running Windows 2000, or *mixed* mode, with domain controllers running both Windows 2000 and Windows NT.

Management Tools

Several MMC snap-ins are used to manage Active Directory

Several different tools are used to manage Active Directory, and all of them are implemented as Microsoft Management Console (MMC) snap-ins. Those tools are:

- *Active Directory Users and Computers snap-in* This tool allows adding, removing, modifying, and otherwise manipulating user accounts, computer accounts, groups, and related resources in the directory.

- *Active Directory Domains and Trusts snap-in* This tool is used to explicitly establish trusts between domains. It also contains a switch that changes a domain from mixed mode to native mode. This switch can be set only once—after a domain has been converted to native mode, it can't be changed back.

- *Active Directory Sites and Services snap-in* The major use of this tool is to define sites and to control how replication happens between those sites.

- *Active Directory Schema snap-in* As its name suggests, this tool is used to examine and modify the directory schema.

Active Directory APIs

Clients use LDAP to access an Active Directory database, but client software also needs some application programming interface (API) to allow developers to issue LDAP requests and receive responses. The IETF defines a standard LDAP API, which is supported in Windows 2000. Active Directory also provides another, more general API called the Active Directory Services Interface (ADSI). And for backward compatibility with applications built using the Microsoft Exchange directory, Active Directory also supports the Windows Messaging API (MAPI).

Active Directory can be accessed through several APIs

Before describing the two most important of these APIs—the standard LDAP interface and ADSI—it's worth noting that most of the time, developers of distributed applications won't use either API directly. While their applications will ultimately rely on some Active Directory API (usually ADSI), that interface is hidden from them. For example, applications built using DCOM or MSMQ are likely to use Active Directory, but these technologies provide their own simpler interfaces for developers. While some kinds of applications, such as scripts created by directory administrators, will directly use the Active Directory APIs, many will not.

The LDAP API Defined in RFC 1823, the LDAP API is specified as a group of C function calls. For the most part, these calls mirror the operations defined in the LDAP protocol. Many of the calls are defined in a synchronous version, where the call blocks until a result is received from the server, and an asynchronous version, where the call returns immediately and the caller must make a later call to retrieve a result. The two types of calls are distinguishable by their names: the synchronous call names end in "_s".

Among the calls defined by the LDAP API are:

- *ldap_simple_bind_s* Establishes a connection to an LDAP server, such as the Active Directory server running on a domain controller.

- *ldap_unbind* Releases a connection with an LDAP server.

- *ldap_search, ldap_search_s* Issues an LDAP Search request. The parameters to this call allow specifying the search options described earlier in this chapter, including the distinguished name of the object at which the search should begin, the depth of the search, what filter should be used for the search, and what attributes to return.

- *ldap_modify, ldap_modify_s* Issues an LDAP Modify request, allowing a client to change one or more attribute values in an object.

- *ldap_add, ldap_add_s* Issues an LDAP Add request, allowing a client to add an object.

- *ldap_delete, ldap_delete_s* Issues an LDAP Delete request, allowing a client to delete an object.

- *ldap_result* Retrieves the result of a previously issued asynchronous call.

The ADSI API In contrast to the standard LDAP API, which is aimed at developers working in C and C++, the ADSI API is defined as a set of COM objects. Those objects allow straightforward access to the directory from any programming language. In particular, the ADSI API is intended to make it easy for administrators to write scripts, using simple languages such as Microsoft VBScript, that make their jobs easier. It's also worth noting that the ADSI API isn't LDAP-specific. Instead, it's intended to be useful as an API to any directory service or, for that matter, to any hierarchal storage mechanism.

Figure 2-16 shows how that generality is provided. To access a particular directory service, a client must load the appropriate *ADSI provider*. This provider presents a set of COM objects to the client, and the client invokes methods in those objects' interfaces to access directory data. The ADSI provider then uses whatever protocol is required to access the directory service in use. The idea is quite similar to ActiveX Data Objects (ADO), which provides generic COM-based access to databases rather than to directory services.

Figure 2-16 *An ADSI provider presents COM objects to its client, and then uses whatever protocol is required to access a particular directory service.*

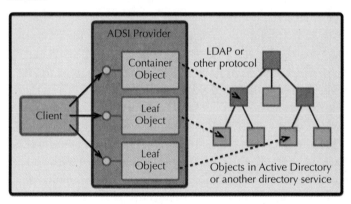

Microsoft supplies ADSI providers for several different directory services, including the Windows NT 4 directory, the Novell NetWare Bindery, and, of course, Active Directory. For Active Directory, the protocol used to access the directory is LDAP, but the basic structure of the COM objects seen by a client remains the same regardless of the underlying directory service.

Various directory services can be accessed through ADSI

An Example Use of Active Directory: Group Policy

There are a huge number of uses for a directory service. Several of the uses for Active Directory are described elsewhere in this book, but one of them is worth a look right now: Group Policy. As its name suggests, Group Policy allows domain administrators to define policies that control the environment seen by a particular set of users and computers in a domain. Windows 2000 then makes sure that environment is applied consistently by enforcing whatever policies are defined. Group Policy can only be applied to computers running Windows 2000, however—machines running older operating systems can't participate.

Here's how the process typically works. An administrator uses the Group Policy snap-in to define a Group Policy object (GPO). In doing this, the administrator specifies the policy settings that GPO should contain (exactly what these settings might be will be described shortly). Next the administrator associates the GPO with a container object in a domain's Active Directory hierarchy. That object can be for an entire domain (that is, it can be the root object in a domain's Active Directory tree), an OU, or a particular site. The policies defined in the GPO will then be applied to all users and computers in that domain, OU, or site.

The same GPO can be explicitly associated with several different directory container objects, making the settings it contains applicable to all of them. Also, a user or a computer might fall within the purview of two or more GPOs, and if that happens, the default is that policies set in all GPOs are applied. In other words, policies defined by a GPO higher in the hierarchy are inherited by any GPOs that appear lower in the tree.[7]

---

7. For domains grouped into a domain tree, GPOs set for a domain higher in the tree are not inherited by lower domains. It is possible, however, to associate a GPO defined in one domain with a domain, OU, or site object in some other domain, although doing this exacts a performance penalty when that GPO's policies are applied and is not recommended in most situations.

For example, Figure 2-17 shows the us.qwickbank.com domain with two GPOs defined. GPO1 defines policy settings A through E, and is associated with the container object for the entire domain. GPO2 defines policy settings X, Y, and Z, and is associated with a particular OU in the domain. In this case, settings A through E defined in GPO1 will be applied to all computers and users in the domain, while the computers and users in the receivables OU will also have settings X, Y, and Z applied.

Figure 2-17 *The policy settings in a GPO are applied to users and computers in a specific domain, OU, or site.*

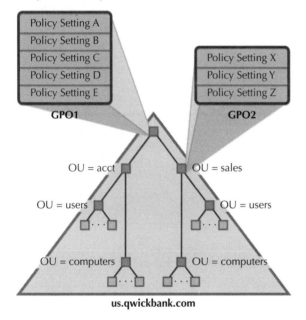

Kinds of Policies

Group policies come in two types, as follows:

- *Computer Configuration policies* Applied on a per-computer basis, these settings get applied to a particular computer in a domain regardless of which user logs into that computer.

● *User Configuration policies* Applied on a per-user basis, these settings get applied to a particular user in a domain regardless of which computer that user logs into.

Policy settings seen by a particular user are a function of all GPOs that apply

Exactly which policy settings a user sees depends on the User Configuration policies applied to that user and on the Computer Configuration policies applied to the computer the user logs into. As shown in Figure 2-18, computer settings are applied to a particular computer when that machine is booted, while user settings are applied when a user logs in. (Some policy settings are also periodically refreshed at an administratively-controllable interval.) Note that policies are applied only to users and computers—they are not applied to groups or any other kind of object.

Figure 2-18 *Computer Configuration policies are applied when a machine boots, and User Configuration policies are applied when a user logs in.*

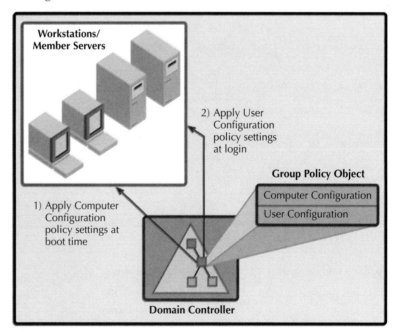

Each computer running Windows 2000 also has a Local GPO (LGPO) that can be configured using Group Policy in much the

same way as with any other GPO. The policy settings it contains are stored and applied on the same machine, however, unlike nonlocal GPOs. And settings defined in a machine's LGPO can be overridden by settings defined in nonlocal GPOs for the domain this machine is part of—the LGPO is the least influential object in the GPO hierarchy.

What Group Policy Can Control

GPOs allow defining policies in several different areas, including registry-based policies, software installation, folder redirection, scripting control, and security. This section describes each of these areas.

Group Policy can control many different aspects of the environment

Registry-Based Policies   This policy category allows an administrator to centrally control settings in the registry of managed machines. Among the things that can be set are:

- Whether various Start menu options, such as the Run command, Search command, or Shutdown command, can be seen by a user.
- Whether a user is allowed to edit the local registry.
- What applications a user is allowed to run.
- The wallpaper and color scheme a user sees.
- Whether a user can run Task Manager.

This is by no means a complete list—many, many more possibilities exist. The key point is that by judiciously using these options (and perhaps others as well), an administrator can exercise a good deal of control over a user's desktop.

Software Installation   When a new user is added to a particular domain, that user typically requires access to some defined set of applications. For example, each user in the us.qwickbank.com domain might need to use Microsoft Excel, Microsoft Word, and a home-grown banking application. It's also often necessary to give existing users access to new applications. Using Group Policy, an

Applications can be made accessible by using Group Policy

administrator can centrally define which applications should be available to users in a domain, an OU, or a site, and then have those applications automatically be made available to those users. To do this, applications can be either *assigned* or *published*.

An assigned application looks to a user as if it's already installed, but is actually installed when it is first accessed

All assigned applications listed in a particular GPO will appear to be available to all users to whom this GPO is applied. A shortcut to the application will appear on the user's Start menu, and the registry will contain information about it. The application itself is not actually installed, however. Instead, its existence is advertised in Active Directory using something called the *class store*. When a user first attempts to start the application, the application's binaries are located, downloaded to the workstation, and installed.[8] From now on, the application will remain installed on this machine; it's only downloaded the first time it's accessed. If a user deletes an assigned application, or even inadvertently removes a necessary part of one, such as a key DLL, this loss will be detected and corrected the next time the application is started—the system will automatically download the missing pieces.

Also, if the user double clicks on a file associated with an assigned application and that application has not yet been installed, it will be automatically downloaded and installed at that point. Suppose, for example, that someone has e-mailed this user a Microsoft Word file, but Word isn't installed on the user's workstation. If Word is an assigned application for this user or computer, double-clicking on the Word file will automatically install Word.

A published application must be explicitly installed by the user

A published application, by contrast, does not automatically appear to be available for use by a user. No shortcut for the application will appear in the Start menu, and no information about it will be preloaded into the workstation's registry. Instead, a user can use the Add/Remove Programs tool to see a list of all published applications, an operation that again relies on the class store. This

---

8. How this works for COM-based applications is described in Chapter 8.

list includes all of the applications that the policy settings applied to this user/computer combination make available as published applications, and a user can explicitly install any applications that are required. Alternatively, as with an assigned application, an attempt by the user to open a file that requires a published application will cause the application to be installed automatically.

Applications that will be either assigned or published are typically packaged using the Windows Installer. These packages are sometimes referred to as .msi files, after their file extension. Once this is done, enough information is available to the system to allow downloading and correctly installing the application as required.

Folder Redirection   These policy settings allow a domain administrator to cause specific folders on a user's desktop to actually point to folders stored on a file server somewhere in the network. A user's My Documents folder might be set to point to a particular place, for example, allowing that user access to its contents regardless of which computer the user logs into. Similarly, the Desktop, Start Menu, and other items can be redirected to a shared server using Group Policy.

> Desktop folders can be redirected to folders on a server

Scripting Control   These policy settings control what scripts are run on a workstation (if any) when the machine boots, when it shuts down, when a user logs in, and when a user logs out. Using the Windows Scripting Host, scripts can be written in VBScript, JavaScript, and other languages. And, of course, scripting Luddites are still free to create traditional MS-DOS command language scripts if they choose.

> Scripts can be run automatically

Security   The policies that can be controlled through a GPO's security settings allow many different aspects of security to be centrally configured. Among the many options included are:

> Many aspects of security can be controlled using Group Policy

- *Password policy*   For example, how frequently passwords must be changed, how many characters those passwords must contain, and how soon a user can reuse an old password.

- *Account lockout policy*   Controls how many failed login attempts are allowed before the account is locked out, and how long that lockout will last.
- *Audit policy*   Controls whether records are kept of every user logon attempt, every access to Active Directory, every security policy change, and more.
- *User rights assignment*   Indicates which users and groups have the right to perform various tasks. These tasks include changing the system time, shutting down the system, performing backups, adding workstations to a domain, and many more.
- *Security options*   Allows changing the names of the built-in Administrator and Guest accounts and many other operations.

A security template allows specifying many security settings at once

To make the task of setting this multitude of security options easier, Windows 2000 defines the notion of a *security template*. A security template is a defined set of security settings, which can include settings for the things listed above and more. Windows 2000 ships with a standard set of security templates, and you can edit these or create entirely new ones using the Security Templates snap-in. Once it's been defined, a security template can be assigned in toto to a particular GPO.

How Policy Settings Are Stored

Information in a GPO is stored in two different places

All the information in a GPO isn't stored in the same place. Instead, a GPO is really an abstraction, as shown in Figure 2-19. The policy settings in a GPO that are relatively small and don't change frequently are kept in Active Directory objects under a *Group Policy Container*, while the information in a GPO that's bigger or that changes frequently is kept in a *Group Policy Template*. Each Group Policy Template is stored in a set of folders on a domain controller—not in the Active Directory database. This information is still replicated, but unlike with Active Directory, the mechanism used to do it is better suited for moving file-oriented data such as Group Policy Templates.

Figure 2-19 *The information in a GPO is divided between the Active Directory database and the file system on a domain controller.*

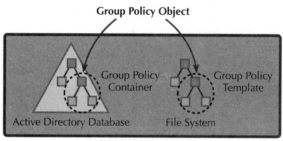

Applying Multiple Policies at Once

As you might imagine, using GPOs can quickly get complex. Suppose a policy setting defined in an OU directly contradicts one specified for the domain. Who wins? The answer is the same as the answer to most interesting questions: it depends. To determine which settings will be in effect for a given user or computer, all GPOs relevant to that user or computer must be applied. First any policy settings contained in the Local GPO are applied, followed by GPOs associated with the site, then the domain, and finally the OU. If the policies defined in the GPOs applied to a particular user or computer conflict, the default is that the policy specified in the last GPO to be applied wins. This means that policies specified at the domain level can override anything specified at the site level, while policies specified at the OU level can override anything specified at the site or domain level. If multiple GPOs associated with multiple OUs must be assigned to the same user or computer, however, the default is that those in the *nearest* OU win. This ordering can seem counter-intuitive, but it was chosen to reflect the most common policy hierarchies in large organizations.

The policies applied to a particular user or computer can be derived from multiple GPOs

And, of course, these defaults can be changed. For example, it's possible to administratively define policies that cannot be overridden. Suppose an organization decides that every user in a given domain must have a password with a specific minimum length. This policy could be defined in a GPO associated with the domain object, and then set so that no other GPO can override it. If desired, it's also possible to stop inheritance of policies so that policies defined at, say, the domain level won't be automatically applied to the OUs in that domain. An administrator can also specify that the policies defined in some GPO should be applied only to members of particular Windows 2000 security groups, allowing fine-grained control of which users and computers feel their effects.

Using Group Policy

In general, fewer GPOs are better

How might an administrator choose to use GPOs in a large, complex domain? In general, defining as few GPOs as possible is a good thing, since managing them requires work. Also, GPOs take time to process. If many GPOs must be applied each time a computer boots or a user logs in, performance can suffer. As always, it's good to keep things as simple as possible.

An obvious approach is to define policies applicable to all users and computers in a domain using a GPO associated with that domain, and then define OU-specific policies in GPOs bound to individual OUs in the domain. While layering GPOs like this simplifies administration, it also hurts performance, since two (or perhaps more) GPOs must be applied at login or boot time. Monolithic GPOs, where every policy required for an OU is contained in that OU's GPO, are harder to administer since they replicate information that might otherwise be kept in a common domain-level GPO, but they're faster to apply. Administrators need to make these tradeoffs in a way that's appropriate for their environment.

Group Policy is anything but simple. Yet the problem it addresses is unquestionably complex. One way to look at Group Policy is to remember that small domains probably won't need its full power, and so will be spared much of its complexity. Large domains, by contrast, are the ones who most need all of this flexibility, and they're also likely to be able to invest the necessary resources to best exploit it. Nothing is free—complex problems tend to require complex solutions.

Upgrading to Active Directory

Moving fully to Windows 2000, domain controllers and all, implies moving to Active Directory—there's no way around it. This is for the most part a good thing, because Active Directory offers a range of powerful services. But making the move to Active Directory and Windows 2000 isn't a simple thing to do for existing domains, especially for large organizations. It requires thought, planning, and effort.

Windows 2000 domains require Active Directory

An essential issue in the transition is deciding on appropriate domain structures. An Active Directory database can hold many more objects than are possible in Windows NT 4, so domains can potentially be much larger. Also, an administrator of a Windows NT 4 domain has control over all accounts in that domain, a fact that has caused many organizations to create multiple independent domains. Active Directory, however, allows delegating administrative authority at the OU level. A single Windows 2000 domain can now have accounts in one OU controlled by one administrator, while accounts in another OU in the same domain are controlled by a different administrator.

The key point to derive from both of these facts is that, for intrinsic technical and administrative reasons, Windows 2000 domains can be larger than Windows NT 4 domains. Organizations that previously had several domains might well find that they can get

Current domain structures should be re-examined and perhaps changed by with just one, and most organizations will probably benefit from combining at least some of their current domains. What were once full-fledged domains can now be just OUs within a single domain.

Choosing the right domain structure can be challenging

Determining how domains should be named and grouped together is also worth a good deal of thought. If one domain won't suffice for an organization, it's a good idea to give domains contiguous domain names and group them into a domain tree. But the existing DNS name structure of an organization can make this a challenging thing to do. The next best option, then, is to group domains with noncontiguous DNS names into a forest. As in a domain tree, domains in a forest all trust each other, and all share the same GC, so it's relatively easy to find information. All domains in a forest must share a common schema, however, which can be challenging to achieve in some organizations.

Moving a domain to Windows 2000 first requires upgrading that domain's PDC

To actually upgrade an existing Windows NT 4 domain to Windows 2000, the domain's PDC must be upgraded first. When this is done, the accounts in the domain are automatically loaded into the Active Directory database. To existing systems in the domain, this new Windows 2000 machine will look exactly like the Windows NT 4 PDC it replaces. Other domain controllers, member servers, and clients in that domain can then be upgraded piecemeal. Domain controllers running Windows 2000 will replicate among themselves using Active Directory's multi-master replication, while those running Windows NT 4 will use the traditional single-master replication. Once all domain controllers have been upgraded, only multi-master replication is used. Even once this is done, however, one domain controller continues to advertise itself as a Windows NT 4 PDC, providing support for any older systems that might exist in this domain.

Planning for and migrating to Active Directory is probably the most demanding part of the move to Windows 2000. Providing a standard directory service, and then using it instead of a plethora of different services, is bound to cause some dislocation. As with any transition, forethought and planning will pay dividends down the road. But once the pain is over and Active Directory is running smoothly in your environment, you'll probably wonder how you ever got by without it.

The effort should be worth it in the end

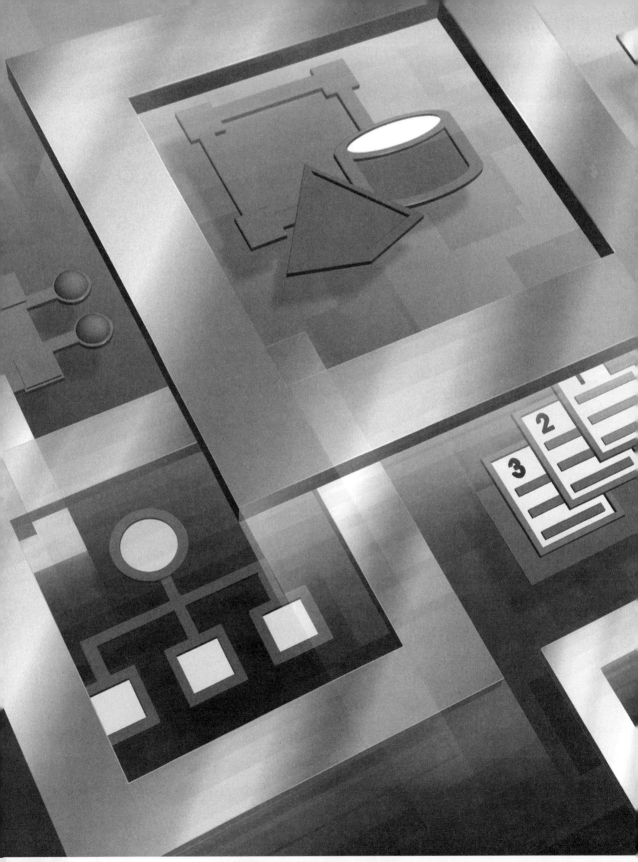

Chapter Three

Distributed Security Services: Kerberos

Distributed security is a non-trivial topic. Yet Microsoft Windows 2000 developers, administrators, and others need to understand the large set of security services this operating system offers and how they are provided. This chapter first examines the basic structure of Windows 2000 distributed security, and then takes a closer look at Kerberos, the most important distributed security technology in Windows 2000.

Distributed security is complicated, but important

Distributed Security in Windows 2000

Although distributed security services were introduced in Chapter 1, it's worth briefly reviewing the four most important of them. They are:

Distributed security comprises several different services

- *Authentication*   Proves you are who you say you are.
- *Authorization (access control)*   Determines what you're allowed to do.
- *Data integrity*   Ensures that data isn't modified in transit.
- *Data privacy*   Ensures that data isn't read in transit.

Another important service, one whose relevance extends beyond distributed security, is *auditing*. Auditing, in general, means keeping a record, sometimes called an *audit trail,* of interesting things that happen on a given system or in a given domain. Exactly what qualifies as interesting can vary, but some common examples of things that might be audited include failed login attempts and password changes. In fact, Windows 2000 can audit a broad range of things in addition to the events just listed, including access to any file, directory, printer, or Active Directory object, and much more.

Every principal has an identity that can be authenticated

One more important security concept is the idea of a *principal*. A principal can be thought of as anything with an account and a password. In Windows 2000, every user and every computer in a domain is a principal, as are some server applications. When authentication occurs, what's really being proven is the principal identity of the parties involved.

Windows 2000 distributed security relies on Active Directory

A strong synergy exists between distributed security services and directory services. Both need to store and access various kinds of information, and both can benefit from replication of that information. Not too surprisingly, then, the distributed security services in Windows 2000 are closely integrated with Active Directory. As shown in Figure 3-1, Windows 2000 does not maintain a separate database for distributed security. Instead, the required information, such as an account and password for each user in a domain, is stored in Active Directory objects. Accordingly, the Windows 2000 Kerberos service runs on a domain controller, allowing it direct access to the Active Directory database.[1]

The Security Support Provider Interface (SSPI)

Security Service Providers are accessed through the Security Support Provider Interface

In Windows 2000, Kerberos, Secure Sockets Layer (SSL)/Transport Layer Security (TLS), NTLM, and possibly other security protocols are each implemented in separate modules called *Security Service Providers (SSPs)*. Access to every SSP is accomplished in the same way: through the *Security Support Provider Interface (SSPI)*. SSPI is based on, although not identical to, the Generic Security Service API (GSS-API) defined by the Internet Engineering Task Force (IETF) in RFC 2078.

---

1. In fact, the Kerberos service runs in the same process as the Active Directory LDAP server.

Figure 3-1 *The Windows 2000 Kerberos service relies on information stored in the Active Directory database.*

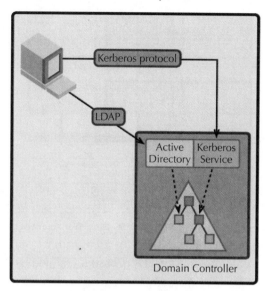

SSPI isn't new with Windows 2000—it's been part of the system since the release of Microsoft Windows NT 3.5. What is new, though, is how broadly it's applied. As shown in Figure 3-2, SSPI provides the common interface between Windows 2000's distributed services and its SSPs. Implementing each distributed security service as an SSP beneath SSPI makes it possible for application protocols to access any security service in the same way.

For the most part, SSPI is not used directly by application developers. Instead, individual application protocols have their own (usually simpler) interfaces. The creator of a DCOM application, for example, uses the security API provided by DCOM, while the creator of an HTTP-based application might use the WinInet interface defined for that environment. Under the covers, though, these interfaces all ultimately rely on SSPI.

Developers usually don't use SSPI directly

Figure 3-2 *All kinds of distributed applications can access distributed security services through the SSPI.*

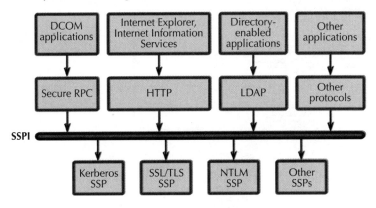

SNEGO allows the client and the server to negotiate which security protocol to use

The support of multiple security protocols raises an issue, however: how do two systems agree on which protocol to use? In Windows 2000, a protocol known as SNEGO is used. Defined by the IETF, SNEGO allows a client's first request to a server to contain an indication of what security protocols that client is willing to use, along with the information that is normally sent for the client's preferred protocol. If the server accepts the client's proposal, it responds with whatever that security protocol specifies. In this most common case, using SNEGO adds no network roundtrips. If the server doesn't support the protocol requested by the client, it sends back an indication of what protocols it does support, and the client tries again. To use SNEGO, applications must make appropriate SSPI requests, and virtually all of Windows 2000's distributed services do this. Kerberos is always the default security protocol choice in the Windows 2000 environment, but using SSPI and SNEGO allows applications to make use of other security protocols as well.

Performing Authorization

Windows 2000 supports the traditional Windows NT authorization mechanism

Kerberos and SSL can both provide authentication, data integrity, and data privacy—exactly how is described in this chapter and the next one—but neither technology addresses authorization. This shouldn't be surprising. Authorization typically takes place on the machine where a server process is running, so it's not a problem that can be solved by protocols such as Kerberos and SSL. But fortunately, Windows 2000 itself has a standard approach to authorization. And like SSPI, this approach is not new—it's been used since the first release of Windows NT.

The basic idea, shown in Figure 3-3, is straightforward: a client contacts a server process requesting access to some resource, such as a file or an object in Active Directory. To identify itself, the client provides its *authorization data,* a set of information describing the user. Once the server has that data, a standard Windows 2000 component called the *Local Security Authority (LSA)* uses the data to construct a *security access token.* The server process being accessed uses this token to impersonate the user by taking on that user's identity, and then tries to access whatever the client is interested in. Files, Active Directory objects, and many other resources have *security descriptors* assigned to them, indicating what kind of access is allowed by various users and groups. Among other things, each security descriptor contains a list of *access control entries (ACEs),* which are sometimes referred to collectively as an *access control list (ACL).* When the impersonating server attempts access, the operating system automatically checks the ACL. If the user the server is impersonating has the right to perform the requested access, the access is allowed; if not, the access is denied.

Resources have security descriptors that contain ACLs

For a client running on the same computer as the server process, the user's authorization data is conveyed by the operating system. If the user is logged on to a different computer than the server process, however, the user's authorization data must be conveyed across the network by Kerberos, SSL, or some other protocol. Authorization data can consist of various things, but perhaps the most important information is a set of *security identifiers (SIDs).* A SID is a globally unique value, and one is assigned to each user and each group in Windows 2000. A running process has associated with it one SID identifying the user whose identity it's running under, and other SIDs identifying the groups that user

Security protocols can convey authorization data across a network belongs to. A basic problem that must be solved by protocols such as Kerberos is how to securely convey this authorization data from a client process to a server process on some other machine. How Kerberos accomplishes this is described in the next section.

Figure 3-3 *A server relies on a user's authorization data to impersonate that user, and then attempts access to a particular object.*

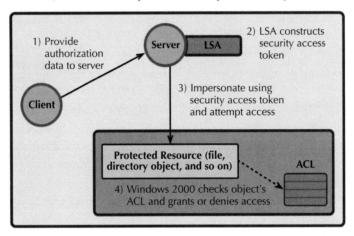

Understanding Kerberos

Kerberos is a mature technology

Kerberos, named after the three-headed dog that guards Hades, was created at the Massachusetts Institute of Technology (MIT) in the early 1980s. The current version, Kerberos version 5, has been published by the IETF as RFC 1510, and Windows 2000 implements the protocol as described in this standard. Despite its relative age, however, Kerberos has not been an especially widely used technology. By making Kerberos the core security protocol in Windows 2000, however, Microsoft has guaranteed that this relative obscurity is over. Given the popularity of Microsoft's technologies, Kerberos seems destined to be an essential part of many distributed environments.

Although the Kerberos protocol does convey the information necessary to make an authorization decision, authorization is typically performed as already described—Kerberos doesn't provide this service. It does, however, provide the other three security services described earlier: authentication, data integrity, and data privacy. The fundamental mechanisms used to provide all three rely on secret key encryption, so before describing Kerberos, it's necessary to outline the basics of how secret key technology works.

Secret Key Encryption

In secret key encryption, the same key is used to encrypt and decrypt data. Suppose, for instance, that you want to send me a private message indicating that the QwickBank Corporation has been sold. As shown in Figure 3-4, you can encrypt that message using some key value. You can then send me the resulting encrypted information, sometimes called the ciphertext, without fear of anyone else reading it (assuming you've chosen a strong encryption algorithm and an appropriate key). To decrypt the message, I must use the same key that you used for encryption.

Secret key encryption requires two parties to share a single key

Figure 3-4 *In secret key encryption, the same key is used for encryption and decryption.*

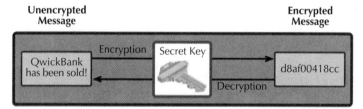

Secret key encryption has some very nice features. Perhaps the most important are that the keys can be short—common lengths are 56 bits and 128 bits—and that encryption/decryption operations are relatively fast. But secret key encryption also has a

Distributing secret keys is a problem

significant drawback: the problem of key distribution. If you and I wish to exchange encrypted messages, we must both have the same key—it's a shared secret between us. But suppose you create this secret key; how do you securely transmit it to me? You could always e-mail it to me, but sending an unencrypted key across the Internet is hardly secure. Solving the problem of key distribution is perhaps the hardest issue in using secret key algorithms, and how Kerberos addresses it is described later in this chapter.

Many different secret key algorithms are in use today. One of the most common algorithms is still the Data Encryption Standard (DES), which uses an eight-byte key. DES dates from the 1970s, however, and it's showing its age. Today, virtually no one views DES as an especially secure algorithm. Instead, other secret key algorithms are becoming more widely used, including Triple-DES (which, as its name suggests, is a souped-up version of the original DES), RC2, and RC4.[2]

Kerberos Fundamentals

Kerberos relies primarily on secret key encryption

Kerberos always provides authentication, and if an application requests it, can also provide data integrity and data privacy. All three of these services are performed using secret key encryption,[3] so encryption keys are an important part of Kerberos technology. Rather than require its users to invent special keys, Kerberos can derive encryption keys from ordinary passwords. But those passwords aren't used to encrypt the actual data sent between clients and servers. Instead, password-based keys are used only during login, as described later in this chapter, and other dynamically created keys are used to encrypt and decrypt data sent across the network.

---

2. "RC" stands for "Ron's Code," after Ron Rivest, the creator of both algorithms.

3. Although Windows 2000 Kerberos also allows logging in using smart cards and public key encryption, an option that's described in the next chapter.

The key a principal uses to log in is really a *hash* of that principal's password. A hash algorithm (sometimes called a *message digest* algorithm) produces a bit string that is derived from the information being hashed, but that can't be used to recover the original input value. In other words, hashes are one-way: given, say, a hashed password value, it's not possible to recover the original password.

A password can be hashed to produce a secret encryption key

In Windows 2000, users have passwords, server applications that want to authenticate their users have passwords, and all computers in a domain have passwords. Anything with a password qualifies as a security principal, something whose identity can be authenticated. The Kerberos *Key Distribution Center (KDC)* runs on a domain controller, where it has access to the hashed password for every principal in its domain. (This information is stored in each principal's Active Directory object, kept on the same domain controller.) By default, the cleartext password itself is not stored in the directory—only a hashed version is kept there. To allow password synchronization with other directory services, an administrator can cause a user's original cleartext password to be stored along with the hashed version if desired. Whichever option is chosen, each principal's password information is stored only in an encrypted form, using the strongest level of encryption available. Despite this protection, however, domain controllers should still be kept physically secure. A determined attacker with unlimited time to successfully crack your domain's most important systems is something you definitely want to avoid.

Kerberos can access hashed passwords stored in Active Directory

The Kerberos protocol allows negotiating which encryption algorithm should be used, and Kerberos implementations have traditionally defaulted to DES with its 8-byte keys. Windows 2000 Kerberos supports DES, but its default choice for an encryption algorithm is RC4.[4] RC4 is both faster and more secure than DES

Windows 2000 Kerberos defaults to RC4 for encryption

---

4. 128-bit keys are used in the North American release. U.S. export laws for strong cryptography are changing as this book goes to press, however, so this key length might also be available internationally by the time you read this.

today, and in a standard Windows 2000 environment, all Kerberos encryption uses this newer algorithm.

Proving I know a key can let me prove who I am

How secret key encryption can be used to send data privately is obvious, but how it can be used for authentication is a little less so. To see how this might be done, imagine that you and I share a key, and suppose I send you some message encrypted using that key. If you use this key to decrypt the message, and that decryption works correctly, then this message must have been encrypted using that same key. If only you and I know that key, this message must have come from me. By proving knowledge of a key in this way, I can prove my identity—I can authenticate myself without ever transmitting the key itself.

Using secret key encryption in this simple way for authentication would not be very practical, however. It would require each client/server pair to share a secret key, which means that each of us would need a separate key for every service we wished to access securely. This is not a very appealing prospect. How, then, is it possible to effectively use secret key encryption for authentication? The answer is provided by Kerberos.

Tickets are used to prove identity

Tickets   When a client wishes to prove the user's identity to a server application on some other system, that client must somehow provide the server with an appropriate *ticket*. Each ticket allows a specific client to prove the user's identity to a specific server application, such as a particular DCOM application. As shown in Figure 3-5, a Kerberos ticket contains both encrypted and unencrypted information. Although the picture shown in the figure is somewhat simplified, the unencrypted part of a ticket contains two primary pieces of information: the name of the Windows 2000 domain in which this ticket was issued (the Kerberos standard uses the term "realm" rather than "domain"), and the name of the principal this ticket identifies.

Figure 3-5 *A Kerberos ticket contains various fields, most of which are encrypted.*

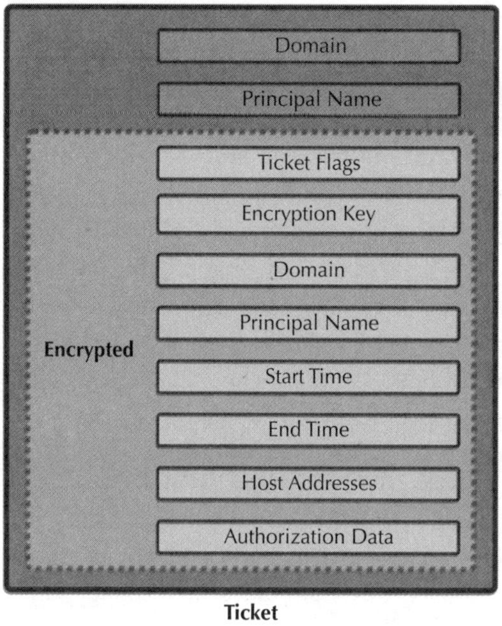

	Domain
	Principal Name
Encrypted	Ticket Flags
	Encryption Key
	Domain
	Principal Name
	Start Time
	End Time
	Host Addresses
	Authorization Data

Ticket

The encrypted part of the ticket contains quite a bit more information. Among the more interesting fields are the following:

- Various ticket flags, some of which are described later.
- An encryption key, commonly referred to as a *session* key, that can be used to encrypt information exchanged between the user named in this ticket and the ticket's target server.
- Encrypted copies of the user's domain and principal name.
- The start and end times for this ticket's validity.
- One or more IP addresses identifying the user's system.
- The user's authorization data, which can be used by the server to determine what this user is allowed to access.

All of those fields are encrypted using the key (that is, the hashed password) of the server application this ticket targets. Note that neither the user nor any attackers listening on the network can read or modify the encrypted fields in a ticket, since they don't know the server password that was used for encryption.

The fields carrying the ticket's start and end times are worth some extra explanation. Every ticket has a finite lifetime, which means that an attacker has only a limited period in which to crack the ticket's encryption, making a successful attack more difficult, and that a stolen ticket can be used only until it expires. (Actually, using somebody else's ticket requires knowing more than just the ticket itself, as is described later.) A lifetime limit also means that every user's tickets expire periodically, which could be a nuisance. Fortunately, Windows 2000 will automatically renew a user's tickets as long as that user remains logged in.

Interactive Login   When a client wishes to prove the user's identity to a server, it must acquire a ticket to that server. In fact, virtually the entire Kerberos protocol is devoted to acquiring and using tickets. Before launching into a description of how the protocol works, however, it's worth taking a moment to explain the notation used in the rest of this chapter. I've mostly adopted what has become the standard Kerberos notation, which is:

- K_X The secret key (that is, the hashed password) of X, where X is a client user (C), a server application (S), or the KDC itself (K).
- $\{anything\}K_X$ Anything encrypted with X's secret key.
- $\{T\}K_S$ A ticket encrypted with server S's secret key. In other words, this is a ticket for server S. (The notation is a bit imprecise, since the entire ticket isn't encrypted.)
- $K_{X,Y}$ A session key used between X and Y.
- $\{anything\}K_{X,Y}$ Anything encrypted with the session key used between X and Y.

The first time a user requests a Kerberos ticket is when that user logs in to some account in a Windows 2000 domain. From the point of view of the user, the process is simple: type a login name, a domain name, and a password into some client machine, and then wait for the login to succeed or fail. What's actually going on, however, is not quite so simple.

The Kerberos protocol is invisible to users

As shown in Figure 3-6, the user's login request causes the client machine to send a message to a KDC running on a domain controller. The message contains several things, including:

A user requests a ticket-granting ticket at login

- The user's name.
- Pre-authentication data, which consists of a timestamp encrypted using K_C, a hash of the user's password, as a key.
- A request for a *ticket-granting ticket (TGT)*. A TGT is just an ordinary ticket, like the one shown in Figure 3-5, and as with all tickets, it is used to prove a user's identity. But the TGT is used in a slightly special way: as we'll see, the Kerberos SSP on the client presents the TGT to the KDC when requesting tickets to specific server applications.

Figure 3-6 *At login time, a user gets a TGT and a session key that can be used to request other tickets.*

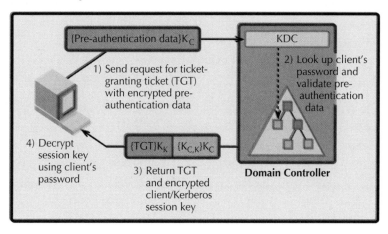

	When this request arrives at the domain controller, the KDC looks up the entry associated with the user's principal name in the domain's Active Directory database. From this entry, the KDC extracts a hash of the user's password, and then uses this value to decrypt the pre-authentication data. If that decryption works—if it results in a very recent timestamp—the KDC can be certain that this user is who he or she claims to be, since the user has demonstrated knowledge of the correct password. (Note that this was done without having that password sent over the network. To provide its services, Kerberos never requires sending a user's password across the network.) If the decryption fails, however, the user must have entered the wrong password, and the login will fail.

The KDC verifies the user's initial request

If the pre-authentication data is correctly validated, the KDC next builds and sends back to the client machine what it asked for: a ticket-granting ticket. This ticket, like all tickets, contains the user's name and the name of the domain in which it was issued, along with a session key, $K_{C,K}$, generated randomly by the KDC, the valid start and end times for this ticket, and various flag values. In the Authorization Data field, the TGT contains Windows 2000 SIDs and other information identifying the user and the groups the user belongs to (this information is extracted from the user's entry in Active Directory). As always, the encrypted part of the ticket is encrypted using the key of the server to whom this ticket will be sent. Since the TGT is used only to request other tickets, and since only the KDC can give out tickets, the encrypted part of the TGT is encrypted using K_K, the key of the KDC itself.

If all is well, the KDC sends the user a TGT

The session key $K_{C,K}$, which the KDC sends back to the client machine along with the TGT, has the same value the server placed in the TGT. This session key is sent encrypted using the user's hashed password as a key. When the client machine gets that message, it uses the hash of whatever password the user has entered to decrypt the received session key. In Windows 2000 Kerberos, this decryption will always work, since only users who demon-

The KDC also sends the user an encrypted session key

strate knowledge of the correct password by means of the pre-authentication data will get this information sent to them at all.

Sending pre-authentication data is optional in the Kerberos standard, but it's an option that Windows 2000 Kerberos always uses. Non-Microsoft Kerberos implementations, however, don't typically use it. If an account has been configured to allow it, a Windows 2000 domain controller can also accept requests without pre-authentication data. This lets the Windows 2000 KDC be used with Kerberos clients that don't generate that information. In this case, the user's identity is verified when the received session key is decrypted, step 4 in Figure 3-6. If the correct password is entered, decryption of the client/KDC session key $K_{C,K}$ will succeed. If the user types the wrong password, however, that decryption will fail, and the user will not know the session key. And as described in the next section, getting tickets to other services requires knowing this key.

One more concern is worth addressing here: what happens if no KDC is available? Preventing a user from logging into his machine, even if the entire network is down, is a bad idea. To allow local login in the event of network or server failures, a hashed version of the user's password and user name is stored on his or her machine. If no KDC is accessible, the information entered by the user at login is checked against this stored data. If they match, the login succeeds.

Local login is possible if the KDC is inaccessible

Network Authentication   Once a user has successfully logged in, that user is likely to begin accessing services running on other computers in the network. To do this securely, the user must at a minimum have some way of proving his or her identity to those services. In Windows 2000, the Kerberos SSP can present a TGT to the KDC, requesting a ticket to a specific service.[5] To distinguish

Given a valid TGT, the KDC will issue service tickets

---

5. The function in the KDC that gives out tickets to specific services is sometimes referred to as the ticket granting service (TGS).

them from TGTs, these tickets are sometimes called *service* tickets, but the format is identical for both types. That ticket is then sent to the target service, which can use it to determine exactly who this user is. (In fact, immediately after acquiring a TGT, every client completes the login process by requesting a service ticket for its own computer, allowing it to prove its identity to local services.)

A service ticket authenticates a user to a specific service

Suppose, for instance, that a user wishes to access a DCOM server application (called, say, Server S) running on some remote system. The user will load the client half of the application, and this client will attempt to create a remote DCOM object. If the application uses Kerberos for authentication, however, that client application will need to acquire a ticket on behalf of its user before it can access the remote server. Recall that each ticket authenticates a particular user to a particular service, and since the client part of a distributed application runs on behalf of the user, that client acquires tickets that prove the user's identity to the server.

When the client application makes its first remote request to the server, a ticket request is made to the KDC, as shown in Figure 3-7. Programmers do not generally code this request explicitly. Instead, the developer of the application just requests that Kerberos be used and everything else happens under the covers. This request contains several things, including:

- The user's TGT.
- The name of the server application for which a service ticket is requested, which in this case is Server S.
- An authenticator proving that this TGT belongs to this user. The authenticator contains the current time and the user's name, and it is encrypted using the session key $K_{C,K}$ that was received at login.

Figure 3-7 *A TGT is used to request a session ticket to a specific server application, and then that session ticket is used to prove the user's identity.*

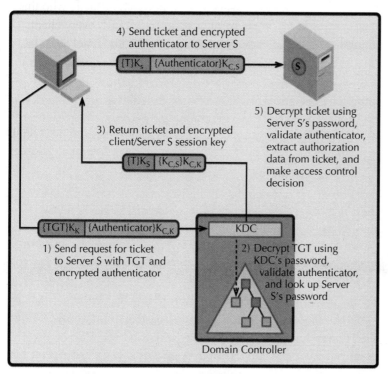

When the KDC receives this request, it decrypts the TGT (recall that only the KDC knows K_K, the key used to encrypt this ticket), and then extracts the session key $K_{C,K}$ from the ticket. It then uses this session key to decrypt the authenticator. The authenticator serves two purposes. First, because it is encrypted using the client/KDC session key, it proves that the user is who he or she claims to be, since as described earlier, the only way to get this session key is to type the correct password at login. If the KDC's attempted decryption of the authenticator is successful, the client must be in possession of the correct session key.

Authenticators prove the user's identity

Second, because the authenticator contains a timestamp, it prevents an attacker from grabbing a user's TGT off the network, and then presenting the TGT as its own. A new authenticator is created each time a ticket is used, and because the timestamp is encrypted using the session key, known only to the client and the KDC, a valid authenticator can't be created by anyone else. To prevent a malevolent third party from saving and later resending authenticators (an example of what's known as a *replay* attack), a KDC will reject any authenticator whose timestamp is too old. By default, an authenticator's timestamp must differ by no more than 5 minutes from that of the server that receives it, but this setting can be changed administratively.[6] To further ensure that the user isn't presenting a stolen ticket, the KDC also verifies that the IP address in the TGT matches the IP address of the system that sent the request.

The KDC copies some
information from the
TGT into each service
ticket it issues

If everything checks out, the KDC will believe that this user is who it claims to be, and will send back the requested service ticket. The KDC copies some fields from the TGT into the new service ticket, including the user's name, domain, and authorization data. It sets the service ticket's flags and start/end times appropriately, and generates a new random session key, $K_{C,S}$, which it places in the ticket. (As described shortly, that session key can be used to encrypt information sent between the client and Server S.) The KDC then encrypts this new ticket using K_S, Server S's secret key, and sends it back to the client, along with the new session key $K_{C,S}$. To prevent attackers from learning this new key, it's sent encrypted using the session key shared by the KDC and the client.

The receiving system
decrypts the service
ticket to verify the
user's identity

Finally, the goal of this entire exercise can be achieved: the user can prove his or her identity to the server application. On its first request to Server S, the client presents the service ticket it just received along with an authenticator encrypted using $K_{C,S}$. This

---

6. This implies that the clocks on machines using Kerberos must be at least loosely synchronized, so Windows 2000 uses the IETF-defined Simple Network Time Protocol (SNTP) for clock synchronization.

information is sent as part of whatever protocol is being used between client and server. With DCOM, for example, the ticket and authenticator are carried in a field in the appropriate DCOM packet. However it's sent, the receiving system decrypts the ticket with its secret key, extracts the session key $K_{C,S}$ from the ticket, and then decrypts and validates the authenticator. If everything checks out, the user's identity information is extracted from the ticket—principal name, domain name, and authorization data—and made accessible to the server application. All of this work is done by the Kerberos SSP—the developer of the server application doesn't have to worry about it.

Although Kerberos itself doesn't directly address the problem, the information about the user that's extracted from the received ticket is commonly used to make an authorization decision. Exactly how this is done is up to the creator of the server application. The application might use the authorization data to impersonate the user, taking the standard Windows 2000 approach to authorization described earlier, or it might do something much simpler, such as look up the user's name in a list of users authorized to perform some function. How authorization is performed, or even whether it's performed at all, is not Kerberos's bailiwick. Instead, Kerberos focuses on guaranteeing that the identity a user is claiming in a service ticket truly identifies that user.

The receiving system can make an authorization decision in any way it likes

To make sure this is all clear, let me summarize why this authentication process works. Since the service ticket the user presented was encrypted using Server S's secret key, and since only the KDC (along with Server S, of course) knows that key, this ticket must have been created by the KDC. And since the KDC will only give out service tickets to users who can prove they know the right password by correctly encrypting the pre-authentication data, this user must be who he or she claims to be. Presented together with a valid authenticator, a Kerberos ticket allows a user to reliably prove his or her identity to a server.

Kerberos also allows a
server to prove its
identity to a client

But what about the reverse problem? We've just seen how Kerberos authenticates the client to the server, but how can the client be certain that the server is who it claims to be? It might be possible for an attacker to install a spurious version of Server S, and then acquire sensitive information by fooling the client into thinking it was the real Server S. To prevent this, the Kerberos standard defines an option for *mutual authentication,* an option that should be requested by pretty much every application. Now not only does the client prove the user's identity to the server, the server must also prove its identity to the client. To do that, the Kerberos SSP on the server creates a message containing the timestamp from the client's authenticator encrypted using the client/ Server S session key, $K_{C,S}$. When this message is received by the Kerberos SSP on the client, it can use its copy of the session key to decrypt it. If the client's Kerberos SSP finds the timestamp it just sent, it can be certain that the server knows the session key, too. And since learning the session key required decrypting the server's ticket, which required knowing the server's password, this server must be who it claims to be.

Providing Data Integrity and Data Privacy   All of the complexity described so far has focused on how Kerberos provides just one security service: authentication. Recall, however, that Kerberos can also provide data integrity and data privacy, two other useful services. Because the exchanges just described have left the client and server in possession of a shared session key, though, providing these services is straightforward.

Data can be accompa-
nied by an encrypted
checksum to provide
data integrity

To guarantee that no attacker can modify transmitted data without being detected, the Kerberos SSP on any system that's sending data can compute a checksum on each packet it sends and transmit that checksum with the packet. The checksum value is a function of the data it's based on, so if the data is changed, the checksum must also change. But sending just a packet and a checksum isn't sufficient—an attacker could grab the packet, modify the data, recompute a new checksum on the new data, and send it on its way. To prevent this from happening, the data's sender computes the checksum on not just the message itself, but on the message and other information, and then encrypts the result using the session key. (By default, Windows 2000 Kerberos uses the Message Digest 5 [MD5] checksum algorithm, and the checksum is encrypted using RC4, although other options are also supported.) No attacker can create a valid checksum for modified data, since no attacker knows the correct session key. The result is that the receiver of a packet can always detect any attempt to modify the contents of that packet. And as always, this work is done by the Kerberos SSP—application developers need only request the service.

Finally, providing data privacy is simple. Since client and server share a session key, the Kerberos SSP on each machine just uses this key to encrypt data it sends to the other. Note that data privacy implies data integrity, since all attacker modifications to encrypted data in transit on the network will be detected.

Data can be encrypted to provide data privacy

An application using Kerberos isn't required to use either its data integrity or its data privacy service—their use is typically requested through the appropriate API—and using them can hurt performance. But choosing not to use these services leaves openings for attackers, so it's up to each application developer to decide how to make this trade-off.

Other Kerberos Topics

Kerberos provides fundamental security services in a distributed environment: authentication, data integrity, and data privacy. But there's more to this technology than we've seen so far. This section looks at a few slightly more advanced Kerberos topics.

Managing Tickets and Keys   Once a client acquires a ticket, it stores the ticket, along with its associated session key, in a ticket cache on the client system. The client can use both the key and the ticket itself over and over until the ticket expires—that is, up to

Once acquired, tickets are cached on the user's machine

the time contained in the ticket's End Time field. And, as already mentioned, Windows 2000 Kerberos automatically refreshes both kinds of tickets when they expire, so users aren't required to perform a new login when their TGTs expire.

Passwords for server applications are stored on that application's machine

Kerberos also requires that every principal have a password, as shown earlier, from which that principal's secret key is derived. Each user is responsible for remembering his or her own password, but how can server applications store their passwords? The answer is that each server application can have its own password stored locally, encrypted in a secure part of the registry. Like all passwords, this one should be changed periodically, although it's up to an administrator to do this—the system will not automatically change a server application's password.

Another option, one that's probably easier and safer, is to configure a server application to use the password of the machine principal on the system it's installed on. This minimizes the number of passwords that must be managed, and because the machine principal password is automatically changed on a regular basis, it gives administrators one less thing to do to maintain a secure environment.

Delegation   In the example described earlier, suppose the user has already authenticated itself to Server S. Server S can now impersonate the user and attempt to access something on its local system, such as a file. In this case, the access checking built into Windows 2000 will grant or deny the access based on the file's ACL. All of this works naturally if the resource being accessed is on the same machine as the server.

But what if it's not? Suppose that to carry out whatever task the user is requesting, Server S must make a request to another server, Server T, running on another machine. Even though Server T's direct user will be Server S, access is being requested on behalf of the original user, not Server S. For this to work correctly, the user needs some way to pass its identity to Server S, allowing Server S to make further remote requests on its behalf.

Kerberos supports this idea through *delegation,* as shown in Figure 3-8. If a client application requests it, a user's TGT and its associated session key can be passed to another server, such as Server S. (Sending just the TGT wouldn't be enough, since the session key is needed to construct the authenticators sent along with the TGT.) Like all tickets, the TGT is encrypted, but to ensure that attackers can't steal the TGT's associated session key off the wire when it's passed from client to server, that key is sent encrypted using the session key the client shares with Server S.

Delegation allows a server to take on a user's identity passed to it from a client machine

Figure 3-8 *One server can access another server on behalf of an original user by requesting a new ticket.*

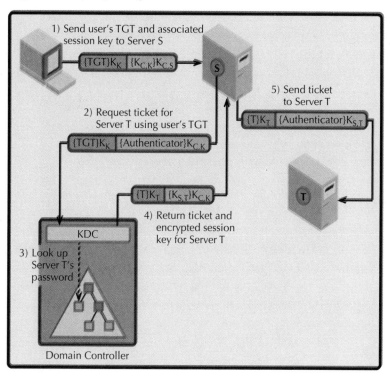

The TGT passed by the client to Server S must have the FORWARDABLE flag set in its Flags field. Server S can then present this TGT to a KDC and request tickets to other services even though the IP address in this TGT won't match Server S's IP

address—the FORWARDABLE flag tells the KDC that it's okay to ignore this discrepancy. Also, a client machine can only send its TGT and associated session key to a server if that server's account in Active Directory is marked as trusted for delegation in the domain. It wouldn't do to allow users to delegate their identity to just any server they run across.

To see how this all works, suppose the client passes a user's TGT and associated session key to Server S with the FORWARDABLE flag set. If Server S needs to access Server T on the user's behalf, it can present this TGT along with a valid authenticator to the KDC, requesting a new ticket for Server T. This new ticket will contain the user's identity, just like the original ticket, but will be encrypted using Server T's password. When Server S presents this new ticket to Server T, again with a valid authenticator, Server T will behave as though it is receiving a request directly from the client.

Kerberos Between Domains   Everything described so far assumes that the client, server, and KDC are in the same domain. Kerberos also allows authentication between clients and servers in different domains, although the process is slightly more complex than what we've seen so far.

A client can request a TGT to a KDC in another domain

To authenticate itself to any server application, no matter what domain the machine running that application is in, a client must acquire a ticket to that server. But only a KDC in the same domain as the target server can issue that ticket, since only it knows that server's password. If a client wishes to authenticate its user to a server in a different domain, then, it must request a ticket to that server from a KDC in that foreign domain. As is always the case, requesting a ticket from a KDC requires presenting a TGT to that KDC. The fundamental problem, then, is for the client to acquire a TGT to the KDC in the foreign domain. Once it has this, it can request and use a ticket to the target server in the normal way.

For this to be possible, the two domains must have a trust relationship between them. How cross-domain trust works in Windows 2000 is described in more detail in the next section, but the critical thing to know right now is that when a trust relationship is created between two domains, a key is also created that is known only to those two domains. This shared key can be used to encrypt a ticket that's passed between the two domains.

Cross-domain access requires a trust relationship between domains

Figure 3-9 shows how the process works (although authenticators have been omitted from the diagram for simplicity). As shown in the figure, suppose a client in the domain us.qwickbank.com wishes to access Server Q in the europe.qwickbank.com domain. The client begins by presenting its TGT to the KDC in its own domain, us.qwickbank.com, requesting a TGT to the KDC in europe.qwickbank.com. The us.qwickbank.com domain's KDC responds by sending back a TGT that the client can use to request tickets from the KDC in the europe.qwickbank.com domain. This ticket is encrypted using K_x, the key that's shared between the two domains.

Once it has this TGT, the client then presents it to the KDC in the domain europe.qwickbank.com, requesting a ticket for Server Q. (The client finds a domain controller for this foreign domain using DNS, just as it would any domain controller.) The KDC in europe.qwickbank.com decrypts the TGT presented by the client using the key it shares with us.qwickbank.com's KDC. If the TGT is valid, this KDC then looks up Server Q's password in its Active Directory database and uses it to build a ticket for Server Q. It then sends this ticket back to the client, who can present it to Server Q.

The mechanics of using Kerberos between domains are simple. All that's required is adding the single extra step of getting a TGT for a foreign domain's KDC (and again, this is done automatically by the Kerberos SSP—application developers don't have to worry about it). But think about what the KDC in europe.qwickbank.com is implicitly assuming in this example: it's trusting the KDC in us.qwickbank.com not to give out TGTs to it without first validating the client's identity. In other words, by accepting a TGT encrypted with the key it shares with this other domain, europe.qwickbank.com is trusting the KDC in us.qwickbank.com to behave correctly. For cross-domain authentication to work, the two domains involved must trust each other.

Figure 3-9 *A client can request tickets in another Windows 2000 domain after first acquiring a TGT to that domain's KDC.*

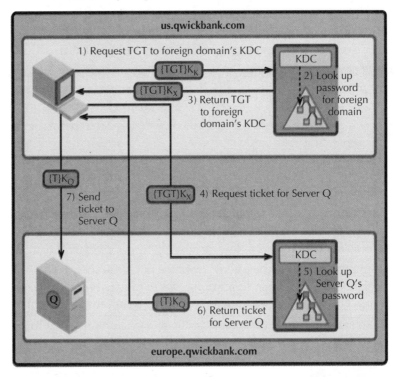

Trust Between Domains Establishing direct trust between two domains requires that those domains share a password, which can then be used as an encryption key to create TGTs to each other's KDCs. In an organization with only a handful of domains, explicitly establishing trust between all of them wouldn't be much work. In an organization with many domains, however, explicitly managing all of the trust relationships could be challenging. With Windows 2000, this fortunately isn't required. Unlike Windows NT 4, which requires explicit management of trust relationships among domains, Windows 2000 lets administrators do significantly less work.

First of all, when a new domain is added to a domain tree or forest, Windows 2000 automatically establishes a two-way trust relationship between the two domains. Put more concretely, a shared key is automatically created by the system and stored in the Configuration data of each domain's Active Directory database. This key is used to encrypt TGTs sent to the other domain, as just described. You don't have to accept this default—it's possible to administratively create one-way trust relationships—but by definition, all domains in a domain tree or forest must have two-way trust.

All domains in a domain tree or forest must trust each other

Think about a domain tree such as the one shown in Figure 3-10, however. The root domain in this tree, qwickbank.com, has two other domains below it. One of these domains, in turn, has its own child domains. By default, each domain has a two-way trust relationship (that is, a shared key) with its parent and its immediate children. But what about domains that are two levels away in the tree? Are shared keys required between, say, the root domain and the domains at the bottom of the tree?

Fortunately, the answer is no. Kerberos provides *transitive trust,* which is a fancy name for a simple idea. The idea is that if the qwickbank.com domain trusts the europe.qwickbank.com domain, and if that domain trusts france.europe.qwickbank.com in turn, then there is automatically a two-way trust relationship between qwickbank.com and france.europe.qwickbank.com. In fact, as already stated, every domain in a domain tree or forest has a two-way trust relationship with every other domain in that tree or forest. Domains need to share keys only with their parent and immediate children—Kerberos takes care of the rest.

Transitive trust allows a domain to trust other domains with which it doesn't share a key

Figure 3-10 *Domains in a domain tree or forest all have transitive trust.*

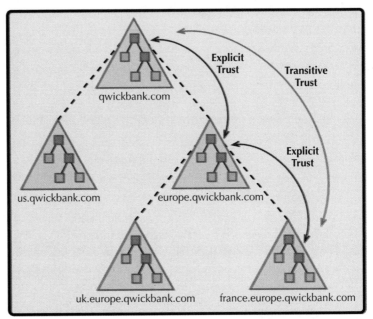

Here's how transitive trust works. Suppose a client in the domain qwickbank.com wishes to access Server R in the domain france. europe.qwickbank.com. The client's domain has a trust relationship with (that is, its KDC shares a key with) the domain europe.qwickbank.com, which in turn has a trust relationship with france.europe.qwickbank.com (so their KDCs share a key, too). The client first requests a TGT from its own KDC to the KDC in europe.qwickbank.com. The client then contacts that KDC, presents the TGT, and requests another TGT for the KDC in france.europe.qwickbank.com. Once the client has the other TGT, it presents this TGT to france.europe.qwickbank.com's KDC and requests a ticket to Server R in that domain. Because the client has presented a valid TGT, this last KDC happily provides the requested ticket. As long as trust relationships (and shared keys) exist for the length of the path, everything works. Like all tickets, tickets to KDCs in other domains are of course cached on client machines, allowing them to be used over and over once they're acquired.

Transitive trust is nice, but it's not always the right solution. Suppose you'd like to establish a trust relationship between a Windows 2000 domain and a Windows NT 4 domain, for example. Since Windows NT 4 doesn't support Kerberos, the best you can do is create a traditional one-way trust link between these domains—transitive trust isn't possible. This kind of relationship is referred to as *nontransitive* trust. An administrator might choose to create a nontransitive trust relationship in each direction, allowing users in both domains to be authenticated to services in either domain, but this must be done explicitly. Another situation where nontransitive trust is required, even in a purely Windows 2000 world, is when a trust link is established across forest boundaries. Transitive trust between domains in different forests isn't possible, so administrators must manually create nontransitive trust relationships as needed for this situation.

Windows 2000 also allows creating nontransitive trust relationships

Interoperability with Non-Microsoft Kerberos Implementations

By making Kerberos mandatory in Windows 2000, Microsoft has guaranteed widespread use of this technology. But other vendors have also implemented Kerberos, which raises the question of how well Microsoft's version will interoperate with products from other vendors. The ideal answer would be that as long as Microsoft and other vendors follow RFC 1510, the official standard for Kerberos version 5, all the products should interoperate with no trouble. Unfortunately, things aren't that simple.

Multi-vendor Kerberos interoperability requires some effort

First, as already described, Windows 2000 Kerberos defaults to RC4 for encryption. Since Microsoft also supports DES, however, this isn't really a problem. When talking to a non-Microsoft Kerberos implementation,[7] Windows 2000 Kerberos will happily negotiate using DES instead of RC4 (and it's possible to configure specific accounts with DES as the default encryption algorithm, making this negotiation more efficient).

---

7. The term *MIT Kerberos* is sometimes used to refer to non-Microsoft implementations of the protocol.

Recall also that Microsoft's Kerberos uses pre-authentication data during login, while most other implementations do not. As already mentioned, however, it's possible to configure specific accounts so that a Windows 2000 domain controller won't require pre-authentication data during login. This allows clients with non-Microsoft Kerberos implementations to successfully acquire TGTs from a Windows 2000 Kerberos server.

By default, Windows 2000 Kerberos hashes passwords to keys in a non-standard way

A more significant issue stems from the fact that Windows 2000 Kerberos is an upgrade to Windows NT 4's existing security protocol, NTLM. Like Kerberos, NTLM uses a hash algorithm to derive secret keys from user passwords. But NTLM uses an algorithm known as MD4, while standard Kerberos uses an MIT-defined *string-to-key* function. Upgrading a Windows NT 4 domain to Windows 2000 does not force users to change their passwords, and so Microsoft's Kerberos allows using secret keys derived using MD4. The domain's administrator can cause changed passwords or those for new accounts to use the MIT standard string-to-key function to derive secret keys, and can even require all users of the domain to change their passwords. Unless this is done, however, Windows 2000 Kerberos won't interoperate with products from other vendors because it uses a different algorithm to convert passwords into secret keys. By making the choice of supporting MD4, Microsoft kept things simple for the most common case—upgrading an existing domain without requiring new user passwords—while making interoperability possible with some extra work.

What's sent for authorization data isn't defined by the Kerberos standard

Another important issue exists, as well. As was shown in Figure 3-5 on page 93, every Kerberos ticket contains a field named Authorization Data. In the Windows 2000 Kerberos implementation, that field contains a user's SIDs and more. Other Kerberos implementations send other information in that field, however, because RFC 1510 leaves undefined exactly what its contents should be. Since the Authorization Data field can be used by a server system to make an access control decision (Windows 2000 compares its SIDs to ACLs, for example), what's in this field matters.

Figure 3-11 shows one possible scenario. Suppose a client in a non-Windows 2000 Kerberos realm wants to access an application called Server V, running on a machine in a Windows 2000 domain. As with any cross-domain access, the client can ask its own KDC for a TGT to the foreign KDC, which in this case is the Windows 2000 KDC. Assuming there's a trust relationship between these two domains, that TGT will be granted, allowing the client to request a ticket to Server V. The client can then present this ticket to Server V to authenticate its user.

Figure 3-11 *With some extra effort, Windows 2000 Kerberos can interoperate with other Kerberos version 5 implementations.*

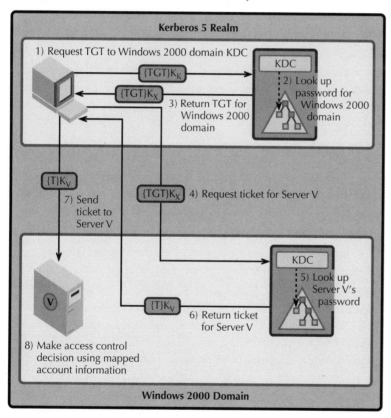

Since Server V is running in a Windows 2000 domain, however, it would like to use the information in the ticket's Authorization

Data field to decide whether this user has the right to do whatever it's requesting. Yet the ticket the user supplies won't have the Windows 2000–defined values in this field. How could it? Those values are ultimately acquired from the user's TGT, and since the initial TGT was issued by a non–Windows 2000 KDC (most likely one running on a UNIX system), there's no way for the appropriate SIDs, and other information, to get into this field.

A non-Microsoft ticket can be mapped into a Windows 2000 account

Yet every ticket does carry the name of the principal it represents as a character string. Windows 2000 allows an administrator to configure a mapping between a principal name extracted from a Kerberos ticket and an account in a given domain. When a user presents a ticket that doesn't contain the appropriate Windows 2000 information in its Authorization Data field, the user will be assigned the required information from whatever Windows 2000 account has been mapped to it. The server makes an access control decision based on this information.

Other interoperability scenarios are also possible

Scenarios simpler than that shown in Figure 3-11 are also possible. For example, a client computer running Windows 2000 can log in and acquire tickets from a non–Windows 2000 KDC. The client can then present those tickets to server applications running on non–Windows 2000 systems to authenticate a user. Conversely, a client computer running, say, UNIX can directly access a Windows 2000 KDC to acquire tickets, and then use those tickets to authenticate a user to applications running on Windows 2000 servers. Both of these options require some administrative work to establish, but they can make life easier for organizations already using a non–Windows 2000 implementation of Kerberos.

In a perfect world, the Windows 2000 Kerberos implementation would interoperate with other implementations without any extra work. In the world we live in, though, both the installed base of Windows NT and the incompleteness of the Kerberos standard make this ideal unachievable. Still, while combining products written by different vendors requires some effort, it can be done.

How Kerberos Improves on NTLM   There's one last point about Kerberos that's worth addressing: why did Microsoft bother with it? In previous versions of Windows NT, network authentication was handled by NTLM. Why make us change? How is Kerberos better than NTLM?

There are several answers. First, as we've already seen, Kerberos provides features that aren't available in NTLM. Delegation and transitive trust are both available with Kerberos, but neither is possible with NTLM. Also, Kerberos is typically faster than NTLM, since each NTLM client authentication requires a server to contact a domain controller. In Kerberos, by contrast, a client can supply the same ticket over and over, and the server can use just that ticket to authenticate the client. There's no need for the server to contact a domain controller each time a client needs to be authenticated. And finally, Kerberos is a multi-vendor standard, so it allows secure interaction between the Microsoft world and other vendor environments. Establishing this interaction requires some work, but it's far better than using a purely proprietary solution such as NTLM.

Kerberos provides useful features that aren't available in NTLM

Any way you look at it, Kerberos qualifies as progress. It's nice to see this powerful, secure, but long-neglected protocol move into the limelight. After years of languishing in relative obscurity, Kerberos has finally hit the big time—it's about to become ubiquitous.

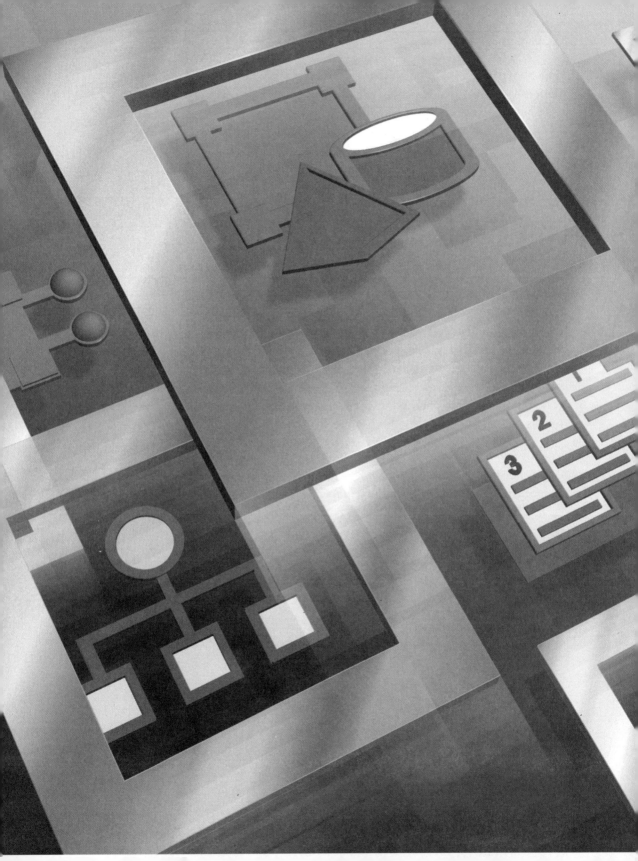

Chapter Four

Distributed Security Services: Public Key Technology

Public key technology is one of the greatest ideas of the twentieth century. Elegant, powerful, and eminently useful, it's likely to eventually be ubiquitous. Today, public key solutions underlie the exploding world of Internet commerce, and the technology is applied in other areas as well. To use it effectively, a *public key infrastructure (PKI)* must be created, providing a necessary set of supporting services. Without this, the beautiful ideas at the core of this technology are much less useful.

In Microsoft Windows 2000, every domain will use Kerberos—it's the core protocol for distributed security. In contrast, it's possible for organizations to successfully use Windows 2000 while completely ignoring its support for public key technology. Most organizations probably won't be willing to do that, however, so it shouldn't be surprising that Windows 2000 provides a great deal of built-in support for public key technology. This chapter describes that support, beginning with an introduction to the basics of public key technology. It then describes the PKI features provided by

Public key technology depends on a public key infrastructure (PKI)

Windows 2000, and concludes with a look at the Secure Sockets Layer (SSL)—today's most widely-used public key-based security protocol—and a brief examination of how public key technology can be used with Kerberos.

Understanding Public Key Technology

Understanding how public key technology works and what's required to manage a public key environment is important for both developers and administrators. As this technology gets more widely used, its terminology and concepts work their way into many aspects of a distributed environment. Although several public key encryption algorithms are in use today, this section generally assumes a commonly used choice, both in Windows 2000 and elsewhere: the Rivest-Shamir-Adelman (RSA) algorithm, named after the three men who created it.

Keys and Encryption

Secret key technology requires two communicating principals to know the same key

In a secret key algorithm, such as the Data Encryption Standard (DES) or RC4, the same key is used to encrypt and decrypt data. For secure communication, then, two communicating principals must each know that key. As described in the last chapter, this leads ineluctably to the problem of key distribution—once created, how is a secret key passed to all those who must know it? While Kerberos provides a way to securely distribute keys, that solution assumes that all principals involved in secure communication share—directly or indirectly—trusted Key Distribution Centers (KDCs) and that each of those principals shares a key with one of those KDCs.

In public key technology, every principal has a public key and a private key

Public key technology takes a quite different approach. Rather than sharing a single key among two or more principals, public key technology assigns two separate keys, often referred to as a *key pair*, to each principal. One of those keys is kept private—only the principal knows it. The other key is made completely public, and so is available to anybody. These private and public keys have a relationship to one another—they're not just random numbers. And, of course, knowing a principal's public key doesn't allow determining that principal's private key. Windows 2000 provides mechanisms for generating key pairs, but the really interesting thing to note right now about these two keys is this: anything transformed using one key in the pair can be returned to its original state only with the other key.

Suppose you want to send me a message informing me that QwickBank has just been sold, for example, but you don't want anyone else to know this information. With secret key encryption, you and I would both need to know the secret key used to encrypt the message, raising the problem of key distribution. But with public key encryption, key distribution is no longer a problem. In theory, at least, all you have to do is acquire my public key, then use it to encrypt the message, as shown in Figure 4-1. This key by definition isn't secret, so I can send it to you in any way I like, such as via an Internet e-mail message. And because anything encrypted with my public key can be decrypted only with my private key, which I alone know, only I can read this encrypted message. If I want to send a response, I can acquire your public key, then use it to encrypt messages that only you can read. With public key encryption the problem of key exchange that bedevils users of secret key encryption vanishes.

A principal can use its public key to encrypt data

Figure 4-1 *In public key encryption, anything encrypted with a principal's public key can be decrypted only with that principal's private key.*

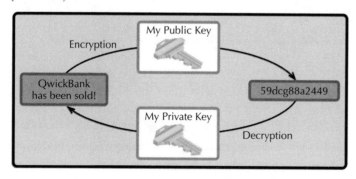

A principal can use its
private key to create
digital signatures

Further, just as anything transformed using my public key can be recovered only with my private key, anything transformed using my private key can be returned to its original state only using my public key. Since anybody can know my public key, using my private key to encrypt data doesn't make much sense. I can, however, use my private key to prove my identity by creating a *digital signature.*

A principal's public key
can be used to verify a
digital signature

Exactly how digital signatures work is described in the next section, but the general idea is this: Suppose I want to send a message informing you that QwickBank has been sold, and I want you to be certain that this message is from me. As shown in Figure 4-2, I can use my private key to sign the message, creating a digital signature, then send this signature along with the message. You can then use my public key to verify the signature you receive. Since only I know my private key, only I could have created this signed version of the message, so it must be from me. By proving that I know my private key, I can authenticate myself.

Figure 4-2 *Information signed with a principal's private key can be verified only with that principal's public key.*

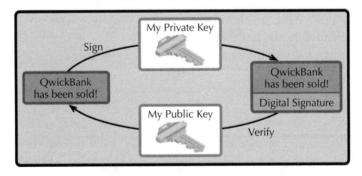

Public key encryption is a great technology, but it has a few drawbacks. For one thing, the keys tend to be quite long. Unlike DES with its 8-byte keys or RC4 with keys of 5, 7, or 16 bytes, RSA keys are commonly 512 bits (64 bytes), 1024 bits (128 bytes), or more in length. In addition, not just any pair of strings can be used as public and private keys. Instead, the two values must have a well-defined relationship, which means you can't simply choose, say, your name and address as your private key. The point is that unlike keys used with secret key algorithms, which are short enough to be derived from simple passwords, the keys used in public key technology are essentially impossible for people to remember.

This isn't a serious problem for public keys. Since their values don't need to be confidential, they can be stored pretty much anywhere. But storing private keys is a much tougher issue. They're too big to easily remember, but they must be stored in such a way that attackers can't access them. How Windows 2000 addresses this problem is described in more detail later in this chapter, but fundamentally, it supports two different approaches: store the private key on disk somewhere, encrypted using some other key, or store it on a *smart card*. A smart card is a device the size of a credit card that contains processing power and memory—it's a tiny computer mounted on a piece of plastic. The card's memory contains your private key and other information, and the processor is capable of performing public key encryption and decryption operations using that key. With a smart card, your private key need never leave the card—all operations are done on the card itself. To prevent an attacker from stealing your identity by stealing your smart card, each card also has a personal identification number (PIN) that you must enter to use it.

Private keys can be stored encrypted on disk or on smart cards

Smart cards require smart card readers. Windows 2000 provides standard software support for smart card drivers, but making smart cards popular requires making smart card readers popular, too. We can probably expect smart cards and smart card readers to become more widely used over the next few years, but until then, most users of public key technology in Windows 2000 domains will store their private keys encrypted on disk.

Smart cards require smart card readers

Public key technology is generally slower than secret key technology. Both encryption and decryption using RSA can be 100 to 1,000 times slower than the corresponding operations using DES.

Public key and secret key technology are often used together

As a result, public key algorithms are rarely used to encrypt the actual data sent by users. A more common approach is for a sender to use the public key of the receiver to encrypt either a secret key, such as a DES or RC4 key, or information that can be used to create a secret key.[1] Only the receiver can decrypt this secret key, since only it knows its private key. Once it has done this, sender and receiver now share a secret key that can be used to efficiently encrypt any data they exchange. Using public key technology to exchange information from which a secret key can be derived, then using secret key encryption for transmitted data, is exactly what's done by SSL, as is described later in this chapter.

The relative slowness of public key operations threatens to obviate one of its greatest benefits, which is the ability to authenticate a user. If encrypting an entire message using a private key is potentially too slow to be practical, how can a principal use public key technology to prove its identity? The answer is described next.

Digital Signatures

Encrypting a message's hash with the private key of its sender produces a digital signature

Rather than encrypt an entire outgoing message using a private key, a sender can create and send with a message a digital signature. The process of creating a digital signature is illustrated in Figure 4-3. To begin, the sending system computes a hash (also referred to as a message digest or a checksum) from the message itself. Just as with Kerberos—described in the last chapter—this value is a function of the message itself; changing a bit in the message would (with a very high probability) result in a change in the hash. For SHA-1 (Secure Hash Algorithm-1), a commonly used hash algorithm, the resulting value is 20 bytes long. The sender encrypts this relatively short result using its private key, an operation that's much faster than encrypting the entire message. The resulting encrypted hash is the message's digital signature.

---

1. Note that throughout this book, a *secret* key is one used with a secret key algorithm such as DES or RC4, while both *private* and *public* keys are used with a public key algorithm such as RSA.

Figure 4-3 *To create a digital signature, the sender uses its private key to encrypt a hash of the message.*

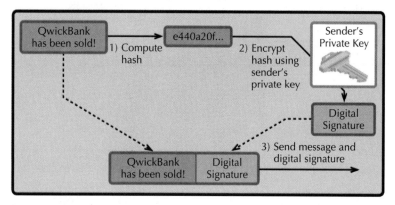

When the message arrives, its receiver must verify that the digital signature is correct, a process illustrated in Figure 4-4. To do this, it computes a hash of the received message by applying the same algorithm used by the sender. It then uses the sender's public key to decrypt the digital signature that accompanied the received message and compares the results. If the newly computed hash matches the decrypted hash, the signature is valid, and the receiver can be certain of the sender's identity. If they don't match, either the message has been modified in transit or it wasn't signed by the sender whose public key was used to verify the signature.

A receiver verifies a digital signature using the sender's public key

Figure 4-4 *To verify a digital signature, the receiver of a message computes the hash, decrypts the received signature using the sender's public key, and compares the results.*

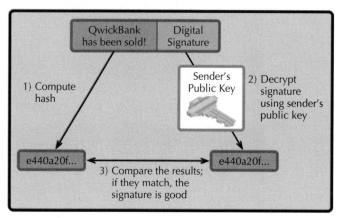

Digital signatures provide both authentication and data integrity. They do not, however, provide data privacy. If a message's contents must be protected from prying eyes, it should itself be encrypted—just signing the message isn't enough.

Yet for a receiver to rely on a digital signature to authenticate the sender of a message, that receiver must have a reliable way of knowing the sender's public key. In some cases, this is not a problem. If the sender and receiver are friends, for example, the receiver might already know the sender's public key, or they might simply trust one another to send the correct public key. But digital signatures should also be reliable even when the sender and receiver are complete strangers. Reliably learning the sender's public key in this situation is a somewhat challenging problem, but it's one that must be solved for digital signatures to be really useful.

One simple solution is for the sender to include its public key with every signed message it sends. Attractive as this sounds, it's not sufficient. To see why, suppose an attacker uses his own private key to create a digitally signed message, then sends that message to an unsuspecting receiver along with the attacker's own public key. The attacker can claim to be anybody, say, the President of the United States. How can the receiver detect whether the sender is lying? After all, the public key sent with the message will correctly decrypt the message's digital signature. To detect the fraud, the receiver must be able to tell that this is not really the President's public key. But how can the receiver do this? Put more generally, how can a receiver know to whom a particular public key really belongs?

To solve this problem, and to make digital signatures a truly effective method for authentication, there must be some way for the receiver of a message to reliably associate a public key with the identity of the principal to whom that key belongs. There must be a mechanism that binds together a principal's public key and name such that a receiver will believe that the key really does belong to that principal. Fortunately, there is a way to do this: using certificates.

Certificates

A *certificate*, often called just a "cert" by the cognoscenti, is nothing more than a string of bytes divided into several different fields. Most certs used today follow the format defined by version 3 of the International Telecommunications Union (ITU) X.509 standard. (The Internet Engineering Task Force [IETF] has produced a slightly more approachable description, available in Request for Comments [RFC] 2459.) A slightly simplified version of an X.509v3 certificate is shown in Figure 4-5. Among its fields are the following:

A certificate contains a principal's name, its public key, and more

- *Version*   Indicates which version of the X.509 standard this certificate conforms to.
- *Serial number*   Contains a unique identifier for this certificate. This can be used for revoking certificates, as described later in this chapter.
- *Signature algorithm*   Indicates the algorithm used to produce the digital signature this certificate bears.
- *Issuer*   Contains the name of the organization that issued this certificate.
- *Valid from and valid to*   Indicates the validity times of the certificate (that is, when the certificate begins being valid and when it will expire).
- *Subject*   The name of the principal whose public key is contained in this certificate.
- *Public key*   The public key of that principal.
- *Various other fields*   Some of these other fields are referred to as *extended attribute fields.* Some extended attributes are standard, while others can be defined in vendor-specific ways. How the most important of these fields are used in Windows 2000 is described later in this chapter.

Version
Serial Number
Signature Algorithm
Issuer
Valid From
Valid To
Subject
Public Key
Other Fields
CA's Digital Signature

Certificate

Every certificate is digitally signed by its issuer

Every certificate ends with the digital signature of its issuer. Like all digital signatures, a certificate's signature is created using the private key of that issuer—which is usually some organization—and it can be verified using the issuer's public key. A certificate is not encrypted, and nothing in it is secret. But since it includes the digital signature of whoever issued it, anybody who encounters this cert can verify that it really was created by the signer, and that the certificate hasn't been modified since it was signed.

Certificates are issued by certification authorities (CAs)

To see how certificates can solve the problem of reliably learning someone's public key, it's necessary to look at how they are created. The issuer of a certificate is commonly referred to as a *certification authority (CA)*, and if I wish to acquire a certificate for myself, I must first find an appropriate CA to give me one. (Exactly what constitutes an "appropriate CA" will be described shortly.) Once I've chosen a CA, I can present it with my name and my public key. Somehow, I must prove to the CA that I am who I claim to be and that this really is my public key. How I do this depends on the CA. If the CA is an organization within the company I work for, it might require that I prove I am an employee. If the CA is an external organization, it might require my driver's license or passport or some other form of identity, and it might do things such as run a credit check on me to verify my existence. The point is that I somehow prove my identity and my public key to the CA. The CA then issues a certificate containing those two things plus the other information listed previously. By signing the certificate, the CA is expressing its belief that I am who I claim to be and that this really is my public key.[2]

Now, when I send you a digitally signed message, I can send along with it not just my naked public key, but instead my public key wrapped inside a cert. You can then use the public key of the CA that issued my certificate to verify the digital signature on that certificate. If that signature is valid, you can extract my name and public key from the certificate, secure in the knowledge that this really is my public key. You can now safely use my public key to verify the digital signature on my message, thereby authenticating me as the sender of the message. This process is illustrated in Figure 4-6.

A certificate can be sent with a digitally signed message

Figure 4-6 *The receiver of a digitally signed message and certificate can verify the certificate's signature, extract the sender's public key from that certificate, then use that key to verify the message's digital signature.*

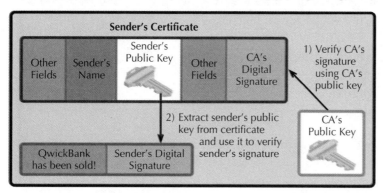

---

2. All of this assumes that no attacker has learned the CA's private key. In fact, for the entire edifice of public key technology to work correctly, every principal must keep their private key utterly secure—only they can know it. The minute somebody else knows my private key or yours or, worst of all, a CA's, problems arise.

Windows 2000 includes software to generate and manage certificates

To act as a CA requires having software or hardware that's capable of generating certificates. To perform this function, Windows 2000 includes Microsoft Certificate Services. Certification services are described in more detail later in this chapter, but the main thing to know right now is that Windows 2000 does provide a way to create and manage certificates.

A CA's public key can be extracted from a certificate

Certification Hierarchies If you're still with me, you might have noticed a potential problem with this scenario. Given that verifying a certificate's digital signature requires knowing the public key of the CA that issued this certificate, how can this public key reliably be acquired? The usual solution is to acquire that public key in the same way other public keys are acquired: from a certificate. CA's themselves can have certificates, and so a CA's public key can be extracted from its own certificate. But who issues a CA's certificate? Whose digital signature does that certificate bear?

A root CA has a self-signed certificate

There are a couple of possible answers. If this CA is what's called a *root* CA, its certificate is self-signed. That is, the CA produces the signature on its certificate using its own private key. Verifying the signature of a self-signed certificate requires securely acquiring the public key of that CA, perhaps through downloading it from the CA's Web site or in some other reliable way, then using it to check the digital signature on the certificate. Determining which CAs you trust to sign their own certificates—which CAs you're willing to accept as root CAs—is a serious matter, and how Windows 2000 controls this is described later in this chapter.

An intermediate CA's certificate is signed by the CA above it

Another alternative is for a CA's certificate to be issued by some other CA. In this case, checking the digital signature on a CA's certificate requires learning the public key of the CA that issued it. It's common to organize CAs into a hierarchy, with a root CA, which has a self-signed cert, atop one or more levels of *intermediate* CAs (also called *subordinate* CAs). Each of these intermediate CAs has a cert signed by the CA above it in the hierarchy. How this looks is shown in Figure 4-7.

Figure 4-7 *A hierarchy of CAs can be created, with one or more levels of intermediate CAs beneath a root CA.*

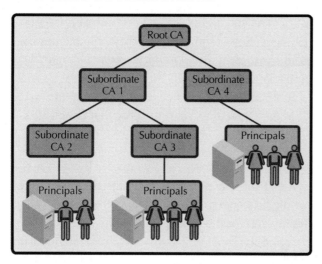

As Figure 4-7 suggests, a common practice is for the root CA to issue certificates only to CAs at the next level below it in the hierarchy, then for those CAs to issue certs to the next level, and so on. How many levels exist in a CA hierarchy can vary. A simple structure might have just a single CA that issues certs directly to principals, while a more complex structure might involve several levels. A large organization, for example, very likely could not get by with a single CA—routing all requests for certificates to one server would be impractical—so some kind of distributed certification hierarchy would be needed. Also, different certificates can be issued for different purposes—sending secure e-mail, logging into a domain, and so on—and so different CAs can be used to create different kinds of certificates.

Think for a moment, though, about what's required to verify the digital signature of a principal in this case. With a hierarchy of CAs, not only is that principal's certificate needed, but so are the certificates of every CA above that principal in the hierarchy. To allow you to verify my digital signature, then, I might well need to provide you with not only my cert, but also with a whole series

Higher-level CAs commonly issue certificates only to other CAs

Verifying a digital signature might require a certification chain

of certs. This group of certificates is commonly referred to as a *certification chain* (or sometimes, as a *certification path*). This chain consists of a list of certs and all but the last cert contains the public key of the CA beneath it in the CA hierarchy. Only the last certificate, commonly known as an *end-entity certificate*, actually contains the public key of a principal. The idea is that each certificate signer's public key can be extracted from the certificate that precedes it in the chain, then used to verify that certificate's signature.

Figure 4-8 illustrates a certification chain generated by the CA hierarchy in Figure 4-7. The lowest certificate in the chain is for the principal whose digital signature is ultimately being verified—that is, it's the end-entity cert for the principal who's being authenticated. Between it and the root certificate appear two intermediate certificates, each issued by the appropriate intermediate CA in the hierarchy. At the top is the self-signed root certificate, from which the highest-level public key is extracted when the process of verifying this certification chain is performed.

Figure 4-8 *In a certification chain, each CA's public key is extracted from a certificate issued by a CA above it in the hierarchy. The root CA has a self-signed certificate.*

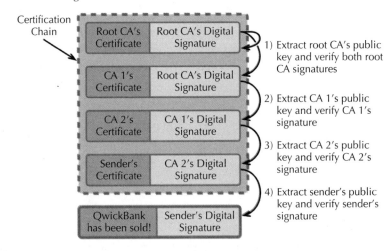

Controlling Which CAs Are Trusted The idea of public key encryption is simple and beautiful, but as should be apparent by now, applying it takes some work. And we still have a few more ideas to discuss.

Suppose I send you a digitally signed message along with a certificate issued by some CA. If you use the CA's public key to verify the certificate's signature, then extract my name and public key from that certificate, all you can really be sure of is that the CA believed that this was my public key. A CA that you don't trust— say, the CA run by your major competitor—might choose to issue bogus certificates. If you don't trust the CA that issued the certificate, you can't trust that the public key included in that certificate really belongs to the principal the certificate names. In other words, if I send you a digitally signed message and a certificate, you can only authenticate me if you trust the CA that issued the certificate.

Relying on a certificate requires trusting the CA that issued that certificate

A CA hierarchy makes things even more interesting. In a hierarchy, trusting the root CA means that you believe it will not issue certs to unreliable lower-level CAs. If you believe that a particular root CA might issue certificates to lower-level CAs that could issue bogus certs, you should not trust that root CA.

Which CAs should you trust? In general, organizations are automatically willing to trust their own CAs. If the company you work for has established its own internal certification hierarchy, for example, you probably are willing to trust that none of those CAs will issue bogus certificates. But what if you want to use digital signatures to authenticate information exchanged with another company? To address this problem, several firms are in business today to act as trusted CAs. Among the best known of these are VeriSign, Thawte, and Belsign, but many more exist. Depending on the exact kind of certificate requested, these firms might go to a good deal of trouble to verify that a principal really is who it claims to be.

Choosing which CAs to trust is an important decision

Yet within a particular Windows 2000 domain, who should decide which CAs are trusted? Requiring—or even allowing—each individual user to make this decision is almost certainly a bad idea. A better approach is to allow an administrator to specify which CAs are trusted for that domain, then have some way to enforce those choices.[3] This is exactly the approach Windows 2000 takes, and how it's accomplished is described later in this chapter.

Certificate Revocation Lists   Suppose I join a company and that company's CA issues me a certificate. I can then use this certificate together with my private key to prove my identity to anybody who trusts my company's CA not to issue bogus certificates. But suppose I quit–or worse, get fired—for committing some heinous act. My now former employer likely is no longer willing to vouch for my identity, yet I still have the bytes that comprise the certificate they gave me. Or suppose someone steals my private key so that I'm no longer the only one who can generate digital signatures that appear to be from me. My certificate can no longer be used to authenticate me. In both of these situations, the underlying problem is the same: once it's issued, how can a certificate be revoked?

One answer is just to wait. Every certificate has an expiration date, so once that date passes the certificate will no longer be useful. Certificate lifetimes are commonly measured in years, though, so a more immediate solution—one that doesn't require waiting for quite so long—is also required. *Certificate revocation lists (CRLs)*[4] provide this solution. Each CA can maintain and

Windows 2000 allows centrally controlling which CAs are trusted

Certificates must sometimes be revoked

A CA's revoked certificates can be contained in a certificate revocation list (CRL)

---

3. Just to be clear, the notion of which CAs are trusted in a particular domain is independent of the notion of cross-domain trust described in Chapter 3. Trust between Windows 2000 domains is based on Kerberos, a secret key-based technology. CA trust is relevant only when public key-based technologies are used.

4. This acronym is sometimes pronounced "krills," like the sea creatures.

make available a CRL that indicates which of the certificates it has issued have been revoked. Each revoked certificate is identified by its serial number, which is contained in a field in all certs. Whenever a certificate is used, such as during the process of verifying a digital signature, the CRL of the CA that issued the certificate can be checked to make sure the certificate has not been revoked.

CRLs also play a role in determining which CAs to trust. After all, trusting a CA means believing that all of the certificates it has created are valid. To be trustable, then, a CA must regularly publish an up-to-date CRL that allows users of its certificates to determine whether any of its certificates have been revoked. And CRLs themselves have expiration dates, which allow their users to know when to fetch new versions.

Managing Public Key Technology in Windows 2000

Understanding the fundamentals of public key technology is undoubtedly important, but it's only half the battle. One reason why public key technology, invented some 20 years ago, has been slow to become ubiquitous is that creating the necessary infrastructure to use it effectively is no small endeavor. Windows 2000 represents Microsoft's first attempt to build broad support for this technology into the operating system. The remainder of this section describes the major components of that support.

CryptoAPI

In much the same way that Windows 2000 exposes distributed security services through a single *Security Support Provider Interface (SSPI),* it also hides encryption services beneath a common API. Called CryptoAPI, this interface allows access to any *Cryptographic Service Provider (CSP)* installed on the system. CSPs are analogous to the Security Service Providers (SSPs) used with the

Cryptographic Service Providers are accessed through CryptoAPI

SSPI, but rather than encapsulating distributed security services, they instead encapsulate cryptographic services.

CryptoAPI helps applications use security technology more flexibly

Hiding the details of encryption from the applications that use it is a good idea for a number of reasons. First, keeping applications independent of the encryption technology they use allows those applications to be more flexible, since CryptoAPI allows installing and using different encryption providers for different purposes. Second, this approach makes life easier for application developers who might wish to know as little as possible about encryption. Third, because the governments of many countries have laws that control importing, exporting, and sometimes even using strong encryption software, this kind of modularity is especially important with encryption technology.

With CryptoAPI, applications can remain independent of the actual encryption technology being used. Rather than being tied to a specific algorithm, an application can just make standard CryptoAPI calls. Depending on which CSPs are available on its system, an application will get whatever degree of security is available. This allows application developers to create software that uses encryption without having the applications themselves be subject to export control. The CryptoAPI architecture shifts the burden of export issues from the application developer to the CSP developer. Since there are many more of the former than the latter, this is a good thing.

Applications use CryptoAPI to create key pairs, work with digital signatures, and more

CryptoAPI exposes its services through a set of C function calls, and as shown in Figure 4-9, it's used by various Windows 2000 applications.[5] This API allows applications to create key pairs, encrypt and decrypt data, create hashes (also called checksums or message digests) and digital signatures, verify those digital

---

5. Kerberos, Windows 2000's core protocol for distributed security, isn't shown in Figure 4-9 because Kerberos doesn't use CryptoAPI. Instead, the Kerberos SSP contains its own copies of Microsoft's DES and RC4 implementations.

signatures, and more. Among the users of CryptoAPI are the Windows 2000 implementation of SSL and Microsoft Certificate Services. CryptoAPI does more than just allow access to CSPs, however—it also supplies code providing important services such as building a certification chain.

Figure 4-9 *SSPs and others can access cryptographic services through CryptoAPI.*

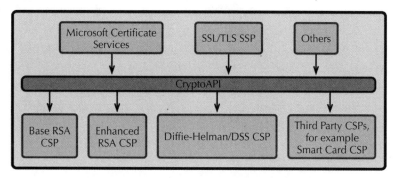

Windows 2000 potentially includes several different CSPs. Depending on where you live, your Windows 2000 system might include:

Windows 2000 includes several CSPs

- *The Base RSA CSP* Implements RSA with 1024-bit keys, along with both RC2 and RC4 with 56-bit keys. Because of its relatively short key lengths, this CSP is available worldwide without an export license. It also implements MD5 and SHA-1 for producing message digests.

- *The Enhanced RSA CSP* Implements RSA with keys as long as 16 kilobytes (although a key this big would very slow to use), RC2 and RC4 with 128-bit keys, DES, and Triple-DES. All of these algorithms provide effective, hard-to-break security (with the probable exception of DES), and so the Enhanced RSA CSP is available without an export license only within North America.[6]

---

6. U.S. export laws are changing as this book goes to press. This statement might no longer be true by the time you read this.

- *A Diffie-Hellman/DSS CSP*   Implements the Diffie-Hellman algorithm for key exchange and the U.S. Government's Digital Signature Standard (DSS).

CSPs must be digitally
signed by Microsoft

Third parties supply other CSPs. A smart card supplier, for example, must implement an appropriate CSP for use with its cards. But CSPs themselves can be a sensitive issue—remember, governments are very touchy about encryption software. Because of this, in Windows 2000 every CSP executable must be digitally signed by Microsoft. This signature is checked when the CSP is loaded, which prevents insertion of arbitrarily strong encryption software. Even access to the CSP software development kit (SDK) is controlled—it can't be freely downloaded from Microsoft's Web site. This means that it's not possible for a hacker somewhere in the world to write a CSP, install it into Windows 2000, and suddenly have built-in access to strong encryption. While it would have been technically possible to allow this, governments aren't in general overjoyed about making strong encryption easy to use, and so Windows 2000 restricts what CSPs can be used.

Storing Private Keys and Certificates

CSPs need someplace
to store information

CSPs implement public key and (sometimes) secret key encryption algorithms, as we've seen. But CSPs typically also need some mechanism to store information. The user of a particular workstation might have a key pair, for instance, which means that this user's private key and certificate (containing the corresponding public key) must be made available on that machine. In other cases, only the certs themselves need to be stored—there's no associated private key to keep track of. For example, when an application uses a CSP to verify a digital signature, that application might present a certification chain with the signature. To validate the signature, the CSP needs access to every cert in that chain, but it doesn't need access to any of the private keys that correspond to those certs.

For smart card CSPs, each user's private key and certificate are stored in hardware on the user's card. For software CSPs, however, private keys and certificates must be stored on disk somewhere on the user's machine. Each CSP can potentially define its own scheme for storing private keys, but Windows 2000 also provides some standards. For certificates, Windows 2000 defines several separate *certificate stores*, including the following:

Certificates used for different purposes are kept in different certificate stores

- *Personal store*   Stores end-entity certificates for individual users of a machine or for specific computers. These users will typically need to create digital signatures, an operation that requires a private key, so each of these certificates has stored with it a reference to its associated private key.

- *Trusted Root CA store*   Contains certs from trusted root CAs in some certification hierarchy. Windows 2000 ships with several self-signed root certificates from commercial CAs already loaded into this certificate store, and others can be added administratively. All certificates stored here are self-signed.

- *Intermediate CA store*   Contains certs used in building certification chains. These are typically certs issued by intermediate CAs that are part of a hierarchy but are not root CAs

- *Enterprise Trust store*   Rather than storing certs directly, this store contains *Certificate Trust Lists (CTLs)*. What CTLs are and how they're used is described later in this chapter.

For all of these options, certificates are actually stored in the registry, and all are accessible to CryptoAPI when it's hunting for the certificates it needs to validate a digital signature. In the example shown in Figure 4-10, the Personal store contains only a certificate for User A. This certificate was issued by CA 2, a CA belonging to the hierarchy shown earlier in Figure 4-7, so it has been

CryptoAPI can access any of the certificate stores

Distributed Security Services: Public Key Technology

digitally signed by that certification authority. Because this is a cert for a specific user of the computer storing the certification information, the Personal store also contains a reference to where the private key associated with this certificate can be found. The Intermediate CA store contains certificates from CA 1 and CA 2, both part of the CA hierarchy shown earlier, and CA 8, which belongs to a different CA hierarchy. CA 2's certificate was issued by CA 1, and so carries CA 1's digital signature. CA 1's certificate was issued by the root CA X, while CA 8's certificate was issued by a different root CA, CA Y. Finally, the Trusted Root CA store contains self-signed root certificates from CA X and CA Y. If CryptoAPI on a system with the certificate stores illustrated in Figure 4-10 were asked to validate something that had been digitally signed by User A, all the necessary certificates to accomplish this (and some that aren't needed, too) are already on hand: a self-signed root certificate for CA X, intermediate certificates for CA 1 and CA 2, and the end-entity certificate for User A.

Active Directory can also store certificates

Certificates can also be stored in Active Directory. Any user object in the directory, representing some user's account, can contain one or more certificates for that user in an attribute of the type userCertificate. This allows anybody with the right permissions to access those certificates, making them easily available in a distributed environment.

CSPs can store private keys in various places

While Windows 2000 provides a common storage area for certificates that can be accessed by any application, each CSP can potentially provide its own containers for storing private keys. For a smart card CSP, the container and the private key it contains are physically resident on the card. For the Base RSA and Enhanced RSA CSPs, however, the containers for private keys are stored in the Windows 2000 Application Data folder as part of a user's profile information (they're not kept in the registry, as was done in Windows NT 4). Stored private keys are encrypted using a secret key algorithm that relies on a master key. This key, in turn, is encrypted with a derivation of the user's password.

Figure 4-10 *Windows 2000 has several logically distinct certificate stores.*

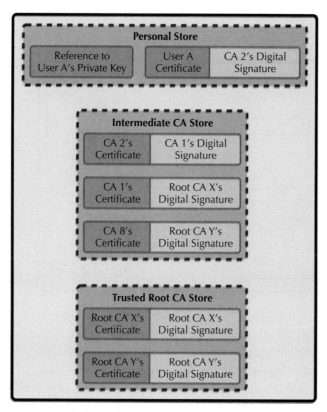

By default, a user's private key stays in the CSP's key storage, which (without smart cards) usually means on the hard drive of the machine on which the key was created. If the *roaming user profile* option is turned on, however, a copy of the user's private key is also uploaded to a file server when the user logs off. When the user logs in from another system, the login process will acquire a ticket to the file service on the machine that contains that user's profile, then download the private key and other profile information to the user's system, as shown in Figure 4-11. Since the private key is encrypted using the master secret key mentioned earlier, storing the private key on some share on a file server in the network is a reasonably safe thing to do.

Private keys can be stored locally or downloaded when a user logs in

Figure 4-11 *If the roaming user profile option is turned on, a user's private key will be kept on a file server and downloaded to the user's workstation at login.*

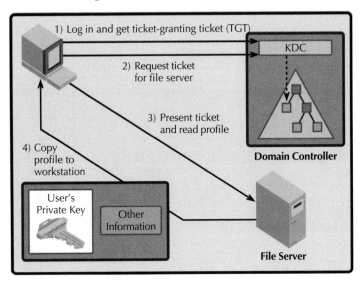

Microsoft Certificate Services

Certificates are a critical part of any public key infrastructure. While external firms such as VeriSign could theoretically supply all the certificates an organization needs, being able to produce certs on your own is much more convenient. (It's also cheaper, since those firms typically charge for each cert they issue.) And even third parties in the business of producing certificates need some mechanism to actually create them. Microsoft Certificate Services, a standard part of Windows 2000, provides this mechanism. It can be used by companies that want to act as public CAs or by organizations that need to produce certificates for their own use. Whichever category an organization falls into, Certificate Services provides the intelligence required to create and manage X.509 certificates. And ultimately, Certificate Services relies on services provided by some CSP and accessed via CryptoAPI.

Clients can request certificates from Certificate Services in various ways, including via Hypertext Transfer Protocol (HTTP), through DCOM, and by telling it to read information from a file. The request itself is sent in a standard format called PKCS #10,[7] and it must indicate the purpose for which this certificate will be used. For example, certificates can be issued for purposes such as authenticating clients, authenticating servers, signing e-mail, signing executable code, and others. The result of the request is an X.509v3 certificate, returned in another standard format called PKCS #7.

Certificates can be requested in various ways

To make it easier to build requests, an administrator can use *certificate templates* that contain the basic parameters for a given type of request. An individual request can then simply plug in the user-specific values it requires. Windows 2000 includes a number of predefined certificate templates for common kinds of requests, so an administrator can often just use one that already exists. Certificate Services also allows adding custom policy and exit modules that enforce whatever rules an organization believes are important. For example, a CA at some organization might use a policy module that looks up each user requesting a certificate in the company's list of current full-time employees, then issue certs only to requesters found on this list.

Certificate Services can be customized using policy modules

While an organization might have only a single CA, creating a multilevel CA hierarchy allows for greater security. This is because higher-level CAs can be kept offline in a physically secure location, making them much more difficult for an attacker to access. Whatever choice is made, CAs implemented with Windows 2000 Certificate Services must be configured as either of two types: *Enterprise* CAs and *Standalone* CAs. The most important difference between the two is that an Enterprise CA is integrated with

Certificate Services supports Enterprise and Standalone CAs

---

7. "PKCS" stands for Public Key Cryptography Standards, the name of a group of standards defined for use with various public key technologies. PKCS #10 defines a standard format for requesting certificates.

the security and directory services of a domain, and so can automatically issue a certificate when it receives an authenticated request from a user in that domain. A standalone CA, by contrast, generally requires requests for certificates to be explicitly approved by an administrator or in some other way.

An Enterprise CA can automatically issue a certificate when a user requests one

In fact, an Enterprise CA can only be deployed as part of a Windows 2000 domain—it requires Active Directory. Before issuing a cert to a requesting user, an Enterprise CA looks up that user in Active Directory, satisfying itself that this user really exists in this domain and that the user is allowed to ask for the type of certificate being requested. If so, the requested cert is automatically issued—no human intervention is needed. Also, Enterprise CAs can be configured to publish the certs they create and their CRLs in Active Directory.

A Standalone CA generally requires human intervention to issue a certificate

A Standalone CA, by contrast, does not require access to Active Directory, and so is not required to be part of a Windows 2000 domain. It certainly is possible for a Standalone CA to belong to a domain, however, and if it does, it can publish information into Active Directory just like an Enterprise CA. But Standalone CAs don't automatically verify users in Active Directory, and they don't typically issue certs without explicit human intervention.

Standalone CAs are useful in some situations

Most CAs in most organizations will be Enterprise CAs, but there are a few cases where Standalone CAs are the right choice. For example, think about how a commercial CA such as VeriSign would use this type of software. Automatically issuing certs when users request them, as Enterprise CAs do, would make very little sense—a commercial CA commonly performs some offline checks to verify a user's identity. A Standalone CA's requirement for human intervention before issuing a certificate matches this situation well. Standalone CAs are also useful for an organization that creates its own CA hierarchy. While most of the CAs in this hierarchy will be Enterprise CAs, the root CA should be a Standalone CA.

Recall that the root CA issues certs only to the CAs directly beneath it in a hierarchy, not to end users. While using a Standalone CA to issue certs to users would be inconvenient—it's better to let an Enterprise CA verify the user's existence using Active Directory, then automatically issue the cert—relatively few CAs are directly beneath the root. Even more important, certifying a new CA beneath the root in a CA hierarchy is a critical task, one in which the human intervention a Standalone CA requires is probably a good thing. Finally, using a Standalone CA at a hierarchy's root allows physically securing the machine that CA runs on—it need not be available online.

Depending on its type and position in a CA hierarchy, an installed instance of a CA using Windows 2000 Certificate Services can be configured as one of four types:

Certificate Services supports Root and Subordinate CAs

- *Enterprise Root CA* Acts as the highest level CA in a hierarchy. Enterprise Root CAs are intended to issue certificates only for use by other CAs—they shouldn't issue certs for direct use by users. Because they're at the root of the CA hierarchy, each Enterprise Root CA has a self-signed certificate.
- *Enterprise Subordinate CA* A non-root CA in some enterprise's hierarchy. Its certificate is signed by another CA, such as an Enterprise Root CA or another Enterprise Subordinate CA.
- *Standalone Root CA* Like an Enterprise Root CA but does not issue certs without human intervention.
- *Standalone Subordinate CA* Like an Enterprise Subordinate CA but also does not issue certs without human intervention.

To manage a Windows 2000-based CA that uses Certificate Services, an administrator uses the Certification Authority Microsoft Management Console (MMC) snap-in. This tool allows performing basic tasks such as backing up and restoring a CA's data, along with more advanced functions such as revoking certificates, approving requests, and explicitly forcing publication in Active Directory of a new CRL for an Enterprise CA.

Acquiring Keys and Certificates

A user gets a key pair and a certificate through enrollment

Each principal that wants to use public key technology for authentication or anything else must first acquire a key pair, along with a certificate containing the public key in that pair. The process of acquiring and installing this key pair and certificate is called *enrollment*. In Windows 2000, the enrollment process depends on CryptoAPI, Microsoft Certificate Services, and more.

Enrollment relies on a COM component

Windows 2000 provides two different user interfaces for enrollment: the Certificates snap-in, usable only with Enterprise CAs, and a simple Web-based interface, usable with CAs of either type. The actual work of enrollment is done in both cases by a COM component called the Certificate Enrollment Control. To begin the process, shown in Figure 4-12, a user accesses this control in some way. In practice, this commonly means that the user accesses a Web page that in turn invokes the services of the enrollment control, or uses the Certificate Request wizard in the Certificates snap-in to do the same thing. However it's accessed, though, the control relies on CryptoAPI to generate a new public key pair. Exactly how this is done depends on which CSP is used. The Base RSA CSP produces a key pair entirely by using software, for example, while a smart card CSP might rely on the card's hardware to create key pairs (although this can be slow). However it's done, the private key of the newly created pair is placed in the key storage for whatever CSP is used to create it. With the Base RSA CSP, for example, the private key is stored on the hard drive of the user's machine, as described earlier, while a smart card CSP stores the private key on the card.

Figure 4-12 *Enrolling a new user requires generating a key pair, creating a certificate containing that pair's public key, then storing the principal's private key and certificate in the appropriate places.*

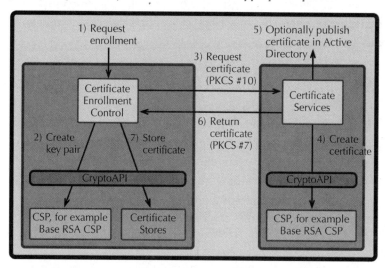

The public key is returned to the enrollment control, which wraps it, the principal's name, and other information into a PKCS #10 message. This message is then signed with the requester's private key and sent off to Certificate Services. Certificate Services builds a certificate using the information in the request, then sends it back as a PKCS #7 message. The server might also publish the new cert in the user's object in Active Directory. Once the cert has been returned to the requesting machine, the enrollment control stores it in the appropriate place, such as the client machine's Personal store (along with a reference to the associated private key) or, with smart cards, both in the Personal store and on the card itself. Everything is now ready for use. Note that, throughout this process, the user's private key is never sent across the network, so there's no danger of that key being acquired by an eavesdropper.

The enrollment process creates a key pair and certificate, then stores them in the proper places

One more point worth mentioning is that for some applications, such as Internet Protocol (IP)-level security, computers themselves must have key pairs and certificates. Using Group Policy, it's possible to cause all computers in a domain, organizational unit (OU), or site to automatically request enrollment. Using this automatic certificate request feature can make life simpler for administrators when keys and certs are needed for each computer.

Managing Certificate Revocation Lists

CRLs can be stored in Active Directory

Windows 2000 Certificate Services allows publishing CRLs in Active Directory—that is, storing them in a directory object that's accessible to clients. When a new Enterprise CA is created that's part of a Windows 2000 domain, that CA adds an entry in Active Directory for its CRL. An administrator can add a cert to the CRL of the CA that issued it using the Certification Authority snap-in. By default, a new version of the CRL is published to Active Directory once a week, but this can be changed using the Certification Authority snap-in.

Certificates can contain the location of a CA's CRL

For a system using a certificate to determine whether that cert has been revoked, there must be some way to find the CRL of the CA that issued the cert. To allow this, every cert produced by a Windows 2000 CA contains an extended attribute field called the CRL Distribution Point (CDP). This field holds the name of the Active Directory entry, expressed as an LDAP URL, that contains the CRL for this CA. To check the CRL for a particular certificate, all that's required is to read this field, access the CRL in Active Directory, and see if this cert is on the list. If it is, the certificate is no longer valid.

Certs issued in other ways—that is, certs that aren't issued by Windows 2000 Certificate Services—can also contain a CDP attribute. If they do, the URL in this field can be accessed to find the appropriate CRL. There's a standard format for CRLs, one supported by many suppliers, which makes multivendor use possible. To perform this access, protocols such as HTTP or LDAP might be used on either an internal network or across the Internet.

Controlling Certificate Trust

In Windows 2000, each computer in a domain has its own set of certificate stores. If a computer has the certificate for some CA in its Trusted Root CA store, this says two things about that computer's trust in the CA. First, that machine (and by extension, the software running on that machine) trusts this root CA. Second, that machine also trusts every CA in the CA hierarchy beneath this root CA (unless one of those CAs has a revoked or expired certificate). This means that which root CA certificates find their way into a machine's Trusted Root CA store is critically important. Trust the wrong root CA and havoc can ensue.

CAs with self-signed certificates in the Trusted Root CA store will be trusted as root CAs

Determining which root CAs you trust is a human process, not a technical one. As already mentioned, Windows 2000 automatically installs certificates from several commercial CAs in a machine's Trusted Root CA store. It's also potentially possible for a machine's user to install root CA certificates in the Trusted Root CA store on her own machine, but these will be trusted only by her, not by any other users of that machine. In a typical domain, however, the best approach will be for a domain administrator to determine which root CAs should be trusted.[8] Once this choice has been made, there must also be some way to centrally enforce that decision. Windows 2000 provides several ways to do this.

People must decide which CAs to trust

The first and simplest choice is this: in a Windows 2000 domain where all root CAs are implemented using Windows 2000 Certificate Services, self-signed certificates for those root CAs are automatically placed in the Trusted Root CA store of all machines in the domain when the root CA is installed. This makes sense, since presumably all machines and users in a domain should trust certificates issued by its own root CAs.

Some CA certificates are automatically placed in the Root CA store

---

8. Allowing each end user to decide which CAs to trust would generally be a bad idea, since most end users would have no idea what criteria to use. Of course, it can also require some effort for administrators to determine which CAs are trustworthy, but that's the kind of work they're paid for.

Some CA certificates are
placed in the Trusted
Root CA store using
Group Policy

The second choice is most useful for an organization that has its own root CAs but in which those CAs are not running on Windows 2000 machines. In this case, Group Policy can be used to write the certificates for those root CAs into the Trusted Root CA stores. Using a Group Policy option called the *trusted root certification authority*, an administrator can specify which CA certificates should be placed in the Trusted Root CA store of all Windows 2000 computers in a site, a domain, or an OU.

Finally, an organization can use a Windows 2000 feature called *enterprise trust policy*. In this case, an administrator creates and digitally signs some number of Certificate Trust Lists (CTLs). A CTL contains one or more foreign root certificates—certificates issued by root CAs that aren't in this domain's own CA hierarchy. Each CTL must be signed using a private key whose associated certificate chain ends in a root certificate contained in the Trusted Root CA store, such as an administrator's private key. Stored with each root certificate hash in a CTL is an indication of what the certificates issued by that foreign root CA are trusted for. Some CAs might be trusted only to issue certificates for secure e-mail, for instance, while others might be trusted to issue certificates for many purposes. This extra feature is one reason why a domain administrator might choose to use CTLs rather than just add more certs to the Trusted Root CA store. Once it's been defined, a CTL can be published to all machines in a site, a domain, or an OU via Group Policy. The CA certificates it contains will then be automatically added to each machine's Enterprise Trust store. When a certification chain is verified but found to terminate in a root certificate that's not in the Trusted Root CA store, the Enterprise Trust store is then searched to see if that root certificate is contained in a valid CTL. If it is, and if the certificate is being used for a purpose that matches those allowed for its issuing CA in that CTL, that chain is considered to be trusted.

Putting the Pieces Together: Validating a Digital Signature

To get a sense of how all of this fits together, it's useful to describe how the process of validating a digital signature really works. What's involved is shown in Figure 4-13. The hard work is hidden—it's done by CryptoAPI—but knowing what's going on is useful nonetheless, if only because it illustrates how all the technology described in this chapter is actually used.

Figure 4-13 *Validating a digital signature might require locating certificates, checking CRLs, and more.*

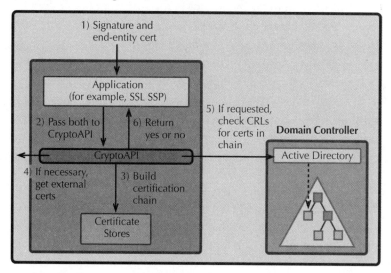

To begin, suppose some application has acquired a digital signature and either the end-entity certificate or the complete certification chain for the principal who created that signature. This application might be, for example, an IIS server that's just received this information from some client. Assuming this information was provided as part of an SSL exchange, as described later in this chapter, the SSL SSP will rely on CryptoAPI to validate the signature. The goal is to determine whether the client really is who it claims to be.

Validating a digital signature can require finding certificates, checking CRLs, and more

In a Windows 2000 environment, validating a digital signature requires several things. First, the validation process must be able to construct a certification chain stretching from the end-entity cert to the root CA, and that chain must contain only valid, unexpired certificates. In the simplest case, the principal whose signature is being checked will have provided a complete certification chain. Even if that principal supplied only an end-entity cert, however, the validation process must somehow be able to construct the appropriate chain. Also, the certificate for the root CA in this chain must already be present in the Trusted Root CA store, which means that the machine on which the IIS server is running trusts that root CA and all subordinate CAs in its hierarchy. And, of course, all signatures on all certificates in that chain must check out correctly, guaranteeing both the integrity and the authenticity of the certs themselves. Finally, the principal's digital signature must itself be correct, proving that it was constructed using that principal's private key.

CryptoAPI does the work of signature validation

In the example shown in Figure 4-13, only a signature and an end-entity certificate have been provided, and the SSL SSP passes both of these things to the appropriate CryptoAPI call. CryptoAPI must now acquire the certificates it needs to construct a complete certification chain up to a root CA. It begins this process by attempting to locate the certificate for the CA that issued this end-entity cert. That certificate might already be stored on this machine in one of the certificate stores, so CryptoAPI will first check there. If it's not found, CryptoAPI looks in an extended attribute field in the end-entity certificate, a field called Authority Information Access. This field contains a URL that tells CryptoAPI where to find the cert for the CA that signed the certificate. By following this URL, CryptoAPI can retrieve that CA's certificate. If this certificate is from a root CA—that is, if the certificate is self-signed—the process can stop here. If the certificate is not from a root CA, CryptoAPI must next find the certificate for the CA that signed this cert. As before, it first searches the local machine's certificate stores for that certificate. If it's not found there, CryptoAPI once again extracts from this newly acquired cert the URL indicating where to find the certificate of the CA that signed it. This process continues until CryptoAPI constructs the complete certification chain.

As CryptoAPI constructs the certificate chain, it verifies that each link is valid, as shown in Figure 4-8 (on page 130). If requested by the application, CryptoAPI will also locate the CRL for each certificate it finds and check to see if that certificate has been revoked. If any cert in the chain has been revoked, the process of validating the digital signature will fail. And throughout this process of acquiring the certificates in this certificate chain, newly acquired certs are placed in the Intermediate CA store on this machine.[9] If these certs are needed in the future, they can then be found locally rather than accessed across the network.

Once all this has been done, CryptoAPI attempts to validate the signature. If all goes well, and if the certificate at the top of the chain was found in the Trusted Root CA store or is part of a valid CTL, the signature is validated, and the call returns successfully. If anything goes wrong, however, the CryptoAPI call returns a validation failure to the application that invoked it.

Authentication based on digital signatures and certificates is a reasonably complicated process. This is especially true when the entire PKI edifice—CA hierarchies, smart cards, and the rest—is taken into account. Still, the complexity is largely hidden, so users and even developers don't see it. And because it's so powerful and so broadly applicable, public key technology is finding its way into more and more applications.

Public key technology is becoming widely used

---

9. Newly found root certificates are not automatically added to the Trusted Root store, however.

Understanding SSL

Windows 2000 makes SSL potentially accessible to various applications

Kerberos is the core security protocol in Windows 2000, but it's not the only choice. The SSL protocol can also be used by some kinds of Windows 2000 applications. Although its most common users today are browsers and Web servers, recall that SSL is implemented in Windows 2000 as an SSP, accessible through the SSPI. This means that other application protocols can potentially make use of SSL as well.

SSL is most commonly used on the Web

Still, SSL shines today for Web-based applications. Suppose, for example, that you want to allow users from a partner company to access, across the Internet, a Web site on your organization's internal network. Doing this securely requires at least some way to authenticate those users. If the partner company is running in a Microsoft Windows NT or Windows 2000 environment, you could theoretically choose to establish trust links between your domains and your partner's domains using NTLM or Kerberos (although you're likely have trouble making these approaches scalable). Another solution, though, one that scales well and doesn't depend on your partner using Microsoft operating systems, is to use SSL.

SSL can provide authentication, integrity, and privacy

Once you understand how public key technology works—signatures, certificates, and the rest—understanding SSL is easy. Like Kerberos, SSL can provide authentication, data integrity, and data privacy. For authentication, SSL relies primarily on digital signatures and certificates. SSL does not use public key technology to provide data integrity and data privacy, however. Instead, SSL uses public key encryption to exchange the information necessary to construct a secret key, then uses that secret key along with an algorithm such as RC4 to provide integrity and privacy. For data integrity, SSL appends a checksum to each transmitted packet, much like Kerberos. For data privacy, SSL encrypts the data in each packet sent over the wire.

The SSL specification is full of options. For example, a client and server can choose which encryption algorithms they will use and whether mutual authentication is required. The Windows 2000 implementation of SSL, an SSP which Microsoft sometimes refers to as *Secure Channel* or *SChannel*, supports the IETF-standard Transport Layer Security (TLS) protocol as well as versions 2 and 3 of SSL. It also supports Private Communications Technology (PCT), Microsoft's enhancement to SSL version 2 that has been largely obsoleted by SSL version 3 and, more recently, by TLS. Throughout this section, however, I'll simply use the name "SSL," and what follows describes SSL version 3 specifically.[10]

The Windows 2000 SSL implementation supports multiple versions of the protocol

The SSL Protocol

On the Internet, where SSL is most often used, requiring each client to have its own certificate and private key can be painful (today, anyway). Requiring this of each secure server is not too much to ask, however, since there are many fewer servers than clients. Accordingly, it's common to use SSL only for one-way authentication, to prove to the client that the server really is who it claims to be. But if both client and server have their own private keys and certificates, SSL can also be used for mutual authentication. This section shows how both options work.

SSL allows either server-only or mutual authentication

SSL with Only a Server Certificate   Figure 4-14 shows what happens when a client with no certificate and private key of its own uses SSL to communicate with a server that does have a certificate and private key. As the figure shows, the process begins with a ClientHello message sent from client to server. This message, like all SSL information, is sent over TCP or another connection-oriented transport protocol, and it contains several pieces of information. The most important of these are a random number (whose use will be described shortly), a session identifier, and a list of proposed encryption algorithms.

SSL commonly runs over TCP

---

10. In fact, the TLS and SSL specifications define a negotiation mechanism. The SChannel SSP first proposes TLS, then attempts to negotiate use of SSL version 3 if necessary.

Figure 4-14 *If only the server has a certificate and private key, SSL can be used to authenticate the server to the client and to securely create a secret key known to both client and server.*

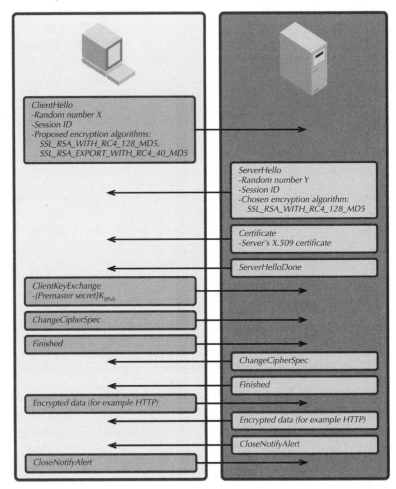

ClientHello
-Random number X
-Session ID
-Proposed encryption algorithms:
  SSL_RSA_WITH_RC4_128_MD5,
  SSL_RSA_EXPORT_WITH_RC4_40_MD5

ServerHello
-Random number Y
-Session ID
-Chosen encryption algorithm:
  SSL_RSA_WITH_RC4_128_MD5

Certificate
-Server's X.509 certificate

ServerHelloDone

ClientKeyExchange
-{Premaster secret}K_{SPub}

ChangeCipherSpec

Finished

ChangeCipherSpec

Finished

Encrypted data (for example HTTP)

Encrypted data (for example HTTP)

CloseNotifyAlert

CloseNotifyAlert

If this is the client's first request to this server, the session identifier field will be empty. If not, this field can contain a value that identifies a previous session that the client wishes to resume. This value was provided by the server during that previous session, and it serves an important purpose for a critical class of SSL users: Web browsers. To understand why this value is significant, think about what happens when you browse the Web. When your browser accesses a Web page using HTTP, each page you access typically requires setting up and tearing down a TCP connection to transfer that page's data. (In fact, several TCP connections might be used for a single page, one for the page's text and one for each graphic element on the page.) In a single browser session, comprising one set of interactions between you and some Web server, your browser might create and destroy many different TCP connections. Requiring a complete SSL connection exchange for each of them would make secure browser access intolerably slow. If a client indicates that it wishes to resume a previous session, however, the client can reuse much of the existing information from that session. The result is a much faster SSL connection process for multiple TCP connections used within the same browser session. The session identifier field makes this possible.

The list of encryption algorithms contained in the ClientHello message in Figure 4-14 indicates the choices that the client is willing to use. In the example shown in the figure, the client is proposing two commonly used algorithms (although several more are defined):

The client proposes a list of encryption algorithms

- *SSL_RSA_WITH_RC4_128_MD5*   Requests RSA for exchanging secret key information, RC4 with a 128-bit key to encrypt exchanged data, and MD5 as a hash algorithm;
- *SSL_RSA_EXPORT_WITH_RC4_40_MD5*   Also requests RSA, RC4, and MD5, but specifies using only a 40-bit key for RC4 encryption of exchanged data. As its name suggests, software supporting this option can be exported from the U.S. without a license, which is not true for this example's first proposed choice.[11]

---

11. Once again, the laws are changing as this book goes to press. This statement may not be true by the time you read this.

The server sends back its
choice for an algorithm
along with its certificate

In response to a ClientHello, the server sends a ServerHello message. This message contains another random number, along with an encryption algorithm selected by the server from the options proposed by the client. It also contains a session identifier, which is the value a client can supply in a future ClientHello message if it wishes to resume this session at a later time. After the ServerHello message, the server sends the client a Certificate message containing its X.509 certificate, followed by a ServerHelloDone message.

The client sends the
server a byte string
encrypted using the
server's public key

The client now sends a ClientKeyExchange message. What's contained in this message varies depending on the algorithm selected in the exchange just described. The example here uses RSA,[12] today's most common choice, so the message contains something called a *premaster secret*. This value is generated randomly by the client, then encrypted using the server's public key, denoted as K_{SPub} in the figure, which the client has extracted from the server's certificate. Since only the server knows its private key, only it can decrypt the premaster secret. Both client and server perform some slightly complicated hashing on this value to produce a 48-byte *master secret*. This master secret is used along with the random numbers exchanged on the Hello messages to generate the secret keys used for data integrity and data privacy.

Both sides derive a secret
key, then can exchange
encrypted data

The client now sends a ChangeCipherSpec message, which is always the same—it has no variable parameters. All it means is, "Let's begin using the encryption algorithm and key we've agreed to." Finally, the client sends a Finished message that contains a hash of various standard information. This message is encrypted using the encryption algorithm and key just agreed to—it's the first message sent protected in this way.

---

12. The Windows 2000 implementation of SSL also supports using the Diffie-Hellman algorithm for exchanging key information.

The server responds with a ChangeCipherSpec message of its own followed by a Finished message. As before, this Finished message is encrypted using the algorithm and key agreed to earlier in this protocol exchange. Both sides can now send encrypted information securely, using whatever application protocol they wish, since each side knows a secret key (derived from the master secret) that an eavesdropper can't determine.

After all encrypted data has been sent, the server sends a CloseNotifyAlert message, which is simply a fixed byte string, and the client responds by sending a CloseNotifyAlert message of its own. These messages indicate that the secure connection is being closed.

As the example in Figure 4-14 shows, SSL allows a client to be certain that the server is who it claims to be (assuming, of course, that the client trusts the CA that issued the server's certificate, or if a certification chain is used, trusts the root CA in that hierarchy). The client's certainty is based on the server's ability to decrypt the premaster secret sent in the ClientKeyExchange message. Since this value is encrypted using the public key extracted from the server's certificate, it can be decrypted only if this really was the right certificate for this server, that is, only if the server knows the corresponding private key. If the server can successfully send encrypted information that the client can decrypt, it must have successfully decrypted the premaster secret the client sent it, and so it must be who it claims to be.

The SSL exchanges just described let the client authenticate the server

In this example, the client is not authenticated. It's common for Internet applications to authenticate a client by prompting the user for a name and a password. Since both client and server now possess the same secret key, that information can be sent over an encrypted channel, which makes this a fairly safe solution. A more complete solution, though, would be to give the client its own certificate, allowing SSL to provide mutual authentication. How this works is described next.

SSL with Both Client and Server Certificates   The example
shown in Figure 4-15 is much like the case just described, except
that in this next example, mutual authentication is used—both the
client and the server have their own private keys and certificates.
Unlike Kerberos, in which client authentication only is the default
and server authentication an option, SSL reverses the priorities:
server authentication only is the default. In fact, SSL won't allow
authenticating a client if the server doesn't also provide a certificate to authenticate itself.

The process shown in Figure 4-15 begins just as in the previous
example, with each side sending a Hello message containing a
random number, a session identifier, and more. As before, the server next sends its certificate. But unlike in the previous example,
the server follows the Certificate message with a Certificate-
Request message. This message contains a list of certificate types
acceptable to the server, such as certificates usable with RSA, and
a list of the CAs this server trusts to issue those certificates.

The client responds by sending its X.509 certificate, using the
same message format that the server used to send its certificate.
This message is followed by the ClientKeyExchange message,
which, as in the previous example, contains a random value encrypted using the server's public key. Next, the client sends a
CertificateVerify message, which contains a complex hash value
that the client has digitally signed. The server can also compute
this hash value, then extract the client's public key from the newly
received certificate and use it to validate the digital signature.

Figure 4-15 *If both the client and server have certificates, SSL can provide mutual authentication.*

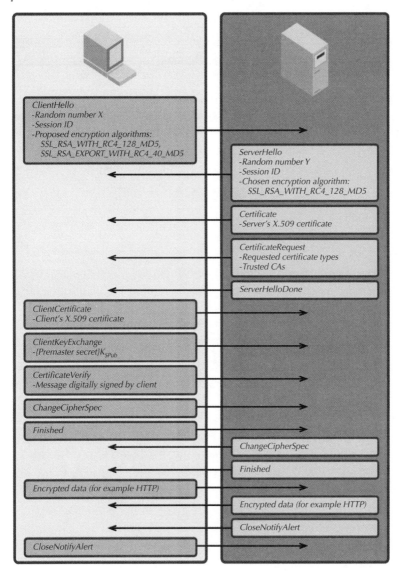

As in the previous example, the client can be certain of the server's identity because the server will demonstrate that it has correctly decrypted the premaster secret sent in the ClientKey-Exchange. The server can be certain of the client's identity because the client has provided a digital signature along with a certificate. Once each party has verified the other's identity, the exchanges proceed as in the previous example: the client sends Change-CipherSpec and Finished messages, and the server responds with these same two messages. As before, the two parties can exchange encrypted data, then mark the end of the connection with an exchange of CloseNotifyAlert messages. The only difference between this scenario and the previous one is that now the client proves its identity using a certificate and a digital signature.

SSL in Windows 2000

The SSL protocol is a multivendor standard, so by definition, every implementation must send the same information across a network. But some important aspects of using SSL aren't addressed by the standard, which means that Windows 2000 must address those issues in a vendor-specific way. Among those aspects are how the information needed to make an authorization decision is acquired and, in a Windows 2000 domain, when to choose SSL over Kerberos.

SSL doesn't define how authorization should be done

Getting Authorization Data   While SSL can't be used for direct login to a Windows 2000 domain, it can be used to provide security for distributed applications. Kerberos and SSL can both provide authentication, data integrity, and data privacy, but neither one provides authorization. As described in the previous chapter, however, a Kerberos ticket carries authorization data, such as security identifiers (SIDs) identifying the client and the groups the client belongs to. The receiving system's Local Security Authority (LSA) uses this information to build a security access token and allow the server to impersonate the client. In the standard authorization model, Windows 2000 itself can then check the appropriate ACLs and make an authorization decision.

Accomplishing this same thing with SSL requires a bit more work. The SSL protocol conveys no tickets, and in fact no field in any SSL packet carries Windows 2000–specific authorization data. If a client identifies itself with only a certificate, how can a server acquire the information it needs to impersonate the client?

The answer is shown in Figure 4-16. When an SSL client authenticates itself by presenting its certificate and a digitally signed message, the server system first examines the certificate. If this certificate was created by Microsoft Certificate Services, it has an extended attribute field that contains the client's User Principal Name (UPN). If this field is present, it is looked up in the global catalog to find the client's user object in Active Directory. Once this object is found, the client's authorization information is returned to the server system, which can then use it to make an authorization decision.[13]

The client's authorization data can be looked up in Active Directory

Figure 4-16 *A server can acquire authorization data by querying a domain controller using information from the certificate.*

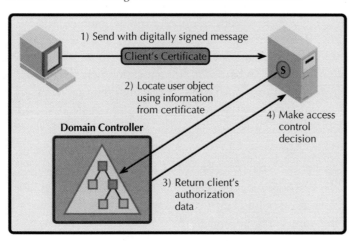

---

13. This information is not returned by means of LDAP. Instead, the server machine uses an authenticated RPC connection to connect to the domain controller, then conveys the required authorization information back to the server.

If the client's certificate was not produced by Microsoft Certificate Services, though, it most likely won't contain the client's UPN. In this case, the Issuer name or Issuer and Subject names in the certificate are used as a lookup key to find an associated user object in Active Directory that contains a mapping specifying these names. This object represents a particular user account in Active Directory, and so once again, the proper authorization information can be located and returned to the server. Note that this second case implies that someone has created a mapping between a particular certificate and a specific user object in Active Directory. In other words, the correlation between certs and users must be created administratively for certificates that are not created by Microsoft Certificate Services.

SSL can scale well, which is good for Internet use

Kerberos or SSL?   Why have both Kerberos and SSL? In fact, providing strong support for both of these protocols in Windows 2000 makes good sense. Because SSL is based on public key technology, clients and servers aren't required to share Kerberos servers (directly or indirectly). This allows SSL to scale better, which is a big reason why it's so popular on the Internet today.

Public key technology is arguably less mature than Kerberos

Public key technology is relatively slow, however—distributed applications that use Kerberos for authentication will generally perform better than those using SSL. More important, if Windows 2000 used only SSL for distributed security, all of its users would be dependent on the relative complexity of public key technology. Every domain would be required to configure and use a public key infrastructure consisting of CAs, CA hierarchies, and more. One can argue that the experience and knowledge required to bet the farm on public key technology just isn't here yet, although that time is fast approaching.

Kerberos remains the core security protocol in Windows 2000

In Windows 2000, Kerberos is Microsoft's primary choice for security within an organization. As we've seen, Kerberos-based security can be used both inside a domain and between different domains, and it can scale to support large numbers of users. It seems likely that SSL will remain the dominant security protocol for Web-based applications on the Internet and might be used for Web-based applications on intranets as well. But in a Windows 2000 environment, the core security protocol is unquestionably Kerberos.

Microsoft has stated its belief that both Kerberos and public key-based technologies such as SSL will coexist for some time. The widespread use of SSL on the Internet and the general attractiveness of public key technology, together with the requirement for Kerberos imposed by Windows 2000, make this prophecy very likely to come true.

Using Public Key Technology with Kerberos

As originally deployed by MIT, Kerberos required only secret key encryption. Today, however, there is an IETF specification for using smart cards and public key technology to acquire a Kerberos ticket-granting ticket (TGT), and Windows 2000 supports this option. Using this approach eliminates one of the potential weaknesses of Kerberos, which is its reliance on passwords chosen by users. In standard Kerberos, if I can guess or steal your password, I can log in as you. With a smart card-based login, this is no longer true. Assuming your private key is stored only on your smart card, I can't pretend to be you without both having that smart card in my possession and knowing the card's PIN.

Windows 2000 Kerberos allows logging in using smart cards instead of passwords

This smart card option is sometimes referred to as PKINIT, and how it works is shown in Figure 4-17. Rather than entering just a password on login, the user inserts a smart card into a smart card reader, then enters the appropriate PIN for that card. The user's certificate is read from the smart card, then sent to the KDC with a digitally signed request for a TGT. (The certificate information is carried in place of the preauthentication data normally sent in Windows 2000 Kerberos.) The KDC validates the certificate by checking its digital signature, which might require constructing a certification chain. (In Windows 2000, a user's certificate must have been issued by an Enterprise CA to be used for login.)

A client sends a digital signature and certificate to authenticate its user

Assuming the certificate information supplied by the user checks out, the KDC extracts the user's public key from the certificate, uses it to verify the supplied digital signature, then looks up this user's entry in the Active Directory database.

Figure 4-17 *A client can use a smart card to acquire a Kerberos TGT.*

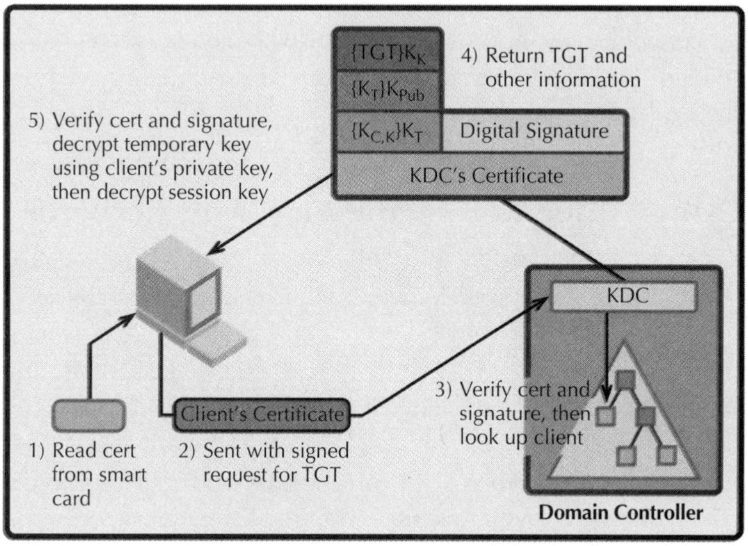

The KDC verifies the signature, then sends back a TGT

The KDC then returns a TGT encrypted with the KDC's secret key $K_{K'}$ just as in standard Kerberos. The KDC also sends back an encrypted session key $K_{C,K'}$ just as before, but the key used to encrypt this session key is no longer derived from the user's password. Instead, the KDC randomly generates a temporary secret key K_T, uses it to encrypt the client/KDC session key, then sends this temporary key along as well. The temporary key is itself sent encrypted using the client's public key $K_{Pub'}$ which the server extracted from the certificate the client supplied. And to prove to the client that this really is the correct KDC, the encrypted session key is digitally signed using the KDC's private key. Finally, to allow the client to verify this signature, the server also sends back its certificate or certification chain.

When this message arrives at the client, several things happen. First, the client verifies the received digital signature, satisfying itself that this message came from the correct KDC. Next the client uses its private key to decrypt the temporary secret key K_T sent back by the server. Once it knows this key, the client can then decrypt the session key $K_{C,K}$, and just as in a traditional Kerberos login, the client now has a TGT and a valid client/KDC session key.

PKINIT changes only how the TGT and its associated session key are acquired—everything else in Kerberos works just as before. In an environment where smart cards are common, PKINIT can provide an extra measure of security for Windows 2000 domains. And by combining Kerberos and public key technology, PKINIT provides an effective union of today's two leading solutions for distributed security.

Combining Kerberos and public key technology exploits two leading security solutions

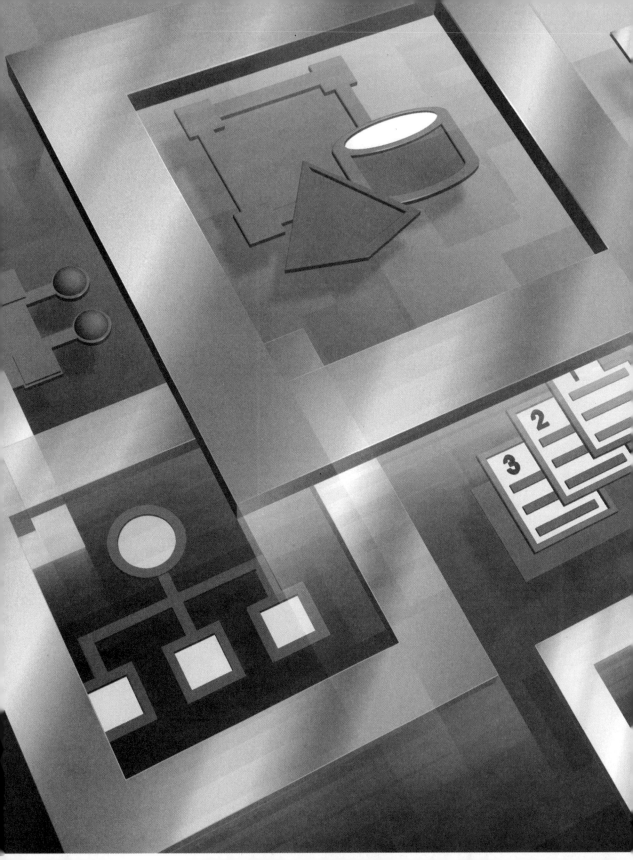

Chapter Five

Component Services: COM and DCOM

No technology is more fundamental to Microsoft Windows 2000 software development than the Component Object Model. COM is used in some way by nearly every application written on this and other Microsoft operating systems. Even applications that span multiple systems can use COM in its slightly extended form known as Distributed COM (DCOM).

Writing software for Windows 2000 means using COM

Windows 2000 introduces COM+, a substantially extended version of this core technology. This chapter gives a concise overview of the fundamentals of COM, most of which are unchanged by COM+. For an examination of what COM+ brings, see Chapter 8.

Understanding COM Objects

In COM, clients access services provided by *COM objects*. The first question to answer, then, is what is a COM object? Like other kinds of objects, a COM object is a software abstraction that encapsulates two things: *data* and *methods*. An object's data, also referred to as its *state,* is the information stored in memory by the object, while its methods are code that allows the object

A COM object has data and methods

to provide its services. For example, a COM object that allows a sales representative to place an order might contain data such as the items that are currently part of this order and the time the order was created. The methods for the object could include ways to add an item to the order, delete an item from the order, submit the order, determine what time the order was created, and more.

Methods are grouped into interfaces

Like methods in programming languages, a COM object's methods can have parameters. For instance, a method to add an item to an order might take an integer parameter containing the stock number of the item to be added. In COM, methods must be grouped into *interfaces,* and each COM object implements some number of interfaces. (This number is virtually always greater than one, for reasons explained later in this chapter.) The order object just mentioned might put all methods related to building an order in one interface, for example, while all methods concerned with information about the order, such as when it was created, might be grouped into a second interface. Interfaces expose only an object's methods—the data is encapsulated, accessible only through the methods in the interfaces the object implements. And as shown in Chapter 1, each interface an object provides is by convention illustrated as a small circle connected to the object.

Clients invoke methods using interface pointers

Each COM object has one or more clients—other pieces of software that use its services. To access an object's services, a client must invoke the methods that object provides. Before invoking the methods in a particular interface, a client must acquire an *interface pointer* to that interface. Depending on the programming language the client is written in, this might or might not be seen by a programmer as a true pointer; but whatever it looks like, it allows the client to call methods in the interface it references. As Figure 5-1 shows, it's common for a client to hold more than one interface pointer to the same COM object, one for each interface whose methods it wishes to invoke.

Figure 5-1 *To invoke the methods in a particular interface, a client must hold an interface pointer to that interface.*

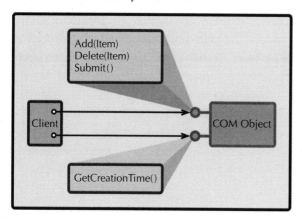

Before diving into a more detailed description of interfaces, it's important to emphasize that COM objects can be created in and used from many different programming languages. In fact, a COM object and its client might or might not be written in the same language. Because COM defines language-independent standards for client/object interaction, that doesn't matter. The most common language choices today among COM developers are Microsoft Visual Basic, C++, and Java, but nearly every development tool available for Windows 2000 and other Microsoft operating systems supports COM in some way. Each of the three most popular languages for working with COM has its own notion of what an object is. Those notions are broadly similar to one another and to COM's definition of an object, but none of them are exactly the same. Writing software that uses COM requires understanding COM's view of objects—it's always the same, no matter what programming language is used—then grasping how that view is mapped into a particular language.

Not too surprisingly, C++ developers can take the most detailed, painfully low-level view of COM if they choose to. They can also use higher-level tools such as the popular Microsoft ActiveX

COM objects can be used with many different programming languages

Template Library (ATL) to hide many of the details. Visual Basic programmers, by contrast, always have a substantial amount of COM's details hidden from them. This makes it easier to use COM from Visual Basic, but also a little more frustrating—the Visual Basic/COM mapping isn't to everyone's liking. And finally, Java's native view of objects serendipitously turns out to be very similar to COM's. Microsoft's Java virtual machine (JVM) exploits this similarity by supporting a direct mapping from Java objects to COM objects and vice versa. If the Microsoft JVM is used, Java is probably the most natural language for COM developers because of the straightforward mapping between the two kinds of objects.

Interfaces

COM defines an in-memory layout for interfaces

In COM, a client never holds a reference to a running object as a whole. Instead, the client interacts with the object only by invoking methods through interface pointers. From a client's point of view, then, a COM object is primarily seen as a collection of interfaces. And regardless of the language an object is written in, COM interfaces always conform to a defined in-memory structure. By nailing down the exact memory layout for how a client invokes methods in an object, COM makes it possible for clients written in one language to work with objects written in another.

COM has three kinds of interfaces

Kinds of Interfaces   In a perfect world, one interface style could be used with all combinations of client and object. In the imperfect world in which COM exists, however, this is not the case, and so there are three different kinds of COM interfaces. Each one was created for a particular reason during COM's evolution, although if COM were being created today this diversity might not exist.

The first interface type, vtable interfaces, were originally defined for C++

The first choice, *vtable* interfaces, was initially designed with C++ in mind. Also known as *custom* interfaces, their in-memory structure mirrors the way methods are invoked in popular C++ compilers (including Microsoft Visual C++). This makes it straightforward to implement vtable interfaces in C++ and very efficient to invoke methods through vtable interfaces in COM objects written in C++.

Today, vtable interfaces are also easy, fast, and commonly used with Visual Basic and Java. But when COM was first introduced in 1993, vtable interfaces weren't suitable for use with Visual Basic. For one thing, Visual Basic programs had a challenging time invoking methods using a C++–oriented interface structure. But this wasn't the only problem vtable interfaces posed for Visual Basic. A more intractable issue was one faced by any technology that tries to allow interaction between clients and objects written in different languages: how do you translate data types defined in one language into those defined for the other? Suppose an object written in C++ is being used by a Visual Basic client. What happens if one of the methods an interface on that object implements takes a pointer as a parameter? Visual Basic has no support for pointers, so calling that method from a Visual Basic client becomes all but impossible. A more subtle but no less pernicious problem occurs when the two languages involved both support a particular data type, but do it in different ways. Both C++ and Visual Basic support character strings, for example, but the way they do it differs. How can these problems be addressed?

COM's initial answer was to define a second type of interface, officially known as *dispatch* interfaces but more often referred to as *dispinterfaces*. Dispinterfaces were created to allow Visual Basic programs to effectively implement, and act as a client of, COM objects. The in-memory layout of a dispinterface is slightly different from that of a vtable interface, which makes invoking methods from Visual Basic easier. (In fact, every dispinterface relies on a particular vtable interface called IDispatch.) Also, methods in dispinterfaces are allowed to have parameters of only a limited number of data types. Unlike vtable interfaces, whose methods are allowed to contain virtually any parameter type that's defined

The second interface type, dispinterfaces, were originally defined for Visual Basic for C++, dispinterfaces are basically restricted to parameter types that are available in Visual Basic (although dispinterfaces are also commonly used with Java today as well). Because using dispinterfaces is sometimes referred to as *automation,* an interface whose parameter types are drawn only from this limited set is said to be *automation-compatible.*

When parameters are passed to and from a dispinterface method, those parameters are packaged into one or more *variants.* A variant contains a value of any automation-compatible type and also includes an indication of what type it contains. For example, a particular variant might contain some integer value and a tag identifying its data as a long integer. Variants are very convenient for Visual Basic programmers—Visual Basic does all the work of translating parameters to and from this format.

The third interface type, dual interfaces, merges the first two interface types

Today, Visual Basic has advanced, and it's now possible for a Visual Basic client to access or implement COM objects using vtable interfaces as long as those interfaces are automation-compatible. And a third type of interface is also available, called a *dual* interface. A dual interface essentially combines the in-memory layout of a vtable interface and a dispinterface, allowing methods to be invoked using either interface's style. Dual interfaces must still be automation-compatible, however, making them suitable for use with Visual Basic and Java. In fact, COM objects created in Visual Basic default to using dual interfaces to expose their methods.

Every interface has a name

Identifying Interfaces To invoke the methods in a particular interface, a client must acquire a pointer to that interface on some running COM object. Exactly how this is accomplished is described later, but it's probably obvious that acquiring this pointer requires some way for the client to identify the interface it's interested in. In other words, interfaces must have names.

In COM, every interface has two names. One of those names is used by people, so it's just a character string. By convention, the names of COM interfaces begin with the letter "I". The interfaces on the order entry object mentioned earlier might have names like IOrderEntry and IOrderStatistics, for example. This first style of name is easy for people to remember and to use when talking about COM objects.

Human-readable interface names usually start with "I"

This kind of interface name is not unique, however. It's entirely possible (and completely legal) for two different people to define two different interfaces and each name their interface IMyInterface. Yet to get an interface pointer to the correct interface, a client must have some way to uniquely name the interface it's interested in. Therefore, each interface must also have a name that identifies it and no other.

While this second kind of name must be globally unique, it doesn't have to be at all friendly for people to use—it's intended for use only by software. Accordingly, every COM interface is assigned a value known either as a Universally Unique Identifier (UUID) or a Globally Unique Identifier (GUID). (The terms are used interchangeably, but I'll primarily use the latter in this book.) A GUID is a 16-byte value that's unique in time and space. The GUID assigned to a particular interface is known as its interface identifier (IID). Once an IID (that is, a GUID) has been assigned to an interface, that IID will identify only that particular interface forever.

Every interface also has a globally unique IID, specified with a GUID

Since GUIDs are globally unique, you can't just make one up whenever you define a new interface. Instead, there are a couple of different ways to acquire GUIDs. The hard way, an approach that's not often used, is to request a GUID from Microsoft. The easy way to get one, though, is to run a simple software utility on your desktop machine. Each time you use this tool, it produces a

GUIDs are typically created using a software tool

new GUID, one that's guaranteed to be globally unique.[1] And while one important use of GUIDs is as IIDs, they're also used to name other things, as we'll see.

Defining Interfaces   A COM interface is a very simple concept— it defines only what a client needs to know to invoke the methods it contains. Because of the diverse ways in which COM is used, however, there are a few choices for how interfaces are defined.

IDL can be used to define interfaces

The most formal and in some ways most powerful way to define an interface is using COM's Interface Definition Language (IDL). The syntax of IDL was originally derived from C, and COM's IDL is actually based on the IDL defined for the Open Group's Distributed Computing Environment (DCE). If the order entry interface described earlier were a vtable interface, here's how it might look in IDL:

```
[ object,
    uuid(A7CD0D00-1827-11CF-9946-493655354000) ]
interface IOrderEntry : IUnknown {
        import "unknwn.idl";
        HRESULT Add([in] int item);
        HRESULT Delete([in] int item);
        HRESULT Submit();
}
```

---

1. How is it possible for each of us to run the same software independently on all of our machines, yet be sure that the values produced by that software are all different? The answer lies in what a GUID consists of. Its two primary elements are a timestamp indicating when it was created and the Medium Access Control (MAC) address of the network card installed in the machine on which it is created. The timestamp guarantees that every GUID produced on this machine is different (and the GUID-generating software notices and compensates for clock setbacks). The MAC address guarantees that no other GUID produced at the same time will be identical to this one, since MAC addresses are assigned by a central authority and thus are globally unique. The result is a value that's easy to produce but still guaranteed to be unique. And to address the security concerns of some organizations, Windows 2000 can generate GUIDs that obfuscate the creating system's MAC address rather than dropping it unchanged into the GUID.

Using IDL is the most flexible way to define a COM interface, but it's also the most complex. It's often used today by C++ developers, who are generally a hardcore bunch with a high tolerance for pain. Visual Basic encourages a somewhat lower complexity threshold, however, so it allows defining COM interfaces in Visual Basic itself—there's no need to learn IDL unless you want control over every aspect of your interface definition. Given that IDL is not a simple language, that is a good thing.

Other approaches to defining interfaces are also possible

However they're defined, COM interfaces share one common trait: they are by definition immutable. In other words, once an interface has found its way into the world—once it has clients—the rules of COM prohibit making any changes to this interface. During development, of course, interfaces can and do change, but once they're in use they must change no more. From now on, the GUID serving as the IID for a particular interface will always identify that interface and no other. If a new method or even just a new parameter must be added, an entirely new interface with its own IID must be defined—it's not possible to define a new version of an existing interface. This rule can seem nonsensically strict at first sight, but it turns out to be central to how COM handles version control, a subject described later in this chapter.

Once it's in use, a COM interface can't be changed

Interface Inheritance   COM allows one interface to inherit from another. This means that rather than explicitly repeating the method definitions of an existing interface in a new one, the definer of the new interface can just reference the existing interface and its methods will automatically be included. This can be convenient, and as we'll see, there's one case where it's essential.

A new COM interface can inherit from an existing one

COM supports only single inheritance, which means that an interface can directly inherit from only one other interface at a time. Also, only an interface's method definitions are inherited, not the actual implementation of the methods in that interface. That means that COM has no support for implementation inheritance.

COM allows only single inheritance

When a developer writes code for an interface that inherits from some other interface, that developer must somehow supply code for all the methods in both interfaces. Of course, the implementation inheritance built into languages such as C++ can be used to do this, so developers really aren't forced to re-implement the same methods over and over. Still, COM itself provides no support for inheriting actual method implementations. And for better or worse, Visual Basic—the most widely used language on Microsoft operating systems—provides only limited support for COM's interface inheritance. This fact significantly contrains the utility of this feature.

Visual Basic uses properties extensively

Properties   COM objects expose interfaces that contain methods—nothing more. But some programming languages, notably Visual Basic, depend extensively on the notion of *properties*. A property is a value an object contains, one that can be read and/or modified. For example, a COM object representing an order being submitted might have properties such as Customer and Order Number. To work well in a Visual Basic environment, COM objects must be able to support this idea. And they can.

A COM object can also have properties

A readable property is implemented in COM by a method in some interface that allows accessing the property's value. If that property can also be modified, the interface will contain another method that allows changing its value. From the point of view of the COM object, a property is just data it maintains whose value can be read and possibly changed by calling the appropriate methods—there's nothing special about it. But allowing clients written in Visual Basic to view these methods through their own native metaphor of properties makes life much easier for Visual Basic developers.

It's fairly common today to see COM objects described in terms of their methods and properties, especially in documentation aimed at Visual Basic programmers. There's even explicit support in COM IDL for defining methods that allow getting and setting a property's value. While purists might complain, the existence of

Visual Basic–oriented properties in COM is really just another example of the challenges inherent in creating a system object model that can be used effectively with many different programming languages.

Classes

In object technology, a class is generally thought of as a template for a set of similar instances. For example, the class Bridge might have instances such as Golden Gate, Brooklyn, and Pont Neuf. Classes in COM are much like this. A COM class is implemented by some chunk of code that can be used to create one or more instances of COM objects, each of which is of the same class.

Most COM classes are assigned a class identifier, usually written as CLSID. The COM classes available for general use on a given computer, together with their CLSIDs, are listed in that machine's registry. Given a CLSID, it's possible to find the file containing the code that implements this class by looking in the class's registry entry.

CLSIDs are GUIDs, so no two classes will ever have the same name. Having unique names for classes is important because, as we'll see, classes created by any number of organizations might reside on a single machine or in a common distributed environment. If those classes were named with simple character strings, it would be possible for two different classes to wind up with the same name. Since a class's name is used when creating instances of that class, as described in the next section, name collisions would be problematic.

At the same time, it's not very convenient for programmers to work with CLSIDs, since 16-byte GUIDs aren't very friendly. To minimize this problem, COM also allows assigning each class a *programmatic identifier,* more often referred to as a *ProgID.* ProgIDs are just character strings, so they're easy for developers to use and remember, and they can be translated into CLSIDs when required. This translation relies on the system registry, which can contain a

Every COM object is of some class

A COM class is often assigned a CLSID

CLSIDs are GUIDs, which means they're globally unique

A class can also be named with a human-readable ProgID

mapping from ProgID to CLSID for any COM class installed on the system. ProgIDs aren't strictly guaranteed to be unique, but it's common to use naming conventions (such as beginning all ProgIDs allocated by a specific company with a trademarked name owned by that company) to make collisions unlikely. And in any case, ProgIDs are just a convenience—a class's true name is its CLSID.

Objects of a given COM class will generally implement a particular group of interfaces. For example, all objects of the COM class identified by CLSID_X could implement the interfaces IOrderEntry and IOrderStatistics. It is legal, however, to change the set of interfaces supported by objects of a particular COM class over time either by adding new interfaces or by dropping support for older ones. This kind of change doesn't require changing the CLSID. Instead, since a COM class really refers to a particular set of code, all that's required is changing what that code does. When an instance of that class is created from the modified code, that instance will reflect whatever functionality the code currently implements.

The code for a COM class can be contained in a DLL or an EXE

The code implementing a COM class can be packaged as a stand-alone executable, commonly called an EXE file, or as a dynamic link library (DLL). Both are common today, although for reasons described later in this book, the advent of COM+ makes building classes as DLLs significantly more attractive. COM objects implemented in EXEs always run in a separate process from their client. COM objects implemented in DLLs, however, can't run in their own process. Instead, this kind of object will run in either the same process as its client or, with the help of a "surrogate" of some type, in another process.

A COM component can run in the same process as its client or in another process

A COM class implemented in a DLL runs in an *in-process* (or just *in-proc*) server, while a COM class implemented in an EXE runs in either a *local* server, if it's on the same machine as the client, or a *remote* server, if it's on another machine. These three possibilities, illustrated using two computers in the QwickBank domain, are shown in Figure 5-2.[2] There's another term that's important here, too, which is *component*. I'd argue that there is no definition for this broadly used word that everyone in the software world agrees on, but in COM, a component is just a file, either a DLL or an EXE, that contains the code for one or more COM classes. In fact, you can think of the word "component" as interchangeable with the word "server" as it's used in this paragraph. There's nothing fancy or abstract about this definition, and it doesn't cover every use of this term in our industry, but for COM, it's accurate.

Figure 5-2 *COM objects can run in in-proc, local, or remote servers.*

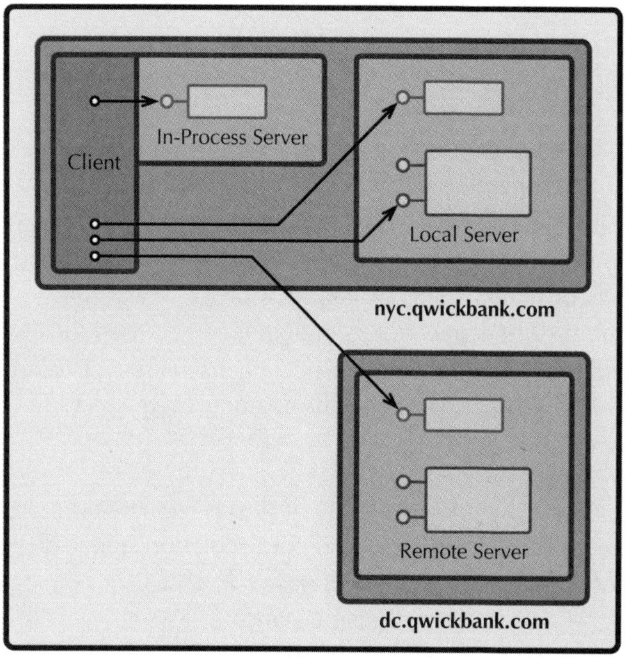

---

2. Although it's not shown in the figure, DLLs running in a surrogate process can also be accessed remotely. As described in Chapter 8, this is especially important with COM+.

Creating Object Instances

In a typical object-oriented programming language, the developer defines a class, then uses some built-in language operation to create instances of that class at run time. In C++, for example, invoking the *new* operator with the name of a class causes the creation of a new instance of that class. COM is a system object model rather than a language-specific approach, but it also allows clients to create instances of COM classes—COM objects—by calling an appropriate function. Exactly what this function looks like depends on the programming language in use, since each language has its own mapping to COM. I'll begin by describing how COM object creation looks to a C++ programmer, then describe what a Visual Basic or Java programmer sees.

A C++ client can call CoCreateInstance to create a new instance of a COM class

Creation Basics   To create a new instance of a particular COM class, a C++ programmer can call either of two standard functions: CoCreateInstance or CoCreateInstanceEx. Both of these functions are implemented by the COM runtime library, more often called just the runtime, which is a standard part of Windows 2000 and other Microsoft operating systems. Both CoCreate-Instance and CoCreateInstanceEx can be thought of as COM analogs of the C++ *new* operator. Although it can be used locally, CoCreateInstanceEx turns out to be especially useful with DCOM as described later in this chapter, so the example here uses only CoCreateInstance.

When a client calls CoCreateInstance, it passes in several parameters, the most interesting of which are shown in step 1 of Figure 5-3. Most important, the client passes in a CLSID, indicating the class it wants to create a new instance of. The client also passes in an IID, indicating the first interface to which it wants a pointer on the newly created object.

CoCreateInstance looks up the specified class in the COM+ Catalog

When that call is made, the COM runtime searches the local machine's COM+ Catalog for the specified CLSID, as shown in step 2 of Figure 5-3. The COM+ Catalog is a logical entity that really consists of two separate things: the system registry and a database named RegDB, a new addition with COM+ in Windows 2000. All components containing COM classes that can be created using CoCreateInstance are listed in the registry, and all *configured* components also have various attributes stored in RegDB. As described in Chapter 8, a configured component can use extra services provided by the COM runtime. In this chapter, however, we're concerned with what are now called *unconfigured* components. Prior to the release of Windows 2000, these were the only kind of COM components possible, and developers are still free to create this kind of traditional COM software. RegDB stores no information about unconfigured components—everything about them is kept in the registry—so as Figure 5-3 shows, there's no RegDB entry for CLSID_Y.

Figure 5-3   *A client can call CoCreateInstance to create an instance of a COM class.*

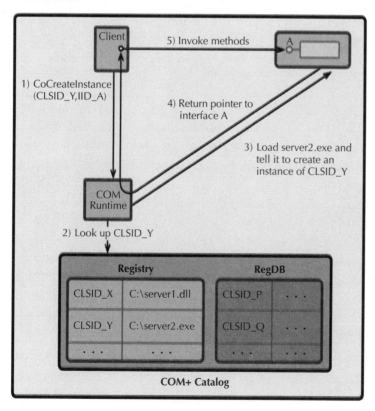

The object is created and
one interface pointer is
passed back to the client

The COM runtime next extracts the filename that's stored in the registry with CLSID_Y, in this case server2.exe. This file contains the code that implements this class, so the COM runtime causes this file to be loaded. Once this has been done, the COM runtime then instructs this newly loaded code to create an instance of the specified class, as shown in step 3 of Figure 5-3. The newly created object then passes an interface pointer back for the interface whose IID the client passed in the CoCreateInstance call, as shown in step 4. Finally, the runtime returns this interface pointer to the client, and the client can call methods on the new object, as shown in step 5.

Several variations of this basic structure are possible. For example, if the required code for this class has already been loaded, COM can allow the creation request to be handled by this running copy—reloading the component isn't required for every request. Also, in Windows 2000, creating any COM object also creates a *context* for this object. Contexts are especially useful with configured classes, however, so they're described more fully in Chapter 8.

Visual Basic clients can
create COM objects us-
ing CreateObject or *new*

The creation process is exactly the same in Visual Basic and Java as it is in C++—CoCreateInstance ultimately gets called, the COM+ Catalog is searched, and so on—but it looks a little different to the programmer. In Visual Basic, a client can call the CreateObject function rather than CoCreateInstance, passing in a ProgID rather than a CLSID. The Visual Basic runtime system translates this ProgID into a CLSID using the registry, then performs essentially the same process shown in Figure 5-3. A Visual Basic client can also use Visual Basic's *new* operator to create a COM object. To do this, the Visual Basic programmer declares an appropriate variable, then assigns that variable the result of the *new* call. Which of the object's interface pointers is returned is determined by this variable's type.

Things are even easier in Java. The programmer always invokes Java's *new* operator—there's no special COM creation function. Because Java's notion of objects is so close to COM's—both allow an object to have multiple independent interfaces, for example—the Microsoft JVM can map standard Java language syntax for working with objects into calls on COM objects.

Java programmers can just call *new* to create a COM object

Class Factories   When a client calls CoCreateInstance (or one of its analogs in Visual Basic or Java, which eventually resolve to the same thing), the COM runtime causes a new instance of some COM class to be created, as just described. To the client, how this happens is magic—it just makes the request and the object springs into existence. To the person who writes that code for that COM class, however, it might not be magic. That developer might need to explicitly implement a *class factory*.

Object creation often relies on class factories

A class factory is a COM object that implements the standard interface IClassFactory. When the COM runtime creates a new instance of a COM class, it is really invoking a method in IClassFactory named CreateInstance. It's also possible for C++ clients to acquire their own pointers to this interface and directly create new instances, although this option is not readily available to developers working in Visual Basic or Java.

Each class factory object implements IClassFactory

A developer creating a COM class in C++ can write the code for the required class factory by hand. As always, C++ offers COM developers the maximum potential for both control and pain. Alternatively, a C++ developer can use a toolkit such as ATL that provides a standard class factory implementation. It's probably fair to say that a majority of C++ developers today take this second route, since class factories aren't especially interesting things to write. Developers working in Visual Basic or Java need never worry about class factories—the runtime systems of these languages provide them automatically when they're needed. Wherever they come from, however, class factories play an essential part in the creation of COM objects.

Developers seldom need to explicitly write class factories

Not all objects are
created using
CoCreateInstance

Creation in an Object Model   There are cases where using CoCreateInstance to create every COM object a client needs is overkill. Sometimes, it's easier to use this standard creation function to create just one object, then have that object provide its own mechanisms to create objects of the same or different classes. When COM objects are used in this way, they are sometimes said to comprise an *object model*.

One object can expose
methods that create
other objects

For example, the services provided to a human user by Microsoft Excel can also be accessed by applications. To allow this, Excel implements a number of different COM classes, each of which provide some group of methods.[3] But a client uses CoCreateInstance (or its analog in Visual Basic or Java) to create only one object instance. Methods in this object can return interface pointers to other newly created COM objects of various classes. Creation of these objects does not rely on the registry, nor do these classes necessarily have CLSIDs. Instead, the object model is defined as a hierarchy, where objects lower in the tree are created by objects higher up. Clients can still hold direct interface pointers to objects below the tree's root, but the registry was involved in creating only that root object. How this might look is shown in Figure 5-4.

The Universal Interface: IUnknown

There are a couple of important questions that haven't been answered yet. First, we've seen that a client gets one interface pointer on a newly created COM object when that object is created. But since COM objects typically support multiple interfaces, how do clients get pointers to other interfaces on the object? Second, I've described how COM objects are created, but how are they destroyed? Since COM is widely used today, and since our machines' memories aren't filled with old COM objects, there must be some mechanism that makes them disappear.

---

3. Those methods are all exposed via dispinterfaces. By writing simple programs in Visual Basic or other languages that use the COM objects embedded in Excel, it is possible to automate work that was otherwise done manually. This was one of the early uses for dispinterfaces, and it's why using them is sometimes called automation.

Figure 5-4 *In some cases, a client uses CoCreateInstance to create the root of a COM object hierarchy, then uses methods in that object to create other objects in the tree.*

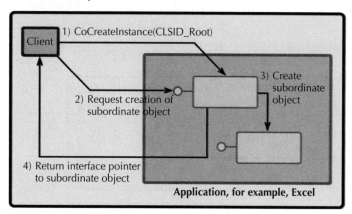

Both of these problems are solved by the methods in IUnknown, COM's most fundamental interface. Every COM object must support IUnknown, which is why virtually all COM objects support two or more interfaces—an object offering just IUnknown wouldn't be very useful. In fact, every interface on every COM object must inherit from IUnknown, which means that given any interface pointer on any COM object, a client can always invoke the methods in IUnknown. Important as it is, though, there are only three methods in this interface: QueryInterface, AddRef, and Release. As described next, the first of these allows a client to request new interfaces to a COM object, while the last two are used to control how long a COM object lives.

Every interface on every COM object inherits from IUnknown

Acquiring New Interface Pointers to an Object A client can get its first interface pointer to a new COM object when that object is created. Once it has this pointer, it can call IUnknown::QueryInterface on the object to request pointers to other interfaces this object may support. Figure 5-5 shows how the process works.

Recall that every interface inherits from IUnknown, which means that all of IUnknown's methods can be called on any interface pointer. When a client calls QueryInterface, it passes in the IID of the interface to which it would like a pointer. If the COM object

QueryInterface allows requesting a new interface pointer from an object

implements the specified interface, the QueryInterface call will return a pointer to the interface. If the object doesn't implement the interface, the QueryInterface call will return null.

Figure 5-5 *A client calls IUnknown's QueryInterface method to acquire a new interface pointer on a COM object.*

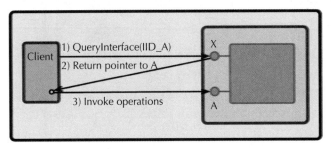

As usual, how this call looks depends on the programming language the client is written in. A C++ client makes direct calls to QueryInterface. However, Visual Basic and Java clients don't; instead, both languages invoke this method under the covers when required. As always, COM is the same in every case. What varies is how COM's mechanisms are mapped into each programming language.

QueryInterface is important for versioning

QueryInterface is a very simple method. Despite its simplicity, however, it underlies how COM handles versioning of objects. Because it allows a client to safely determine whether an object supports an interface before invoking methods in that interface, clients can use an older version of an object, one supporting fewer interfaces, without breaking. While it might receive fewer services from an older object than it would like, the client isn't forced to invoke a particular method (and possibly crash) to determine whether an object supports it.

COM relies on reference counting

How COM Objects Are Destroyed   Since clients explicitly create objects, there must also be some way to destroy them. Some programming languages, such as C++, allow clients to explicitly delete objects once they're been created. COM isn't like this, however. In COM, there's no standard mechanism that allows a client to directly destroy an object. Instead, a COM object's lifetime is controlled using a technique called *reference counting*.

The idea is simple: every COM object keeps track of how many outstanding interface pointers it has, maintaining this value in its reference count. When a client first creates a COM object, the object will have one outstanding interface pointer, and so the value of this object's reference count will be one. If that client uses QueryInterface to acquire another interface pointer on this same object, the object must increase its reference count to two. When a client is finished using an interface pointer, it must call IUnknown::Release on that interface pointer. When it receives this call, the object subtracts one from its reference count. Once the client has called IUnkown::Release on all of the interface pointers it holds on this object, the object's reference count will have gone to zero. When this happens, an object typically destroys itself.

A client must call Release when it is done using an object

It's perfectly legal for the client of an object to pass an interface pointer to some other client, however. If nobody tells the object this has happened, its reference count won't correctly reflect the number of outstanding interface pointers it has. Accordingly, whenever an interface pointer is duplicated, such as when that pointer is passed to another client, an AddRef call must be made to the object. This causes the object to increment its reference count by one, correctly accounting for the new interface pointer. And as always, the user of this new interface pointer must call Release when it's through using the object.

A client must call AddRef when an outstanding interface pointer is duplicated

Reference counting is a nice idea, and it allows intelligently controlling a COM object's lifetime in an environment where no single client can reliably know when it's safe to destroy an object. For clients written in C++, developers must correctly code calls to Release and AddRef. For clients written in Visual Basic and Java, however, these calls aren't generally required. Instead, the language runtime for both environments calls Release and AddRef as needed. As usual, life is simpler for non-C++ developers.

Invoking Methods

Most methods are invoked synchronously

By default, calling a method on a COM object is a synchronous operation. In other words, the client makes the call, the method executes, and then the call returns, with the client waiting patiently the entire while. Until the call returns, the client thread that invoked the method is blocked.

Calls can also be made asynchronously and can be cancelled

In Windows 2000, COM clients can also invoke methods asynchronously. Asynchronous calls don't make the client block while waiting for a response. Instead, the call returns immediately, allowing the client to go about its business while the call is executing. Although it's more complex for the programmer, this style of method invocation can sometimes improve performance significantly. Clients can also cancel in-progress calls, whether made asynchronously or in the traditional style. This section describes both of these options, beginning with cancellation.

Canceling Calls   Suppose a client makes a synchronous call on some COM object. Especially if this object is running in another process or on another machine, it's possible this call will take longer than the client wishes to wait. In situations like this, it's useful to have some way to cancel an in-progress call.

Calling a method on a call's cancel object can cancel an in-progress call

Windows 2000 adds a straightforward mechanism for doing this.[4] Whenever a synchronous call is made by some thread, a cancel object is created that implements the ICancelMethodCalls interface. To cancel this call, a second thread in the client can call CoGetCancelObject, passing in the identifier of the thread that made the call. Doing this returns a pointer to the ICancelMethodsCalls interface of the cancel object for the pending call. To cancel the call, the second thread just invokes ICancelMethodCalls::Cancel on that cancel object.

---

4. For C++ programmers, at least, the audience at which this mechanism is aimed.

Asynchronous Calls   Synchronous calls are inherently simple to understand, but asynchronous calls, sadly, are somewhat less so. Supporting them is optional—if a COM object accepts any asynchronous calls, it implements ICallFactory, an interface containing only the method CreateCall. When a client wishes to invoke methods asynchronously, it calls ICallFactory::CreateCall on the target object, passing in the IID of the interface on which it plans to invoke those methods. This call returns an interface pointer to a *call object* that the client will actually make method calls on.

Asynchronous calls rely on a call object

Asynchronous calls are defined on a per-interface basis—either every call in an interface can be invoked asynchronously or none of them can. To make an interface callable asynchronously, its creator marks it with a special IDL attribute. This allows a tool called the Microsoft IDL (MIDL) compiler to generate an asynchronous definition of this interface with each of the interface's methods split in two. The client calls one method, assigned a name starting with "Begin_", when it wishes to invoke the method. This method includes all of the input parameters defined for the original method. The client can call the second method in the pair, assigned a name starting with "Finish_", when it wishes to retrieve the results of the method. For example, think back to the methods in the IOrderEntry interface shown earlier in this chapter. If this interface were marked as asynchronous, each of these methods would be divided into a pair of methods. The Add method, for example, would be split into Begin_Add and Finish_Add, while Submit would become Begin_Submit and Finish_Submit. The client is free to do whatever it wishes between its calls to a Begin method and its corresponding Finish—it's not required to wait—although a particular call object can handle only one asynchronous call at a time.

Asynchronous interfaces divide every method in two

To the object that implements it, an asynchronous method is no different than any other method. Once invoked, the method executes, then typically returns some results. Once the call returns to the client process, however, the proxy for the Begin method informs the call object that the method has completed. To determine

A client can learn when an asynchronous call has completed or can cancel the call before completion when an asynchronously invoked method has completed, the client can invoke the Wait method in an interface called ISynchronize implemented by the call object. If the value this method returns indicates the call is finished, the client can invoke the appropriate Finish method to retrieve the results. And if it wants to, a client can invoke the Cancel method in the ICancel-MethodCalls interface to cancel an asynchronous call while it's still executing.

Asynchronous calls have some limitations. First, they work only with vtable interfaces—methods in dispinterfaces and dual interfaces can't be called this way. Second, they're a little more complex to use than ordinary synchronous calls. Still, the performance benefits they bring can sometimes make the effort worthwhile.

Queued Components also allows non-blocking calls

Windows 2000 also provides one more way to invoke methods on COM objects without waiting for a response. Called Queued Components (QC), it uses a Microsoft Message Queuing (MSMQ) to convey requests and their parameters between client and object. QC is described in Chapter 9.

Threads and Apartments

A server process can contain multiple threads executing at once

In a simple running program, there's only one thread of execution and only one thing happens at a time. For more complex software, however, especially server software that will be accessed by several clients at once, this simple approach isn't very effective. Having only one thread means that all but one client will be waiting, a situation that doesn't lead to happy users. A better approach is to allow a single running program to have multiple threads of execution. Now multiple clients can be serviced at once, and everybody's happier.

To make multi-threaded servers possible, COM provides apartments

Everybody except the developer of that software, that is. While Windows 2000 and most other modern operating systems provide good support for threads, writing multi-threaded code is not for

190   Chapter Five

the faint of heart. To make threads more manageable for developers, COM introduced the idea of *apartments*.

Each process can contain one or more apartments. As Figure 5-6 shows, any executing COM object runs inside exactly one apartment. Apartments have traditionally come in two types—single-threaded apartments (STAs) and multi-threaded apartments (MTAs)—although as described shortly, Windows 2000 introduces another type as well. A process can contain one or more STAs, and each STA can contain one or more COM objects. Each STA has only a single thread, one that's shared by all the objects in that apartment. At any given time, only one object in a particular STA will be executing—the one that is currently using that apartment's thread. Like an STA, an MTA can also contain one or more COM objects. A given process has at most one MTA, however, and each call to an object in the MTA happens on a distinct thread. Because of this, it's possible for multiple methods in a single object in a process's MTA to be executing simultaneously.

COM provides single-threaded apartments (STAs) and multi-threaded apartments (MTAs)

Figure 5-6 *A COM object can run inside an STA or an MTA.*

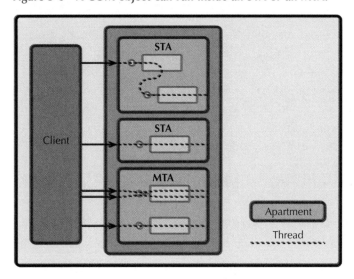

For a COM class implemented in an EXE, the kind of apartment it runs in is determined by the type of thread on which it is created. In C++, a thread calls CoInitializeEx to create a new apartment, and objects created by that thread will by default run in that apartment. A parameter on this call determines what kind of apartment is created. As of Visual Studio 6, however, Visual Basic is limited to STAs, so Visual Basic programmers don't need to worry about controlling this option.

DLL components have their threading model configured in the registry

For a COM class implemented in a DLL, the kind of apartment it runs in is determined by a threading model value stored in the registry for that component. DLLs for which this value is set to Apartment will have their objects instantiated in an STA, while DLLs for which this value is set to Free will run in the MTA of whatever process they're loaded into. A DLL can also be marked as Both, which means its objects will be created in whatever apartment its creator resides in, even if its creator is running in a process's MTA.

Single-threaded apartments can protect objects from concurrent access

One advantage of running COM objects in an STA is that the developer of those objects need not worry as much about concurrent access. Because there's only a single thread in the apartment, only one method in one object in that apartment can be executing at any one time. The process as a whole can still be multithreaded—each STA has its own thread—but the developer's life is greatly simplified. STAs also allow applications with thread affinity to work correctly. Thread affinity means that once a chunk of code, such as a method in an object, has been assigned to a particular thread or group of threads, that code must always run on that thread or group. Up through version 6, every Visual Basic application has thread affinity, but Visual Basic 7 promises to remove this limitation. STAs are also useful for objects that present a user interface—they fit well with this kind of code.

The big advantage of running COM objects in the MTA is that truly multi-threaded objects can provide better performance. Objects capable of running in the MTA are significantly more complex to create and debug, however, than objects that run only in an STA. This is because the programmer who creates them must write code allowing safe access to these objects by multiple clients.

Multi-threaded apartments allow concurrent access at the cost of greater complexity for programmers

Now that you have a basic idea of what apartments are, it's time to reveal the truth: in Windows 2000, they matter less than in previous releases. The primary reason for this is that COM+ recasts the notion of apartments in terms of contexts, and allows exploiting a new choice called the neutral apartment (also called the thread-neutral apartment, or TNA). A great deal of existing COM code relies on apartments for dealing with concurrency and thread affinity issues, but going forward these problems will likely be addressed in a somewhat different way. The changes COM+ brings to this area are described more fully in Chapter 8.

Traditional apartments become less important with the arrival of COM+

Marshaling

Think about what happens when a client invokes a method in a COM object. Most often, the client and the object will be in different apartments, processes, or machines (and now with COM+, in different contexts). To deal with this, invoking a method in a COM object commonly requires some intermediary to package the parameters of the call into a standard format—a process called *marshaling*. Those packaged parameters are then transferred via some appropriate mechanism across the boundary, whatever it is, that separates the client from the object. Once they arrive, the called object must *unmarshal* the parameters, converting them from the standard format in which they arrived to a format the object can handle.

Invoking methods usually requires marshaling and unmarshaling

COM provides two basic approaches to marshaling. The first, called standard marshaling, relies on *proxies* and *stubs,* code that may make use of *type libraries*. The second option, custom marshaling, also uses proxies and stubs, but allows developers more flexibility. Both approaches have pros and cons, and both are used today.

Standard Marshaling

To understand marshaling, think first about what an interface really defines. It's nothing more than a group of methods, each of which has a name and possibly one or more parameters. Those parameters must appear in a defined order, and each is of some type. To correctly package a call to a method—to marshal that call—requires knowing the parameter types of that method and the order in which they appear. Similarly, unmarshaling requires knowing this same information to make sense out of what's received and to correctly invoke the method. The problem, then, is to acquire a suitable proxy/stub pair, then somehow supply the proxy and stub with the information they require. In COM applications written for Windows 2000, the most common way to do this is using a system-supplied proxy/stub pair that's sometimes referred to as the *universal marshaler*. To get the information needed to marshal and unmarshal calls, both the proxy and stub rely on a type library.

Often called a *typelib,* a type library contains machine-readable information that describes the interfaces supported by a particular COM class. That information can be stored in its own file, a file which by convention has a name ending in .tlb, or it can be placed in the same file as the code for the COM class it describes. However it's done, the information in a type library is essentially the same as that contained in the IDL definitions for this class's interfaces (if IDL definitions exist). The big difference is that an IDL file is just text, intended to be read by people and tools such as the MIDL compiler. A type library, by contrast, is meant to be read by programs.

Type libraries can be produced by development environments, such as Visual Basic, or by the MIDL compiler. Once it exists, a type library can be used for all sorts of things. For example, a Visual Basic programmer can browse his machine, examining the capabilities provided by whatever COM classes are installed. Doing this actually accesses the type library for each of those classes. One very frequent use, however, is for marshaling.

Type libraries are used for marshaling and other purposes

Figure 5-7 shows how typelib-driven marshaling works. When a client invokes a method in some interface, the universal marshaler proxy uses information from the type library to determine how to correctly marshal this call. The packaged parameters are conveyed to the object, where the universal marshaler stub has access to a copy of the same type library. It uses this information to unmarshal the call, then invokes the method in the target object. Rather than requiring a specific proxy/stub pair for each interface, the universal marshaler is a generic service that relies on type libraries to perform its function. Once a class's type library has been installed and registered, marshaling can happen.

Figure 5-7 *The universal marshaler can use a type library to acquire the information needed to package and unpackage a call's parameters.*

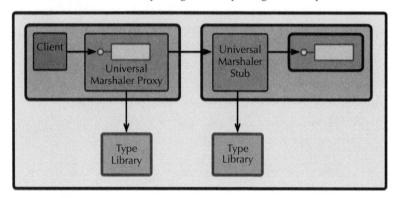

It's also possible to perform marshaling without using type libraries. Feeding an IDL file into the MIDL compiler produces an interface-specific proxy and stub pair, each of which can be installed and registered on the appropriate system, then used to marshal and

Marshaling can also be performed by interface-specific proxy/stub pairs unmarshal calls to the methods in that interface. While typelib-driven marshaling initially supported only dispinterfaces and was slower than using interface-specific proxies and stubs, both of those limitations have been overcome. As a result, interface-specific proxy/stub pairs are less commonly used today.

Custom Marshaling

Custom marshaling allows the developer to control how marshaling is done

Suppose you need to do something unique, maybe even a little idiosyncratic in marshaling. What can you do? Standard marshaling is easy to use, but it doesn't offer much flexibility for applications that might need it. COM's designers anticipated this possibility. If desired, COM developers can implement custom marshaling. Doing this requires the developer to implement the standard interface IMarshal. Once this is done, how parameters are packaged and unpackaged can be customized by the developer—there are no hard and fast rules.

Custom marshaling can, for example, be used to pass objects by value rather than by reference

For example, suppose you wish to pass an entire COM object from one process or machine to another. One way to do this would be to somehow extract all of the object's data, then pass that data across the process or machine boundary as parameters to one or more method calls. All of this could be done using the standard marshaling technique described earlier. Another solution, however, would be to use custom marshaling to move the entire object's data at once. Now, passing an interface pointer to this object won't just transfer the pointer, as it normally does, but instead move all of the object's data. Sometimes referred to as marshal-by-value, it's a good example of the kind of thing that can be done using custom marshaling.

Apart from its complexity—implementing it is not for beginners—custom marshaling has a few other drawbacks. For example, implementing call cancellation requires some extra work, and custom marshaling can't in general be used with configured components. Still, although it's not used very frequently, there are times when custom marshaling offers just the right solution for a specific problem.

Distributed COM

When COM was first released in 1993, clients and objects were required to be on the same machine. With the release of DCOM in 1996, this restriction was eliminated. Today, clients can access COM objects across apartment, process, and machine boundaries at will. As this section shows, DCOM does not change the fundamentals of COM. Instead, it provides extensions that allow communication between objects and their clients connected by a network.

DCOM allows a client to communicate with objects running on another machine

Creating a Remote Object

To create an object on the same machine, a client can call CoCreateInstance or one of its corresponding functions in another programming language. A client can also create an object on another machine using this call. Figure 5-8 shows how the process works.

Figure 5-8 *By replacing the name of a local file with the DNS name of a remote machine, CoCreateInstance can be used to create objects across a network.*

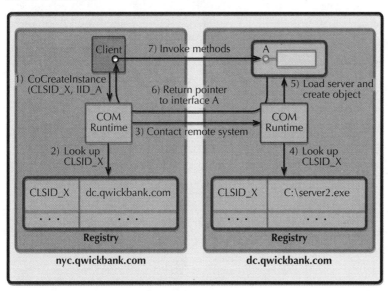

The CoCreateInstance call works as always: the client passes in a CLSID and the IID of the first interface to which it wants a pointer, step 1 in Figure 5-8, and the COM runtime looks up the CLSID in the COM+ Catalog, as shown in step 2. (Once again, the focus in this chapter is on unconfigured components, so all information about this class is stored in the registry—there's nothing in RegDB. This is why Figure 5-8 shows only the registry.)

When the COM runtime looks up that CLSID in the registry, however, it finds not a filename, as in the local case already described, but the name of another machine. (This is usually a DNS name, although other options are also supported.) Rather than create the object on the local machine, the COM runtime contacts the computer whose name it found in the registry—step 3 in Figure 5-8—telling it to create an object of that class. The COM runtime on that remote machine looks up the CLSID specified by the client in its local registry, as shown in step 4, then loads whatever file is named there. As in the local case, the object is created, shown in step 5, and a pointer to whatever interface the client requested is retrieved from the object and returned to the client, as shown in step 6. In step 7, the client uses this pointer to invoke methods in the new object. From the client's point of view, everything happens just as in the local case, although the process probably takes a little longer.

In some cases, however, configuring each client's local registry to point to a particular server machine isn't feasible. To avoid this, a client can call not CoCreateInstance but rather CoCreate-InstanceEx. One difference between the two calls, as Figure 5-9 shows, is that CoCreateInstanceEx allows a client to explicitly specify the name of the machine on which the object should be created. To further speed up the process of creation, this call also allows a client to specify a group of interface pointers that should be returned on the new object rather than just one.

Figure 5-9 *CoCreateInstanceEx allows a client to explicitly specify the machine on which an object should be created.*

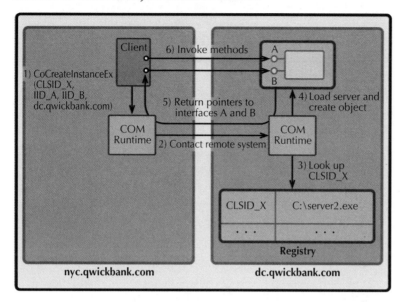

Now there's no requirement to change the client's registry to contain the name of the remote server for a particular CLSID. Instead, the object will be created on the machine whose name is passed into the CoCreateInstanceEx call. And since it's common for a client to create an object and then acquire several interface pointers to it, returning many pointers at once avoids issuing many remote (and thus relatively slow) calls to IUnknown::QueryInterface on the new object.

Accessing a Remote Object

Once a remote object has been created, it can be accessed just like any other COM object. Obviously, though, some protocol must be used to convey requests and responses between the client and server machines.

The protocol used by DCOM is known as Object RPC, and it's really just a slight enhancement to the Microsoft RPC protocol (which was itself based on the RPC protocol used by the Open Group's DCE). In Microsoft Windows NT 4, Object RPC ran over both connection-oriented transport protocols such as TCP and connectionless transports such as UDP. Two different RPC protocols were used in each case, so the behavior seen by applications was the same—all messages were transferred reliably. Both kinds of transport protocols were supported because each one offered better performance in some situations. In Windows 2000, however, only connection-oriented transports are supported—DCOM applications no longer use UDP. This change was made because improvements in the Windows 2000 TCP implementation made it uniformly faster than UDP for use with DCOM, so allowing the option no longer made sense. DCOM applications written for Windows NT 4 will still work in a Windows 2000 or mixed environment, however, because those applications implicitly negotiate which protocol to use. When talking with Windows 2000 systems, they'll always choose TCP.

Providing Security

When a client invokes methods in a COM object running in the same process, security is not an issue. (It isn't even really possible, since the client and object share the same address space.) When a client invokes methods in a COM object running in a different process on the same machine, security is provided by the local operating system. But when a client invokes methods in a COM object running in a different process on a remote machine, security becomes a much more serious concern.

DCOM doesn't mandate any particular security protocol. In Windows 2000, DCOM applications can use either Kerberos or the legacy NTLM protocol to provide authentication, data integrity, and data privacy. For authorization, however, DCOM itself does provide some services. DCOM servers can also use the standard authorization mechanisms provided by Windows 2000, impersonating their clients and then attempting access to an ACL-protected resource.

The security services provided by DCOM can be broadly divided into two categories: *activation* security and *call* security. Activation security controls which clients have the right to create objects on a remote machine, while call security controls which clients have the right to invoke which methods in remote objects. Call security itself has two sub-options: *automatic* security and *per-interface* security. In automatic security, a client or server can set all of its security options (collectively referred to as its *security blanket*) at once. In per-interface security, these options can be set differently for each interface the process is using.

DCOM provides activation security and call security

Automatic security is relatively simple to use. A DCOM client or EXE server can make one call, CoInitializeSecurity, to specify all of its security choices. Since it sets several options at once, this call has a number of parameters. One of the most interesting parameters is the setting for authentication level, among the choices for which are:

Automatic security allows setting all of a process's security options with one call

- *None* No authentication is performed.
- *Connect* Performs authentication only when a connection is initially established.
- *Call* Performs authentication on every call.
- *Packet* Performs authentication for each packet that's sent.
- *Packet Integrity* Performs authentication for each packet that's sent and provides data integrity for each packet.
- *Packet Privacy* Performs authentication for each packet that's sent, provides data integrity for each packet, and provides data privacy for each packet by encrypting its data.

The authentication level chosen by a client can be different from that chosen by a server. In this case, the higher of the two levels is chosen. This means, for instance, that a server can always require clients to use at least a certain level of authentication. Also, if NTLM is used, the server will authenticate the client, but the client can't be certain that the server is who it claims to be. Kerberos, which becomes the default for DCOM applications in a Windows 2000 environment, does provide mutual authentication as was described in Chapter 3.

Another parameter in CoInitializeSecurity sets the impersonation level that will be used for calls made by this process. The possible choices for this parameter and their meanings when made to a server process on another machine are:

- *Identify*   The server process can learn the client's identity, but can't use it to impersonate that client while accessing system objects.
- *Impersonate*   The server process can use the client's identity to impersonate the client, but it can't pass this identity to another server process running on a different machine. This means that the impersonating server can't make a request to another server process on another machine asking it to also impersonate this client.
- *Delegate*   The server process can use the client's identity to impersonate the client, and it can also pass this identity on. That is, the impersonating server process can make a request to another server process on a different machine asking it to also impersonate this client, this server process can make a similar request to another server process on yet another machine, and so on. This ability is new in Windows 2000, and it relies on the delegation capabilities of Kerberos.
- *Default*   The COM runtime sets a default value based on the security choices set for this client.

Cloaking allows delegation, where a server takes on a client's identity

For a client to pass on its identity to all the server processes that might eventually handle its request, it must have turned on *cloaking*, another new Windows 2000 feature. Cloaking allows a thread in a server process to make a request "cloaked" in the identity of the client that thread is impersonating. Using cloaking, client C can call server S, server S can call server T, and server T can call server U, yet server U will still see its caller's identity as C. Because each server called the next in line while cloaked, each call was made under the original client's identity.

Unlike the process-wide options set with CoInitializeSecurity, per-interface security allows clients and servers to set different security blankets for different interfaces. To do this, clients and servers use methods in the standard interfaces IClientSecurity and IServerSecurity, respectively. The options that can be set include those just described for controlling the authentication level and impersonation. The big difference is that those options can be set differently for each proxy (and thus for each interface) on which a client is invoking methods.

Per-interface security allows setting different security options for different interfaces

For the most part, DCOM's security features build on what Windows 2000 provides: Kerberos, Microsoft's Security Support Provider Interface (SSPI), and the rest of the system's security infrastructure. What's added are standard ways to access these services and support for authorization, a problem that can't be solved by a security protocol.

In a broadly similar way, every technology described in the rest of this book builds on COM. With the exception of the Windows NT/Windows 2000 line of operating systems, COM is surely the most important technology introduced by Microsoft in the 1990s. In the chapters that follow, I'll describe how COM is used to define data access mechanisms, access transaction processing services, build Web-based applications, and more. There's no way around it: working in the Windows 2000 distributed environment means working with COM.

COM is a critically important technology

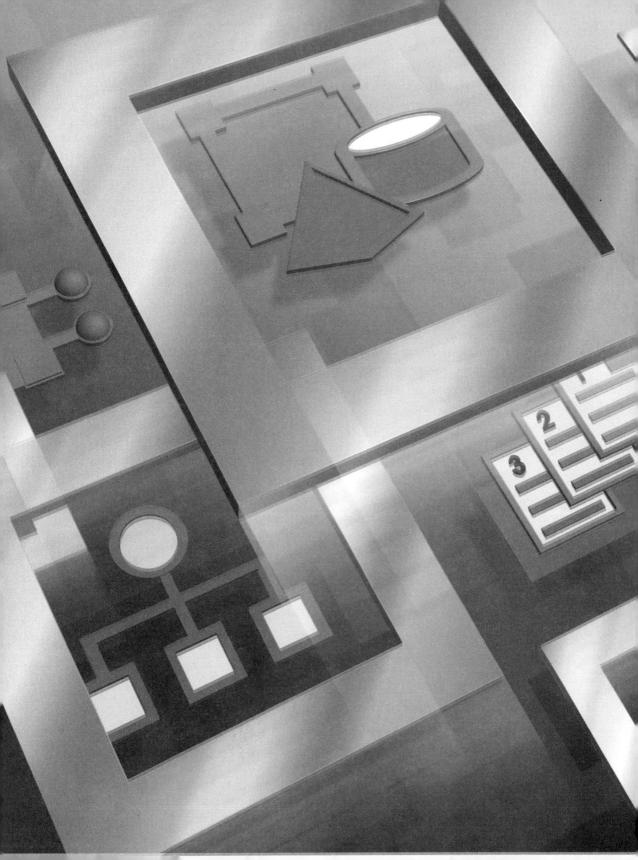

Data Access Services

Most applications work with some kind of data. If there's enough of it, that data is typically stored in a database management system (DBMS), and applications access it through some kind of application programming interface. A commercial DBMS usually provides its own proprietary API, but Microsoft has also defined several standard interfaces that can be used for accessing a variety of data sources in a more or less common way.

Accessing stored data is part of most applications

Defining a single interface that can be used to access many data sources isn't an especially easy problem, and Microsoft's solutions to this problem have gone through several iterations. Today, Microsoft Windows 2000 applications can use three primary data access interfaces, collectively referred to as the Microsoft Data Access Components (MDAC). Those interfaces are:

Microsoft has defined several different data access interfaces

- *Open Database Connectivity (ODBC)* The oldest interface of the three, Microsoft ODBC defines a set of C function calls focused on accessing relational databases through Structured Query Language (SQL) queries.
- *OLE Database (OLE DB)* Created in the mid-1990s, Microsoft OLE DB is specified as a group of COM classes and interfaces. While it supports access to relational databases using SQL, OLE DB is also designed to be useful for accessing more general data sources, including those that don't support SQL.

- *ActiveX Data Objects (ADO)* Like OLE DB, Microsoft ADO is specified using COM, and it's intended to allow access to both relational and non-relational data. The biggest difference between the two is that ADO is significantly simpler to use than OLE DB.[1]

Figure 6-1 shows the relationship among these three data access interfaces. As the figure shows, a client can use any of them directly to access a data source. ADO is always implemented on top of OLE DB, however, and the OLE DB interface might or might not be implemented on top of ODBC.

Figure 6-1 *An application can use any of ADO, OLE DB, or ODBC to access data.*

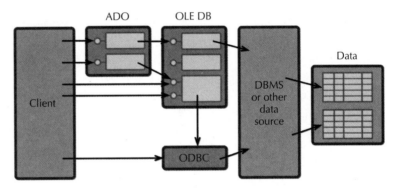

Open Database Connectivity

ODBC is a widely used interface

ODBC is based on the SQL Call-Level Interface defined by the industry consortium once know as X/Open and now called The Open Group. Various organizations have created database-specific *ODBC drivers,* software that accesses a particular DBMS yet provides the standard ODBC interface to its clients. ODBC has

---

1. The name "OLE Database" is a relic of the era when Microsoft assigned the "OLE" label to technologies that used COM. The name "ActiveX Data Objects" is a relic of the era when Microsoft assigned the "ActiveX" label to technologies that used COM. Thankfully, Microsoft's marketing mavens appear to have largely ended the practice of assigning broad marketing labels to COM-based technologies.

been very successful—drivers exist for DBMS's from Microsoft, Oracle, Sybase, IBM, and many other vendors—and despite being relatively old, it's still a widely used technology.

ODBC includes several dozen function calls. Among the most important of these are:

ODBC targets C applications that issue SQL queries

- *SQLConnect*   Establishes a connection to a database using a specific ODBC driver.
- *SQLPrepare*   Passes a SQL statement to a DBMS, allowing the DBMS to compile the statement.
- *SQLExecute*   Tells a DBMS to execute an already-compiled SQL statement.
- *SQLExecDirect*   Passes a SQL statement to a DBMS and tells it to compile and execute it immediately.
- *SQLFetch*   Retrieves one or more rows from the result returned by an executed SQL query.
- *SQLGetData*   Returns the values of one or more columns in a row retrieved using SQLFetch.
- *SQLBindParameter*   Allows defining variables into which the results of a SQL query should be directly copied.
- *SQLDisconnect*   Releases a connection to a DBMS.

By today's standards, ODBC is a more than a little archaic for several reasons. First, because it's defined as a group of C function calls, it's not easily accessible from languages such as Microsoft Visual Basic[2] or Java. In addition, ODBC was designed as an interface for accessing relational DBMS's using SQL. This addresses a large part of the data access problem, but doesn't completely cover the terrain. To allow use from other languages and to allow non-SQL access to data, something else is required.

Today, ODBC isn't enough

---

2. Although Microsoft did define Remote Data Objects (RDO), an earlier COM-based interface designed specifically to allow Visual Basic developers access to ODBC drivers.

OLE Database

OLE DB is a more
general interface
based on COM

Unlike ODBC, OLE DB is defined as a group of COM objects rather than as a set of C function calls, and it's general enough to be implemented over a variety of data sources. Rather than focusing exclusively on access to SQL-accessible data, as does ODBC, OLE DB strives to be useful for accessing a variety of data stored in a variety of ways.

OLE DB providers exist
for a number of different
data sources

With OLE DB, application developers use an *OLE DB provider* for a particular data source rather than an ODBC driver. Like an ODBC driver, a provider allows access to that data source, whatever it is, through the common interface defined by OLE DB. Microsoft provides a number of OLE DB providers, each focused on accessing a particular type of data. Among the most interesting of these are:

- *The Microsoft OLE DB Provider for SQL Server and the Microsoft OLE DB Provider for Oracle*   Allow access to Microsoft's SQL Server DBMS and to Oracle's DBMS, respectively.
- *The OLE DB Provider for ODBC*   Allows accessing any existing ODBC driver through an OLE DB interface. While some native OLE DB providers exist, such as the SQL Server and Oracle providers just mentioned, this provider allows using OLE DB (and thus ADO) to access any data source for which an ODBC driver exists.
- *The Microsoft OLE DB Provider for Microsoft Active Directory Service*   Provides read-only access to information in Active Directory.
- *The Microsoft OLE DB Persistence Provider*   Can be used to save information accessed through OLE DB and ADO to disk. How this is accomplished is described later in this chapter.

OLE DB is relatively
complex to use

While OLE DB providers remain the foundation of Microsoft's approach to data access, the OLE DB interface is too complex for the average developer to work with (and too complex to summarize here, as well). Furthermore, the COM objects that comprise OLE DB expose their services through vtable interfaces using the full range of COM Interface Definition Language (IDL) data types. Taken together, these two characteristics make OLE DB unsuitable for mainstream application development. Microsoft still promotes OLE DB as the interface of choice for providing low-level access to various data sources, yet something else is required, too: an interface that everyone can use as the standard way to access all types of data.

ActiveX Data Objects

Today, the data access interface that Microsoft most encourages developers to use is ADO. ADO is really nothing more than a set of COM objects that provide a simplified veneer over OLE DB. Unlike OLE DB, however, the objects in ADO expose their services using dual interfaces. And while OLE DB objects commonly have many interfaces, each ADO object exposes all of its methods through a single interface. C++, Visual Basic, and Java are all capable of accessing COM objects with multiple interfaces, but very simple languages such as Microsoft Visual Basic, Scripting Edition (VBScript) are not. Accordingly, ADO can be used effectively from virtually any language in the Windows 2000 environment. Given ADO's status as the most popular data access interface for new applications, the rest of this chapter is devoted to a more detailed look at ADO 2.5, the version shipped in the first release of Windows 2000.

One important note about terminology: Throughout this discussion, the word "client" refers to whatever software is using ADO to access a data source. It's possible for that client software to be running on a desktop machine, but in a three-tier application, the model assumed throughout this book, the ADO client is typically running in the middle tier on the server. Don't be confused; in the modern world, an ADO client isn't necessarily found on a client machine—that is, on the user's desktop.

ADO is COM-based, but simpler than OLE DB

ADO clients can run on the desktop or on a middle-tier server machine

An Overview of ADO

ADO defines three primary classes of COM objects—Connection, Command, and Recordset—and a few subsidiary ones. Taken as a group, these objects make up what's known as the ADO object model. The most fundamental of the three is the Connection object. Its methods allow a client to establish a connection with a specified data source, such as a particular Oracle database. Because ADO is implemented over OLE DB, the client identifies a specific OLE DB provider that it will use to access that data source.

As its name suggests, an ADO Command object can contain a command that can be compiled and eventually sent to a data source. For example, if the data source is a relational database, the command might be a SQL request such as the following:

```
SELECT Salary FROM Employees WHERE Name='Smith'
```

ADO allows other options, too—Command objects aren't required to use SQL—but since relational databases are still the most commonly used data source with ADO today, SQL queries are the most common choice. If desired, commands can instead specify an existing stored procedure in the database that should be executed.

The third key object in the ADO object model is the Recordset object. When a client has established a connection with a particular data source and issued a command, it's likely that command will return a result. For example, the SQL query just mentioned might return a set of records (also called rows) from the relational database against which it's executed. This result is returned to the client in a Recordset object, and the contents of the Recordset can then be examined or modified by the client.

While Connection, Command, and Recordset are the three most important COM classes defined by ADO, there are also several other interesting classes of objects. Among them are the following:

- *Field*   Each Recordset object contains one or more records. Each record contains one or more values, and each of those values can be seen by a client as a Field object. To examine or change the values in a record in some Recordset, the client can access the Field objects that contain those values.

- *Record*   As its name suggests, a Record object can be used to represent and access a particular row in a Recordset object. But Records can also be used more generally. For example, a group of Record objects can be organized into a tree, then used to access hierarchical data such as a group of files beneath a particular directory in the Windows 2000 file system. New with ADO 2.5, Record objects are described in more detail later in this chapter.

- *Stream*   Stream objects contain strings of bytes. Those bytes might be the contents of a file in the file system, a chunk of memory, or something else. Like Record objects, with which they're often used, Streams are new with ADO 2.5 and are described in more detail later in this chapter.

- *Parameter*   Some commands issued to a data source need never change. Others, though, can retain a standard format while still allowing replacement of some parts. For example, in the following SQL query it might be useful to allow replacing only the name that is searched for:

```
SELECT Salary FROM Employees WHERE Name='Smith'
```

To make this easy to do, a Command object can have a Parameter object associated with it. That object might represent, say, the name that's used in this SQL query. By changing just this parameter, an ADO client can use the same Command object for many different queries.

- *Error*   If an error occurs during the execution of a method on an ADO object, one or more Error objects can be returned. The client can examine these objects to determine what went wrong.
- *Collection*   A Collection object provides an easy way to reference a group of related objects. For example, a Connection object has an Errors collection that allows access to all Error objects that were created for a single failure. Similarly, all of the Field objects in a single Recordset can be accessed through that Recordset's Fields collection object, and all the Parameter objects associated with a particular Command object can be accessed through that object's Parameters collection.

Some ADO objects are created in the usual COM way, through a client call to CoCreateInstance or CreateObject or *new* or whatever else is appropriate in the programming language being used. For example, Connection, Command, and Recordset objects can all be created in this way. Clients do not directly create all ADO objects, however—some are created implicitly. For example, using a Command object to execute a query that returns data will automatically create a Recordset object. And some ADO objects, such as Error objects, are never explicitly created by clients. Instead, these objects are created as required by another ADO object when it needs to report an error.

ADO events can inform a client when an asynchronous operation has completed

An OLE DB provider can provide support for both synchronous and asynchronous operations, so ADO clients might have both options available. In the synchronous case, a client makes some request, then waits for it to complete. With asynchronous operations, the client need not block waiting for a response. For example, a client can execute a command asynchronously, then do something else without waiting for the command to complete. When the requested operation finishes, the client is notified through a callback to an event handler function. In other words,

ADO automatically calls a function provided by the client, informing it that some operation has completed. These callbacks, referred to more generally as *events,* can also happen before an operation begins, allowing an ADO client to examine the parameters that will be used, change those parameters, or affect the operation in some other way.

The goal of this chapter is to give you an architectural understanding of how ADO works. To do this, the next several sections take a closer look at how clients use the objects ADO defines.

Opening a Connection

The most general way to open a connection to a data source is shown in Figure 6-2: create a Connection object, set its ConnectionString property, then invoke its Open method. The value of ConnectionString identifies the data source to connect to along with other required information, such as a user name and password for that data source. This string can be a simple Data Source Name (DSN) such as "DSN= mydb", a URL, or something else. It's also possible to pass a connection string directly on a call to a Connection object's Open method—you don't have to set the property separately.

A Connection object's ConnectionString identifies the data source to connect to

Figure 6-2 *A client can create a connection to a data source by invoking a Connection object's Open method.*

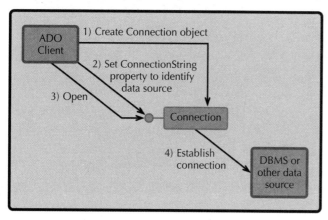

The client can set other properties on the Connection object to control behavior. For example, the ConnectionTimeout property controls how long the ADO interface will wait for a connection to be established before returning an error. Similarly, the value the client assigns to the object's CommandTimeout property controls how long the ADO interface will wait for a response to queries issued on this connection before giving up and returning an error.

Clients can also open connections using Command or Recordset objects

A client can also open a connection to a data source without explicitly using a Connection object. One way to do this is for the client to set the ActiveConnection property of a Command object to a connection string. ADO still creates a Connection object when the command is executed, but it's hidden from the ADO client. Alternatively, a client can pass a connection string as a parameter on a Recordset object's Open method, which results in the same behavior: a Connection object is created but hidden from the ADO client. Both of these approaches are useful for executing single commands against a data source, but since both create a new Connection object every time a command is executed, they're too inefficient for clients that make many requests on the same connection.

Executing a Query

The results of calling a Connection object's Execute method are returned in a Recordset

Not too surprisingly, ADO provides several different ways to define and execute a query against a data source. For a client that already has a Connection object, the simplest approach is shown in Figure 6-3. (To make the examples more concrete, the discussion here assumes that the data source is a relational DBMS, but remember: ADO allows access to other kinds of data as well.) The client invokes a Connection object's Execute method, passing in the query as a string. If this query results in one or more rows of data, the Execute method will return an interface pointer to a newly created Recordset object that contains that data. If the query doesn't return data (maybe it's a SQL UPDATE statement, for example), no Recordset is returned.

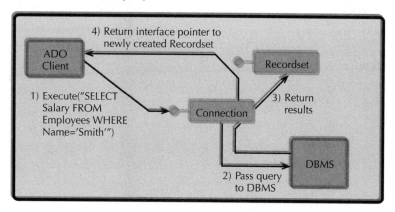

Another way to execute operations, shown in Figure 6-4, is to create and use a Command object. Once this object exists, the client can set its ActiveConnection property to contain either a connection string or an association with an existing Connection object. Next, the client can set the Command object's Command-Text property to contain the query, then invoke that object's Execute method. Like the Connection object's Execute method, this call returns an interface pointer to a newly created Recordset object if the query returns data. Alternatively, the value of the CommandText property can identify a stored procedure or something else—it need not be a literal SQL query.

A client can invoke a Command object's Execute method to run the query stored in this object

Although it's not shown in Figure 6-4, a Command object can also be used to define a query with parameters. Those parameters can be applied to the query defined in the object's CommandText property, or they can be parameters for a stored procedure that's already been created in the database. To do this, the client invokes a Command object's CreateParameter method, passing in values that describe this parameter. The client then appends this new Parameter object to that Command object and executes the query. For later executions of the same command, the client can change just the values of one or more Parameters rather than define a completely new query.

Queries in Command objects can have parameters

Figure 6-4 *An ADO client can also store a query in a Command object's CommandText property, then invoke the object's Execute method.*

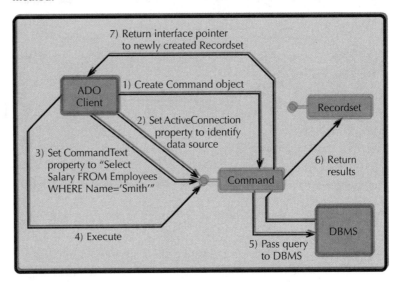

By setting other properties on a Command object, an ADO client can control various aspects of the command's execution. For example, a client can set a Command object's Prepared property to TRUE, instructing the data source to compile the query when it is first executed. While this makes the query's first execution somewhat slower, it makes subsequent requests significantly faster, since they will use the compiled version. A client can also control how long the ADO interface will wait for a response to a particular query by setting the CommandTimeout property of that query's Command object.

Queries can be executed using a Recordset's Open method

Finally, ADO provides one more way to define and execute queries: a Recordset object's Open method. A client can specify the desired query in several ways, including passing in a SQL statement, identifying an existing Command object that contains a query, or naming a stored procedure. The client also passes in a connection string or a reference to an existing Connection object, along with a few more parameters. As shown in Figure 6-5, the query will be executed and the results, if any, placed in the Recordset object on which the method was invoked.

Figure 6-5 *An ADO client can simultaneously open a connection and execute a query using a Recordset's Open method.*

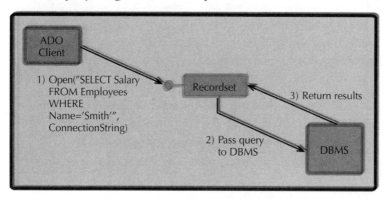

Examining the Result of a Query

Recordsets are fundamental to ADO, since they provide a client with its most commonly used view of data. In the scenarios just described, no matter how a query was executed the data it returned was contained in a Recordset object. As a result, Recordsets are the most complex kind of object in ADO, with a plethora of properties and methods. Because they're central to how ADO works, they're worth a detailed look.

Conceptually, a Recordset object contains some number of records, each of which consists of one or more fields. Each Recordset object has a *cursor*, allowing a client to step through the records in the object. Various kinds of cursors are defined by ADO, although which ones are available depends on the data source in use. The cursor always points at a particular record in a Recordset, and the client can change which record this is by invoking methods on that Recordset object. For example, the methods MoveNext and MovePrevious move the cursor forward and backward one record in the Recordset, respectively, while MoveFirst

ADO clients most often work with data stored in a Recordset

Each Recordset provides methods that let a client work with the data it contains and MoveLast move the cursor to the first and last record. A client can also use a Recordset's Move method to position the cursor forward or backward by a specified number of records, or its AbsolutePosition method to move the cursor to a specific record in the Recordset. Figure 6-6 gives a logical view of the contents of a Recordset object returned by some query. This object has four records, each with three fields, and its cursor is currently pointing at the Recordset's second record.

Figure 6-6 *A Recordset object contains some number of records, each with one or more fields. The Recordset's cursor points at the current record.*

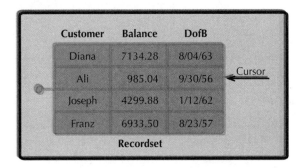

Once a client has an interface pointer to a Recordset object, it typically wishes to access the object's data. One way to do this is to invoke the Recordset's GetRows method. This method copies all or part of the Recordset's contents, as specified by the client, into a two-dimensional array that the client supplies. The client can then examine the array's contents at will.

The data in a Recordset's current row is accessible via the Recordset's Fields collection

A more common approach to examining a Recordset's contents, however, is to examine the fields in one or more rows individually. To allow this, every Recordset object has an associated Fields collection object. This object in turn references one Field object for each column in the Recordset. The fields referenced by a Recordset's Fields collection at any given time are those in the record currently pointed to by the cursor.

For example, given a Recordset with the contents and cursor position shown in Figure 6-6, the Fields and Field objects would be as shown in Figure 6-7. To access the values in this row of the Recordset, a client can loop through the Fields collection object and access the properties of each of the corresponding Field objects. The most important of those properties are Name and Value, which (not surprisingly) contain the field's name and value, respectively. In Figure 6-7, the Name property in the first Field object contains "Customer", while the Value property contains "Ali". As an ADO client moves the cursor through each record in a Recordset, the values in the Field objects change, reflecting whatever values are in the current record. The process can seem cumbersome, but in fact, it turns out to be fairly straightforward to use in client code.

Figure 6-7   *A Recordset's Fields collection references a group of Field objects, with each object containing the value of one field in the current record.*

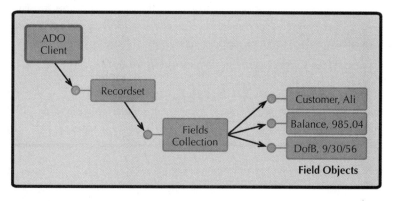

Making Recordsets Persistent

Once a Recordset has been created and populated, an ADO client can use the OLE DB Persistence Provider to cause that Recordset and its contents to be saved as a file on disk. To do this, the client calls the Recordset's Save method, passing as parameters an indication of where the Recordset should be saved and the format that should be used. The client might specify a filename on the

A Recordset's data can be saved to disk

local machine, for example, or give a URL on a remote Web server. You can save the Recordset in one of two formats: Microsoft's Advanced Data TableGram (ADTG) format, which is the default, or a format described using the Extensible Markup Language (XML).

A saved Recordset's data can be loaded back into a new Recordset

To retrieve the information in a saved Recordset, a client can invoke the Open method on an existing Recordset object, passing as a parameter an indication of where the saved Recordset data can be found, such as a filename. The information in the persisted Recordset will then be copied into the Recordset on which the Open call was made. Alternatively, a client can call a Connection object's Execute method, again passing in a filename or some other indication of where the persistent Recordset is located. In this case, the call returns a Recordset object that contains the information in the persistent Recordset.

Modifying Data

To read the results of a query, an ADO client can examine the values contained in a Recordset object, as described earlier. A client can also set those values, allowing it to modify data in the data source. How this happens is shown in Figure 6-8.

Figure 6-8 *A client can create and populate a Recordset object, change one or more of its values, then update the underlying data source with those changes.*

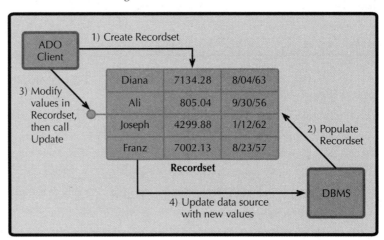

Chapter Six

The process begins by creating and populating a Recordset. This can be done by getting the Recordset returned as the result of executing a query using a Connection or Command object, or by explicitly creating and populating the Recordset. Once the client has a pointer to that Recordset, it can read its values through the Fields collection, as just described. The client can also change those values, however, by setting the Value property of each Field object. Using the cursor to step through the records in a Recordset, the client can make changes to multiple values in multiple records. Once all the changes have been made, the client calls the Recordset object's Update method, and the underlying data source is updated with the new values. (And of course, there is another way to do this: a client can directly pass one or more field name/value pairs as parameters on the call to Update.)

It might also be possible for a client to modify data in an underlying data source without using a Recordset object. For example, assuming the underlying data source is a relational DBMS, the client can use an ordinary SQL UPDATE statement, executed using, say, a Command object, to modify stored data. In many cases, such as with a typical relational DBMS, this style of update will be more efficient.

A client can modify data in a Recordset, then apply those changes to a data source

Locking Data

When a client first examines a populated Recordset object, the data in that object is usually a copy of some part of the underlying database from which that data was obtained. While the client is working with the data in the Recordset, some other client might be interested in reading or modifying the same data in the database. But should this other client be allowed to do this? In some cases, allowing another client to access the underlying data will cause no problems at all. If both clients are just reading the data, for example, there's no reason not to allow simultaneous access to the same information. If both wish to change the data, however, or even if one client wishes to read it and another to change it, allowing simultaneous access can lead to problems.

A client often wishes to lock data for its exclusive use

To avoid these problems, clients can set a Recordset's LockType property. This value is set before the Recordset is opened, and it has four possible values:

- *Readonly*   The default value. The values in the Recordset can't be changed by the client, and the data source does not lock the underlying data. Data copied into a Recordset that has this value set for its LockType property can still be read or modified in the data source by other clients.

- *Pessimistic*   The data source locks a record in the database when this Recordset's client first modifies a field in that record. No other client can modify or even read the information in those locked database records until the client calls Update on the Recordset. This option guarantees that the data won't be changed in the underlying database while the client is modifying the copy in the Recordset, and it also guarantees that changes to the data in this Recordset that are later applied to the underlying data source will succeed. It can hurt performance, though, since other clients that wish to modify or read these records are locked out until the client has completely finished with the Recordset.

- *Optimistic*   The data source does not lock records in the database as they are read into the Recordset, but the client is still free to change values in the Recordset. When the client calls this Recordset's Update method, the data source momentarily locks each record in the database as the update is applied. This raises an obvious question: what happens if some other client has changed the record's value in the meantime? This is why the approach is called "optimistic"—the client is hoping this won't happen. If it has, the data source will return an error to the client for each row that has been changed, and those updates will fail. The goal of optimistic locking is to increase the number of clients who can access the data, and thus increase the performance of applications using this database. If a client must always see the most current values for every record, however, or doesn't wish to deal with the errors that can arise, Pessimistic locking is a better choice.

- *BatchOptimistic*   This option is used together with the UpdateBatch method and disconnected Recordsets, as described later in this chapter.

A particular data source might not support all four LockType options, so what's available can vary. Still, choosing the best kind of locking is an important part of building an application that produces the correct results and performs well.

Using Transactions

Put simply, a transaction is a group of events in which either all of the events happen or none of them do. A very common example of a transaction occurs when a client must make two or more changes to data in a database. For example, suppose that a QwickBank customer wishes to transfer $100 from her savings account into her checking account. Doing this requires subtracting $100 from this customer's savings account and adding the same amount to her checking account. It's likely that both of those events are really just changes to database records, since today, money is often just blips on a disk. If only one of the events takes place, either the customer or the bank will be unhappy—somebody will have lost money. To produce a consistent result, one that leaves both customer and bank satisfied, either both operations or neither of them must be performed. In other words, the two events must belong to a single transaction.

A transaction is an all-or-nothing set of events: either all occur or none occur

ADO allows clients to inform a data source when a transaction should begin and when it ends. An ADO client's request to start a transaction is typically passed to a transaction manager function implemented by a DBMS. All work performed on this database by

An ADO client can rely on a data source to provide transactions

the client until it indicates otherwise will now be considered part of the transaction. When the client is finished with the operations in this transaction, it has two choices. If it tells the DBMS to commit the transaction, all of the work it has performed will be made permanent. If it tells the DBMS to abort the transaction, all of the changes the client has made in this transaction will be rolled back—the database will return to the state it was in before the transaction began. While the client demarcates the boundaries of the transaction, thereby indicating which operations it should include, the DBMS itself actually makes sure that the transaction remains an all-or-nothing affair.

A client can control transactions in a data source using ADO's Connection object

As shown in Figure 6-9, an ADO client can start a transaction by invoking the BeginTrans method of the Connection object on which the transaction should take place. This request is passed on to the transaction manager function in the underlying data source, which does whatever is required to start a transaction on this connection. The client then issues the queries that should be part of this transaction. These queries can be made in any of the ways described earlier, as long as all of them use this same Connection object. After performing all the operations that should be part of this transaction, the client invokes either the CommitTrans or RollbackTrans method on that Connection object. These two methods tell the data source to commit or rollback the transaction, respectively, and once again the data source does whatever is required to end the transaction appropriately.

It's common for clients to use many transactions in sequence. To make this easier to do, an ADO client can set the Connection object's Attributes property to cause a new transaction to be automatically started immediately after the current transaction ends— that is, right after the client's CommitTrans or RollbackTrans call completes. This allows the client to perform a series of transactions without repeatedly calling BeginTrans to start each one.

Figure 6-9 *An ADO client can rely on a DBMS's built-in transaction manager to ensure that either all the operations in a transaction occur or that none of them do.*

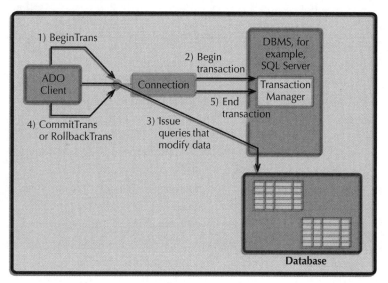

In general, transactions in a database imply locking—isolating—the data that's accessed within that transaction. Imagine, for example, an ADO client that wishes to transfer money between two bank accounts. Doing this requires incrementing one account and decrementing the other, as described earlier. Yet if the data involved in this transaction—the two account balances—remained accessible to other clients all the while, another client might examine or, even worse, modify one of the account balances in the middle of the transfer transaction. If this transaction were rolled back, any value the second client read from either balance might no longer be valid, depending on exactly when that value was read. And if the second client modified either balance, that change could be lost, since the first transaction must by definition restore the account balances to their original values if it's rolled back. The bottom line is that a transaction should be able to securely lock the data it's using, preventing other clients from accessing it.

Transactions generally imply locking of data

How a transaction sees
data in use by other
transactions is
controlled by the
Connection object's
IsolationLevel property

And yet achieving good performance can sometimes require loosening the rules. In particular, it might be OK in some cases for a client in a transaction to work with data that's also part of another transaction in progress at the same time. To control this, the client can set the IsolationLevel property of the Connection object the transaction is being performed on. The value a client chooses for this property affects the behavior of all transactions performed using this Connection object. The possible values for this property (some of which have two different names in ADO) are:

- *adXactReadUncommitted/adXactBrowse*   A transaction can read current values in the database even if those values are changes made by another transaction that hasn't yet committed. This is sometimes called a *dirty read,* and it can increase performance for applications that don't depend on seeing fully consistent data, such as some kinds of decision support solutions, because clients don't have to wait for locks to be released to get to the data. But many, perhaps most, applications won't use this option. Having access to the intermediate state of a transaction in some ways violates the very notion of what a transaction is,[3] and it can produce incorrect results.

- *adXactReadCommitted/adXactCursorStability*   This transaction will never read data that another transaction has changed but not yet committed—that is, there will be no dirty reads. This is what you'd expect with transactions, and it's the default in ADO. If a client looks at the same data twice within a single transaction, however, that data might look different the second time, producing something

---

3. It's common to define a transaction as having the *ACID* properties. The letters in the acronym stand for Atomic, meaning that either all of the transaction's operations are performed or none of them are; Consistent, so that the transaction makes logically correct changes to the data involved; Isolated, so no other transactions see the transaction's data while it's in an intermediate state; and Durable, which implies that hardware or software failures after the transaction has ended won't change its result. In fact, however, depending on the degree of isolation chosen by the client, all of these properties might not hold.

referred to as a *nonrepeatable read*. This is because it's possible that other transactions using this data have committed in the meantime, and so new rows might have been added or some values changed between the two reads.

- *adXactRepeatableRead* Like adXactReadCommitted, this transaction will never read data that another transaction has changed but not yet committed. Furthermore, if a client looks at the same data twice within a single transaction, this isolation level will prevent the client from seeing any changes to data made by transactions that committed between those two accesses. In other words, clients will experience neither dirty reads nor nonrepeatable reads. If the client looks at the same data twice within a single transaction, however, the second read will still see any extra rows that have been added by other committed transactions that were running simultaneously; these added rows are sometimes referred to as *phantoms*.

- *adXactSerializable/adXactIsolated* This transaction will not see any changes at all made by other transactions. Even if the client examines the same data twice within the same transaction, and other committed transactions have changed that data or added new rows between those two reads, this isolation level guarantees that none of these changes will be visible to the client. In other words, clients issuing transactions with this isolation level are guaranteed not to experience dirty reads, nonrepeatable reads, or phantoms.

- *adXactChaos* A client can see this value for the IsolationLevel property of its transaction object if the data it's interested in is currently part of a transaction that's running at a higher isolation level. The client is not allowed to make changes to that data.

- *adXactUnspecified* This value is returned by the underlying data provider, and it means that the provider can't determine what isolation level is being used.

Data sources aren't required to support all IsolationLevel values. If a requested isolation level isn't supported by a particular data provider, that provider can return a higher level. For example, if a client requests adXactRepeatableRead and the underlying DBMS doesn't support this option, the Connection object's IsolationLevel property might actually be set to adXactSerializable, a higher level of isolation. ADO also allows nested transactions, if the provider supports them. A client can begin one transaction, then begin another transaction nested inside the first one. Nested transactions are an appealing idea, but be careful—many data sources don't support them.

One more important point remains to be made about ADO's methods for controlling transactions: many, maybe even most, ADO clients will never use them. Instead, three-tier applications will use the transaction facilities provided by COM+. COM+ applications should never call BeginTrans, CommitTrans, or RollbackTrans (and if they do, the calls will return errors). Instead, transactions are started and ended by the COM runtime library, as described in Chapter 8.

Closing a Connection

To close a connection associated with a Connection object, a client can invoke that object's Close method. As described earlier, it's also possible to create a connection without explicitly using a Connection object, by calling the Open method on a Recordset. Connections opened in this way can be closed by calling the Recordset's Close method.

Connection Pooling

Opening and closing database connections, however it's done, is an inherently expensive operation (where the word "expensive" is a euphemism for "slow"). One approach is for a client to open a connection, use it as long as necessary, then close it only when the client is completely done with it. This works just fine for many kinds of clients, and it's a common approach in two-tier applications. However, for transactional COM objects—an important class of ADO clients—acquiring and holding a database connection isn't usually possible. For reasons described in Chapter 8, these objects can't usually work this way. Instead, they must frequently acquire and release database connections. To make this more efficient, both ODBC and OLE DB (and thus ADO) support connection pooling.

The idea is simple. When an ADO client requests the first connection to a particular DBMS, the underlying OLE DB provider must actually create a new connection. When the client closes that connection, however, the connection is not actually destroyed. Instead, the still-open connection is placed in a pool maintained by the OLE DB Pool Manager. The next time a client in this process needs a connection to this database, it can reuse a pooled connection rather than creating a new one. Figure 6-10 shows how this looks.

To speed things up, open connections can be pooled and reused

Figure 6-10 *Database connections are pooled and reused for better performance.*

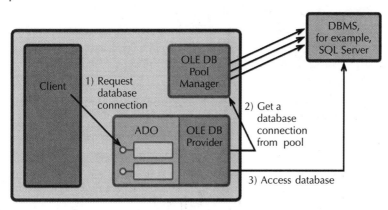

Pooling database connections is a good idea, and it can significantly improve performance. There are a couple of limitations worth keeping in mind, however. First, connections can only be shared among clients in the same process—pools don't span process boundaries. Also, a database connection can be reused by a client only if the connection exactly matches that client's requirements. If a pooled connection exists but has security requirements that don't match those of a potential new client, for instance, that client can't use this connection.

Disconnected Recordsets

As described so far, a Recordset object is always associated with an open connection to some data source. It's possible, however, for an ADO client to create and populate a Recordset, then release the connection it's associated with. The Recordset object can be maintained by the client with no associated connection, and so it's referred to as a *disconnected* Recordset. Disconnected Recordsets are commonly used to pass data from the middle tier to a desktop client via DCOM, and the description here assumes that this is what's being done.

A disconnected Recordset can be used to pass data from the middle tier to a desktop machine

To create a disconnected Recordset, an ADO client such as a COM object running on a middle-tier server machine first sets a property called CursorLocation on either a Connection object or a Recordset object to indicate that a client cursor should be used. The client then opens a connection in the usual way, populates a Recordset, and releases the connection. An interface pointer to that Recordset can now be passed to the desktop client.

Passing an interface pointer to a disconnected Recordset passes the contents of the Recordset as well

But when an interface pointer to a disconnected Recordset object is passed across the network to a desktop client, the entire Recordset—contents and all—is passed, not just the pointer. (Under the covers, this relies on COM's custom marshaling, but this detail is hidden from an ADO user.) This makes it straightforward to pass a disconnected Recordset and the data it contains from the middle tier of a three-tier application to the desktop client.

Disconnected Recordsets can also be used to modify data

Once it has received the Recordset, a client can modify the data it contains, then have those changes applied to the data source. To do this, the client passes the changed Recordset back to the middle tier. (Once again, the client just passes the interface pointer, but the entire contents of the Recordset are actually transferred.) The COM object in the middle tier then reconnects to the data source by calling the Recordset's Open method. Once this has been done, the COM object invokes the Recordset's UpdateBatch method, and the changes are applied to the data source. Figure 6-11 shows how this process looks.

Figure 6-11 *A disconnected Recordset can be passed across the network to a desktop client, modified, then used to update the data source its values came from.*

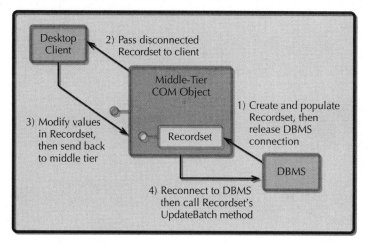

A disconnected Recordset cannot maintain locks on data in the underlying database—its connection to the database is gone. This makes it impossible for a disconnected Recordset to have a LockType of Pessimistic. If a client wishes to modify the rows in a disconnected Recordset, then apply those changes to the data source, the Recordset's LockType must be set to BatchOptimistic. As always with optimistic locking, it's possible that the data being updated has changed since the Recordset was populated. If this happens, the call to UpdateBatch returns one or more errors to the client. Despite this limitation, however, disconnected Recordsets are very useful, especially in three-tier applications.

Disconnected Recordsets must use a flavor of optimistic locking

Records and Streams

The initial ADO releases were biased toward relational databases

Unlike ODBC, both ADO and its big brother OLE DB are intended to allow access to more than just SQL-oriented data. Yet the ADO objects described so far still display something of a SQL bias. Recordsets seem clearly designed to handle the result of a SQL SELECT, for example, and Command objects are very well suited for compiling and executing parameterized SQL queries. This makes a good deal of sense—after all, SQL used with relational DBMS's is by far the most common way to access structured data today.

Record and Stream objects target accessing data that's not stored in a relational database

But other kinds of data can be interesting, too. For example, think about the enormous amount of data stored in ordinary files today, or the vast quantities of useful information locked away in e-mail archives. Neither of those kinds of data can be easily accessed using SQL queries, yet it would be nice to allow clients to get at this information using the familiar ADO interface. As originally defined, ADO wasn't quite right for accessing either of these kinds of data. To address this limitation, ADO 2.5 adds two new COM classes—Record and Stream—that weren't part of earlier ADO releases. Both of these object types are useful for working with data such as files and e-mail, information that previously wasn't easily accessible through ADO. Be aware, however, that providers aren't required to support these new classes, and so they aren't available in all environments.

A Record object can potentially be used to access data in a file or e-mail message

Record objects can be created in the usual way: CoCreateInstance, *new,* or whatever else is appropriate in the programming language of the ADO client. Once it exists, however, a Record object can be populated without executing a SQL query. Instead, an ADO client can invoke the object's Open method, passing in a URL. The URL might name either a directory somewhere in a machine's file system, a particular file, an e-mail message, or something else appropriate for the provider being used. Whatever it identifies, the named information is now accessible via this Record object.

ADO clients can use Record objects to access unstructured information, such as the contents of a particular file, or hierarchically organized information, such as a group of files and file directories. To support these possibilities, each Record object has a RecordType property with one of three values:

Record objects can be organized into hierarchies

- *Simple* Indicates that this Record has no child nodes. For example, if the URL used to populate this Record object names a simple file, the object's RecordType property will have this value.

- *Collection* Indicates that this Record does have child nodes. If the URL used to populate this Record object names a directory in the file system, for example, the object's RecordType property will have this value.

- *Structured Document* Indicates that this Record represents a compound file. Compound files (also known as structured storage) have their own internal hierarchical structure consisting of directory-like storages that contain streams or other storages. Many desktop applications, including Microsoft Word, Microsoft Excel, and lots more, store their information using this format. If the URL used to populate the Record object identifies, say, a .DOC file created by Microsoft Word, the object's RecordType property will have this value.

Because a Record object is intended for accessing non-SQL data, the methods it offers are quite different from those implemented by other ADO objects. These methods include:

- *CopyRecord* Allows copying a Record's contents to another location.

- *DeleteRecord* Allows deleting the entity a Record represents. For example, accessing a file using a Record object and then invoking that object's DeleteRecord method will delete the file.

- *MoveRecord*   Allows moving the entity that a Record represents. This method can be used to move a file from one directory to another, for example.

- *GetChildren*   Returns an ADO Recordset object. Each row in this Recordset represents the information below the Record object on which this method is called, if there is any. For example, if GetChildren is invoked on a Record object that represents a directory in the file system, the resulting Recordset will contain a row for each file and directory directly beneath this one.

A Record object can also derive its data from a row in a Recordset

It's also possible for an ADO client to populate a Record object by basing it on an existing Recordset object. If this is done, the data in the Record object is taken from the fields in the current record in the Recordset (although other fields can also be added by the underlying provider). While Record and Recordset objects don't offer exactly the same methods, a client can manipulate data in a Record in much the same way as it would in a Recordset. In fact, the fields in a Record object can be accessed using a Fields collection, just like the fields in a Recordset.

As already described, Record objects can represent unstructured data, such as the contents of an ordinary file. An ADO client can access that data by opening a Stream object associated with that Record object. As its name implies, a Stream simply contains a string of bytes that can be read or written by an ADO client using the Stream object's methods.

A client accesses data in a Stream object as a string of bytes

To access data, the client creates a Stream object, then invokes its Open method, passing in a reference to an existing Record object. Alternatively, a Stream can be opened directly with a URL that specifies a particular file. If this is done, the Stream will contain the contents of that file. It's even possible for an ADO client to create a Stream directly in memory, using it as a buffer that can be written to and then saved.

Records and Streams both focus on allowing access to unstructured data, data that's not typically accessible using SQL queries. Because their purpose varies somewhat from the more conventional ADO objects (such as Recordset), their use is also somewhat different. Still, these two kinds of objects represent progress in fulfilling ADO's goal of allowing access to all kinds of information through a single data access interface.

Related Technologies for Accessing Data

ADO is a useful interface for accessing information stored in a relational DBMS or, with the addition of Records and Streams, in a hierarchical structure such as a file system. There are many other kinds of information, however, and many potential ways to access it. As a result, ADO has evolved a few cousins, each focused on a particular type of data access.

ADO Extensions for Data Definition Language and Security

While the objects in ADO allow accessing data, they don't provide a generic way to examine and modify the schema describing that data. To remedy this, Microsoft has defined the ADO Extensions for Data Definition Languages and Security, called ADOX for short. ADOX defines a set of COM objects for use with ADO that give clients the ability to read and modify the description of some set of data. It also allows granting and revoking access permissions on tables, and controlling other aspects of data security. Although ADOX attempts to define a generic way to carry out these operations, all of its features aren't fully supported by all OLE DB providers, so exactly what's available varies depending on the data source being accessed.

ADOX defines a generic interface for accessing schema and security information

ADO Multidimensional

A primary goal of ADO is to allow clients easy access to data stored in the two-dimensional tables typical of a relational DBMS. Yet a substantial number of DBMS's today allow storing and querying multidimensional data—data contained in structures with more than two dimensions. Perhaps the most common application of this kind of data is in On-Line Analytical Processing (OLAP), a popular use of business data today. Imagine, for instance, a user who issues a query examining how sales of a particular product vary over a 12-month period in six different regions. Each of these variables can be thought of as a dimension, and the data being examined can be envisioned as a cube. (In fact, this data often has more than three dimensions, but it's still commonly referred to as a cube).

ADOMD defines a generic interface for accessing multidimensional data

ADO (Multidimensional), or ADOMD, adds objects to ADO that allow working with cubes and multidimensional data in general. Working with this kind of data can be inherently complex, and ADOMD is not a simple thing. Still, especially for OLAP applications, ADOMD can provide a useful generic interface. And as usual, the features of this ADO extension won't be available with every OLE DB provider. Instead, an OLE DB provider that wishes to be accessible through ADOMD must qualify as a multidimensional data provider (MDP) as defined in Microsoft's OLE DB for OLAP specification.

Remote Data Service

RDS provides a simple way to issue queries and get results

In a three-tier application, one very common sequence of events is the following: a desktop client issues a SQL query, then passes that query to the middle tier. This query is passed to a DBMS and an ADO Recordset is created containing the result of the query's execution. The data in this Recordset is then returned from the middle tier to the desktop client where it gets displayed to the user. One way to make all this happen is to write a custom client, pass the query to a middle-tier COM object using DCOM, then pass the result back as a disconnected Recordset. But think of the case where the client is Microsoft Internet Explorer, so the protocol used to access the middle tier is HTTP, and all the application needs to do is run a simple query—there's not really enough business logic to justify writing a COM object. Solving this common problem in a straightforward way is the goal of the Remote Data Service (RDS).

RDS is implemented as a small set of COM objects. One of these, called the DataSpace object, runs on the desktop and allows a client to create another COM object on the middle tier. This simple DataSpace object exposes only a single method: CreateObject. If the client is communicating with the middle tier via DCOM, calling this method is like calling CoCreateInstance or another of COM's standard creation functions. If the client is Internet Explorer, however—the most common scenario with RDS—it communicates with the middle tier via HTTP. In this case, the DataSpace object passes the create request to Internet Information Services (IIS) using HTTP rather than the DCOM protocol. In either case, an appropriate proxy is returned to the newly created object, allowing the client to invoke its methods.

The RDS DataSpace object allows creating a remote COM object over DCOM or HTTP

As already described, a typical RDS client wants to invoke a SQL query. To make this as simple as possible, RDS provides an object that runs on the middle tier called the DataFactory object. A client can use the DataSpace object to create an instance of a DataFactory object, then pass a SQL query to the DataFactory by invoking its Query method. The DataFactory object uses ADO to run the query, placing the results in a Recordset object. This Recordset is then appropriately marshaled and returned to the client as a disconnected Recordset, whether the protocol in use is DCOM or HTTP. All of this is shown in Figure 6-12.

The RDS DataFactory object allows executing a SQL query on a server

It's common to use RDS from a VBScript program embedded in a Web page that gets loaded into Internet Explorer. The middle-tier object—a DataFactory or perhaps a custom business object specified by the client—still typically uses ADO, and the client sees only Recordsets. As with other disconnected Recordsets, the client can optionally make changes to the Recordset it receives, then have those changes applied against the data from which that

Recordset was created. And to make displaying the contents of this Recordset easy, RDS provides a third COM object, the DataControl object, to bind the Recordset to an ActiveX control on the client. Although it's not shown in Figure 6-12, this object can be used for things such as associating the returned Recordset's data with a grid object running inside Internet Explorer on the user's desktop.

Figure 6-12 *VBScript code in a Web page loaded into Internet Explorer can use RDS to issue SQL queries to a database accessed through IIS.*

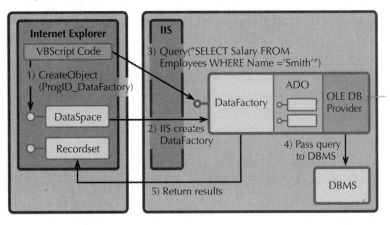

Accessing data, especially data stored in a DBMS, is fundamental to building many, many types of applications today. Going forward, most applications written for Windows 2000 will probably use ADO to access data. Yet for a modern three-tier application built for Windows 2000, ADO is not enough. While ADO allows its clients to use transactions, those clients might also need to makes changes to data managed by multiple DBMS's. If those changes must all belong to a single transaction, ADO alone won't suffice. To solve this problem, Windows 2000 includes the Distributed Transaction Coordinator, the topic of the next chapter.

ADO is used by many, perhaps most, three-tier applications built for Windows 2000

Chapter Seven

Distributed Transaction Services

Accessing data is a critically important part of many, many applications. As long as data is just being read, life can be simple. When applications must make changes to data, however, things necessarily get more complicated. For instance, as described in the previous chapter, it's often the case that for a group of changes, all of them must be performed or none of them should be. In other words, modifications to data are often grouped into transactions.

Two or more events, such as changes to data, can be grouped into a transaction

If all the changes an application makes in a particular transaction are handled by the same DBMS, that DBMS can itself provide support for transactions, and a client can access that transaction service through an interface such as ADO. But what if an application wishes to make changes in two databases managed by two different DBMS's residing on two different machines? Recall, for instance, the money transfer example described earlier, in which money was being transferred from a savings account to a checking account. Suppose that rather than being maintained in the same DBMS, savings accounts are maintained in a Microsoft SQL Server database on a Microsoft Windows 2000 server machine while checking accounts are held in an Oracle database running on a UNIX system. How can money be moved from one account to the other within a single transaction, since neither DBMS knows

Transactions spanning multiple databases or different technologies present special problems

everything that's going on? Or suppose an application wants to combine a database update with something else, such as sending a message via Microsoft Message Queuing (MSMQ), and make sure that either both events happen or neither one does. Transactions certainly can include things other than changes to data in a database, so once again, the transaction support provided by a single DBMS won't suffice; more is required.

DTC can ensure that all participants in a distributed transaction do the right thing

What's needed is something that's able to keep track of all the participants in a particular transaction—even a distributed transaction whose work is spread across multiple machines—then act as a coordinator, ensuring that all of those participants do the same thing and either commit or abort the transaction. In Windows 2000, that feat is accomplished by the Microsoft Distributed Transaction Coordinator (DTC). DTC isn't new with Windows 2000, but it's a key part of the distributed services this operating system provides.

DTC is usually used by the COM runtime rather than directly by application developers

It's important to point out that although it is possible for applications to use DTC directly, it's rare. Instead, applications that require distributed transactions will typically rely on the transaction services provided by the COM runtime, which builds on DTC but hides it from the application developer. How this happens is described in the next chapter. Nevertheless, understanding how COM uses transactions ultimately requires knowing how DTC works, so for this and other reasons, DTC is well worth a look.

The DTC Environment

The DTC transaction manager is accessed through OLE Transactions, a set of COM interfaces

As shown in Figure 7-1, any computer running Windows 2000 can run a DTC transaction manager. A client application can directly access its local DTC transaction manager through a group of COM interfaces called *OLE Transactions*.[1] Using those interfaces, that client can tell the DTC transaction manager when a

---

1. Like OLE Database, the OLE Transactions name is a relic of the era when Microsoft applied the OLE label to COM-based technologies. Don't be confused—neither of these has anything to do with OLE compound documents.

transaction begins, then eventually indicate whether to commit or abort that transaction's work. The DTC transaction manager bears the primary responsibility for passing this information to other DTC transaction managers that might be involved in this transaction and, ultimately, to the software that's carrying out the work involved in the transaction.

Figure 7-1 *The DTC transaction manager communicates with resource managers through OLE Transactions or the standard XA interfaces.*

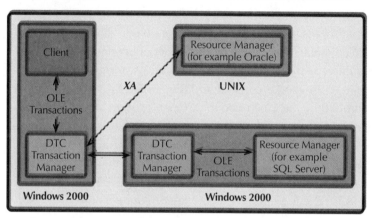

From DTC's point of view, anything that can participate in transactions qualifies as a *resource manager (RM)*. The most common example of an RM is a DBMS such as SQL Server or Oracle, but MSMQ and other products are also capable of acting in the role of an RM. DTC does not itself actually make permanent the work performed within a transaction when that transaction commits, nor does it get involved in locking any data involved in a transaction. Instead, data is locked and work is committed by the resource manager. A DBMS, for example, will rely on its own internal transaction manager to ensure that a group of changes are all committed or all rolled back. Also, DTC does not get involved in telling RMs what work to do as part of a transaction. Instead, it's up to the client to somehow convey its requests to the appropriate RMs. For a DBMS, a client typically accomplishes this through ADO, ODBC, or some other database access interface,

A DBMS, a message queuing system, and anything else that can participate in a transaction qualifies as a resource manager while other RMs provide their own APIs. DTC's role is purely to coordinate the transaction, making sure that every participating RM knows what to do and when to do it.

DTC can work with resource managers that support either OLE Transactions or XA

For the DTC transaction manager to tell a variety of RMs what to do, some standard interface must exist to allow this communication. RMs from Microsoft, including SQL Server and MSMQ, implement interfaces defined as part of the OLE Transactions specification for this purpose. As Figure 7-1 shows, those RMs can communicate with their local DTC transaction manager as prescribed by OLE Transactions.[2] RMs from other vendors, however, typically implement another standard set of interfaces known by the not-especially-descriptive name of *XA*. Originally created by the multi-vendor consortium X/Open, the XA standard is now controlled by the Open Group, X/Open's successor. An RM that doesn't implement OLE Transactions—a set that includes many widely used DBMS's—can communicate indirectly with a DTC transaction manager using XA, whether it's running on Windows 2000 or another operating system such as UNIX. Exactly how this works is described in more detail later in this section.

Two-Phase Commit

Whether communication happens via OLE Transactions or XA, the primary job of the DTC transaction manager is always the same: it must first make sure that every resource manager participating in a particular transaction knows what to do—commit or abort—and then report back to the client what actually happened. It's quite possible, for instance, that even if a client specifies that a transaction should commit, one of the RMs involved decides for reasons of its own to abort the transaction.

---

2. Although it's not shown in the figure, RMs can also run on the same system as the DTC client, allowing both to use a single instance of the DTC transaction manager.

Whatever happens, it's the DTC transaction manager's responsibility to report an outcome to its client.[3]

Once the client has told the DTC transaction manager whether a given transaction should commit or abort, the transaction manager must pass this request on to the RMs participating in that transaction. You might imagine that the transaction manager could just tell each RM whether to commit or abort, then tell the client what happened. Making sure that every RM does the same thing, however, either all committing or all aborting, requires a bit more complexity than this. Rather than just directly telling the RMs what to do, the DTC transaction manager relies on a widely used algorithm known as *two-phase commit* (sometimes shortened to just *2PC*).

DTC uses the well-known two-phase commit algorithm to end a transaction

The basic idea of two-phase commit is not hard. To see how it works, suppose a client tells its local DTC transaction manager to end a transaction, requesting that all the work performed in the transaction be committed. To accomplish this, the transaction manager begins phase one of the 2PC algorithm by sending a Prepare message to each RM involved in the transaction, asking whether they are prepared to do what the client has requested. Exactly how this message gets sent varies, as described in the next section, but it can potentially involve creating a hierarchy of transaction managers, all controlled by a root transaction manager on the DTC client's machine. Each RM then responds with a message that essentially says either, "Yes, I am ready to commit," or "No, I'm not ready." Phase one of the two-phase commit algorithm ends when the transaction manager has received one of those two responses from all the RMs in the transaction.

In phase one, DTC asks each RM if it's prepared to commit

---

3. As with ADO, the word "client" here means DTC's client, not the client machine on the user's desktop. While it's possible for this desktop machine to act as a DTC client, it's far more common for software running in the middle tier to play this role.

In phase two, DTC tells
each RM what to do:
commit or abort

In phase two of the algorithm, the transaction manager actually
tells the RMs what they should do. If in phase one the transaction
manager received a "Yes" message from every RM involved in the
transaction, the transaction manager sends a Commit message to
each of them. Each RM then commits the transaction, making permanent all changes in the transaction, and returns an indication
of this act to the transaction manager. If the transaction manager
received any "No" messages in phase one, however, that means
that all the work performed by all the RMs in the transaction must
be aborted. (Remember, a transaction is by definition an all-or-
nothing affair). In this case, phase two consists of the transaction
manager sending each RM an Abort message, followed by a response from each RM indicating that it has aborted the transaction. In either situation, the right thing occurs: either all of the
transaction's work is made permanent or none of it is.

Problems can arise if
machine or network
failures happen at the
wrong time

This is a lovely story, and most of the time it works as just described. But it doesn't take too much thought to realize that even
using two-phase commit, things can still go wrong. Suppose, for
example, that the network connecting the computer running one
of the RMs in this transaction and the root transaction manager
crashes between phase one and phase two. Or suppose that the
machine running an RM crashes after phase one is completed but
before it has received the message in phase two. What happens?
How is the transaction ever resolved?

DTC and every RM
maintain log files
to allow recovery
from failures

To help solve these kinds of problems, each DTC transaction manager maintains a log file. Every transaction that a transaction
manager takes part in is recorded in this log. Each RM also
maintains a log, storing information about all transactions in
which it is currently involved. After a system crash and restart,
transaction managers and RMs examine their various log files to
determine what actions they should take to make sure everything is resolved correctly.

For example, suppose the machine some RM is running on crashes. Any transactions involving that RM that are currently in progress and have not yet been ended by the client will be aborted—since one of the RMs in these transactions has failed, these transactions can't possibly succeed. But what about transactions that were in the process of performing two-phase commit with this RM when the crash occurred? The RM's machine will eventually be restarted, and so the RM will find these transactions in its log when it begins running again. But what should it do with them? Were these transactions committed or aborted while the RM was down?

From the point of view of that RM, these transactions are *in doubt*, since it can't determine by itself what it should do. To solve this problem, the RM contacts a DTC transaction manager, asking it about the ultimate fate of each in-doubt transaction. This RM then does whatever that transaction manager says it should do, committing those transactions that committed during the RM's absence, and rolling back those that were aborted during that time. This process can actually get quite complicated. The DTC transaction manager that this RM is querying might itself need to contact another transaction manager higher in the hierarchy to determine what to do, and this transaction manager might need to query one that's higher still. Whatever the situation, once any system crashes or network failures have been corrected, DTC works together with the RMs to ensure that for each in-doubt transaction, all RMs do the same thing: all commit or all abort. And fortunately, the root transaction manager is never in doubt about the transaction's fate—it always knows what the outcome should be.

A restarted RM can query DTC to learn what to do with any in-doubt transactions

But even this isn't always sufficient. It's true that if you just wait long enough, DTC and the RMs will work together to guarantee that everything works out, even in the face of system or network failures. But recall that each RM participating in a transaction will also typically lock the data it's working with. Keeping this data

With some kinds of failures, human intervention might be required to correctly end a transaction locked (and thus inaccessible to other transactions) while waiting for, say, a new hard disk to be delivered and installed, would be completely unacceptable. Customers would no doubt be unhappy, for example, if their checking account was inaccessible for several days. In cases like this, an administrator can use the Component Services administrative tool in Windows 2000 to force an in-doubt transaction to commit or abort. This kind of manual intervention isn't the most appealing option, but when it's not feasible to keep all of a transaction's data locked until the systems involved are running again, it's the only choice.[4]

A DTC Example

Imagine that a client running on a Windows 2000 system wants to move money from a savings account maintained in a SQL Server database on another Windows 2000 machine to a checking account kept in an Oracle database running on a UNIX system. What does DTC actually do to allow this distributed transaction to take place?

The DTC client starts a transaction, then issues the first query in that transaction

Figure 7-2 shows the first steps. To begin, the DTC client uses OLE Transactions to tell its local DTC transaction manager to begin a transaction (although recall that, as described in the next chapter, this client will most often be the COM runtime rather than a user-written application). Once this is done, the client issues a SQL query to the SQL Server database requesting that it subtract the desired amount from the target savings account. The API the client uses to do this is very likely ADO, but the calls it makes are ultimately dependent on either an OLE DB provider or an ODBC driver. Before issuing the query, the client can inform the database

---

4. One way to increase the availability of DTC is to use the Microsoft Cluster Server (MSCS). When used on two computers clustered together using MCS, the DTC transaction manager runs on only one of the cluster's nodes at a time. Its log, however, is stored on a disk accessible to both clustered machines. If the machine running the transaction manager goes down, another copy is automatically started on the other machine in the cluster. Since the two machines share the same disk, this new transaction manager can use the same transaction log as did its now-dead sibling, picking up where it left off.

driver that a DTC-controlled transaction is in progress by calling an appropriate function (such as ODBC's SQLSetConnectOption), passing in the identifier of a particular DTC transaction. When the client actually issues the query, this information is passed on to the database (the RM) along with the query. Once the RM receives this request, it joins the transaction (in the jargon of transaction people, the RM *enlists* in the transaction) by calling the appropriate OLE Transactions method to communicate with its local DTC transaction manager.

Figure 7-2 *The client tells DTC to begin a transaction, then issues an update to SQL Server.*

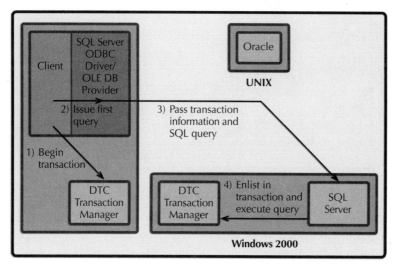

Next, suppose the client issues a second SQL query within this same DTC transaction, this time adding money to the checking account maintained by Oracle on the UNIX system. What happens is shown in Figure 7-3. As before, the client issues the query to the database driver. Because Oracle is running on UNIX, however, the DTC transaction manager is not present on the remote machine. And since Oracle supports XA rather than OLE Transactions, the database driver must bear more responsibility. As before, the driver must be told that this update request is being made within an existing DTC transaction. Now, however, the database driver

The DTC client next issues the second query in this transaction itself must enlist in the transaction by invoking the appropriate OLE Transactions method in the local DTC transaction manager. Once this is done, the database driver passes the SQL query and a transaction identifier to Oracle in a way that's in line with the XA standard.

Figure 7-3 *The client next issues an update to Oracle.*

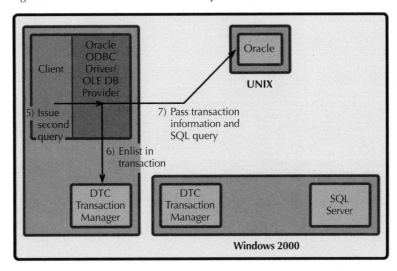

Notice that to participate in a DTC transaction, one of two things must be true. One possibility is that an RM runs on a Microsoft operating system and implements OLE Transactions, as does SQL Server. Alternatively, the driver used to access an RM must be capable of using OLE Transactions to enlist the RM in a DTC transaction and the RM itself must support XA, as is the case with Oracle and many other DBMS's. The key point is that to participate in DTC-coordinated transactions, RMs or the software used to access them must be made DTC-aware in some way.

The DTC client ends the transaction and DTC ensures that all RMs do the same thing: commit or abort

When the client decides to end this transaction, it once again invokes the appropriate OLE Transactions method to do it, as shown in Figure 7-4. This request indicates whether the transaction should be committed or aborted. (While any participant in a DTC transaction is allowed to abort it, only the client that initiated it has the right to commit the transaction.) Upon receiving that request, the local DTC transaction manager engages in a two-phase commit protocol with all RMs that have enlisted in this transaction. For SQL Server, running on a Windows 2000 machine and implementing OLE Transactions, the root DTC transaction manager passes its requests to the DTC transaction manager running on the same machine as SQL Server, which in turn passes those requests on to the DBMS itself. Responses from SQL Server are returned via the same path. However, for Oracle—supporting XA and running on a UNIX system with no local DTC transaction manager—the client's DTC transaction manager makes its requests to the Oracle driver on the client's machine. This driver then forwards the transaction manager's requests to Oracle on the remote system in a way that's in line with XA, with results sent back in the same way.

Figure 7-4 *When the client ends the transaction, the DTC transaction manager performs two-phase commit with the RMs enlisted in this transaction.*

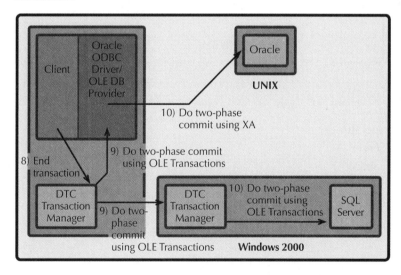

Regardless of the mechanics, the client's DTC transaction manager is in charge. It acts as the root of this transaction tree, sending first phase one's Prepare message, then the final Commit or

Abort message. And although they're not shown in Figure 7-4, each DTC transaction manager maintains a log file as described earlier, allowing recovery in the event of system or network failures.

One final point worth making here is that DTC does not support nested transactions. It's not possible, for instance, for a DTC client to begin one transaction, then start another one that's somehow nested inside the first. Instead, DTC allows only flat transactions, so attempting to start a new transaction within the context of an existing one won't succeed.

Other Topics

By acting as the coordinator of distributed transactions among multiple RMs, DTC provides an important and commonly used service. There are also a few related technologies that, while not so widely used, are worth a look. The final section of this chapter describes these technologies.

The Transaction Internet Protocol

Although a standard part of Windows 2000, DTC is not the only distributed transaction manager in use today

When one DTC transaction manager talks to another DTC transaction manager, they use a DCOM-based protocol defined by Microsoft. But while the DTC transaction manager is the most common choice for Windows 2000, there are many other transaction managers in the world running on many other operating systems. Among the most popular of these are IBM's CICS, BEA Systems' TUXEDO, and various vendors' implementations of the Enterprise JavaBeans (EJB) specification. All of these products can provide their own protocols analogous to the one used by DTC, which means that a plethora of such protocols exists in the world today. Suppose some application wants to group work performed on two or more machines into a transaction, but not all of those machines are running a Microsoft operating system. One option, as just described, is to use an RM that understands XA and whose supporting access software (such as an ODBC driver or OLE DB provider) has been adapted to work with DTC. But suppose the

RM we'd like to use is itself participating in a transaction controlled by a transaction manager other than DTC. How can the DTC transaction manager communicate with other, non-Microsoft, transaction managers?

In Windows 2000, the answer is the *Transaction Internet Protocol (TIP)*. TIP is currently described in an Internet-Draft made available through the IETF, and it specifies a protocol allowing two transaction managers to communicate with one another, regardless of the vendor that created each one. The Windows 2000 version of DTC supports TIP, and extra interfaces have been added to OLE Transactions that allow DTC clients to use this new protocol. Obviously, using TIP to communicate with products from other vendors requires that those products also implement this protocol, but given its status as an IETF-created technology, this is not an unreasonable thing to expect.

DTC supports TIP, allowing coordination with other distributed transaction managers

Figure 7-5 gives a high-level view of how TIP might be used in practice. In the diagram, two Microsoft DTC transaction managers are communicating using their native protocol as usual. The root DTC transaction manager is also communicating with a non-Microsoft transaction manager using TIP.

TIP allows performing two-phase commit

Figure 7-5 *TIP allows the Microsoft DTC transaction manager to communicate with distributed transaction managers from other vendors.*

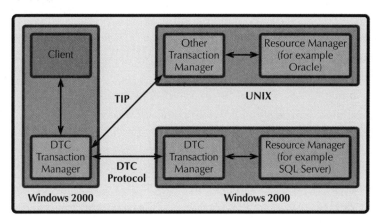

What do transaction managers have to say to one another? Basically all they need to do is exchange the messages required to perform two-phase commit, just as do the DTC transaction managers. Because these messages are very simple, TIP is a very simple protocol.[5] As evidence of this, Figure 7-6 shows a typical set of TIP exchanges.

Figure 7-6 *TIP messages are used to perform two-phase commit.*

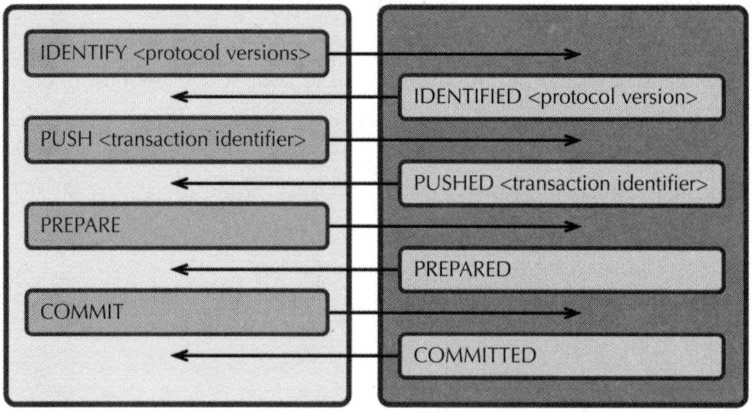

As Figure 7-6 shows, TIP messages are expressed mostly as upper-case words sent in ASCII—the protocol has no fancy binary headers. To begin, the initiating transaction manager (dubbed the *superior* by TIP) can send an IDENTIFY message along with an indication of which TIP versions it supports. The *subordinate* transaction manager can then respond with an IDENTIFIED message, including with this message its choice of TIP version from among the range offered by the superior. Next, the superior transaction manager can send the subordinate a PUSH command, indicating that it wishes to begin a transaction. (TIP also allows the subordinate to pull transactions from the superior if desired.) This PUSH command includes a string of printable characters that the superior uses to identify the transaction. The subordinate responds with a PUSHED command, including another string of

---

5. In fact, the entire TIP spec is only about 15 pages.

printable characters that *it* uses to identify the transaction. These identifiers can be used to reference this transaction later if necessary. For example, if the machine running an RM fails in the middle of the two-phase commit process, the RM will eventually need to query the superior transaction manager to determine whether to commit or abort this transaction. The transaction identifiers sent on the PUSH/PUSHED exchange can be used for this purpose.

From here on, all that's required is to exchange simple, parameter-free messages marking the phases of two-phase commit. To begin the process, the superior sends a PREPARE message to its subordinate, which, assuming all is well, responds with PREPARED. If the subordinate were unwilling to commit this transaction, it might instead send back an ABORTED message indicating this fact. Assuming phase one was successful, the superior will eventually send a COMMIT message, to which the subordinate will respond with COMMITTED. And although other transport protocols could potentially be used, all of these exchanges typically take place over a TCP connection.

Notice what TIP does not define: the protocol has no provision for conveying any information about the actual work being performed in this transaction. For example, Figure 7-5 suggests using TIP with an Oracle database. How the client indicated what data should be changed in that database is not defined by TIP. Instead, TIP is designed to do only one thing: allow transaction managers created by different vendors to work together when committing distributed transactions.

TIP says nothing about how clients make changes to data in RMs

Compensating Resource Manager

Think about what's required to build a resource manager capable of participating in DTC-controlled transactions. First, it must provide some way for its client, such as a middle-tier business object, to access and modify its state. If the RM is a DBMS, for example, a client might use ADO with an appropriate OLE DB provider to

Building a DTC-aware RM is not simple

work with the information it contains. This RM must also be able to take part in the protocol exchanges required for two-phase commit and, depending on the outcome of this process, commit or roll back any changes the client has made to the information it manages, regardless of any failures that might occur. As already described, RMs that do this write records to a log stored on disk, then read these records if necessary to recover after a failure or perform other functions.

In reality, an RM might need to do much more than this to provide correct transactional behavior. A DBMS, for example, provides locking to ensure isolation of the data involved in a transaction. Still, implementing even the core requirements for a DTC-aware RM can be challenging. For an organization creating, say, a new DBMS, the effort required to do this is expected, and so this organization will probably employ specialists in building this kind of software. But suppose you want to create something that can act as an RM with DTC, and you're not a specialist in building this kind of code. Traditionally, you've faced a steep learning curve and a mountain of work.

The CRM provides key parts of a DTC-aware RM's implementation

With Windows 2000, both the curve and the mountain are flattened considerably by the Compensating Resource Manager (CRM). The CRM provides a standard implementation of much of what's required to make an RM DTC-aware. While it doesn't do everything for you, it does make your task considerably easier. For example, suppose you're building an application that stores and modifies information, but because of complexity or cost or something else, you don't want to use a DBMS to manage that information. Instead, let's assume you choose to build your own RM, storing data in ordinary files in the Windows 2000 file system. Your application might still need all-or-nothing behavior, and so your RM would like to take part in DTC-controlled transactions. Yet this feature isn't available with ordinary files in Windows 2000. Since you're writing the RM yourself, though, you can add this ability and make your RM DTC-aware. By providing a standard implementation of some of the code you'll need, the CRM will be useful in building your RM. You'll still have some work to do—the CRM doesn't do everything for you—but it certainly makes the job easier.[6]

Creating a DTC-aware RM using the CRM requires you to build two distinct components. One, called a *CRM Worker*, performs whatever functions your application needs, creating log records as required. The other, known as a *CRM Compensator*, is used when the transaction ends. It can read the log records created by the CRM Worker, and then use that and other information to correctly commit or abort the transaction.

Using the CRM requires implementing a CRM Worker and a CRM Compensator

In this example, the client uses DTC directly, although as always it's more likely that the client will be accessing DTC indirectly through the COM runtime. (In fact, the CRM is sometimes viewed as being part of COM+, but it can be used with or without the COM+ services.) To begin, the client asks DTC to start a new transaction, as shown in step 1 of Figure 7-7. Next, in step 2, the client creates the CRM Worker for this RM. Once it exists, the Worker creates an instance of the CRM Clerk, as shown in step 3, which is a standard component provided with Windows 2000. The Worker then registers an appropriate CRM Compensator with this Clerk. The CRM Clerk enlists this RM in the transaction, as shown in step 4, and the CRM Worker is ready to receive requests to do work within this transaction.

Next, as step 5 of Figure 7-8 shows, the client issues its updates to RM-managed information. This example assumes that two RMs are used: SQL Server and the RM built using the CRM. To access

---

6. In transaction processing applications, it's sometimes necessary to run a *compensating transaction* to reverse the result of a previously committed transaction. Despite its similar name, the Compensating Resource Manager has nothing to do with compensating transactions.

SQL Server, the client probably uses ADO, although this isn't shown in the figure. To access the CRM-based RM, the object uses whatever interface is provided by the implementer of the CRM Worker. As the figure suggests, this is likely to be a COM interface, but this isn't required.

Figure 7-7   *A client creates a CRM Worker, which in turn creates a CRM Clerk.*

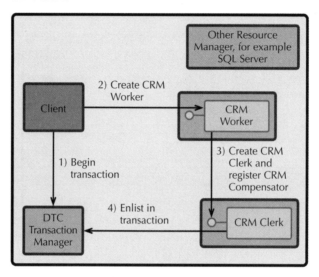

The CRM Worker changes the RM's state and logs these changes

However the requests are made, the CRM Worker is responsible for carrying them out. You must implement this component—it's not provided for you—so its capabilities depend on what this RM does. Most RMs change the state of some data, which might be stored in files or in some other way, in response to requests from their clients. When the transaction those changes are part of ends, the RM must either commit those changes or restore the state to its original values. Furthermore, it must do these things correctly even if software or hardware failures occur. As already described, RMs typically rely on a log to do this.

Implementing a reliable, correct log is nontrivial. Fortunately, the CRM Clerk provides one that can be used by any CRM Worker. In response to requests made by its client, the CRM Worker can record its intention to change the state of data it manages, shown in step 6 in Figure 7-8, then actually make the change, as shown in step 7. Writing the log record first, a process called *write ahead logging*, makes recovery possible even if a failure occurs before the state is changed. The Worker accesses the log through the ICrmLogControl interface provided by the CRM Clerk.

Figure 7-8 *When the client modifies data managed by the RM, the RM logs changes before making them.*

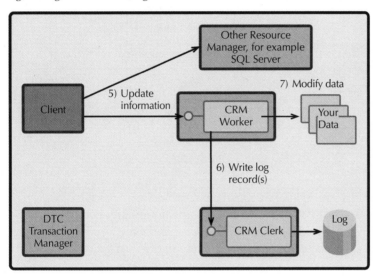

When the client tells DTC to end the transaction, as shown in step 8 of Figure 7-9, DTC communicates with both SQL Server and the CRM-based RM to perform two-phase commit, as shown in step 9. The CRM Clerk receives DTC's requests, then creates an appropriate CRM Compensator for this transaction (recall that the CRM Worker told the CRM Clerk which Compensator to use shortly after the Worker was created). This Compensator does whatever is required to commit or roll back the transaction. As shown in step 11, it can modify data and access the log records created earlier by the CRM Worker to do this correctly.

The CRM Compensator handles transaction commit or abort

Figure 7-9 *When the transaction ends, the CRM Compensator and the CRM Clerk work together to allow the RM to correctly participate in two-phase commit.*

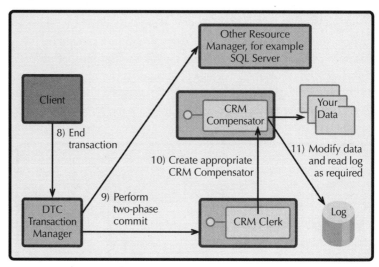

The CRM does not make building an RM trivial—you must still write code to modify data and handle the end of a transaction—but it does make it significantly easier. By providing both a standard log and support for DTC's standard two-phase commit messages, it allows the RM developer to focus on those things that are specific to the problem this RM addresses.

DTC is a commonly used part of three-tier applications built for Windows 2000

Accessing data, whether or not that access is part of a transaction, is fundamental to building applications today. Going forward, most applications written for Windows 2000 will probably use ADO to access data. If those applications also need to make changes to data in multiple resource managers and group those changes into transactions, they will also make use of DTC. But although ADO is used directly by many applications, DTC is not. Getting the full picture of how applications most often use these services in three-tier applications requires understanding the technologies now defined as part of COM+, the subject of the next chapter.

Component Services: COM+

For all but the simplest three-tier applications, it makes sense to wrap the middle tier—the business logic—in COM components, letting clients access those components either via Distributed COM (DCOM) or from a Web browser through HTTP and Internet Information Services (IIS). It also typically makes sense for those COM components to use ActiveX Data Objects (ADO) to access stored data. For some very straightforward applications, these technologies might be all that's required.

But the middle tier of most three-tier applications needs more than this. For example, enterprise applications commonly use transactions, as described in the previous chapter. In some cases, relying on the transaction capabilities provided by a database management system (DBMS) is sufficient, and if it's not, the developer of middle-tier software can use the Distributed Transaction Coordinator (DTC) directly. Yet that developer's life would be significantly simpler if there were one common way for middle-tier components to work with transactions that hid both the variations among different data sources and the complexity of DTC.

Middle-tier COM objects can profitably use many different services

Or consider this: it's common to require that an enterprise application scale to handle hundreds or even thousands of simultaneous clients. Achieving this scalability using only standard COM components is possible, but requires a good deal of work by the application's developers. A common set of mechanisms

Useful services include those for using transactions, for building scalable applications, and more

for building scalable applications, mechanisms that could be used by many different types of applications, would make building scalable three-tier applications easier and quicker. Other problems exist, too—problems that are faced over and over by developers of middle-tier COM objects.

Given this, why not create a common solution? Rather than require each developer to re-create a custom approach, it would make much more sense to provide a standard solution to address these problems. COM+, new in Windows 2000, does exactly that. It provides a set of services that address common problems middle-tier developers face. COM+ includes a few more things, but the bulk of what's provided by COM+ 1.0, the version included with the first release of Windows 2000, is focused on building scalable, transaction-oriented business logic for the middle tier.

From COM to COM+

Microsoft first shipped COM in 1993, with DCOM following as part of Windows NT 4.0 in 1996. Later that same year, Microsoft Transaction Server (MTS) was released as part of the Windows NT 4.0 Option Pack. A second release of MTS a year or so later brought the usual improvements but no radical changes. MTS was based completely on COM—every MTS application was built as one or more COM components—and it provided a useful set of services for building middle-tier business logic in three-tier applications. Yet despite this, MTS was built as an add-on to COM. It made no changes to the fundamental COM infrastructure, instead providing its services in an independent library called the MTS Executive.

In a very real sense, COM+ integrates MTS and COM. The MTS Executive is gone—its functions are now part of the standard COM runtime. As described in Chapter 5, some parts of the fundamental COM infrastructure such as CoCreateInstance have been affected by the arrival of COM+. None of this means that you can't build applications using COM as it was originally defined in 1993—you can. Instead, the major thrust of COM+ is to integrate the services provided by MTS into the standard COM libraries and to provide some improvements along the way. In fact, it's not incorrect to view COM+ 1.0 as incorporating what would have been the third release of MTS. The COM+ services that grow out of MTS include:

- *Automatic transactions*   Rather then require clients or middle-tier components to explicitly define when transactions begin and end, this service allows using transactions in a straightforward, component-oriented way.

- *Object lifetime services*   Using a server machine's resources intelligently is an essential part of creating a scalable application. COM+'s Just-In-Time (JIT) activation service allows objects to be activated only when they're needed, then go away when they're no longer required. The goal is to increase an application's scalability—thus allowing more clients to be supported using the same server hardware—and its correctness. Object pooling, another option provided by COM+, allows an object that's no longer needed to be cached in a pool rather than being destroyed. This object can then later be located in the object pool and reused when it's needed.

- *Threading and concurrency services*   Server applications that aren't multi-threaded but must be accessed by many clients simultaneously can be slow, since each client must wait its turn. Yet writing multi-threaded applications can be remarkably difficult. COM+ provides threading and concurrency services that make it easier for developers to write applications that can be safely accessed by many clients at once.

- *Security services*   Rather than require changing ACLs, or worse, the actual code of an application, COM+ provides authorization services that allow a developer or administrator to control which clients can access which resources by simply configuring an application. COM+ also allows administratively setting an application's requirements for authentication, data integrity, and data privacy, removing the need to include this information in the application itself.

All of these services and more are provided by a new-and-improved version of the COM runtime. To provide the services just listed, the COM runtime can get in the middle of every method call a client makes on a COM object, just as the MTS Executive did in Windows NT 4.

COM+ also adds other services

COM+ also includes various other COM-related services that were first released in Windows 2000, services whose roots aren't in MTS. They include:

- *COM+ Events*   Allowing one component to send an event that is received by many others is a common requirement in application development. A generic service, sometimes called publish-and-subscribe, can be created to make this easier to do. COM+ Events provides this service, representing events as method calls on COM objects.

- *Queued Components*   Most often, a client invocation of a COM object method is synchronous: the client blocks until the call returns. Queued Components brings a form of asynchronous method invocation to COM and DCOM by allowing requests to be carried via Microsoft Message Queuing (MSMQ) rather than over a remote procedure call (RPC) protocol or some other mechanism. Because of its dependence on MSMQ, Queued Components is described in Chapter 9.

- *Component Load Balancing*   When a client calls Co-CreateInstance, there might be several server machines on which that new object could potentially be created. Component Load Balancing provides a service that keeps track of the current load on a group of servers, routing object creation requests to the most available machine. As described later in this chapter, Component Load Balancing is provided as a Technology Preview for the first release of Windows 2000 rather than a fully-supported technology.

- *Miscellaneous other services*   These include Bring Your Own Transaction (BYOT), which allows explicitly joining an in-progress transaction, support for constructors on COM objects, and a few more.

The bulk of what COM+ offers is in the services provided by the enhanced COM runtime. The runtime is a standard part of Windows 2000, and as Figure 8-1 shows, it can sit between COM objects and their clients, intercepting every method call those clients make on the objects. Whether the client is a Visual Basic program running on a desktop machine accessing these objects through DCOM, an ASP script running on the same machine as these objects, or something else, getting between the client and the COM objects that client is using allows the COM runtime to provide a number of useful services. And as the figure shows, the objects using those services are most commonly accessing one or more databases.

COM+ provides its services primarily through an enhanced version of the COM runtime library

Figure 8-1 *Browser and nonbrowser clients can access COM objects through the COM runtime.*

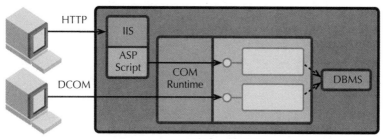

Windows 2000 Server

COM+ Basics

Getting a handle on the services provided by the COM runtime first requires understanding a number of other things. In this chapter, I'll assume that you've read at least Chapters 1, 5, 6, and 7, so that you understand the basics of the Windows 2000 distributed environment, COM, ADO, and DTC. There are a few more ideas that must be introduced as well before we take a closer look at the services the COM runtime offers to applications.

COM+ Applications

A COM+ Application is a group of in-process COM components

To use COM+, business logic must be written as one or (usually) more in-process COM components, that is, as COM classes packaged in DLLs. Once these components have been created, the Component Services administrative tool can be used to group them into *COM+ Applications*. (What COM+ calls Applications were known as Packages in MTS, but don't be confused by this term: a COM+ Application provides only the middle tier of a complete three-tier application.) All of the COM components in a particular COM+ Application will run within a single process, so the way in which components are grouped into Applications determines the process structure.

COM+ supports Server Applications and Library Applications

The two most important types of COM+ Applications are *Server* Applications and *Library* Applications. The key difference between them is that every Server Application runs in its own separate process, while objects created from components grouped into a Library Application run in the process of the client that creates them. As Figure 8-2 shows, it's entirely legal for a single Windows 2000 machine to run more than one Server Application simultaneously. Each will run in its own process, and each process will have its own copy of the COM runtime. And since components that are part of a COM+ Application must be DLLs, some EXE must exist to provide a process for them to run in. The usual choice for this EXE is a simple process shipped with Windows 2000 called the COM+ Surrogate. Although not shown in any figures in this chapter, it is commonly loaded when an EXE is required to host the DLLs in some COM+ Application.

In the figure, Server Application 1 containing components A and B has been loaded into one process, and its objects are being accessed by a client through one instance of the COM runtime. Server Application 2 containing components C and D has been loaded into another process, and a Library Application containing components E and F has been loaded into this same process. Two other clients are invoking methods on objects in one or both Applications, with all of those invocations passing through the COM runtime running in this second process.

Figure 8-2 *Each COM+ Server Application has its own process, while a Library Application does not.*

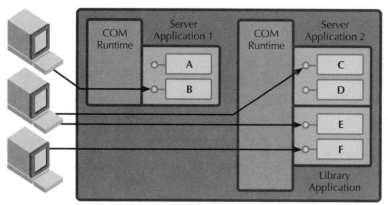

Windows 2000 Server

Once a COM component has been made part of a COM+ Application, that component is referred to as a *configured component*. Recall that components in a COM+ Application must be written as in-process servers, which means that every configured component must be a DLL. In Windows 2000, a COM component that has not been made part of a COM+ Application is sometimes referred to as an *unconfigured component*, something that was mentioned in Chapter 5. A given component can be part of at most one COM+ Application on a particular machine, so there's never any ambiguity about which Application a component belongs to.

Components that are part of a COM+ Application are called configured components

Information about both kinds of components is stored in the registry of the machine on which they reside. For configured components, extra information is also stored in a database separate from the registry called RegDB. The information about configured and unconfigured components in the registry and the information about configured components stored in RegDB are referred to collectively as the COM+ Catalog. Information in this catalog can be accessed either using the Component Services administrative tool, which is an MMC snap-in, or directly through the ICOMAdminCatalog interface implemented by the standard COMAdminCatalog object. When a client creates a new object from a configured component, the COM runtime examines the catalog to learn about the object and determine what services it requires. How this works is described next.

Object Creation in COM+

Clients can remain unaware of what services the COM runtime is providing to objects

To a client running on a desktop machine and accessing configured components on some server, the COM runtime provides its services transparently—a client need do nothing special to use it. Instead, a client creates a COM object like always, invokes its methods, then releases the object when it's no longer needed. The COM runtime silently provides whatever services this object has requested from it.

A configured component's attributes affect the context of objects created from that component

But how does the COM runtime know what those services are? The answer is that every configured component has a set of *attributes* specified for it, which are stored mostly in RegDB. Exactly how the values for these attributes can be set will be described throughout this chapter; the key point to understand now is that when an object is created, the COM runtime examines these attributes and uses them in creating an appropriate *context* for the new object. Based on the information in this context, the COM runtime can determine what services this object requires.

Clients can create objects from configured components using CoCreateInstance as usual

Figure 8-3 illustrates one simple creation scenario. In this example, a desktop client requests creation (also known as *activation*) of the object in the normal way, using CoCreateInstance or whatever call is appropriate in the client's programming language. (This example assumes a DCOM client. With a Web client, the creation call might be issued by an ASP page running on the Windows 2000 server machine that is executing in response to a user request sent via HTTP from a browser.) Although it's not shown in the figure, the client's request causes the COM runtime on the client machine to examine that system's registry as described in Chapter 5, then pass the creation request to the server machine.

Next, the COM runtime on the server system looks up CLSID_X in that machine's COM+ Catalog. There, it finds a wealth of information about the class this CLSID names. Most fundamentally, it learns whether the CLSID references a configured component or an unconfigured component. As described in Chapter 5, if CLSID_X references an unconfigured component, all information about this class is stored in the registry. Assuming that CLSID_X references a configured component, however, the COM runtime finds the same basic information in the registry as it would for an unconfigured class, such as what file contains the code for this class. But the COM runtime also finds lots of information for a configured component in RegDB, including what COM+ Application this component belongs to, the values of the various attributes that have been configured for it, and more. Given all of this information, the COM runtime can now create the object, making sure that it's instantiated in the correct process. The COM runtime also creates the appropriate in-memory context for the object, one that includes all of the settings configured for the class in the catalog.

An object's context is affected by what's in the COM+ Catalog for the object's class

Figure 8-3 *During activation, the COM runtime examines the attributes configured for an object, then creates an appropriate context for that object.*

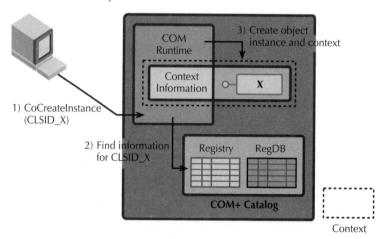

So far, we've been assuming that the creator of an object managed by the COM runtime is a client with no context of its own. But suppose that once this simple client has created a new COM object as just described, this object itself wishes to create another object. Now what happens?

The process can look much the same. As Figure 8-4 shows, however, there are some important differences. As before, the running object X can issue a CoCreateInstance or whatever call is appropriate for its language, and the COM runtime will perform the necessary steps to create the object. As shown in the figure, the runtime looks up CLSID_Y in the COM+ Catalog, then finds the necessary information about this class and uses it to create the object correctly.

An object's context might contain information inherited from its creator

In this case, the object's creator already has a context, and the information it contains must be taken into account during the creation process. If the new object's attributes are exactly compatible with those of its creator, the new object will not have a new context created for it. Instead, it will share the context of its creator. If there are any differences between the two object's requirements, though, which is by far the more common case, the COM runtime will create a new context for the new object. The values it places in this new context will be derived from the information it found in the catalog, of course, but also from the values in the context of the object's creator. Depending on a variety of things, some of the creator's attributes can be passed down to the new object. What these attributes might be is described later in this chapter, but for now it's enough to understand that when one object creates another, the new object's context contains information derived from both the COM+ Catalog and the context of its creator.

A call to an object in another context uses a lightweight proxy

One last point worth making about contexts is that cross-context calls—method invocations between COM objects in the same apartment but with different contexts—entail a bit of overhead. While the stubs and proxies used for calls between machines, processes, or apartments aren't required, calls between objects that share an apartment but not a context do make use of similar software called *lightweight proxies*. The COM runtime creates and uses these proxies automatically, so a developer never sees them. Still, their existence means that sharing an interface pointer across different contexts requires special care from developers.[1]

Figure 8-4 *When one object creates another, the new object can inherit some values from or even completely share its creator's context.*

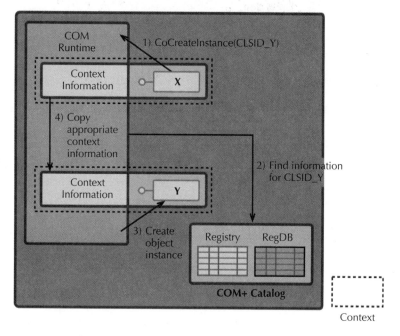

Accessing Context Information

Virtually every object managed by the COM runtime needs to interact with its context and with the runtime itself. To allow this, the COM runtime exposes several different interfaces, each of which contains methods that allow a running object to work with

Objects access their context through IObjectContext and other interfaces

---

1. Catching calls between objects with different contexts is known as *interception*. Microsoft has talked about someday opening up interception, allowing third-party software to insert itself in the call path. In COM+ 1.0, however, this is not possible.

its context information. Among these is IObjectContext, an interface originally provided by the now-defunct MTS Executive. COM+ adds other interfaces that refactor the functions in IObjectContext, providing the same methods but grouping them together differently, and that add a few new features. These new interfaces include IObjectContextInfo, ISecurityCallContext, and IContextState, and they're described later in this chapter. Some might argue that since these new interfaces largely replace the services of IObjectContext, new applications should use them rather than this older interface. Yet IObjectContext remains the simplest way to access the core services of COM+, and so for most of this discussion, I'll assume the use of this traditional interface.[2]

Objects call CoGetObjectContext to get a pointer to IObjectContext

To invoke the methods in IObjectContext, an object must acquire a pointer to this interface. IObjectContext is implemented by an object called ObjectContext (sometimes referred to as the context object). As shown in Figure 8-5, to get an interface pointer to IObjectContext, a COM object can call GetObjectContext (in Visual Basic) or CoGetObjectContext (in C++), which are API functions provided by the COM runtime. Once it has this pointer, the object can call IObjectContext's methods to make use of various services provided by the COM runtime. An important example of these services is automatic transactions, our next topic.

Automatic Transactions

As described in the previous chapter, the all-or-nothing behavior of a transaction is often required in carrying out a business process. While it's possible to control transactions in a DBMS using ADO, or to manage distributed transactions using DTC directly, COM+ provides another solution that's easier and more appropriate for three-tier applications: *automatic transactions*. Under the

---

2. One exception is IObjectContext's CreateInstance method. This method was important in MTS, as it was the only way for one MTS object to create another. Today, although it still works, IObjectContext::CreateInstance is largely a legacy. In all cases, COM objects can now create other COM objects using the standard CoCreateInstance call.

covers, COM+ automatic transactions depend on DTC and, if a DBMS is involved, on the transaction manager functions of that DBMS. But automatic transactions provide a couple of important advantages over either of these approaches.

Figure 8-5 *An object can acquire a pointer to the IObjectContext interface of its ObjectContext by calling CoGetObjectContext.*

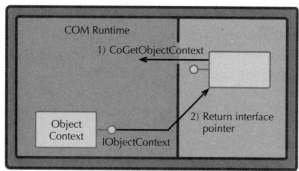

Windows 2000 Server

First, automatic transactions are simple to use. Once the designer and developer of an application understand how they work, creating components that use them is remarkably easy. Second, automatic transactions work very well with applications built from independent components. They allow a single component to be deployed in different ways, in different applications, and still get the transactional behavior it requires. A developer can build a transactional component that does one thing well and then potentially use it in multiple situations. While reusing business logic is an inherently hard problem, the automatic transactions provided by COM+ remove one obstacle to success.

Automatic transactions are simple to use and reuse

How Automatic Transactions Work
To begin understanding how automatic transactions work, think back to the DTC example from the previous chapter. In that example, a DTC client moved money from a savings account maintained in a SQL Server database to a checking account stored in an Oracle database, with DTC ensuring that either both updates

Automatic transactions shield developers from DTC

were executed or neither was. With COM+, a developer can accomplish the same thing without ever being aware of DTC. Instead, the creator of a COM object can implement a method called, say, MoveMoney, that takes three parameters: Source, the account from which money should be subtracted; Target, the account to which money should be added; and Amount, how much money should be moved. A client of that object can then invoke the MoveMoney method, passing in the appropriate values, to cause money to be transferred. By doing a few simple things, the method's implementer can use COM+'s automatic transactions to make sure that both queries succeed or neither does.

The COM runtime can automatically start a new transaction when a method call is made on an object

Figure 8-6 shows the first steps in this process. In step 1, the client invokes the MoveMoney method. (The diagram suggests that the client is a remote system making this call over DCOM, but the client could just as well be, say, an ASP page running on the same machine as the COM object that implements this method.) Because the object on which this call is invoked has been configured to use automatic transactions, this method call is intercepted by the COM runtime. As shown in step 2, the runtime examines the context information for the object to determine whether to start a new transaction. (Exactly how a component is configured to control this will be described shortly.) In this example, the object does require a transaction, so the COM runtime uses OLE Transactions to tell DTC to begin a new transaction.[3]

Resource managers are automatically enlisted in the transaction

The COM runtime then allows the method call to continue by invoking the implementation of MoveMoney provided by the developer of the COM object. This method begins executing, and as shown in step 3, issues its first SQL query, instructing SQL Server to decrement a particular savings account. Just as in the DTC discussion in the previous chapter, SQL Server will enlist in the active DTC transaction, then execute the query, as shown in step 4.

---

3. This is a slight simplification. In fact, the COM runtime puts off starting a transaction until it's really sure that the object will need one, such as when the object issues a database query.

To make these figures as clear as possible, I've omitted some of the details about DTC. Realize, however, that the DTC interactions are just as shown in the previous chapter. Also, although an OLE DB provider is used to access the DBMS's in this example, the interface seen by the COM object is most likely ADO.

Figure 8-6 *A client's method call can cause the COM runtime to begin a transaction, and issuing the first query enlists SQL Server in that transaction.*

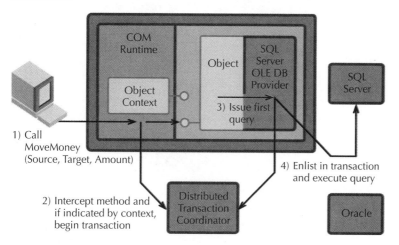

Next, as shown by step 5 in Figure 8-7, the MoveMoney method in the COM object issues its second SQL query, this one aimed at the Oracle database, specifying that money should be added to a specific checking account. Once again, the database is enlisted in the transaction, as shown in step 6, and the query is executed.

Once it has issued both queries, the MoveMoney method can inform the COM runtime that it has completed its work. There are two possible outcomes: either all went well, so the method wishes to commit all the work in this transaction, or something went wrong, which means the method wants to roll back all the work in this transaction. (Perhaps, for instance, there wasn't enough money in the account being debited to satisfy this request, or maybe the request to the Oracle database didn't succeed because of a network failure.) In either case, the MoveMoney

When its work is completed, a transactional object calls SetComplete or SetAbort method can inform the COM runtime of its wishes by invoking a method in IObjectContext, as shown in step 7 of Figure 8-8. If it wishes to commit the transaction, the method calls IObjectContext::SetComplete. If it wishes to abort the transaction, it calls IObjectContext::SetAbort.

Figure 8-7 *Issuing the second query enlists Oracle in this transaction.*

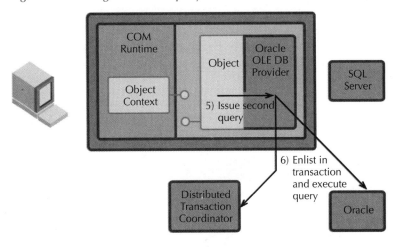

As shown in step 8, the COM runtime responds appropriately. If the object called SetComplete, it uses OLE Transactions to tell DTC to commit this transaction, while SetAbort causes it to tell DTC to abort this transaction. (Note that this is a simple example that includes only a single object in the transaction. Things are a bit more complex with transactions that include more than one object, as is described later.) In step 9, DTC carries out the COM runtime's request, using two-phase commit as described in the previous chapter.

The COM runtime tells DTC to commit or abort the transaction

Finally, once all of this is done and the transaction is ended, the MoveMoney method returns to its caller as shown in step 10. That caller has been entirely unaware of the complexities it has engendered—all it knows is that it asked a COM object to move some money. The fact that a transaction was involved is not directly visible to the caller.

Figure 8-8 *To end the transaction, the MoveMoney method calls SetComplete or SetAbort, and the COM runtime works with DTC to carry out this request.*

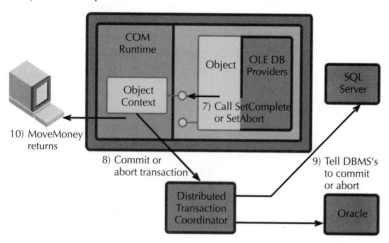

To help get a clear picture of what's happening in this example, here's a simple pseudocode depiction of the MoveMoney method:

```
MoveMoney(Source, Target, Amount)
    Issue SQL query to SQL Server subtracting Amount
        from Source
    Issue SQL query to Oracle adding Amount to Target
    Call GetObjectContext
    If Error Then
        Call ObjectContext.SetAbort
    Else
        Call ObjectContext.SetComplete
```

The method issues both queries, probably using the ADO objects described in Chapter 6, then calls GetObjectContext to acquire a pointer to its IObjectContext interface. If any problems arose during execution of the queries, MoveMoney calls the SetAbort method, while if all went well, it calls SetComplete.[4]

---

4. Note that transactional COM objects don't use any of the ADO methods to control transactions that were described in Chapter 6. Also, there's no simple way to set the isolation level at which a transaction will run. Instead, transactions initiated by the COM runtime always run at the Serializable isolation level, the strictest of the options described in Chapter 6.

The Auto-done attribute
allows not having to call
SetComplete and
SetAbort

As this example suggests, it's very common for every method in a component that's part of a COM+ Application to end with a call to either SetComplete or SetAbort. It's so common, in fact, that COM+ allows setting an attribute that effectively causes one of these calls to be made automatically. Called the Auto-done attribute, it can be set for one or more methods on a configured component. If Auto-done is turned on, the COM runtime will in effect automatically call SetComplete if the method does not return an error (and hasn't explicitly changed the default). If the method does return an error, the Runtime effectively calls SetAbort. The point is to free the programmer from having to end every method with boilerplate calls to SetComplete or SetAbort.

Configuring Components to Use Automatic Transactions

The COM runtime
decides whether to start
a new transaction based
on a component's
transaction attribute

There's one gaping hole in the description so far: how are components configured to allow the COM runtime to know whether to start a transaction when a new method call arrives? The answer is that configured components have a *transaction attribute*. This attribute can potentially be set in a programming environment, such as that provided by Visual Basic or Visual C++, or by using the Component Services administrative tool. However it's set, the value for this attribute is stored with the component's information in RegDB, then read when an instance of a class is created to become part of that new object's context information.

COM+ defines five possible values for the transaction attribute, which are:

- *Requires New* The COM runtime always begins a new transaction when it receives the first method call on an object created from a component with this value for its transaction attribute.

- *Required* If the creator of an object created from a component with this transaction attribute value is not itself part of a transaction, the COM runtime will begin a new transaction when it receives the first method call on this object. If the creator is already part of a transaction, however, the COM runtime will not start a new transaction when the first call arrives. Instead, the work performed by this method will become part of the creator's transaction.

- *Supported* The COM runtime never starts a new transaction when it receives a method call on an object created from a component with this transaction attribute value. If the creator of this object was already part of a transaction, the work performed by this method will become part of that transaction. If the creator did not belong to a transaction, the work performed by this method will not execute within a transaction.

- *Not Supported* As with Supported, the COM runtime never starts a new transaction when it receives a method call on an object created from a component with this transaction attribute value. Furthermore, even if the object's creator was already part of a transaction, the work performed by this method will execute outside of that transaction. Work carried out by methods in objects configured as Not Supported never executes inside a transaction, no matter what. This is the default value for the transaction attribute.

- *Disabled* As with Not Supported, work performed by methods in objects configured as Disabled never executes inside a COM+ automatic transaction. Unlike Not Supported, however, this option tells the COM runtime to ignore an object's transaction attribute value when determining whether it can share the context of the object that created it.

In the example shown in Figures 8-6 through 8-8, the object implementing MoveMoney must have had its transaction attribute set to either Requires New or Required. None of the other possible choices would have resulted in the COM runtime starting a new transaction when the client's call to this method arrived.

An object can check
whether it's running
within a transaction

What if the work performed by a component absolutely must be part of a transaction? It's possible that the component's transaction attribute has been set to, say, Not Supported by an ill-informed administrator. If the application is run in this state, all kinds of havoc might ensue. To prevent this, a method in the object can call IObjectContext::IsInTransaction. If this call returns true, the method is running within a transaction and all is well. If it returns false, however, something has gone wrong and the object can take appropriate action, such as writing an error message and shutting down.

Automatic Transactions with More Than One Object

One transaction can in-
clude work done by
multiple objects

COM+ automatic transactions that involve just one object are fairly simple. In real applications, however, it's common to group the work performed by methods that are in several different objects into a single transaction. For example, an application might include one COM component that knows how to record a customer's order for some product in a database and another one capable of charging the customer's credit card. Placing an order for that customer might well require invoking methods in both objects to ensure that all the work they perform is in a single transaction. It's important, then, to understand how automatic transactions work when multiple objects configured in multiple ways are involved.

The first issue to look at is how a transaction that includes multiple objects ends. The simple example shown earlier had only one object, so the transaction ended when that object called SetComplete or SetAbort. If a transaction includes several objects, however, the situation is more complicated. To understand how COM+ handles this situation, imagine a scenario like that shown in Figure 8-9. In step 1, a client creates a COM object of class A, an object whose code is in a configured component with its transaction attribute set to Requires New. In step 2, the client calls a method in object A. This method call is intercepted and, based on the value for the transaction attribute in this object's context, the COM runtime decides to start a new transaction. Just as in the previous example, the runtime tells DTC to start a new transaction, then passes the call to the actual method implementation in object A.

Figure 8-9 *A client's first method call on an object can cause the COM runtime to tell DTC to start a new transaction.*

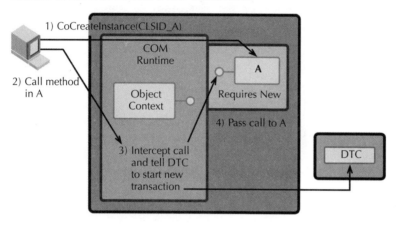

Next, suppose this method in A creates object B, as shown in step 5 of Figure 8-10. Suppose also that, as shown in the figure, B's transaction attribute is set to Required. Any work performed by B will now become part of the transaction already started by the COM runtime. When B is created, some information from A's context is copied into B's, such as an identifier for the transaction that both objects are now part of. The same thing happens in step 7 when A creates object C, which also has a transaction attribute of Required: it joins the existing transaction, and some information from A's context is copied into C's context, as shown in step 8. The three objects A, B, and C can be thought of as forming a transaction tree with A at the root.

Multiple objects in a transaction form a tree

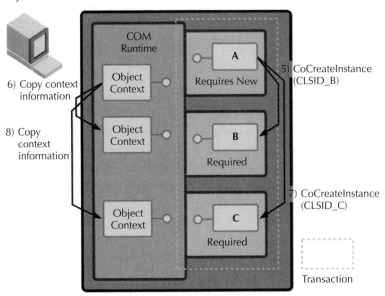

Figure 8-10 *When one object creates another, transaction information from the creator's context can be copied into the context of the new object.*

The root object's call to SetComplete or SetAbort causes a transaction to end

Now suppose that A calls a method in B, as shown in step 9 in Figure 8-11. This method does some work, such as updating a database, then, in step 10, calls SetComplete. The fact that B is done with its work and willing to commit the transaction is recorded in B's context, but the COM runtime does not end the transaction at this point. When more than one object is participating in the same transaction, the transaction ends after the root object calls SetComplete or SetAbort, not when any of the objects lower in the tree make these calls. So when, in step 11, A calls a method in C that does some work, then in step 12 that method also calls SetComplete, the transaction still isn't over.

To decide whether to commit or abort, the COM runtime checks the vote of every object in a transaction

This transaction will end when in step 13 of Figure 8-12 object A calls SetComplete.[5] At this point, the COM runtime examines the contexts of all the objects involved in this transaction—A, B, and C—as shown in step 14. If all objects in the transaction called

---

5. More precisely, the transaction will end when the method in A that calls SetComplete returns control to the COM runtime.

SetComplete, as in this example, the COM runtime will tell DTC to commit the transaction, shown in step 15. If any of them called SetAbort, however, the runtime will instruct DTC to roll back this transaction. Transactions are an all-or-nothing affair, so any breach of consensus means that all the work performed by all the resource managers accessed by all the objects in the transaction must be rolled back. Finally, in step 16, the method called by the client returns and the entire process is complete.

Figure 8-11 *Objects below the root of the transaction tree can't end the transaction by calling SetComplete.*

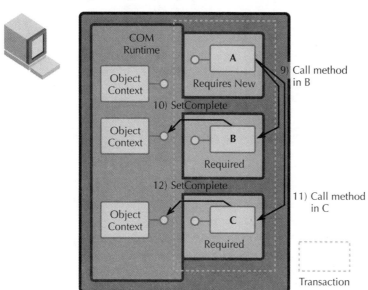

What happens if the root object calls SetComplete or SetAbort, but an object lower in the transaction tree hasn't yet called either one? Somewhat surprisingly, the vote for this lower object will be interpreted as if it had called SetComplete—the default is to commit. Yet suppose an object is participating in a transaction but must return to its caller while still in an intermediate state. It hasn't yet called either SetComplete or SetAbort, but it expects to be called again, at which time it will make one of these calls. In the meantime, though, it's not ready to commit. Yet if the root object calls SetComplete at this point, this object will by default

An object can change its default commit behavior

vote to commit. To avoid this situation, the object can call IObject-Context::DisableCommit before returning to its caller. Doing this changes the object's default vote to be interpreted as if the object had called SetAbort. An attempt to commit this transaction will now cause it to abort, and all of its work will be rolled back. When this object is willing to commit again, it can change its default vote by calling IObjectContext::EnableCommit. When the object is completely done with its work, however, it should call either SetComplete or SetAbort.

Figure 8-12 *The transaction ends when the root object in the transaction tree calls SetComplete or SetAbort.*

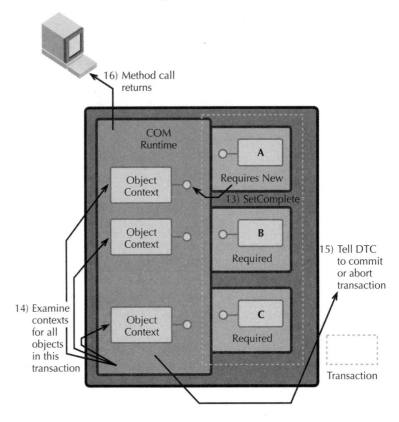

Another interesting issue is how the various transaction attribute settings interact. The example just described showed a relatively simple scenario, where all the work performed by three different

An object marked as Required can join its creator's transaction

objects was grouped into one transaction. Figure 8-13 shows another possibility. Here, a client creates an object from a component whose transaction attribute is set to Required. That object
then creates another object that's also marked as Required. The
client is software running on a desktop machine, and in this example it is not currently part of a transaction. Accordingly, the
first method call this client makes to object A will cause the COM
runtime to start a new transaction, since A requires one and its
caller isn't currently part of any transaction. When A creates and
calls into object B, however, which is also marked as Required,
the COM runtime does not begin a new transaction. Like A, B
must run inside a transaction, but since its creator is already part
of one, B will simply join this existing transaction. All work done
by both objects A and B will be part of the same transaction. And
as already described, this transaction will end when A, the root
object, calls either SetComplete or SetAbort.

Figure 8-13 *The work performed by objects A and B will be in the*
same transaction.

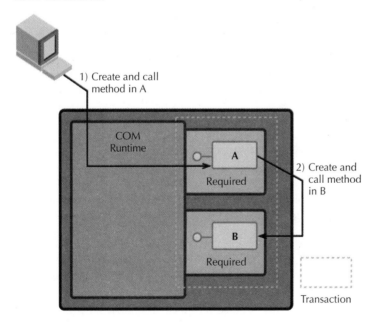

Figure 8-14 shows a slightly more complex situation. As before, a desktop client creates and invokes a method in object A, which is marked as Required, causing the COM runtime to begin a new transaction. A then creates and calls into object B, which in this example is marked as Supported. Supported really means "I don't care—I'll do whatever my creator is doing." In this case, since B's creator is already part of a transaction, B happily joins this transaction. But when A then creates and calls into object C, marked as Requires New, things change. C's transaction attribute setting tells the COM runtime that C insists on having its own transaction, regardless of what its creator is doing. As a result, the COM runtime starts an entirely separate transaction that will include all work done by C. The transaction that includes objects A and B will end when A calls SetComplete or SetAbort, while C's transaction will end only when C makes one of these calls. These two transactions are in no way related—like DTC, COM+ can't be used to create nested transactions—so the outcome of one will not affect the outcome of the other.

Figure 8-15 shows one more possibility. Here, objects A and B are created and used just as in the previous example. Object C, however, marked as Required, is created on another Windows 2000 server machine. This fact makes absolutely no difference— C still joins A's transaction, just as if it were created on the same machine as A. Objects can belong to the same transaction whether they're in the same process, in different processes on the same machine, or in different processes on different machines. The COM runtime and DTC hide the details of the location from developers.

One perhaps surprising point to notice about automatic transactions is that an object involved in a transaction often won't know how that transaction ultimately turns out. In the multi-object transactions just described, for example, the root object might call SetComplete, yet because some object lower in the tree has already called SetAbort, the entire transaction will be aborted. Even in a transaction that includes only a single object, it's possible that the object's SetComplete request might not result in the transaction committing. It's always possible, for example, that a DBMS involved in the transaction decides that it must abort during the two-phase commit process, causing the entire transaction to be rolled back.

Figure 8-14 *Because C is marked as Requires New, two separate transactions are created in this scenario.*

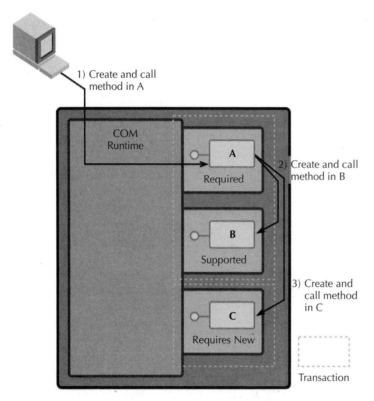

Developers of transactional COM components should strive to create components that do their job, whatever it might be, then issue their vote: SetComplete or SetAbort. Ideally, these components shouldn't care what other components in the same transaction are doing, or even whether there are any other components in the same transaction. In some cases, though, this isn't practical.

An object might inform its caller that it is aborting the transaction

For example, if a component lower in the transaction tree decides that it must call SetAbort, the root object might be able to avoid doing time-consuming work that's doomed to be rolled back anyway. To make this possible, the subordinate object might pass back a parameter to its caller or raise an error to indicate its decision to abort. By checking this value before proceeding, that caller can then decide whether it's worth doing more work.

Figure 8-15 *Objects on different machines can belong to the same transaction.*

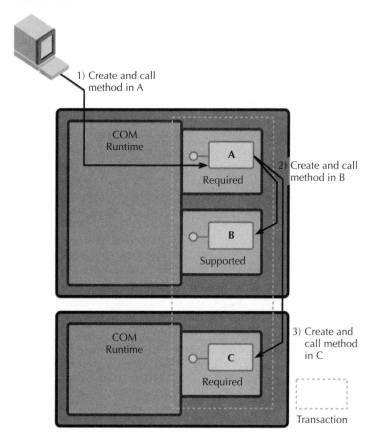

The original client learns whether a transaction commits or aborts

Realize, however, that the original client, such as an ASP page that invoked the first method, always learns what happens, because the client sees the return code of the method it invoked. If all went well, this return code will indicate success. If the transaction aborted, however, even if the abort was caused by a DBMS during the two-phase commit process, the COM runtime will modify the return code sent back by the method, ensuring that the client is informed that its request has failed.

One final topic worth mentioning here is the transaction context object, a standard component provided with COM+. Rather than letting transaction boundaries be established automatically, this object allows a client to explicitly group objects into a transaction. There are two important points to understand about the transaction context object. First, don't confuse it with the object context that provides the IObjectContext interface—despite having similar names, the two are entirely separate. Second, realize that you never need to use this object. The mechanism it provides is built on top of automatic transactions, so you're not really getting any extra functionality. Also, the transaction context object has various limitations—it must run in the same process as its client, for example, which is problematic for remote clients. In general, developers should rely directly on automatic transactions rather than using the transaction context object. It seldom, if ever, buys you anything.

The transaction context object allows a client to group objects into a transaction

Transaction Timeouts

Ideally, every transaction an application executes should be short. Since each transaction typically locks some amount of data, allowing a transaction to last for more than a second or two will make that data inaccessible to other transactions. This can make an application slow, since other transactions might be blocked waiting for a long-running transaction to complete. A good application designer will do her best to ensure that no transaction runs for too long.

Transactions should be short

But there's one situation in which transactions can inadvertently take a long time. Suppose that a transaction executed by object X needs to access both the savings and checking accounts of a particular customer. Suppose also that another transaction, this one

Transactions can deadlock

being executed simultaneously by object Y, needs to access those same two accounts. Now imagine that object X first accesses and locks the savings account, while object Y first accesses and locks the checking account. Each object needs the account locked by the other, and neither can proceed until it gets it. The result, of course, is deadlock—both transactions are stuck.

The COM runtime will abort transactions that exceed their transaction timeout

To solve this problem, the COM runtime enforces a transaction timeout. Set using the Component Services administrative tool, this value controls how long a transaction can last before it is automatically aborted. The default value is 60 seconds, but it can be set to any number between 0 and 3600. Setting the transaction timeout to zero effectively turns it off, allowing transactions to run indefinitely. While this can be useful during debugging, it's not a good thing to do for a production application, if only because deadlocks might go undetected and block indefinitely.

Don't return control to a person during a transaction

The existence of the transaction timeout has a significant impact on the design of a COM+ application. To see why, imagine an object that uses transactions but in which not every method ends with a call to SetComplete or SetAbort. In this case, a transaction will begin when the client makes its first call on this object, but it won't end until the client invokes a method in the object that includes a call to SetComplete or SetAbort.[6] This means that in the midst of a single transaction, control will return to the client. As long as the client invokes a method that calls SetComplete or SetAbort before the transaction timeout period, all is well. But suppose the client returns control to a human user in the middle of an active transaction. People tend to get distracted, and so this user might well get involved in a conversation, decide to get coffee, or do something else that takes longer than the transaction timeout

---

6. It's a rare case, but a transaction will also end if a client calls IUnknown::Release on the root object in a transaction tree. By default, the COM runtime treats this situation as if the root object had called SetComplete, and so will attempt to commit the transaction.

period. If this happens, the transaction will abort, probably leaving this user mystified and unhappy. The upshot is that it's virtually never safe to return control to a human being in the middle of a transaction. Instead, each transaction should be short, and each one should implement a single request as seen by a user.

Automatic transactions are useful, and most COM+ Applications will take advantage of them. Building effective, scalable enterprise applications requires more, however, so the COM runtime (and, despite its name, MTS before it) provides much more. As described next, for example, it provides interesting services for managing an object's state.

Object Lifetime Services

Suppose that, like most banks, QwickBank allows its customers to check account balances, transfer money, and make other requests over the phone. To support this, QwickBank might operate a call center, a group of employees sitting at workstations who spend their days answering the phone and doing work on behalf of the bank's customers. Let's assume that the software these employees use is a three-tier application built on Windows 2000, with Visual Basic clients using DCOM to communicate with transactional COM objects in the middle tier, and with those objects accessing a pair of databases. Figure 8-16 gives a simple picture of how this application might look.

As the figure shows, each client has its own object. With the transactional objects typically used in this kind of application, clients don't generally share objects. While each object accessed directly by a client might well be of the same class, every client has its own distinct instance of that class. This means that if an application has 500 simultaneous clients, there could potentially be 500 objects existing at the same time, each servicing a single client.

Clients of a COM+ Application generally don't share objects

Figure 8-16 *Rather than sharing the objects in a running COM+ Application, each client has its own.*

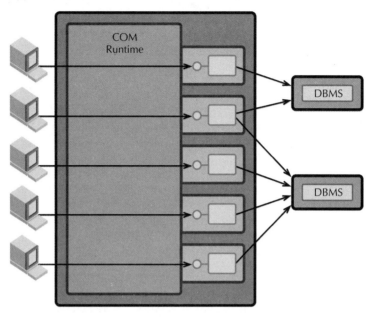

To allow an application to scale well, its objects must share resources

But does this make sense? Is allowing all of these objects to exist all of the time the best use of the available resources on the middle-tier server machine? After all, every running object takes up some memory, uses a thread, perhaps has an open connection to the DBMS, and more. To make this application as scalable as possible, which really means making it capable of supporting the largest possible number of clients with the least amount of hardware in the middle tier, we'd like to make sure that each object is using these resources only when it absolutely needs to. By preventing an object from holding on to resources it isn't currently using, we can allow some other object to use those resources. Especially for applications with a substantial number of clients, forcing objects to share resources like this can significantly improve scalability.

To see how this might work, think about a typical phone call that an employee working in this call center might handle. Imagine that the customer wishes to make two funds transfers: first from account P to account Q, then from account R to account S. When the call begins, she tells the bank employee her name and probably provides other information to verify her identity. Next, she requests the first transfer, reciting the numbers of accounts P and Q along with the amount to transfer, and the employee performs this operation. (In fact, his client software probably invokes the MoveMoney method described earlier.) Because QwickBank has customers all over the country, and because the company's managers have instructed its call center employees to be friendly, the bank employee next asks the customer what the weather is like in her city, and they talk about this for a moment. The customer then gives the account numbers and amount for the second transfer, and the employee once again invokes MoveMoney. Both parties say goodbye, and the phone call ends.

This entire interaction might have lasted for, say, five minutes. But for how much of that time was it really necessary to have an active object running on the middle-tier server on behalf of this client? The answer is almost certainly no more than a couple of seconds, which is the time it took to actually perform the two transactions that were requested. Given this, why have an object hanging around eating up resources for the entire employee/customer interaction? Especially for applications that want to support a large number of clients on the smallest possible middle-tier server, that makes no sense.

Objects used by people sit idle most of the time

One obvious solution would be to have the client software running on the bank employee's workstation explicitly create the object before each transfer, then release it when this single transaction is completed. This would complicate the client code, however, and also burn up a substantial amount of network and machine resources. A better solution, the one provided by COM+, is to provide Just-In-Time (JIT) activation.

JIT Activation

The COM runtime intercepts every client call made to a configured component

JIT activation depends on the fact that the COM runtime can intercept every call made on objects configured to use this service. Figure 8-17 shows a general picture of the path taken by each call the client makes on an object managed by the COM runtime. As described in Chapter 5, calls to objects outside the client's apartment first go to a proxy, then get passed to a stub. With an unconfigured component, the stub will directly invoke the method in the target object. With a configured component, however—one that's been made part of a COM+ Application—the stub invokes a method provided by the COM runtime, which is how the runtime is able to insert itself in the call path. The runtime in turn eventually invokes the actual method in the target object.

Figure 8-17   *Calls to objects in COM+ Applications pass through the usual proxy and stub, then through the runtime itself, before being given to the target object.*

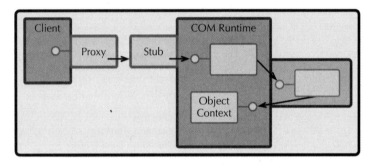

The COM runtime deactivates an object after the object calls SetComplete or SetAbort

When that method completes, however, it very likely calls SetComplete or SetAbort. If JIT activation is turned on for a configured component, which is required for components that use transactions, something interesting happens at this point. Whenever a method in an object using JIT activation calls IObjectContext::SetComplete or IObjectContext::SetAbort, then returns control to the COM runtime, the runtime calls Release on that object and the object is deactivated. The client does not see this directly, however. Instead, deactivating an object places things in the state shown in Figure 8-18: the client has a proxy, which can

Chapter Eight

communicate to a stub, which in turn is connected to the COM runtime. All that's missing is the object itself.

The client isn't aware of the object's demise, however. It still has an interface pointer to a proxy, as always, and so it can happily invoke another method on this object. When this method call arrives at the server, the COM runtime will notice that it has no object to handle the call, and just in time, it will create a new instance of this class, returning things to the situation shown in Figure 8-17. The runtime then invokes the method in the new object, which executes, then probably calls SetComplete or Set-Abort. The COM runtime again releases the object, and the situation reverts to that shown in Figure 8-18. Not until the client calls Release on the object will the proxy and stub be destroyed. Until then, the client can continue making method calls, and the COM runtime will take care of activating and deactivating the object as required.

When a client invokes a method on a deactivated object, the COM runtime creates a new instance of that object

Figure 8-18 *An object that calls SetComplete or SetAbort is deactivated, leaving its stub and proxy in place.*

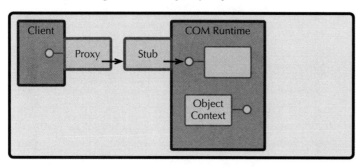

To get a more concrete sense of how this works, think once again about the call center example described earlier. Imagine that the bank employee boots his workstation when he arrives each morning, then starts the client piece of this application. Since we're assuming a Visual Basic client communicating with the middle tier through DCOM, it's very likely that this client issues a CoCreateInstance request immediately upon startup. This

A client can rely on what looks like the same object for many unrelated transactions

causes the object to come into existence, as already described. If we assume that all our fictitious bank employee can do is transfer money between accounts, he will rely on this same object all day, using it for every MoveMoney request he carries out. Unknown to him, however, the object will in fact be activated and deactivated over and over throughout the day.

If the user were at a Web browser rather than a Visual Basic client, requests would arrive at the middle-tier server via HTTP. In this case, each request might cause an ASP page to be executed, and this page would create the object. However, the object will typically be destroyed—not just deactivated—between every request from the user. This is because ASP pages are started when a request arrives from a browser, then destroyed when that request ends. By default, any COM objects a page creates are also destroyed when the page's execution completes. In this scenario, the phone teller would not use the same object all day, but would instead have a new one created for each request he makes.

JIT activation allows an object to exist only when it's needed

Assuming our original example with a Visual Basic client, however, the situation is this: the bank employee is sitting at his workstation waiting for a customer call. That client has issued a CoCreateInstance, so it has an interface pointer to the object whose methods it wishes to invoke. When the customer calls, nothing happens until the bank employee handling this call makes the transfer request. This causes the Visual Basic client to invoke MoveMoney in the object managed by the COM runtime on the middle-tier server, at which point this object is created. As described in the previous section, this method debits one account, adds to another, then calls either SetComplete or SetAbort to end the transaction. When this method returns control back to the COM runtime, the runtime calls Release on the object that implements MoveMoney and it is deactivated. When the customer requests her next transfer, the client invokes MoveMoney again, the object is activated, and the method executes again. When it completes, the object is deactivated and so frees any resources it was using. No matter how long the bank employee is on the phone with this customer, the object exists—and eats up resources—only when it's absolutely needed, that is, only when it is actually executing a method.

As noted earlier, every method in every object need not end with a call to SetComplete or SetAbort. It's possible for a client to make multiple calls to a single object, then have only the last method invoked call SetComplete or SetAbort. In this case, the object will not be destroyed and reactivated on every method call. Realize, however, that if this object is using transactions, the transaction timer will cause the transaction to abort and the object to be destroyed if neither SetComplete nor SetAbort is called within the allotted time period.

For components that don't use transactions, JIT activation can be turned off. But components whose transaction attribute is set to Requires New, Required, or Supported will have JIT activation turned on automatically. Along with the improved scalability described earlier, this leads to another benefit. Because transactional objects are required to use JIT activation, those objects cannot maintain state—in-memory data—across a transaction boundary. When the transaction ends, the object is deactivated and its memory is freed. There is no way around this in COM+: ending a transaction means destroying all in-memory state maintained by the objects participating in that transaction.[7]

A transactional COM object can't maintain state internally across a transaction boundary

Recall that in COM+ an object doesn't necessarily know the ultimate outcome of a transaction. All it knows is what it voted to do: commit or abort. Suppose an object were allowed to maintain state across a transaction boundary, and that the state reflected a change made during this transaction, such as the new balance in a checking account. Now suppose this object called SetComplete, voting

Losing state, then refreshing it, can help make an application more correct

---

7. For this reason, people sometimes say that objects created from configured components are *stateless*. This isn't strictly true, since these objects can sometimes hold state between method calls, and they aren't always required to use JIT activation. Still, it does describe the most commonly used approach.

to commit the transaction it's part of. What happens if that transaction actually aborts? The object is never informed of this, yet the state it's maintaining is incorrect. If the object uses this state to satisfy the client's next method call, perhaps a request to examine the account's balance, it will return the wrong result. Coupling JIT activation with transaction boundaries forces the object to refresh its state, increasing the odds that the values it has will be correct. This coupling not only improves application scalability, it also improves application correctness.

Managing State

JIT activation requires managing state

While JIT activation certainly can help make applications more scalable and more correct, there's no denying that it also makes life harder for developers. Designing applications in which the middle-tier objects don't maintain state internally is a departure from what most developers have done in the past. As a result, using JIT activation requires thinking about an object's state in a new way.

Some objects have no state to maintain

If possible, applications that use this service shouldn't maintain middle-tier state at all. For example, the call center application described earlier might be able to get everything needed for a transaction from the customer, and then simply issue the transaction and get its results. If every transaction requires a new and different set of information, there's no need to maintain any state at all on the middle tier.

Maintaining state can sometimes be necessary, however

Real life is seldom so neat, however. Suppose, for instance, that QwickBank's call center application allows customers to ask questions about several accounts, and that those accounts might exist in many different databases stored in many different machines. Accessing all of this information is likely to be a slow process. To achieve acceptable performance, then, the first query issued for this customer might go out and read all of it, then store it locally. Later requests will be much faster, since the information they need will be readily accessible.

But where should this information be kept? It can't be maintained indefinitely in a transactional object, since that object's state is destroyed after every transaction. Several other possibilities exist, however, as illustrated in Figure 8-19.

Figure 8-19 *There are several different options for storing state when JIT activation is used.*

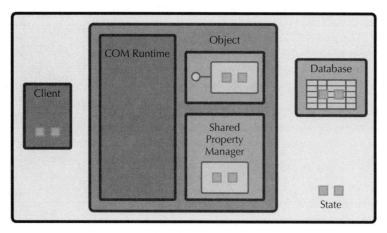

One choice is for a middle-tier object to pass its state back to its client before the transaction it belongs to ends. The client can then pass this state back to the object on the next method call. For small amounts of state, this approach is simple and convenient, but moving lots of information back and forth between the client and the middle-tier machine is problematic. As a result, storing state at the client is not very efficient if the state involved is large.

A client can store state for a deactivated object

Another option is to take advantage of the fact that objects managed by the COM runtime aren't required to use either transactions or JIT activation. If an object's transaction attribute is set to Not Supported, then JIT activation is turned off or the object never does anything that causes deactivation (such as calling SetComplete), this object will never be deactivated. It can create other transactional objects, all of which get deactivated when their transaction ends, but still store state on their behalf between transactions.

A transactional object can maintain its state for a short time

Yet another possibility is to store state in the Shared Property Manager (SPM). The SPM is a DLL that can be loaded into a process with the COM runtime and one or more configured components. An object can store information in the SPM, then pass a reference to that information back to its client. When the client next calls a method in this object, it passes this reference back. The newly JIT-activated object uses this reference to read the stored state from the SPM.

While the SPM is useful, it is relatively simple. It does not, for example, participate in transactions. If an object stores state in the SPM, then calls SetComplete, the transaction might still abort. If this happens, the state stored in the SPM is not rolled back—the SPM does not function as a resource manager. If this stored state is really a cached copy of data in this transaction, such as an account balance, it might not be correct after an abort. Also, cleaning up leftover state in the SPM can be a nuisance if a client crashes unexpectedly. For these reasons, the SPM often winds up being used more to allow objects in the same process to share state than to let those objects store state while they're deactivated.

A transactional object's
state can be stored in a
database

One final choice for storing state is to write it to a database. Once again, the client might be passed a key that's used by a JIT-activated object to identify which information to read back from the database. Since most COM+ Applications access one or more DBMS's, this is often a reasonable choice. Given that most DBMS's cache recently accessed information in memory, it can also be quite fast.

Object Pooling

Whatever its benefits, JIT activation can seem inefficient. Why keep destroying and recreating objects all the time? In fact, however, it's usually not so bad. Recreating an object's state can be slow, since it might require disk access, but recreating the object itself is typically not very time-consuming. There are situations, however, where this is not true. In cases such as these, object pooling can be very useful.

Imagine a COM class whose methods allow accessing a multi-year history of fluctuations in the U.S. prime interest rate. Suppose that every time an object of this class is created it must read a large database of interest rate changes to build this history in its memory, an operation that takes a good deal of time. The object is creating a substantial amount of state that will be useful to any client that uses it. For this object, ordinary JIT activation will be slow, since the object must perform an expensive initialization operation every time it is created.

Extensive initialization can make JIT activating an object slow

Object pooling can help in situations like this. If a component is configured to be pooled, objects created from that component are not destroyed when one of their methods calls SetComplete or SetAbort. Instead, they are placed in a pool with other objects of the same class. When a client invokes a method on a deactivated object of this class, a new instance of that class is not created. Instead, an existing object is chosen from the pool and assigned to that client.

Object pooling allows reusing a pooled object instance rather than creating a new one

One more important example of objects that can have per-class state is objects that maintain open connections to a DBMS. Recall from Chapter 6 that both ODBC and OLE DB automatically provide database connection pooling, allowing an object to avoid the expense of setting up and tearing down new connections. Pooled objects can also maintain open connections to a DBMS, however, as long as any of those connections can be used by any client that might be assigned an object of the pooled class. This allows a developer to implement his own database connection pooling. You might choose to do this, for example, if you want your application to build an initialized pool of open connections before any client requests come in, which is something that's not done by the ODBC or OLE DB pooling mechanisms.

Objects with open database connections can be pooled

Pooling does have some restrictions, however. To be pooled, a component can't have thread affinity—that is, it must be able to run on any thread. In Microsoft Visual Studio 6, this limitation makes it impossible to create pooled components using Visual Basic. Also, resource managers accessed by pooled objects can't be automatically enlisted in a transaction, as they typically are with ordinary transactional objects. Instead, the developer of a pooled object must write code that manually enlists any resource managers that participate in transactions.

An object can control whether it is pooled

An object can control whether it's willing to be pooled by implementing the IObjectControl interface. This interface includes the CanBePooled method, which is called by the COM runtime before an object is deactivated. If this call returns true and the component is configured to be pooled, this object instance will be pooled rather than deactivated. IObjectControl also includes two other methods, Activate and Deactivate, that are called by the COM runtime immediately after an object is activated and immediately before it is deactivated, respectively. They can be used to perform initialization and cleanup operations if desired, even if object pooling is not being used.

Pooled objects can't maintain state on behalf of a particular client

Object pooling is primarily useful for objects that acquire and maintain a significant amount of per-class state that will be useful to any client using an object of this class. It's not useful for objects that maintain specific state information on behalf of a specific client. In other words, you can't use object pooling to maintain per-client state, because there's no way to ensure that a client is assigned any particular object instance on its next method call. In practice, while this feature will improve the performance of some applications, it won't be useful in every situation.

Concurrency Services

Configured components can use Apartment model threading

Chapter 5 described the idea of COM apartments, mechanisms that make it possible to work with multithreaded applications using COM. Since COM+ Applications are always built from DLLs, each configured component can have a threading model set in the registry. One possible choice for this value is Apartment, ensuring that all objects running in a particular single-threaded apartment (STA) will execute on that apartment's lone thread. This was typically what MTS components did, so many existing applications work this way.

As mentioned in Chapter 5, however, Windows 2000 introduces a new type of apartment: the neutral apartment, also referred to as the thread-neutral apartment (TNA). Every process has at most one TNA, but unlike STAs and multi-threaded apartments (MTAs), no thread in a process actually resides in the TNA. Instead, threads can execute in this apartment as required. Going forward, it's likely that many configured components will set their threading model registry attribute to Neutral (or perhaps Both, which also allows running in the TNA) rather than Apartment. To understand why, it's necessary to think about what apartments provide and how the advent of contexts in COM+ affects this.

Most configured components will eventually use threading models other than Apartment

STAs really address two problems: concurrency control and thread affinity. Because all objects in an STA share one thread, only one method in one of those objects can be executing at any given time. This simplifies life for a developer, freeing her from concerns about possible concurrent access to her object. STAs also provide a way to ensure that code with thread affinity, which primarily means code written in Visual Basic, will always run on the same thread.

But starting with Visual Studio 7, Visual Basic is scheduled to no longer have thread affinity, which eliminates one reason for using STAs. If we assume that thread affinity is no longer an inescapable concern (which isn't true at the moment this book is being written but should be soon), then the problem that remains is controlling concurrent access to objects. Rather than depending solely on the traditional notion of apartments to address this, the Windows 2000 COM runtime provides another abstraction: *activities*. Activities first appeared in MTS, and Windows 2000 activities can still behave just as they did in MTS—they have to, or existing code would break—but they can do more as well. Like so much else in the COM+ world, activities are based on contexts.

Configured components can use activities for concurrency control

In COM today, an apartment is really a specific group of contexts within a single process. If the apartment is an STA, only one thing at a time is happening inside it—that is, only one method in any of the STA's objects can be executing at any given moment. An activity is in some ways quite similar. Like an apartment, an activity is a specific group of contexts. As shown in Figure 8-20, however, a single activity can include contexts in multiple apartments. If all of those contexts are in the same process, an activity can also ensure that only one method is executing in any of the objects those contexts contain. In Figure 8-20, for example, two objects in this process's TNA are in the same activity, which guarantees that only one method in one of those objects will be executing at any given moment. Assuming that thread affinity isn't an issue, activities can provide concurrency control in a more flexible way than STAs.

Figure 8-20 *An activity is a group of contexts that can have a single flow of control.*

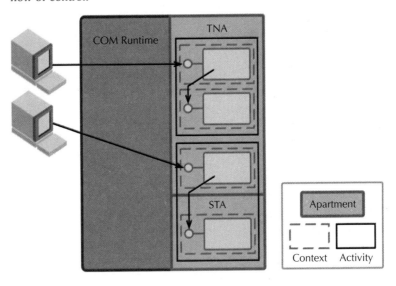

As Figure 8-20 shows, objects running in different apartments, such as the NTA and an STA, or even in a process's MTA, can also have their work synchronized if they belong to the same activity. One thing that makes activities more useful than apartments, however, is that a single activity can contain contexts in multiple processes running on multiple machines. Figure 8-21 illustrates this situation, showing one activity that includes four objects on two different machines. Those objects are running in three different contexts, each of which is in a different type of apartment, yet the COM runtime does its best to ensure that all calls made within this activity are synchronized. Although it's possible to cause multiple methods to execute simultaneously within an activity when the contexts it contains are not in the same process, it's usually true that all calls made within an activity are synchronized.

Figure 8-21 *An activity can span process and machine boundaries.*

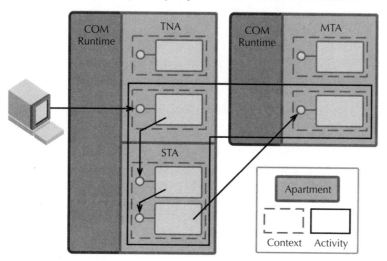

What activity an object runs in, and even whether it runs in one at all, depends on the value of a component's synchronization attribute. Like other attributes of a configured component, this attribute can be set using the Component Services administrative tool. The possible values for this attribute are like those for transactions:

A configured component's synchronization attribute determines how that component uses activities

- *Requires New* An object created from a component with this value for its synchronization attribute will always cause the COM runtime to create a new activity containing that object.

- *Required* If the creator of an object with this value for its synchronization attribute is already part of an activity, this object will join that activity. If the creator is not part of an activity, the COM runtime will start a new activity for the object.

- *Supported* This value causes the object to do whatever its creator is doing. If the creator is part of an activity, this object will join it. If the creator is not part of an activity, this object will execute without the protection from concurrent access that an activity offers.

- *Not Supported* No matter what the state of its creator, an object with this value for its synchronization attribute will never become part of an activity.

- *Disabled* This value indicates that the COM runtime should ignore the component's synchronization attribute when determining which context to place a new object in.

Objects using transactions and/or JIT activation must use activities

For objects that use transactions, JIT activation, and/or run in an STA, which covers the majority of objects in COM+ Applications, activities are required to protect against concurrent access—they can't be turned off. Objects in COM+ Applications that don't use transactions or JIT activation, however, and that can run in either an MTA or TNA have a few more options. By setting the synchronization attribute of a configured component, it's possible to use activities to control concurrent access to objects without relying on STAs. While STAs were a workable solution, the declining need for thread affinity and the rise of contexts makes activities a more attractive approach for controlling concurrent access to many COM objects.

Security Services

As described in Chapter 1, distributed security is made up of several different services, the most important of which are authentication, authorization, data integrity, and data privacy. All of these can be useful in COM+ Applications. In keeping with its general philosophy, COM+ allows requesting these services administratively by setting options on configured components, so developers aren't required to write code to use them.

Authentication, Integrity, and Privacy

A COM+ Server Application's choices for authentication, data integrity, and data privacy are all configured with a single setting. The possible values for this setting are the same as those listed for the authentication level parameter in COM's CoInitializeSecurity call in the "Providing Security" section in Chapter 5. (In fact, COM+ Applications should never explicitly call CoInitializeSecurity.) By default, COM+ Library Applications take on the authentication settings of the process into which they're loaded, so configuring this value is only possible with COM+ Server Applications.

COM+ Server Applications can have administratively configured security settings

Authorization

The COM runtime also provides interesting and useful services for authorization. To get an idea of what it offers, think again about the QwickBank call center application described earlier. Suppose that this application allows the tellers who answer the phone to transfer money between accounts, but requires a manager to stop payment on an outstanding check. Suppose too that the application provides some functions, such as checking built-in performance statistics, that can only be accessed by system administrators. The authorization services built into the COM runtime in Windows 2000 make these kinds of rules quite simple to enforce.

The COM runtime provides authorization services

COM+ authorization depends on the notion of *roles*. A role is a set of Windows 2000 users or groups, and what roles can be used with a particular COM+ Application are defined by its creator. For instance, the QwickBank call center Application might have three roles defined for it: Teller, Manager, and Administrator. But while an Application's creator defines what roles that Application is aware of, she does not specify which users and groups belong to which roles. Because the assignment of users to roles will vary with different installations of the Application, an administrator on the system performs this configuration when it is installed.

A role is a set of users and/or groups

Once roles have been defined for an Application, the access
rights for each role can be specified administratively. As Figure
8-22 shows, role-based authorization is performed by the COM
runtime, not by the objects themselves. As seen by, say, a DBMS,
all of the objects in a COM+ Application can have the same security identity, and all of them can have the same access rights. This
greatly improves the ability to share database connections using
the connection pooling features described in the previous chapter.
Because of JIT activation, objects typically acquire and release
those connections on every method call, so taking advantage of
database connection pooling can help significantly in achieving
good performance.

Figure 8-22 *Role-based authorization is performed by the COM
runtime.*

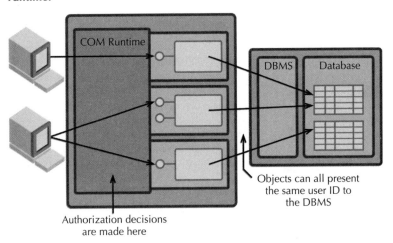

Role-based authorization can be set at the component, interface,
or method level.[8] That is, clients can be granted access to an entire
component, to specific interfaces on a component, or even to particular methods on a component based on their roles. All of this is
accomplished using the Component Services administrative tool—

---

8. Method-level authorization checks are new in COM+—MTS allowed checking
   only for interfaces or entire components.

these settings don't appear in the code of the components themselves. To determine at runtime whether security has been configured for a component, a method in that component can call the method IsSecurityEnabled in the IObjectContext interface of its object context.

Figure 8-23 shows an example of how this might look. Two clients are shown, one in the Teller role and the other in the Manager role, along with three objects, all of which belong to the same COM+ Application. The uppermost object in the figure has been configured to allow access to either Tellers or Managers, and so both clients shown here can invoke any of the methods in any of its interfaces. The middle component has been set to allow access only to Managers, which means that the COM runtime will block calls to any of its methods made from Tellers or Administrators. The bottom component has each of its two interfaces configured differently. The methods in one are accessible to both Tellers and Managers, while those in the other interface can be invoked only by clients in the Administrator role. Accordingly, a call from a Manager will be blocked, as the figure shows. And again, although it's not shown here, access rights can also be granted on a per-method basis if desired.

The COM runtime blocks calls from clients in the wrong roles

Figure 8-23 *Components, interfaces, and methods can be configured to grant access to clients based on roles.*

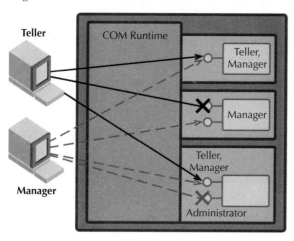

An object can make its own role-based authorization decisions

This kind of *declarative* role-based authorization can be quite useful. There are plenty of situations where it's not enough, however. For example, suppose this application allows tellers who answer the phone to make transfers of up to $100,000, but requires a manager to make transfers for more than this amount. While it would be possible to define two separate methods in one of this COM+ Application's objects, then configure each to allow access only by clients in the correct role, it might be simpler to use a single method. In this case, that method might make use of what's sometimes known as *programmatic* security. This feature relies on IsCallerInRole, another method provided by the IObjectContext interface. This method allows doing just what its name suggests, which is determining whether a caller is in a specific role. In the example just given, the code for the MoveMoney method might use this to check that any client attempting to transfer more than $100,000 is in the Manager role, rejecting the request if this condition isn't met.

Impersonation and Delegation

Role-based authorization isn't always the right choice

Role-based authorization, whether declarative or programmatic, is a fine solution when what you're trying to do is control which clients can execute specific chunks of code in a COM+ Application. Yet this kind of authorization isn't always enough. Think, for example, about the case where you're trying to control which data specific clients can access, rather than which code they can execute. In this situation, you might prefer to use the authorization functions of the DBMS itself to do this.

An object can impersonate its client if necessary

One important reason to make this choice is that database administrators (DBAs) are notoriously reluctant to trust the security of their data to anything but the DBMS. Relying on the role-based authorization in COM+, which must be both programmed and administered correctly to work, might make a DBA very nervous. Also, some kinds of data access, such as allowing specific users access to specific data, can't be provided very effectively using role-based authorization. In cases like these, each object in a

COM+ Application needs to access the DBMS using the identity of the client making the request. In other words, each object needs to impersonate its client. In some situations, an object impersonating a client must also access another process, such as a DBMS, across a machine boundary. Doing this requires delegation as well as impersonation.

The basic ideas of impersonation and delegation were described in Chapter 3, while a bit more about how these features are used in COM was described in Chapter 5. A method in an object that's part of a COM+ Application can impersonate its client just like a method in any COM object. And if the server's account is configured in Active Directory to be trusted for delegation and the client allows it, this server can make calls to other machines using this client's identity. Be aware, though, that impersonation typically means that each connection to a database is established using a specific user's identity. If this connection is pooled, it can be re-used only by that same user. This makes the database connection pooling described in Chapter 6 much less useful.

Learning About an Object's Caller

It's often useful for a running method in an object to learn the identity of the process that invoked it—its direct caller. When a number of objects are used together, each calling a method in the next, it can also be useful to learn the identity of the *original caller*—that is, the process that made the initial method call that got the ball rolling in the first place. To acquire this information, COM+ provides the ISecurityCallContext interface. Using its methods, an object can access a collection of information about its caller. This information includes the Security ID (SID) of the direct caller, the SID of the original caller, the minimum authentication level used on any of the calls in this call sequence, and more. ISecurityCallContext also includes the method IsCallerInRole, providing the same service as IObjectContext::IsCallerInRole, and a few others. ISecurityProperty effectively replaces an earlier

An object can use ISecurityCallContext to learn who its direct and original callers are interface provided with MTS, ISecurityProperty. In fact, COM+ Applications shouldn't use this older interface—some of its methods are no longer guaranteed to work correctly.

Providing good security for distributed applications is never simple. The security services built into the COM runtime can help, especially when role-based authorization fits the bill. But there's no substitute for understanding the problems to be solved and the services available, then thinking hard about the right approach.

Other COM+ Technologies

COM+ includes a rich (one might even say complex) set of features. This section provides short descriptions of a few more services this technology offers.

More on Accessing Context Information

The services provided by the COM runtime are built around the notion of contexts. Methods in IObjectContext, the interface first introduced with MTS, access an object's context, but in Windows 2000, new interfaces are also provided to work with this information. For example, the interface IObjectContextInfo offers the following set of methods:

- *IsInTransaction* Like IObjectContext::IsInTransaction, returns TRUE if the calling object is currently part of a transaction.

- *GetTransaction* Returns an interface pointer to the ITransaction interface of the current transaction. ITransaction is defined as part of OLE Transactions, and so its methods allow detailed access to information about the current transaction. This interface pointer might be used, for example, by a pooled object that needs to explicitly enlist a resource manager in a transaction.

- *GetTransactionId*   Returns an identifier (a GUID) for the current transaction.
- *GetActivityId*   Returns an identifier (a GUID) for the current activity.
- *GetContextId*   Returns an identifier (a GUID) for the current context.

Similarly, the IContextState interface introduced in COM+ allows very fine-grained control of when an object is deactivated and, if the object is part of a transaction, of whether it votes to commit or abort that transaction. These methods probably won't be called by most COM+ Applications—SetComplete and SetAbort in IObjectContext are generally sufficient—but they can be used if needed. The methods in this interface are:

IContextState allows detailed access to the done and consistent bits

- *SetDeactivateOnReturn*   This call sets the *done bit*, controlling whether the object should be deactivated when the method returns.
- *GetDeactivateOnReturn*   Returns the value of the done bit.
- *SetMyTransactionVote*   This call sets the *consistent bit*, controlling whether the object is willing to commit the transaction it belongs to.
- *GetMyTransactionVote*   Returns the value of the consistent bit.

The COM runtime relies on the values of these two bits to determine what action to take when a method returns. When a JIT-activated transactional object begins executing, the consistent bit is set to TRUE and the done bit is set to FALSE. By default, then, returning from a method without changing either of these values indicates that the object is willing to commit the transaction (because the consistent bit is TRUE) and doesn't yet wish to be deactivated (because the done bit is FALSE). While these bits can be

SetComplete, SetAbort, and other methods also set the done and consistent bits explicitly set using the calls just listed, other calls described earlier in this chapter also set these bits. Those calls and their resulting settings are:

- *SetComplete* Sets both the done bit and the consistent bit to TRUE. The object wishes to be deactivated and votes to commit the transaction.
- *SetAbort* Sets the done bit to TRUE and the consistent bit to FALSE. The object wishes to be deactivated and votes to abort the transaction.
- *EnableCommit* Sets the done bit to FALSE and the consistent bit to TRUE. The object does not wish to be deactivated and votes to commit the transaction.
- *DisableCommit* Sets the done bit to FALSE and the consistent bit to FALSE. The object does not wish to be deactivated and votes to abort the transaction.

Setting the auto-done attribute for a method also affects the value of these bits. Before the method is called, it changes the default setting of the done bit to TRUE, indicating that the object wishes to be deactivated when the method returns. When the method does return, the COM runtime determines whether the method completed successfully. If all went well, the runtime sets the consistent bit to TRUE, and this object will vote to commit the transaction. If an error was returned, the runtime sets the consistent bit to FALSE, and the object will vote to abort the transaction.

Constructors

COM objects can have constructors

Many object-oriented programming languages provide constructors when an object is created that carry information used to initialize the new object. Windows 2000 adds this ability to COM objects that are part of COM+ Applications. To take advantage of this ability, a constructor string can be set for a configured component using the Component Services administrative tool. For example, if a component must access a database of customers, and the name of the database will vary depending on the application in which this component is used, that name could be provided as a constructor string.

To use constructors, objects must implement the IObjectConstruct interface. When a new object is created, the method IObjectConstruct::Construct will be invoked by the COM runtime, passing the constructor string as a parameter. This string can then be accessed by the object and used to perform any required initializations.

COM+ Application Proxies

COM clients depend on proxies and perhaps type libraries to marshal method calls made to other objects. Traditionally, those proxies and type libraries were installed and registered manually on the client's machine, and doing this is still perfectly legal. In Windows 2000, however, all of the proxies, type libraries, and other information required to access all interfaces in all classes contained in a particular COM+ Application can be grouped together into an file called an *application proxy*.

A COM+ application proxy contains proxies, type libraries, and other information needed to access a COM+ Application

Application proxies are created using the Component Services administrative tool, and they're always packaged as .msi files suitable for use with the Windows Installer. This means that, given the appropriate Group Policy settings, application proxies can be deployed in Active Directory as assigned or published applications. Once that is done, everything a COM client needs in order to find and communicate with a COM+ Application can be located using Active Directory, then installed automatically. Although an entire COM+ Application can be downloaded on demand, the most interesting (and most common) case is when the COM+ Application is running on a different machine than its client. From now on in this section, I'll assume this situation.

Application proxies can be configured as assigned or published applications, then installed when needed

Recall from Chapter 2 that both assigned and published applications can be configured for either computers or users. I'll first describe what happens when an application proxy is configured via Group Policy as an assigned application, then look at what changes when it's a published application.

The simplest case is when an application proxy is configured as an assigned application for a computer. In this situation, the application proxy will be located using Active Directory and downloaded when that computer boots. When a client attempts to create an object in the COM+ Application referenced by this application proxy, everything it needs to access the Application will already be present.

If the application proxy is configured as an assigned application for a user, an Active Directory query is issued when the user logs in. That results in a minimal install: information is placed in the client's registry, but the application proxy is not actually downloaded or installed. When an application started by this user calls CoCreateInstance or another creation call, the COM runtime goes directly to the file server containing the application proxy, downloads it, completes the install, then performs the creation. There's no need to query the directory again.

Group Policy settings and client-specified flags control whether a published application proxy is downloaded

If the application proxy is configured as a published application for either the client computer or its user, what happens depends on a particular Group Policy setting that applies to the user making the call, and on flags the client can specify on calls to CoCreateInstance and CoCreateInstanceEx. With COM+, two new flag values are available for these calls: ENABLE_CODE_DOWNLOAD, which allows a client to explicitly request downloading of application proxies (or other COM components, for that matter), and NO_CODE_DOWNLOAD, which allows a client to explicitly request that application proxies not be downloaded. A client can also specify no flag, which is what every COM client written before Windows 2000 will implicitly do (since this flag didn't exist prior to COM+).

If the client specifies ENABLE_CODE_DOWNLOAD on a call to CoCreateInstance or CoCreateInstanceEx, the Group Policy setting doesn't matter—if an application proxy that contains the CLSID specified on the creation call exists as a published application, it will be downloaded and installed. If the client specifies NO_CODE_DOWNLOAD, the Group Policy setting also doesn't matter—no application proxy will be downloaded even if one exists. The Group Policy setting only controls what happens when the client specifies neither of these flags and the application proxy is a published application for this user or computer. In this case, the application proxy is downloaded if the Group Policy setting enables download, while it's not downloaded if the setting disables download.

To get a better sense of how this all works, Figures 8-24 and 8-25 show an example of what happens when an application proxy is a published application for a user or computer. As shown in steps 1 and 2 of Figure 8-24, a client's call to CoCreateInstance causes the COM runtime to search the local registry for CLSID_X. If the CLSID is found, everything proceeds normally, and a new instance of that class is created on either the local or a remote system, depending on what's in the client machine's registry. If the CLSID is not found in the client's registry, as is the case here, the COM runtime checks to see whether downloading is enabled for this class, based on the flags and Group Policy settings just described. If it is, the COM runtime automatically issues a query to Active Directory requesting the location of an application proxy for CLSID_X, as shown in step 3. Next Active Directory returns a pathname to this file on some file server machine, and, as steps 4 and 5 show, the client machine downloads and installs the application proxy.

The COM runtime can automatically download and install an application proxy

During installation, all of the proxies, type libraries, registry settings, and other information required to use the classes in this COM+ Application are set up correctly. If the COM+ Application is running on another system, as in this example, this information

An application proxy can copy a remote server name into the client's registry also includes the name of that remote machine. During installation of the application proxy, that name is copied into the client's registry, as shown in step 5.

Figure 8-24 *Issuing CoCreateInstance on a published application can cause an application proxy to be downloaded and installed.*

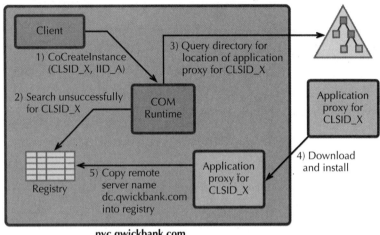

nyc.qwickbank.com

Once a remote server name is installed, creation proceeds in the usual way

From here on, everything proceeds just as if all of this information, including the remote server name, had always been available on the client.[9] As steps 6 and 7 in Figure 8-25 show, the client's COM runtime contacts its sibling on the server machine, which then looks up the specified CLSID in that machine's registry. The creation process is completed in steps 8 through 10, leaving the client free to invoke methods on the new object.

Enabling code download can have unwanted side effects

It's worth pointing out that making application proxies or other COM components published applications, then enabling code download for unsuspecting clients—those that specify neither ENABLE_CODE_DOWNLOAD nor NO_CODE_DOWNLOAD— can be dangerous. First, causing an Active Directory lookup

---

9. This is the mechanism that underlies the example described in Chapter 1, where a client used Active Directory to locate a machine on which to create a COM object.

Figure 8-25 *Once a remote server name has been placed in the client's registry, the remote object is created as usual.*

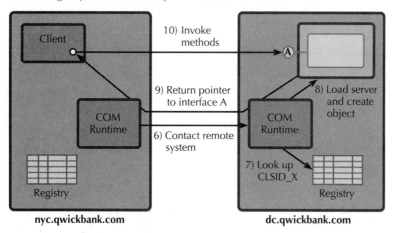

whenever a requested CLSID isn't in the local registry can need-lessly hurt performance, because that CLSID often won't be found in the directory, either. Also, a requested CLSID might be located via the directory, but the code found that implements this class could be part of some large application rather than the specific component a client was interested in. Still, used well, the ability to locate, download, and install application proxies and other components on demand can be quite useful.

Bring Your Own Transaction

The usual way a COM object becomes part of an existing trans-action is that the COM runtime, based on the object's transaction attribute and the transaction status of the object's creator, copies information about a current transaction into this object's context. For example, an object marked as Required that receives a method call from its creator that is already part of a transaction will have had information about that transaction copied from its caller's context into its own. In other words, it will join the transaction.

Objects usually join transactions via the COM runtime

BYOT allows explicitly indicating what transaction an object should join when it's created

Suppose, however, that a client wishes to create a COM object but also wishes to explicitly make this object part of an existing transaction rather than relying on the automatic mechanism provided by the COM runtime. To allow this, Windows 2000 includes a service called Bring Your Own Transaction (BYOT). A client can use it by creating a system-supplied object called the BYOT object, then calling QueryInterface on this object to request a pointer to either of the interfaces ICreateWithTransaction or ICreateWithTIPTransaction. Each of these interfaces provides only the single method CreateInstance. When a client invokes this method in either interface, it passes in the CLSID of the object it wants to create, the interface identifier (IID) of the first interface pointer it wants returned on the object, and a reference to an existing DTC or Transaction Internet Protocol (TIP) transaction. The COM runtime creates the object, then modifies the object's transaction information in its context to make it part of the specified transaction.

Why would you ever want to do this? Why not just let this new object join an existing transaction in the usual way, by configuring its transaction attribute value correctly and letting it join automatically? One possibility is that you'd like to enlist the object in a transaction started by a transaction manager other than DTC that supports OLE Transaction. At the moment, there are no such transaction managers, but the possibility exists. Another example is an application that chooses to start a transaction outside COM+, perhaps as part of integrating legacy code, then needs to include a COM object within that transaction. Without something like BYOT, this wouldn't be possible. Or, a vendor might wish to build a gateway between the world of Windows 2000 transactions, dominated by DTC, and another transaction coordinator. While building this kind of product isn't simple, BYOT makes it possible. It's probably safe to say that BYOT won't be an especially widely used technology, but there are situations where it is exactly what's needed.

COM+ Events

Suppose you want to write one or more COM objects that must take some action when a specific event occurs. For example, imagine what might happen at QwickBank when a check that results in an overdraft on some account is processed. One COM object in QwickBank's system might respond to this event by causing a letter to be sent to the customer informing him of the overdraft. Another object might write a record in a database of overdrafts maintained by the bank, while a third object might check to see how many overdrafts this individual has had recently and perhaps flag him as a problem customer. The point is that the same event might need to be received and processed by several different objects.

Allowing various components to learn about a particular event, then letting each one process it in its own way, turns out to be a frequent pattern in software systems. Often referred to as *publish and subscribe*, this paradigm shows up in all kinds of applications. As a result, many software developers have created their own customized systems for providing this kind of service. As always, though, it doesn't make much sense for many developers to solve the same problem in different ways. A better solution would be for the operating system to provide a standard technology for subscribing to and receiving events that could be used by a large group of applications. In Windows 2000, this service is provided by *COM+ Events*.

COM+ Events provides a publish and subscribe service

Since COM+ Events is based on COM, each event that can be sent is represented by a method. In other words, sending an event to a COM object really means invoking a method in some interface on that object. The sender of an event is referred to as the *publisher*, while the COM object that receives it is a *subscriber* to that event. The same event can have many subscribers, so when a publisher invokes a single method representing this event, sometimes called *firing* the event, one or more subscribers might receive that method invocation. Because of this, methods used with

Publishers invoke methods to send events to subscribers

COM+ Events can have only [in] parameters—they can't return results from the object that receives them. Since the same event can be sent to more than one subscriber, returning results wouldn't make sense—from which of an event's multiple recipients would they come? Also, an event that has more than one subscriber can be delivered to those subscribers in any order. In fact, that order might change each time the event is delivered—COM+ Events makes no guarantees.

To control what events it wishes to receive, an object can create one or more *subscriptions* in the *event store*, part of the COM+ Catalog. These subscriptions can also be created administratively using the Component Services administrative tool. To send an event, a publisher relies on an *EventClass* object. Developers using COM+ Events can also create filters to control exactly which events get sent. The next few sections describe each of these concepts.[10]

Event Classes   To send events, a publisher must register an appropriate EventClass with COM+ Events. An EventClass can be registered either administratively using the Component Services snap-in or programmatically using standard interfaces. Each EventClass must have a CLSID and a ProgID, allowing clients to create instances of this class, and each one must also have a type library describing the interfaces and methods this class supports. Those methods are the events that can be sent using that particular EventClass.

An EventClass groups together one or more events

---

10. COM also provides Connection Points, a simple way for one component to send events to another. Used by ActiveX Controls and other technologies, this mechanism relies on the standard interfaces IConnectionPoint and IConnectionPointContainer. Connection Points require both the sender and receiver of an event to be running when the event is sent, however, and it also has other requirements that closely bind senders and receivers. As a result, this mechanism supports what are sometimes called *tightly-coupled events*. COM+ Events doesn't have these requirements—the sender of an event and its receivers can be much more loosely associated, allowing *loosely-coupled events*.

What an EventClass does not need, however, is any user-written code. Developers using COM+ Events never need to actually implement an EventClass. Instead, once an EventClass has been registered, a publisher can create an instance of that class by calling CoCreateInstance with that class's CLSID (or using an appropriate Visual Basic function passed this class's ProgID). Because a type library was provided for this class, the COM+ Events system can create an object that exposes the appropriate interfaces and methods.

Developers don't write code for EventClass objects

Publishers don't need to write any code for an EventClass because every EventClass object does the same thing. A publisher sends an event by invoking an appropriate method in some interface on its EventClass object. In response, this object delivers the event to each subscriber by invoking the corresponding method in the subscriber's implementation of the interface. Those methods can be invoked like any COM method, using either COM's standard RPC-based mechanisms or COM+'s Queued Components. However it's done, the result is that the subscriber receives the event it has expressed interest in.

When a publisher calls a method in an EventClass object, that object invokes the corresponding method in each subscriber

If desired, a developer creating a publisher can implement *publisher filtering*. This option allows the publisher to intervene in each event a particular EventClass object sends. The publisher might need to do this, for example, if a particular event always needs to be delivered to subscribers in a certain order, or if the publisher wishes to validate that each subscriber has the right to receive this event, or for many other reasons. Publisher filtering requires extra work, but it's useful for some kinds of applications.

Publishers can filter events before they're sent

Subscriptions   Like an EventClass object, a subscription can potentially be created either administratively or by a running object. However it's done, each subscription identifies the subscriber, lists an event this subscriber is interested in, and references the publisher and EventClass from which this subscriber wishes to receive

A subscription associates a publisher with a subscriber

the event. It's also possible for a single subscription to indicate that a subscriber wishes to receive any events sent in a particular interface.

Persistent subscriptions result in creation of an object to receive an event

Subscriptions can be of various types. *Persistent* subscriptions, as their name suggests, are stored on disk and so survive system failures. They can be created either administratively by a human being or directly by a running object, and they allow naming a subscriber using either a CLSID or a *moniker*, which is a standard COM mechanism for naming a specific instance of a class. When an event is delivered for a persistent subscription, the EventClass object will create an instance of the appropriate class, then invoke the method for this event.

Transient subscriptions cause an event to be sent to a running object

Unlike persistent subscriptions, a *transient* subscription can be created only by a running object, and its existence will not survive a system crash. Rather than identifying the subscriber with a CLSID or moniker, the object that creates a transient subscription inserts an interface pointer to itself in the event store. When an EventClass object delivers an event with this type of subscription, it uses this pointer to locate the target subscriber. While persistent subscriptions cause the EventClass object to create a new instance of the subscribing class, this is not true with transient subscriptions. There's no need to create a new instance to receive the event because the instance that created the subscription is still running.

Subscriptions can specify a filter

A subscription can also contain filtering criteria. For example, perhaps a particular object in QwickBank's check processing system only wants to see overdrafts from a specific customer. To allow this, its subscription can specify logical tests that an overdraft event must meet, such as CustomerNumber = 7498, grouping together multiple tests with AND, OR, and NOT. Only events that meet these criteria will be delivered to this object.

Using COM+ Events To make clear how the COM+ Events system works, it's useful to walk through an example. As shown in Figure 8-26, the process begins with either a person or a running process registering an EventClass. Once this is done, subscriptions can be created that are associated with that EventClass (although it's also possible to create subscriptions to an EventClass before that EventClass exists). In this example, those subscriptions are persistent, and each subscriber is identified by a CLSID. When the publisher wishes to send one of these events, it first creates an instance of this EventClass object. Once it exists, this object examines the event store to determine its attributes and who its subscribers are, storing this information in memory for fast access when it's needed.

Figure 8-26 *Once an EventClass has been registered and subscriptions created for it, a publisher can send an event.*

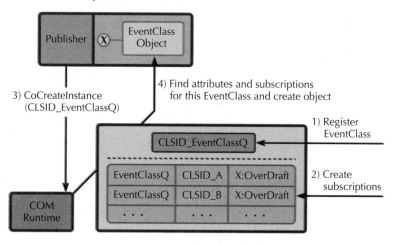

To send an event, the publisher invokes the corresponding method in the EventClass object, as shown in step 5 in Figure 8-27. In this example, the event is represented by a method called OverDraft in interface X. When it receives this call, the EventClass object creates instances of the two classes that have subscribed to this event, shown in step 6, then invokes X::OverDraft in each of those objects as in step 7. If there were any transient subscriptions to the event, the EventClass object could instead just invoke X::OverDraft in the running subscriber, using the interface pointer the subscriber stored with its subscription to locate it.

Figure 8-27 *The EventClass object can create the subscribers, then send them the event by invoking the appropriate method.*

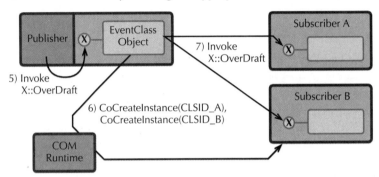

COM+ Events can be a useful tool for many kinds of applications. In fact, it's used by some of the built-in services in Windows 2000. If you need this kind of service, it makes sense to use a standard technology developed and supported by somebody else. Why recreate what already exists?

Component Load Balancing

Distributing client requests across multiple server machines can make an application more scalable

A key goal of COM+ is to allow developers to build scalable applications. One way to make an application support more users is to spread that application across multiple machines, sharing the processing load those users create. In a three-tier scenario, the usual approach with a COM+ Application, this means that clients will be able to create and access the Application's objects on multiple machines.

To make this as efficient as possible, we'd like to spread those objects evenly across the available server systems. Yet requests from clients can be unpredictable. There's usually no way to know in advance which clients will need services at any given time. Manually assigning clients to servers, then, isn't a very effective way to spread the load. While this kind of static configuration will work, it's a sub-optimal solution.

A much better approach is to dynamically spread client requests across the available set of server machines. Doing this allows choosing the machine that's best suited for this request, such as the one that's currently least heavily loaded. This kind of dynamic load balancing is exactly what's done by Component Load Balancing (CLB). As Figure 8-28 shows, a client using CLB issues a standard CoCreateInstance request to a remote system. With CLB, however, all clients direct that request to a single Windows 2000 machine, called the CLB Server. This system keeps track of the current load on all machines configured to be in a particular CLB Cluster. When it receives a creation request from a client, the CLB Server determines which machine in the cluster is most available, then forwards the request to that machine. This system then creates an instance of the requested class, and one or more interface pointers to this new object are returned to the client as usual. From now on, the client invokes methods directly on the object—the CLB server is no longer involved.

Component Load Balancing dynamically balances clients' creation requests across a group of server machines

CLB load balances only creation requests—it doesn't get involved in JIT activation. This means that some clients will derive more benefit from it than others. For instance, in the call center example described earlier in this chapter, I pointed out that a client might create one object in the morning, then use it over and over all day. After every transaction, the object is deactivated, then re-created when its client issues the next method call. In this case, while CLB would get involved in determining which machine the object should initially be created on, the object would live on that machine all day—no further load balancing would occur.

Load balancing isn't done for JIT activation

Figure 8-28 *A client's CoCreateInstance request to a CLB Server is directed to the most available machine in that CLB Cluster.*

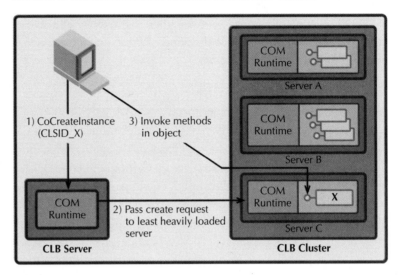

Imagine, though, that the client is an ASP script rather than a DCOM client. ASP scripts commonly create and destroy the COM objects they use every time they are invoked. Now, each request made by a browser will result in the ASP issuing a creation request, which means that CLB could be used each time. The point is that exactly how useful this technology is depends in part on how an application is structured.

CLB works only with configured components

Like the other features described in this chapter, CLB is only available for configured components, those that are part of a COM+ Application. Not all components in an Application need be marked as Load Balanced, but those that are will get the benefit of being created on the least heavily loaded machine. To determine which machine this is, the CLB Server keeps track of how long it takes each one to respond to requests. The faster a machine responds, the more available CPU cycles it must have, and so the lighter its load must be. The CLB Server continually adjusts its notion of which machine is most available as these response times change.

As mentioned at the start of this chapter, CLB is not a fully released technology in Windows 2000. While a technology preview version is available, CLB's complete release is as part of a separate product, shipped a few months later than Windows 2000. This product includes a number of tools for managing a distributed, load balanced environment as well as an enhanced version of the CLB technology included with Windows 2000. Among those enhancements is the ability to replace the algorithm used by CLB to measure the load on servers in the CLB cluster.

CLB is available as a technology preview for Windows 2000

Although CLB is not among them, many of the services described in this long chapter were originally provided by MTS. By merging the functionality of MTS into the standard COM runtime library, Windows 2000 provides a more consistent and more rational implementation of those services. Calling the result COM+ makes some sense, since COM in Windows 2000 is really the traditional COM plus extra services. The changes this new release brings to COM should ultimately make it both more powerful and easier to use.

COM+ is COM plus extra services

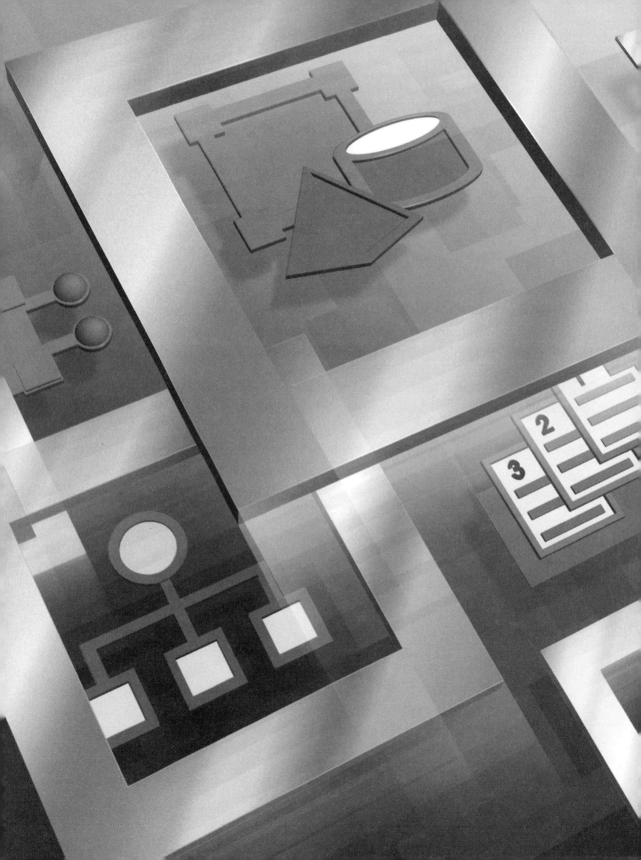

Message Queuing Services

No style of communication is conceptually easier than message queuing. An application using message queuing just builds a message and sends it to a queue. Some other part of the application (or of some other application) can then read the message from the queue. If needed, this reader can respond, again by sending a message into some queue that's later read by the original sender or perhaps by some other application. The process is undeniably simple.

Message queuing is a simple idea

To build real applications, however, there are lots of features you'd like to have available, and so products that support message queuing commonly offer much more than just simple sending and receiving. Microsoft Message Queuing (MSMQ), the message queuing technology built into Microsoft Windows 2000, does exactly this, providing a broad range of features for message-oriented applications. This chapter describes MSMQ 2.0, the version shipped with the first release of Windows 2000.

MSMQ provides more than simple message queuing services

It's worth noting that MSMQ 2.0 systems can be used together with those running MSMQ 1.0. As you'd expect, though, machines running the older version can't use the new Windows 2000 features.

When to Use Message Queuing

When should you use message queuing rather than some other form of communication between distributed processes? The choice is most often between COM/DCOM—where communication between processes or machines typically uses the paradigm of remote procedure call (RPC)—and message queuing. Here are some simple rules that can help you decide when to use each one:

Use message queuing when the sender need not wait for a response

- If the sender must wait for a response from the receiver before proceeding, you might as well use RPC, since a call blocks until a result is returned. RPC is typically simpler to use than message queuing, so if it fits the bill, use it (although Queued Components [QC], described later in this chapter, can make message queuing very nearly as simple as RPC). If the sender need not wait for a result, however, but can usefully do something else in the meantime, message queuing might be a better choice.[1]

Use message queuing when the sender and receiver might not be available at the same time

- If the sending and receiving applications might run at different times, definitely use message queuing—RPC assumes that both client and server are available at the same time. Message queuing can provide reliability even in the event of hardware, software, or network failures, since messages can wait safely in queues until their target receiver becomes available.

Use message queuing when communicating with any of a group of receivers

- If a sender isn't sending to a specific receiver, but instead to any one of a group of receivers, use message queuing. Once a message has been placed in a queue, it is potentially available to any application that can read from that queue. With RPC, by contrast, a client typically makes a call to a specific server, and the identity of that server is known when the call is made.

---

1. The addition of asynchronous method calls to COM, described in Chapter 5, makes this once very sharp distinction a bit fuzzier.

- If requests need to be logged and possibly reprocessed to recover from failures, consider using message queuing. While it's certainly possible to build logging into an RPC-based application, mechanisms to do this are an intrinsic part of MSMQ. As always, exploiting what the Windows 2000 system provides is more efficient than re-creating the same function yourself.

Use message queuing when logging is required

- If your client simply calls some server, gets a response from that server, and then goes on, RPC is fine. But if you need more complex interactions between the parts of a distributed application, use message queuing. With MSMQ, A can send a message to B, who sends one to C and D, who both send response messages back to A. That kind of flexibility isn't possible with RPC.

Use message queuing for complex interactions among senders and receivers

It's tempting to think of performance as a reason to choose either MSMQ or RPC, too. RPC somehow seems like it should be significantly faster than message queuing, since with RPC requests and responses don't have to go through a queue. In reality, though, the performance difference between MSMQ and RPC often won't be an important factor in your choice. MSMQ can be surprisingly fast.

Message queuing is fast

On the downside, though, message queuing imposes more administrative overhead than RPC-based COM and DCOM applications. Once you've installed the appropriate type libraries, stubs, and proxies, those types of applications will work without any further attention. With a message queuing application, life isn't so simple. More initial configuration is required, and administrators might also have periodic work to do when the application is used. Some kinds of queues can fill up, for example, and so perhaps require regular human attention to keep messaging applications running smoothly.

Message queuing imposes administrative overhead

Message queuing is
a distinct technology
from e-mail

Finally, don't confuse message queuing with e-mail. The two can seem very similar (and both are often called just "messaging"), but they have quite different purposes. The simplest way to think about it is to view e-mail protocols as a way to send messages between people, while technologies like MSMQ are designed to send messages between applications. It's theoretically possible that some future version of, say, Microsoft Exchange could be built on MSMQ, but standard protocols for e-mail are already in place. As a result, the historically rooted distinction between technologies for person-to-person messaging and those for application-to-application messaging shows no signs of going away.

MSMQ Basics

As shown in Figure 9-1, the major components of MSMQ are:

- APIs that applications can use to send and receive messages. MSMQ provides two different APIs, and Windows 2000 also introduces QC, which allows using MSMQ to convey calls between a client and a COM object.
- Messages that are created, then sent and received by applications.
- Queues, managed by a queue manager, into which those messages are sent and from which they are received. Queue managers can communicate with each other to send messages from one queue to another.

From these basic components, MSMQ constructs three different kinds of systems, each of which is described in the next section.

Kinds of MSMQ Systems

MSMQ servers provide
queues and can route
messages

As shown in Figure 9-2, the most complete of the three kinds of MSMQ systems is called an MSMQ *server*. An MSMQ server can contain queues and a queue manager, software to route messages between queues, and more. It can also support the MSMQ APIs, and thus support applications that send and receive messages. If

MSMQ is used in a Windows 2000 domain, an MSMQ server must run on at least one domain controller in that domain.

Figure 9-1 *MSMQ applications rely on the MSMQ APIs to send messages to and receive messages from queues.*

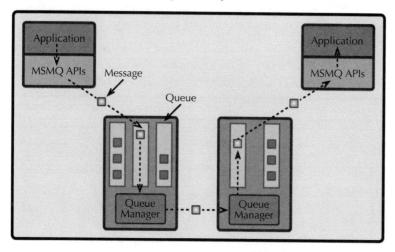

MSMQ also defines two types of clients. An *independent* client supports the MSMQ APIs and also has a queue manager with its own queues. If the client is currently connected to a network, any messages sent by applications running on that machine can be immediately forwarded to an MSMQ server or their destination queue. If the client isn't connected to a network—maybe it's running on your laptop, and you're trying to get some work done while crammed into a coach seat on a long flight—messages sent by the application are stored in the client's own queues. When an independent client is eventually connected to a network, its queue manager will automatically figure this out and forward those messages on to their destinations.

MSMQ independent clients have their own queues

Finally, MSMQ allows *dependent* clients. Like independent clients, dependent clients can support only applications that send and receive messages—they can't act as message routers. But dependent clients are more limited than independent clients. Since they support only the MSMQ APIs, an application running on a dependent

MSMQ dependent clients don't have their own queues

client must have online access to an MSMQ server. In fact, MSMQ servers implement a proxy function solely to support these needy systems. Dependent clients are intended for systems with permanent connections to a network, such as a desktop machine connected to a LAN. Dependent clients have limitations, as is described later in this chapter, but because they have no queues of their own, managing an MSMQ environment full of dependent clients can be simpler than if independent clients are used instead.

Figure 9-2 *MSMQ defines three different types of systems.*

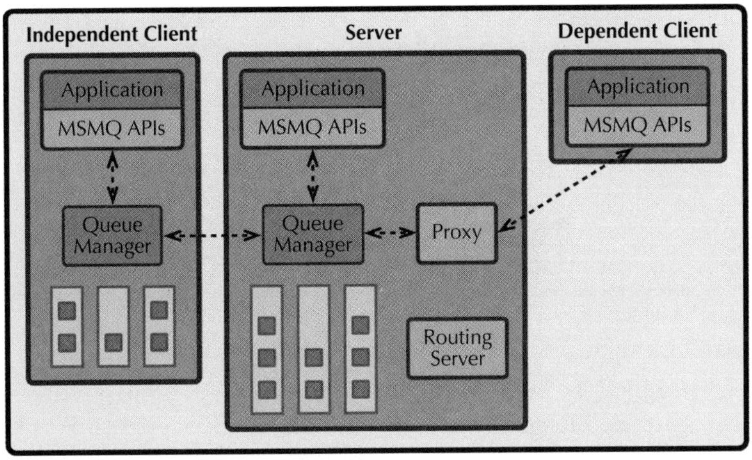

Storing MSMQ Information

MSMQ 1.0 was released in the second half of 1997, well before Active Directory appeared with Windows 2000. Like some other applications, MSMQ originally provided its own specialized directory service called the MSMQ Information Store (MQIS), based on Microsoft SQL Server. In Windows 2000, the information that was kept in MQIS is held in Active Directory, and so MSMQ 2.0 no longer requires SQL Server.

MSMQ 2.0 stores information about queues and other things in Active Directory

In MSMQ 1.0, MQIS helped clients find queues, stored information about each queue, and more. A copy of the MQIS database was kept on one or more MSMQ servers, and changes were automatically replicated among the copies. But storing and replicating this kind of information is exactly what a directory service is for, so MSMQ 2.0 keeps all of this information in Active Directory. And although the original MQIS has been retired, the interface seen by developers remains the same.

MSMQ can also be used by systems that aren't part of a domain— that is, in an environment such as a workgroup where Active Directory isn't present. Doing this limits MSMQ in a number of ways, however, some of which are described later in this chapter.

Understanding Queues

The service MSMQ provides is based on two things: queues and messages. Understanding these two will make clear what MSMQ can do and what you can use it for. Messages are described in the next section; we'll look at queues first.

Types of Queues

MSMQ defines two broad categories of queues. The first, *application* queues, are created by and primarily used by MSMQ applications written by developers. *System* queues, the second category, are created and used by MSMQ itself. Application queues come in four types:

- *Message queues*   Used by applications to send and receive messages. MSMQ users can create either *public* or *private* message queues. If a queue can be located using Active Directory, it's a public queue. If a queue's location isn't in the directory, it qualifies as a private queue. Public queues are useful for applications that need to let other applications locate and use their queues (although even if some other application can find a queue through the directory, that queue's security settings might still prevent access, as described later). If an application uses only a specified set of queues, however, and no other applications will need to use those queues, private queues are probably a better choice.

Applications use message queues to exchange messages

- *Response queues* Used by one application to send responses to another. A response queue is typically just an ordinary message queue that's specified in a particular message as the place to which any responses should be sent.

- *Administration queues* Used for acknowledgment messages sent by MSMQ itself. The kinds of acknowledgments that might be sent are described later in this chapter.

- *Report queues* Used to track message progress. For example, if an application asks MSMQ to trace the route of a message, those MSMQ-generated trace messages are sent to a report queue. In theory, messages generated by applications can also be sent to report queues, however, which is why they are considered application rather than system queues.

The second category of queue, system queues, includes queues used for two different purposes. They are:

- *Journal queues* Used for MSMQ-created copies of messages sent by applications. MSMQ offers two different kinds of journaling. Each MSMQ server and independent client has a *machine journal* that can potentially store a copy of every message sent on that machine. Each queue that is created also has an associated *queue journal* that can store a copy of every message removed from that queue. Both kinds of journal queues are read-only, and applications and MSMQ administrators control what kind of journaling, if any, is done.

- *Dead letter queues* If a message can't be delivered to its destination queue, an application can ask MSMQ to place that message into a dead letter queue. Applications can decide whether they'd like their undeliverable messages sent to a dead letter queue or just silently deleted.

Queue Properties

Every queue has a number of properties. The values of these properties, set by applications and MSMQ administrators, control what a particular queue can be used for and how it behaves. Property settings for public queues are stored in Active Directory, with a cached copy kept on the machine where the queue exists. Property settings for private queues, however, are kept only on the machine where the queue exists—they're not stored in Active Directory. Specific access rights can be granted to a queue's properties, allowing different users varying permissions to read and modify their values.

Queues have properties

The properties a queue can have, along with a short description of each one, are listed in Table 9-1.

Table 9-1   MSMQ Queue Properties

Property	Description
Authenticate	Must messages sent to this queue use authentication?
Base Priority	Priority of this queue
Create Time	Date and time this queue was created
Instance	GUID that identifies this queue
Journal	Is every message removed from this queue copied to a journal queue?
Journal Quota	Maximum size in bytes of this queue's journal queue
Label	Character string describing this queue
Modify Time	Date and time this queue's properties were last modified
Pathname	Name of this queue
Pathname DNS	Name of this queue using a DNS name for the queue's computer
Privacy Level	Must messages sent to this queue be encrypted?
Quota	Specifies the total number of bytes that can be stored in this queue
Transaction	Is this queue transactional?
Type	A user-defined GUID; can be used when searching for a queue

Some queue properties are set by MSMQ and can't be changed by MSMQ applications and administrators. The others are settable by anybody with the right access permissions. Among the more important of a queue's properties are:

Every queue has a Pathname property

- *Pathname* The only property that's absolutely required when creating a queue, a queue's Pathname is a character string identifying the machine the queue is on and giving a name for the queue. For example, a queue used in some application at the QwickBank Corporation might have the value "machine1.qwickbank.com\myqueue". Once this property has been set for a queue, it can't be changed.

The Quota property controls how much data a queue can contain

- *Quota* Specifies the maximum size in bytes that the queue can hold. If the total size of all messages in the queue reaches the specified limit, further attempts to send messages to this queue will fail. The default is to have no quota, allowing a queue to expand until the machine that hosts it runs out of space. (MSMQ also allows specifying a quota for a computer as a whole—it's set as a property of that computer, not as a property of any particular queue on that computer. This quota sets a limit on the total number of bytes that can be stored in all queues on this machine. If it is exceeded, new messages sent to any queue on this machine will be discarded.)

The Journal property controls whether a queue's messages are copied to a journal queue

- *Journal* Controls whether messages removed from the queue will be copied to the queue journal maintained by MSMQ. (This journal is implemented as a journal queue on the same machine as the queue being logged.) While this option allows keeping a record of all messages removed from a queue, MSMQ also allows journaling of sent messages. This is accomplished by setting a property in each sent message and is described later in this chapter. Journal queues are not automatically emptied by MSMQ, so some kind of periodic administrative action is required to keep them from filling up.

- *Base Priority*   Used to make decisions when routing among queues. Messages sent to a higher-priority queue will be routed more expeditiously than those sent to queues with lower priorities. Only public queues have this property—private queues don't support it.

The Base Priority property affects routing

- *Type*   An application-defined GUID that can be used when searching for a queue in Active Directory. For example, QwickBank's developers might define a specific GUID for labeling queues that overdraft notices should be sent to. Any application that needs to send this kind of message can search Active Directory for a queue with this value for its Type property. This approach frees applications from being aware of which machine a queue is on, letting them instead rely on the directory to locate the right kind of queue.

The Type property is used to find a specific kind of queue

- *Label*   A character string identifying a queue or class of queues. Like the Type property, an application can specify a particular value for this property when searching for queues in Active Directory.

The Label property can also be used to find a specific kind of queue

- *Privacy Level*   If this property is set to None, the queue accepts only unencrypted messages. A setting of Body, however, causes the queue to accept only messages that the sender specified should be encrypted (using a message property described later in this chapter). If this property is set to Optional, which is the default, the queue will accept both encrypted and unencrypted messages.

The Privacy Level property controls whether a queue will accept unencrypted messages, encrypted messages, or both

- *Transaction*   If this property is set for a queue, that queue is said to be *transactional* and can accept only messages that are sent within a transaction. Using transactions with MSMQ is a critically important topic, one that's discussed in its own section later in this chapter.

The Transaction property determines whether a queue can participate in transactions

Each queue can also have access permissions defined for it. These access permissions depend on a security descriptor with an access control list (ACL) that's associated with each queue. This ACL indicates which users are allowed to send messages to the queue, which can receive messages from it, and more.[2]

A queue's security descriptor can itself be changed by users with the appropriate permissions, and those permissions can be granted on a very fine-grained basis. For example, a user might have the right to look at but not remove messages stored in the queue. By default, everyone is allowed to send messages to a queue, but if desired, this right can be limited to only specified senders.

Understanding Messages

MSMQ messages are, in one sense, very simple beasts—they're just a group of properties. Since MSMQ tries to offer a powerful, flexible service, though, each message has lots of properties, and understanding what all of them do is not so simple. Table 9-2 lists the properties a message can have, although properties that just contain the length of other properties have been omitted. The rest of this section describes the most important ones.

Table 9-2   MSMQ Message Properties

Property	Description
Acknowledge	Indicates what kind of acknowledgment should be sent
Administration Queue Name	Name of queue to which acknowledgment should be sent
Application Specific	Used to filter received messages
Arrived Time	Date and time the message arrived in the queue

(continued)

---

2. Queues are actually implemented using memory-mapped files in Windows 2000, but a single file may contain messages from several different queues. For this and other reasons, the ACL on each queue is completely separate from the ACL of the file that holds that queue's messages.

Property	Description
Authenticated	Was this received message authenticated by MSMQ?
AuthenticatedEx	Was the MSMQ 2.0 digital signature version used?
Authentication Level	Should this message be digitally signed?
Body	Contents of the message
Body Type	Type of message contents
Class	Type of message: normal, acknowledgment, report
Connector Type	Lets an application such as a gateway set a property usually set by MSMQ
Correlation ID	Correlation identifier
Delivery	Express or Recoverable
Destination Queue	Name of the queue the message was sent to
Destination Symmetric Key	Key for encrypted messages
Encryption Algorithm	Choice for body encryption algorithm
Extension	Used for communication with non-MSMQ systems
First in Transaction	Is this the first message sent in a particular transaction?
Hash Algorithm	Choice for digital signature hash algorithm
Journal	Is message journaled, sent to dead letter queue, or neither?
Label	Application-defined character string for this message
Last in Transaction	Is this the last message sent in a particular transaction?
Message ID	MSMQ-generated identifier for this message
Priority	A number between 0 and 7
Privacy Level	Is this message encrypted?
Provider Name	Cryptographic provider in a non-MSMQ system

(continued)

continued

Property	Description
Provider Type	Type of cryptographic provider
Response Queue	Name of queue to which responses should be sent
Security Context	Contains security information
Sender Certificate	Sender's certificate
Sender ID	Windows 2000 SID of the message's sender
Sender ID Type	Is Sender ID a SID or null?
Sent Time	Date and time message was sent
Signature	Digital signature for this message
Source Machine ID	Identifies machine where this message originated
Time To Be Received	Maximum time for message to be received
Time To Reach Queue	Maximum time for message to reach destination queue
Trace	Controls whether route tracing messages are sent
Version	Version of MSMQ software used by sender
Xact ID	Identifies which transaction this message belongs to
Xact Status Queue	Contains transactional acks sent by non-MSMQ systems

Message Body

The Body property contains a message's data

The most important property in a message is Body. As you might expect, Body contains the data being sent in the message, and it can be up to four megabytes in size. Another property, Body Type, indicates what kind of data is in this message's body. Many types are possible, including integers, character strings, byte strings, and more. The data in the message body can also be a persistent COM object. For example, an application can send the contents of an ADO Recordset in an MSMQ message by simply assigning the Recordset to the message's Body property.

Chapter Nine

Delivery Types

A message's Delivery property determines how that message will be handled and stored by queues. The two possible values for this property are Express and Recoverable. If a message is marked for Express delivery, all queues that handle this message might store it in memory only—the message won't necessarily be written to disk. Messages requesting Express delivery will get to their destination queue very quickly, but they pay a price for this speed. If an Express delivery message is currently resident in some queue and the machine that holds that queue crashes, the message will be lost.

Messages marked for Recoverable delivery, by contrast, are written to disk by the queues that hold them. If the machine holding a queue crashes, the Recoverable messages in that queue will not be lost, since they've been written to non-volatile storage. MSMQ offers a choice, and developers must make the trade-off between more reliable delivery and faster communication.

One obvious case where Recoverable messages should be used is when an MSMQ application running on an independent client is being used with no network connection. If Express messages are sent, they'll be lost if the client (say, your laptop) is turned off before it's reconnected to a network. Setting the delivery property to Recoverable guarantees that the application's messages will be stored on the client's local disk until it's again attached to a network.

Message Timeouts

Some messages are time-critical. If a message has not been received within a certain number of seconds, for example, it might be appropriate to throw that message away. MSMQ defines a pair of message properties intended to be used in this situation. The value of a message's Time To Be Received property specifies the total number of seconds the message will exist after it has been

Express messages are fast, but can be lost due to machine failures

Recoverable messages are slower, but will survive machine failures

A message can be discarded if it takes too long to reach its destination or to be received

sent. If the message is not received by some application within this time period, MSMQ will discard it. Similarly, a message's Time To Reach Queue property specifies the total number of seconds a message has to reach its destination queue. If it doesn't make it in time—maybe the only path to that queue is down, for instance—MSMQ will discard it.

Acknowledgments

MSMQ provides
many kinds of
acknowledgments

The possibility of discarding messages raises another important point: how does a sender know what happens to its messages? Which ones are received correctly? Which ones are discarded? How these questions are answered for a particular message depends on the value of that message's Acknowledge property. This property has five possible values:

- *Full Reach Queue*   Causes MSMQ to automatically send an acknowledgment message indicating that the message has reached its destination queue or that it will never reach it (maybe the value in the message's Time To Reach Queue property has expired, or perhaps the destination queue has reached its quota, or some other failure has occurred). If the message can't reach its destination, one of several different acknowledgment messages is sent depending on the exact reason for the failure. The result is that the sender learns that its message couldn't reach the queue and what went wrong.

- *Full Receive*   Causes MSMQ to send an acknowledgment message indicating that the message has been received or that it will never be received (perhaps because the message's Time To Be Received property has expired).

- *Nack Reach Queue*   Causes MSMQ to send an acknowledgment message indicating that a message can't reach its destination queue (again, perhaps because the message's Time To Reach Queue timer has expired or for some other reason).

- *Nack Receive*   Causes MSMQ to send an acknowledgment message indicating that a message can't be received (for example, its Time To Be Received timer might have expired).

- *None*   MSMQ sends no acknowledgment messages. If the sender does not explicitly set the Acknowledge property, this is the default.

All the acknowledgment messages MSMQ generates are sent to an administration queue specified by the application. To use acknowledgments, the sending application must supply a value in each sent message's Administration Queue Name property to indicate which administration queue should receive the acknowledgment messages.

Message Journaling

One of the nice things about message queuing is that it's easy to keep a record of what messages have been sent. An organization with a strong requirement for effective auditing procedures, such as the fictitious QwickBank company used as an example throughout this book, might find this very handy. An application can set each message's Journal property to determine what, if any, records are kept at the sending system about this message. If the property's value is set to Journal, a copy of this message will be placed in a journal queue on the sending machine. This queue can be examined by other applications interested in knowing what messages have been sent.

The Journal property can cause a copy of every sent message to be kept in a journal queue on its sender's system

What happens to messages that, for whatever reason, can't be received? For messages whose Journal property is set to Dead Letter, the answer is that they wind up in a dead letter queue. If the discarded message was sent to a non-transactional queue, it is placed in the dead letter queue on the machine that decided to discard this message. If the discarded message was sent to a transactional queue, however, it is placed in transactional dead letter queue on the machine that sent the message. Finally, if no value is explicitly

The Journal property controls whether an undeliverable message is sent to a dead letter queue set for a message's Journal property, the default is to do nothing—the message will not be recorded in the journal queue when it's sent, and it won't be forwarded to the dead letter queue if it can't be received.

Message Priority

In a typical application, some messages will be more important than others. For example, messages that submit trades in QwickBank's brokerage application might have priority over those that just inquire about stock prices, and high dollar trades might have even higher priority. MSMQ recognizes this fact, and so each message has a Priority property that applications can set. Defined as an integer value between 0 and 7, messages with higher numbers have higher priority. (By default, MSMQ sets every message's Priority property to 3.) This priority is taken into account when MSMQ makes routing decisions and when messages are inserted into queues. Messages with higher priorities are inserted toward the front of the queue rather than strictly in order of their arrival. Routing among queues also takes message priorities into account, but the queue priority stored in each queue's Priority property takes precedence in making routing decisions.

Sending Response Messages

When an application sends a message to a queue, it might well expect some kind of response. With RPC-based communication such as DCOM, it's obvious who to respond to—the COM runtime keeps track of who a call came from. With message queuing, though, it might not be obvious how to get a response back to the sender of a message. After all, one of the benefits of messaging is the ability to send a message without knowing precisely who's going to receive it. Short of hard-wiring it into the application, how can a sender let the receiver of a message know how to respond? The answer is to use another property of an MSMQ message. By placing the name of some queue in a message's Response Queue property, the sender can inform the receiver where it would like a response to this message sent. Setting this property isn't required, since some applications choose to use only a predefined set of queues. But it does provide a convenient and standard way to let a message's receiver know where a response should be sent. (Don't be confused, though—setting this property in no way obligates the receiver to send a response. Whether a response must be sent is part of the application's semantics, not those of MSMQ.)

A related question is, how can a sender associate responses with the message that engendered that response? Suppose, for example, that an application sends ten messages and gets a response message for each one. There's no guarantee that the ten responses will arrive in the same order as the requests were sent. To allow a sender to figure out which response message goes with a particular request message, MSMQ automatically generates a unique Message ID for each message that's sent. Both the sender and receiver of a message can read this property. The receiver, if desired, can copy this Message ID into the Correlation ID property of any message it sends in response. By remembering the Message ID of the message it originally sent and matching it with the Correlation ID of a received message, the sender can figure out which response matches a sent message. In fact, when MSMQ sends an acknowledgment as required by a message's Acknowledge property, it does exactly this, copying the Message ID of the message being acknowledged into the Correlation ID of the acknowledgment message.

The Correlation ID property can allow the sender to determine which of its messages is being responded to

Accessing MSMQ

MSMQ provides several different ways for applications to access its services. First, there are two different APIs for direct MSMQ access. One of these, aimed at developers working in C and C++, is defined as a set of C function calls. For those working in Microsoft Visual Basic, Java, or even C++, there's another API

MSMQ has both a C API and a COM API

defined as a set of COM objects. It's possible to build, send, and receive messages with either one, but the C API offers access to a few more services than the COM API.

Applications can also access MSMQ using Queued Components

MSMQ 2.0 also includes support for an option called Queued Components (QC). QC allows a COM application to more-or-less transparently use MSMQ as its underlying mechanism for invoking methods on remote objects. QC doesn't allow access to all of the features MSMQ offers, but it does provide a simple, natural interface for developers familiar with COM.

MSMQ APIs

The C API allows access to all MSMQ services

It makes sense to look first at MSMQ's C API, both because it's the most powerful choice and because it provides the foundation for both the COM-based API and QC. Among the most important calls in the C API are:

- *MQCreateQueue*   Creates a new queue in an MSMQ server or an independent client. This queue might be either on the same machine as the application creating it or on some other machine.
- *MQDeleteQueue*   Destroys a queue.
- *MQOpenQueue*   Opens an existing queue. As already described, in MSMQ 2.0 public queues are located using Active Directory.
- *MQCloseQueue*   Closes a queue.
- *MQSendMessage*   Sends a message to a specified queue. The developer specifies the property values this message should have, then passes them as a parameter on this call.
- *MQReceiveMessage*   Receives a message from a specified queue. Messages can be read either synchronously, with the receiving application blocking until the message arrives (or an application-specified timeout occurs), or asynchronously, with the application receiving a notification that a message has arrived via a callback function or

in some other way. An application can retrieve a message, which removes it from its queue, or peek at it, which lets the application examine the message's properties without removing it from the queue. An application can also choose to receive only certain properties of a message—it's not obligated to read the entire message. And finally, by creating and using a *cursor*, applications can examine and receive messages that aren't currently at the head of the queue.

To invoke a function in the C API, the developer must first populate some number of structures with appropriate values, then pass those structures as parameters into the desired function. This is a classic approach to building a messaging API, so it's not surprising that MSMQ offers this option. If you're familiar with the APIs used by other messaging products, this MSMQ interface won't seem strange.

MSMQ also provides a more modern interface that's defined using COM objects. This interface essentially wraps COM objects and interfaces around MSMQ's native C API, allowing a developer to access MSMQ's services by setting properties and invoking methods on these objects.

To create a queue, for instance, an MSMQQueueInfo object is used. The process is simple: the developer can assign the queue's name to the MSMQQueueInfo object's PathName property, then invoke this object's Create method. To open this newly created queue, the application invokes MSMQQueueInfo::Open. This call returns an MSMQQueue object, which can be used to reference the open queue. To get an MSMQQueue object that refers to an existing queue instead of creating a new one, an application can use the LookupQueue method of the MSMQQuery object. This method has various parameters that allow the application to search for queues that meet specific criteria.

The COM API exposes MSMQ's services through a group of COM objects

To build and send a message, the developer creates an MSMQMessage object, sets its properties, then invokes its Send method. Which queue the message gets sent to is controlled via an MSMQQueue object passed as a parameter on this call. To receive a message, an application invokes the appropriate method on the MSMQQueue object representing the queue from which the message should be read. As described earlier, there are lots of options for how a message can be received—applications aren't forced to blindly wait for the next message in the queue.

Queued Components

To use either of MSMQ's APIs—the C interface or the COM-based interface—requires understanding the fundamental send/receive approach that has traditionally characterized message queuing. To an experienced messaging developer, this is no problem. Writing code to open a queue, create a message, send that message, and then perhaps close the queue becomes natural after a while. But to a developer who's more accustomed to an RPC style of communication, such as a COM developer, going through all of these steps can seem burdensome, if not downright stupid. Why not make sending a message as simple as calling a method in a COM object?

QC makes message queuing more like RPC

That is exactly what QC does. First made available in Windows 2000 as part of COM+, QC allows developers to use MSMQ without ever seeing a traditional message queuing interface. Instead, a developer writes code that invokes methods in COM objects, and QC takes care of the details of conveying those method calls using MSMQ messages.

A Recorder captures the calls a client makes

The fundamentals of how this works are shown in Figure 9-3. In the figure, a client invokes one or more methods in an interface implemented by the COM object with which this client wishes to communicate. None of those methods is actually sent to the object, however, until the client is done using that object. As defined by QC, a client is done using an object either when the transaction those method calls are part of commits (if the calls are made within a transaction) or when the client calls Release on the interface pointer on which the calls were made. Until this happens, the information in these method calls is stored by a QC component called the *Recorder.*

Rather than forcing the developer to understand the format of data in messages, QC relies on the standard COM infrastructure to perform marshaling. Once this is done, the calls are sent to the destination COM object as MSMQ messages. At that system, the server containing the target object listens for incoming messages, and then hands them off to another QC component called the *Player.* Once again, standard COM marshalling is used, and the Player transforms each received request into the corresponding method invocation on the target object.

A Player issues calls to the target object

Figure 9-3 *Using QC, a client can send MSMQ messages by invoking methods on COM objects.*

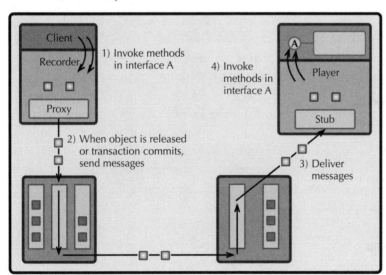

Interfaces used with
QC can have only
input parameters

Of course, using MSMQ rather than COM's more traditional mechanisms to convey method calls imposes some limitations. Most important, methods that can be invoked this way can only contain [in] parameters, and they can have no return values. This shouldn't be surprising; after all, if the client is a transactional COM object, the method-invoking messages aren't sent until the transaction the object belongs to ends. But due to just-in-time (JIT) activation, ending the transaction will also deactivate the object, which means there's nothing left to receive any return values even if they could be sent. The point is that QC is a one-way communication method. If the target object wishes to send responses using QC, it must invoke methods in an interface supported by the original client or send information back in some other way. Two-way communication requires two separate one-way paths.

Only configured compo-
nents can be accessed
using QC

Components whose methods can be invoked using QC must be configured components—that is, they must be part of a COM+ Application.[3] Like other configured components, components using QC can rely on COM's role-based security for authorization, although objects accessed via QC cannot impersonate their clients. Also, for an interface to be usable with QC, all of its methods must follow the rules listed earlier—[in] parameters only and no return values. If that is the case, the IDL for that interface can be marked with the QUEUABLE attribute, and the decision whether these methods can be invoked using QC or COM's normal mechanisms can be made for this component administratively rather than when it is written. This can be handy, since it allows the same component to be used with or without QC, depending on how it is configured. It's even possible for the same component to behave differently at different times, choosing between DCOM and QC at runtime.

---

3. QC clients need not be part of a COM+ Application, but QC itself must nonetheless be available on the client's machine. This means that those clients must be running on a Windows 2000 system.

Some developers, especially those with experience in writing message queuing applications, will have no trouble using MSMQ's more traditional APIs. But for the ever-growing number of COM-oriented developers, QC is likely to be simpler to use. And it's hard to argue with the benefits of having both choices available.

MSMQ Security Services

Like any distributed application, an application communicating via message queues is potentially exposing itself to attackers on the network. To guard against those attacks, MSMQ provides a variety of security services. For the most part, MSMQ silently provides security services when asked—applications need do nothing more than request them. To participate in secure communication, MSMQ machines can either be part of one or more Windows 2000 domains or be organized into a workgroup (although the absence of Active Directory makes some services unavailable in this latter situation).

MSMQ provides built-in security services

Authentication and Data Integrity

MSMQ allows authenticating the sender of a message using digital signatures. Recall from Chapter 4 that digital signatures also provide data integrity, guaranteeing that the receiver can detect whether changes were made to the message while it was in transit. Authentication is an option requested on a per-message basis, and as is generally the case with security services, choosing to use it reduces MSMQ performance. To accomplish authentication, MSMQ can insert as properties in a message an X.509 certificate containing the public key of the user sending the message and a digital signature created with that user's private key. MSMQ uses the services of CryptoAPI and an appropriate cryptographic service provider (CSP) to transparently create the digital signature

MSMQ provides authentication and data integrity using digital signatures

when the sender requests it.[4] Note that whether authentication is used is controlled entirely by the sender—there's no way for a message's receiver to demand that authentication be used (except, of course, by discarding any unauthenticated messages it receives or by configuring a queue to receive only authenticated messages).

MSMQ allows using both *internal* and *external* certificates. An internal certificate and its associated private key are generated and managed by MSMQ itself, and the certificate identifies its subject with a Windows 2000 SID. This option does not require creating certification authorities (CAs) with Microsoft Certificate Services or some other product. An external certificate, by contrast, is one generated by any external CA, and identifies its subject using standard X.509 naming. If an application using MSMQ runs solely within one or more Windows 2000 domains, an internal certificate is probably sufficient. MSMQ automatically creates an internal certificate when a new user requires one, and most organizations will trust its simple built-in CA. If your application must send messages outside the Windows 2000 world, however, such as through gateways to other operating systems or other message queuing products, or if you wish to rely solely on CAs outside MSMQ, external certificates can be used. Whichever option you choose, the certificate must be registered in Active Directory before it can be used, something that can be done programmatically or administratively.

Whatever the source of the certificate, messages containing a digital signature are verified by the MSMQ queue manager when they are received. (How digital signature verification works is

---

4. By default, MSMQ uses MD5 as its hash algorithm for digital signatures. If desired, the sender of a message can specify a different algorithm using the message's Hash Algorithm property. For this to be successful, however, both the sending and receiving systems must have a CSP installed that implements the new choice.

described in Chapter 4.[5]) As with creating the signature, this verification relies on an installed CSP accessed via CryptoAPI. If the signature is valid, the queue manager then looks up this certificate in Active Directory and extracts the SID for the user who registered the certificate. If the message contains a SID in its Sender ID property, the queue manager next compares this SID with the SID found in the directory. If they match, authentication succeeds. If the SIDs aren't the same, the message is discarded, and if one was requested, a negative acknowledgment is sent. And if no SID is contained in the message, this final check isn't made—the message is considered to be authenticated if its digital signature was verified.

If only a few authenticated messages will be sent, an application can send its certificate explicitly with each one. Alternatively, an application that sends many authenticated messages can create a *security context*. Once this is done, MSMQ will automatically extract the information necessary to attach a certificate to each message. Once a message's sender has been authenticated, the receiver of the message can also create a security context, then use that information to impersonate the sender. Impersonation might be useful if the receiver needs to make an authorization decision, for example, or if it must send the message on under the identity of the original sender.

Applications that send many authenticated messages can create a security context

Data Privacy

Providing data privacy means encrypting the contents of a message, and MSMQ allows two ways to do this. The simplest choice, available only to applications running in a Windows 2000 domain, is

If requested, MSMQ will encrypt a message before sending it

---

5. When verifying signatures using external certificates, MSMQ does not rely on the standard Windows 2000 certificate stores described in Chapter 4. Instead, external certificates must be registered in the personal certificate store provided by Microsoft Internet Explorer. In fact, MSMQ makes no attempt to determine whether the CA that issued an external certificate is trusted. It's up to the application to determine which CAs it trusts to issue external certificates.

to request this service from MSMQ. To do this, the sender sets the Privacy Level property in the message, and as with authentication, the MSMQ queue manager silently provides the service.

Message encryption uses secret key algorithms

The message receiver need do nothing special to read an encrypted message. Instead, by the time the receiver sees it, an MSMQ queue manager has already transformed the message back to its original form. By default, MSMQ encrypts data using RC2, but an application can request RC4 instead by setting a message's encryption algorithm property. The available key lengths, and thus the security of the encryption, depend on what CSPs are available. Both the sender and the receiver (but not intermediate systems) must have installed a CSP that supports the chosen algorithm. Note that messages sent between dependent clients and their assigned MSMQ server are always sent unencrypted, because there's no queue manager on the dependent client—only the MSMQ API libraries are present.

Providing data privacy in the world of message queuing poses some interesting problems. Chief among them is this: since a sender can send an encrypted message to an unknown receiver, how is it possible for sender and receiver to agree on what encryption key should be used? Because public key encryption is generally too slow to use for encrypting the actual message, the key in question is for use with RC2 or RC4, both of which are secret key algorithms. But how can the sending queue manager securely transfer this key to the destination queue manager?

MSMQ sends a secret key by encrypting it using the destination queue manager's public key

To solve this problem, each queue manager has a public/private key pair. When it needs to send an encrypted message, the sending queue manager randomly generates an RC2 or RC4 secret key. It encrypts the outgoing message using this secret key, then encrypts the secret key itself using the public key of the destination queue manager. When it receives this message, the destination queue manager uses its private key to decrypt the secret key the message contains, then uses this secret key to decrypt the message's contents.

An MSMQ application can also itself encrypt a message's body using the built-in data privacy services of Windows 2000. To do this, the application essentially performs the steps just described: it creates a secret key and uses it to encrypt the message's body, then uses the public key of the receiving queue manager to encrypt this key. All of that information is then sent in the message, and the receiving queue manager decrypts it as already described. Although it's more work, this option is useful when the sending and receiving systems aren't part of a domain and thus can't use Active Directory to find the receiving queue manager's public key.

Auditing

An MSMQ application or administrator can ask MSMQ to automatically keep a record of various events for one or more queues. This auditing function allows an administrator to keep tabs on who is doing what in an MSMQ environment. For example, a queue can be set to record every attempt to open a queue, every attempt to change a queue's permissions, and more. While it can lead to huge event logs, auditing can nonetheless be a very useful tool in a secure environment.

MSMQ can audit various events

MSMQ and Transactions

Although the most common use of transactions today is with databases, recall from Chapter 7 that transaction processing people use the generic term *resource manager* to refer to anything managing changes that are part of a transaction. And database management systems aren't the only things that can act as resource managers. MSMQ, too, can be a resource manager.

MSMQ can act as a resource manager

To get a sense of what this means and why it's so useful, think about the QwickBank example described in Chapter 1. In this application, a client request to the banking COM object might make changes to one or more databases that contain information about customer accounts. For example, a call to the MoveMoney method can transfer money between two accounts, modifying the database record containing each account balance. Recall that QwickBank's policy is to send customers written confirmation of transfers over $10,000, and that this policy is implemented by having the MoveMoney method send an MSMQ message to another system indicating that a large transfer has occurred. That system eventually reads the message, prints a letter, and causes it to be sent. This is a good example of where message queuing is useful, since the user making the funds transfer needn't wait for this request to be received and processed.

Yet it's entirely reasonable to demand that either both of these things happen—the account balances are changed in the databases and the message is sent requesting written confirmation—or neither one does. It wouldn't make much sense for a customer to receive a letter confirming her large transfer when the transaction that accomplished this transfer actually aborted. The simplest way to avoid this situation is to make the funds transfer and the act of sending the MSMQ message that triggers the letter part of the same transaction.

Transactions can be useful in other MSMQ scenarios as well. Because of this, MSMQ provides several options for supporting transactions. All of them, however, depend on the idea of a transactional queue.

Transactional Queues

To allow a queue to participate in a transaction, its Transaction property must be set when the queue is created. Once this is done, this *transactional queue* will be capable of acting as a resource manager under the control of DTC (and indirectly of a COM+ Application). An application can only send a message to a transactional queue if the application is currently part of a transaction, although it's legal to receive a message from a transactional queue even if you're not currently in a transaction. Messages sent to transactional queues are sometimes called *transactional messages*, and they contain special attributes that mark them as part of a transaction.

MSMQ certainly doesn't require you to use transactions when sending or receiving messages. You might find, however, that many, even most, of your applications are sending messages to transactional queues. Here's a big reason why: for non-transactional queues, MSMQ doesn't guarantee either in-order delivery or exactly-once semantics for messages. In other words, a group of messages sent to a non-transactional queue can be delivered in a different order than they were sent, and some of those messages can be delivered more than once. If a message requests, say, a deduction from your QwickBank savings account, having it delivered twice is not an appealing prospect. For transactional queues, however, MSMQ can guarantee both in-order delivery and exactly-once semantics. In this case, one transmission is guaranteed to result in one message appearing in the destination queue, and MSMQ promises to deliver all of your messages in the order in which they were sent. If you know that your messages must be delivered in order and only once, a requirement for many applications, use transactional queues.

Transactions guarantee in-order delivery and exactly-once semantics

Kinds of MSMQ Transactions

MSMQ applications can use transactional queues in several different ways. Which one you choose depends on your exact requirements. This section describes each of the options.

COM+ Transactions   One very common way to use transactional queues is for an MSMQ application to be implemented using transactional COM objects. In this case, the application ultimately relies on DTC, as shown in Figure 9-4, just like the objects in any COM+ Application. The figure omits some of the details shown in earlier chapters, but the fundamental idea is the same. The only difference is that now both MSMQ and a DBMS are acting as resource managers, and both automatically enlist in the transaction.

COM+ Applications can include MSMQ sends and receives in a transaction

Figure 9-4 *MSMQ can act as a resource manager accessed by a transactional COM object.*

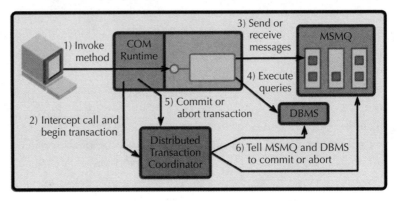

For a more concrete example, think once more about the QwickBank application. In the process of moving money between two accounts, the application (implemented as a COM configured component with its transaction attribute set to, say, Required) makes changes to databases and sends a message to a transactional queue. If all goes well, the COM object calls SetComplete and the transaction commits. Committing the transaction causes two things to occur: the DBMS makes the changes to the database permanent, and MSMQ sends the message. Because the queue was marked as transactional, any message sent to it is held until the transaction the message is part of completes. If the transaction is committed, the message is sent. If the transaction is rolled back, however, the message is removed from the queue—it never gets sent. Both the database changes and the sending of the message either happen or don't happen, which is exactly as it should be for this application. And as already mentioned, the act of receiving a message can also be part of a transaction—if the transaction commits, the message is permanently removed from the queue. If it aborts, however, the message is returned to the queue, waiting to be received again.

Using transactional queues with COM+ Applications is common

In this scenario, the COM object sends and receives MSMQ messages as always (although those requests must be made on a transactional queue), and the COM runtime silently takes care of the transaction. One drawback of this approach is that it requires writing the application as one or more COM objects, which might not always be appropriate. If an application wishes to include a receive operation as part of a transaction, for example, this approach requires that the receive request be issued by a COM object that's already part of a transaction. This can sometimes be awkward to accomplish. Still, a large number of MSMQ applications are built in this way.

DTC External Transactions   Rather than let the COM runtime communicate with DTC to start and end transactions, an application using MSMQ is free to communicate with DTC directly, as shown in Figure 9-5. This is no different from any other application that uses DTC. As described in Chapter 7, if an application's developer understands the OLE Transactions interfaces, she is free to issue MSMQ sends and receives within an explicitly defined transaction. Like a DBMS, MSMQ acts as a resource manager, behaving appropriately when the transaction ends. Recall, however, that understanding and using OLE Transactions is not simple, so this approach is not especially common. In most cases, developers will choose to let the COM runtime manage transactions, as just described, instead of doing it themselves.

MSMQ applications can control transactions using DTC

Figure 9-5   *MSMQ applications can use DTC to directly control transactions.*

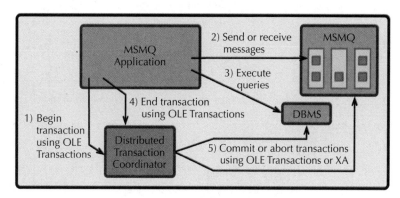

MSMQ can look like an
XA-compliant resource
manager

XA-Compliant Transactions Here's another possibility: suppose you'd like to use MSMQ within a transaction, but your transaction coordinator is not DTC. This means that your application is using some non-Microsoft transaction product, but you'd like MSMQ to participate in its transactions. In this case, you still want MSMQ to act as a resource manager, and this is possible. To see how, remember that the standard XA interface, mentioned in Chapter 7, is supported by transaction coordinators from many vendors, allowing them to communicate with resource managers to carry out transactions. MSMQ doesn't support XA—it only understands the Microsoft-specific OLE Transactions interfaces—but all is not lost. Along with its usual function as a transaction coordinator, DTC is capable of acting as an XA-to-OLE Transactions translator. As shown in Figure 9-6, a transaction coordinator that doesn't speak OLE Transactions (that is, pretty much every transaction coordinator in the world except Microsoft's DTC) can still include MSMQ operations in a transaction by relying on DTC to translate. As long as the transaction coordinator speaks XA, as most do, the combination of the DTC translator and MSMQ will act like a standard XA-compliant resource manager.

Figure 9-6 *MSMQ can look like an XA-compliant resource manager by relying on the DTC to translate XA into OLE Transactions.*

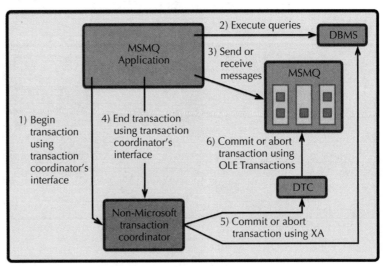

MSMQ Internal Transactions Finally, as shown in Figure 9-7, MSMQ also supports internal transactions. This option doesn't rely on the COM runtime, DTC, or any other software that's not part of MSMQ itself. Because of this, MSMQ internal transactions can't include work performed by some other resource manager, such as a database management system, in a single atomic operation. Instead, an MSMQ internal transaction allows an application to group several sends and receives on a queue into an atomic unit. MSMQ itself ensures that all the operations happen or none of them do. And because the only way to ensure exactly-once delivery of an MSMQ message is to use a transactional queue, MSMQ provides a special option that allows doing a single send with an internal transaction. That message is guaranteed to be delivered exactly once, but no other operations are included in this transaction.[6]

Internal transactions are provided by MSMQ itself

Figure 9-7 *MSMQ internal transactions guarantee delivery, but don't rely on anything outside of MSMQ itself.*

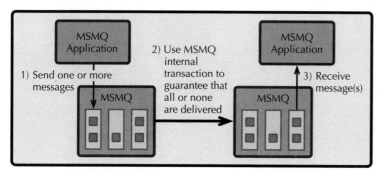

MSMQ does some standard things to every message sent to a transactional queue. For example, MSMQ sets the Priority property of all transactional messages to zero. This makes sense, since MSMQ guarantees in-order delivery of transactional messages

---

6. One could reasonably argue that the use of the term "transaction" in this case is a misnomer, since the word usually implies two or more operations grouped together. Because MSMQ requires transactions of some kind to ensure exactly-once delivery, however, allowing a single send to be its own transaction is sometimes necessary. And from MSMQ's point of view, more than one operation must complete successfully to perform the transaction.

sent to a particular queue. If different messages had different priorities, received messages could be placed in a queue in an order different from that in which they were sent. MSMQ also sets the Delivery property of every transactional message to Recoverable, ensuring that those messages will survive system crashes. And if a transactional message is undeliverable, that message is always sent to a special transactional dead letter queue on the machine that sent it.

Allowing MSMQ to participate in transactions makes it much more useful. Defining several different ways for this to happen makes understanding this topic more challenging, but it also increases the number of situations in which transactional queues can be used. As always, it's up to an application's designer to make the trade-off between correctness and complexity.

Routing in MSMQ

MSMQ attempts to establish a direct connection between sender and receiver

Suppose an MSMQ independent client sends a message to a queue on some MSMQ server. The simplest and fastest way to get that message to its destination queue is for MSMQ on the client to establish a transport-layer connection, usually using TCP, with MSMQ on the machine that contains the target queue. If establishing a direct connection is possible, this is exactly what MSMQ does.

If necessary, MSMQ will route a message from sender to receiver

But what if it's not possible? What happens when the client and the server are on different networks, for example, and a direct connection isn't possible? In this situation, MSMQ performs its own routing. To decide what route a message should take, MSMQ can take advantage of queue priorities, message priorities, and some administratively set parameters. If the destination system is not currently available, MSMQ will keep trying to deliver the message until it either succeeds or is forced to delete the message.

Although it's not required, MSMQ is usually deployed in an environment using Windows 2000 domains, which means that Active

Directory is available. As described in Chapter 2, Active Directory supports the idea of a *site*. A site consists of a defined group of IP subnets, and all systems within that site should be connected by fast links.

MSMQ exploits this notion, automatically handling routing within a single site. To route messages between sites, however, an MSMQ administrator must define the available paths that messages might take. A connection used to route messages between two sites is called a *routing link*,[7] and two MSMQ servers acting as *site gates* can be directly connected via this link. The administrator can assign a cost to each of these links, and these link costs are used by MSMQ to make intelligent routing decisions when passing messages between sites. Figure 9-8 shows an MSMQ environment with two sites, site gates, and a routing link between them.

MSMQ routes messages between sites via a routing link

Figure 9-8 *MSMQ connects sites with a routing link.*

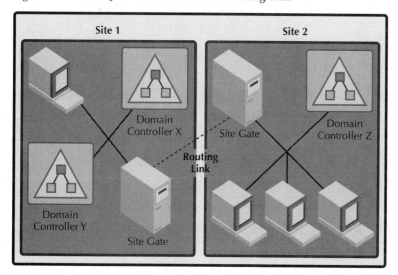

---

7. MSMQ 1.0 defined its own notion of sites, and so routing links were originally named site links. In Windows 2000, the term "site link" refers to connections used by Active Directory to replicate information between sites. An MSMQ routing link is an entirely separate idea.

An administrator can configure several independent clients within a site to always send messages through the same MSMQ server, an option called *session concentration*. The result is a star-like logical topology, where even messages from one independent client to another are sent first to the MSMQ server at the center of the star. Session concentration can reduce the network bandwidth used by MSMQ at the cost of adding an extra hop to the path between those clients. Site gates also allow intersite session concentration, since all messages sent to and from a particular site must go through the site gate. This simplifies the network's routing topology, although the number of hops that some messages must take might increase.

Session concentration allows all messages to be routed through a single MSMQ server

Connecting MSMQ to Other Systems

MSMQ is a fine technology, but it's not the only messaging product in the world. Similarly, Windows 2000 is a popular operating system, but it's far from the only system in use today. To be really useful, then, MSMQ must be able to interwork effectively with other messaging products and other operating systems.

To make this possible, gateways can be created from MSMQ to other messaging technologies. For example, Microsoft makes available the MSMQ-MQSeries Bridge, a gateway that links MSMQ with IBM's MQSeries, another popular message queuing product. While protocol gateways can in general be challenging to administer and use, the asynchronous nature of message queuing makes mapping between different queuing products less painful than, say, doing real-time translation between different RPC protocols.

Microsoft makes available an MSMQ-MQSeries gateway

To link with e-mail, MSMQ includes the Exchange Connector, allowing messages sent with MSMQ to be delivered via e-mail and vice versa. Microsoft also provides a Messaging API (MAPI) Transport provider, allowing any client that supports MAPI to send and receive messages using MSMQ. As might be expected,

The MSMQ Exchange Connector provides a gateway between message queuing and e-mail

moving messages from e-mail to MSMQ has some limitations—
attachments aren't always allowed, for example—but it can still
be very handy. For example, suppose that the QwickBank application described earlier needs to inform a bank manager whenever
a funds transfer occurs of more than $100,000. One solution would
be to write an MSMQ application for this and install it (and MSMQ)
on each manager's system. Another, probably simpler, choice
would be for the MSMQ application to send that notification as
e-mail using the Exchange Connector. Now the bank manager
can learn about the error without using a special application—
the news just arrives in e-mail.

MSMQ 2.0 is a standard part of Windows 2000, but at the time
this book is being written, Microsoft did not provide MSMQ 2.0
clients for Windows 95, Windows 98, or Windows NT 4.0.
MSMQ 1.0 clients are available from another company, Level 8,
for a range of other operating systems, including various UNIXs,
OpenVMS, MVS, and the AS/400. With this third-party support,
MSMQ has perhaps the strongest multiplatform story of any of
Windows 2000's distributed services.

Level 8 sells MSMQ clients for non-Microsoft operating systems

Message queuing is unquestionably a good idea, and there are
plenty of problems for which it's just the right solution. A complete set of distributed services, something that Windows 2000
aspires to provide, can't exist without support for message queuing. Although it probably hasn't received the attention it deserves,
MSMQ is likely to be used in more and more Windows 2000
applications.

Message queuing is a necessary service in a distributed environment

Chapter Ten

Web Application Services

It's probably fair to say that most distributed applications built today allow access from a Web browser. Making an application Web-accessible potentially allows anyone to use it, since browsers have become ubiquitous. Doing this can also allow access from anywhere, since the Internet has become ubiquitous, too. While it's still common to build a custom client that uses DCOM to remotely communicate with business logic on a server, allowing at least the option of browser-based access has become almost obligatory.

The fundamental model of Web access is not especially complex. Clients, which are typically Web browsers such as Microsoft Internet Explorer, send requests to a Web server, such as Microsoft Internet Information Services (IIS) 5.0, the Web server included in Microsoft Windows 2000. These requests are made using the Hypertext Transfer Protocol (HTTP). The Web server responds with a stream of information, which is also sent via HTTP and is commonly annotated using the Hypertext Markup Language (HTML).

Most applications must allow browser access

Browsers access Web servers via HTTP, retrieving HTML-annotated information

More complex, however, are the different ways in which the information returned by the Web server can be generated. If the Web server is IIS, what it returns can come from several sources, as shown in Figure 10-1. Those sources include:

- *Ordinary files*   These files contain HTML, which is simply read by IIS and sent to the browser. The HTML in these files can also contain simple embedded programs, commonly called *scripts.* Written in relatively simple languages such as JavaScript and Microsoft VBScript, these scripts are executed by the browser when it receives them.

- *Common Gateway Interface (CGI) applications*   CGI was the first widely used technology for interfacing applications with Web servers. A CGI application, commonly written in a language such as Perl or C++, can be passed parameters sent by its client, then return HTML and other information that it has dynamically generated in response to the client's request. Each client request launches a new process to handle that request.

- *Internet Server API (ISAPI) extensions and filters*   ISAPI is similar to CGI in that parameters sent from a browser can be passed to an application through a simple interface implemented by IIS, with results again sent back to the browser. Unlike CGI, ISAPI applications are written as DLLs, usually in C++, which makes them more efficient but also more difficult to write.

- *Active Server Pages (ASPs)*   Just as an HTML file can contain scripts that are sent to and executed by a browser, it can also contain scripts that are executed by IIS itself. An ASP page is script stored in an ordinary HTML file but executed by the server, with results sent back to the browser. Typically created with relatively simple languages such as VBScript, these programs take input from browsers and return results, much like CGI applications and ISAPI DLLs. They're significantly easier to write, however, and so ASPs are the most commonly used approach to building IIS applications today.

Figure 10-1 *The information returned by IIS can come from several sources.*

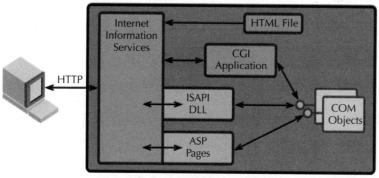

Windows 2000 Server

The last three of these options—CGI applications, ISAPI DLLs, and ASP pages—can also create and use COM objects, which allows them to access transactional COM applications, stored data through ActiveX Data Objects (ADO), Active Directory through the Active Directory Services Interface (ADSI), Microsoft Message Queuing (MSMQ), and more. To understand how all of this works, it's useful to begin with a brief description of Web technology basics.

IIS applications can use COM objects

Web Basics

The Web has become so popular so fast that nearly everyone in the Western world has a basic idea of how it works. Still, understanding the services Windows 2000 includes for building Web-accessible applications requires knowing a bit more than the average user about what's really going on. The goal of this section is to provide that knowledge.

Accessing HTML Files

As every schoolchild knows, accessing information on the Web requires giving your browser the Uniform Resource Locator (URL) of whatever you're interested in. A URL commonly contains the name of a protocol, the Domain Name System (DNS) name of a

A URL can reference an HTML file on a server machine

server to access using that protocol, and some kind of path to a resource, such as a file, on that server. For example, if you type the URL *http://www.qwickbank.com/info.htm* into your Web browser, you're asking the browser to first use DNS to find the IP address of the machine that corresponds to the name www. qwickbank.com. (This step was shown in the example in Chapter 1; to keep things simple, I won't mention it again in the discussion here.) Your browser will then use HTTP to access that machine and return the contents of the file info.htm. The filename in this sample URL ends in .htm, indicating that the file contains HTML. In this simple case, IIS needs only to read the file and send it back to the browser to be rendered, as shown in Figure 10-2. If you're at all familiar with HTML, you'll recognize that this simple example just displays the heading "An HTML Example", then displays the word "Hello" between horizontal lines.

Figure 10-2 *A request specifying the URL* http://www.qwickbank.com/ info.htm *causes IIS to send back the contents of the file info.htm.*

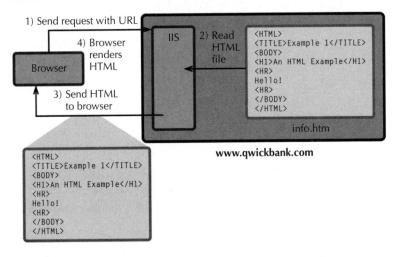

Requesting an HTML file that contains an embedded script to be executed on the client is very similar. Once again, the browser sends a URL that names an HTML file on some server, that server returns the file, and the browser renders it, as shown in Figure 10-3. The difference is that because the file contains a script, the

HTML files can contain scripts to be executed by the browser

browser will execute the commands in that script and display the result.[1] Although I won't describe the details here, the very simple script shown in Figure 10-3 displays much the same information as the previous example: a heading followed by the word "Hello" between horizontal lines.

Figure 10-3 *HTML sent by IIS can contain scripts—simple programs that are executed by the browser.*

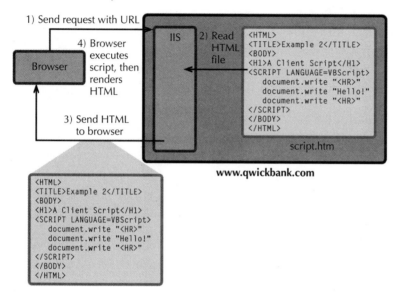

As already described, though, a URL might also name a file that contains not just HTML but instead some kind of executable code. Exactly what that code looks like depends on what kind of application this is: CGI, ISAPI, or ASP. In all these cases, however, IIS loads the specified file and the application executes. The result the application generates, typically information wrapped in HTML, is handed to IIS, which sends it back to the browser for rendering.

A URL can reference an application on a server machine

---

1. Although it's not shown here, it's also possible for an HTML page to request downloading a type of COM component called an ActiveX control. When the control is downloaded, it can be executed inside Internet Explorer, interacting with the user and with any script code on that page.

To create that result, the application might access a database, invoke other applications, or perform any other required processing. Building Web-accessible applications is the focus of this chapter, and so it's examined in much more detail later.

Understanding HTTP

It's entirely possible to use a Web browser while having no idea how HTTP actually works. It's also possible, but not especially desirable, to build Web applications in the same state of ignorance. Grasping some of the fundamentals of Web-based development requires knowing at least a few things about this widely used protocol.

HTTP defines a set of methods that clients can invoke

Protocol Basics   HTTP is not especially complicated. It defines a group of methods, each of which is used for a particular purpose, that can be invoked by browsers. The method name and its parameters are sent as simple character strings across a TCP connection, with the results returned the same way. Among the most interesting HTTP methods are:

- *GET*   Allows a client to retrieve information. The response to a GET request contains a message body along with some basic header information, such as the type of information the body contains. The possible set of types— known as Multipurpose Internet Mail Extensions (MIME) types—includes text/html, image/gif, image/jpeg, and many more. The requests for HTML files shown in the earlier figures were actually made using the GET method.

- *HEAD*   Returns the same information as GET, except that the message body is not returned.

- *POST*   Allows a client to send information to a Web server. Input entered by users through forms is commonly sent using this method.

Before an HTTP method is invoked, a Secure Sockets Layer (SSL) exchange can occur as described in Chapter 4. In this case, the HTTP exchange will be encrypted during transit. This combination of HTTP and SSL used together is sometimes referred to as HTTPS. When a browser accesses a typical Web page, that page might contain several different elements: HTML, references to various graphics files, and more. All of the elements in the page are not transferred in a single HTTP request, however. Instead, multiple GETs are issued, each for a specific part of the page.[2] In HTTP 1.0, a separate TCP connection was established for each GET. In HTTP 1.1, supported today by IIS and many other Web servers, multiple GET requests can occur over a single TCP connection. Yet even then, the Web server itself doesn't keep track of the fact that all of these requests are from the same client. To the server, each GET is independent—it doesn't care that they're all from the same browser. Another way to describe this kind of behavior is to say that the interaction is *stateless*, because the receiving HTTP implementation maintains no state about its clients. The server simply sends back whatever information is requested by each GET, viewing every request as completely independent from any other. HTTP was originally intended for accessing static files containing HTML, so this model made perfect sense.

In a world of dynamic Web-based applications, however, it makes much less sense. To see why this simple approach can cause problems, imagine that you wish to access your QwickBank accounts via the Internet. Using your browser, you probably log on by entering your name and password, then perhaps make various requests: check an account balance, transfer funds, and so on. To you, all of these requests take place in a single "session"—you log on once,

HTTP treats each method invocation as an independent request

Building Web applications typically requires tracking sessions

---

2. To make loading a page look more even to the user, and perhaps to make it faster, Internet Explorer creates several threads to handle a single user request, then has each one issue a GET for an element on that page.

transact your business, then leave. But the HTTP protocol has no intrinsic support for the notion of sessions. To it, each request you make is independent of all the others. To let you log on once, then let all the various pages you're using have access to the information you initially entered, such as your name, requires somehow grafting the notion of a session onto a series of stateless HTTP interactions. To allow this kind of state management, HTTP allows using cookies. How this works is described next.

Creating Sessions: Cookies   A cookie is simply a byte string that gets passed back and forth between a Web server and a browser. This cookie can contain anything—by default, IIS uses a fairly complex algorithm to generate it based on the current time, some random values, and more—but whatever it contains, the cookie must be unique for each client. If IIS receives a request from a browser that does not contain a cookie, it can create one and return it to the browser. The browser stores this cookie in memory or possibly on disk, then sends it back to the server with each request. This allows IIS to determine that a group of requests are all part of the same session, since each request contains the same cookie.

A cookie allows a Web server to recognize requests made on the same session

IIS can begin a new session when it receives a request from a cookie-less browser. But how can it know when a session ends? One solution is for an application to explicitly inform IIS that a session has ended. Another is to set a timer for each session, and if no requests come from the browser within that time period, to unilaterally terminate the session. It's also possible that a user might begin making requests again after the initial session times out, but before either the user's browser or IIS have been restarted. If this happens, those requests will carry the same cookie, but IIS will nevertheless begin a new session for this user.

A session can time out if the user makes no requests for a while

Some Web application environments, such as ASPs, provide explicit support for sessions. An ASP developer can completely ignore cookies and instead rely on IIS to manage sessions. Other

ASPs provide built-in support for cookie-based session management

environments, however, provide no intrinsic support for sessions other than the ability to send and receive cookies. Developers of CGI applications and ISAPI DLLs who wish to group requests into sessions, for example, must explicitly work with cookies to do this—there's no built-in support.

If a cookie is used solely to group multiple HTTP requests into a single session, then the cookie's value is irrelevant. As long as it's different from every other cookie this server sees, the Web server will be able to determine which requests belong to the same session. And by default, cookies are deleted from the client when the browser is shut down. It's possible, however, to both store useful information in the cookie and to cause a browser to store the cookie on disk for future use. For example, if a Web application asks the user to enter a name, this name can be placed in a cookie and sent back to the browser. If the application has set an expiration date on the cookie, the browser will write it to disk on the client machine, deleting it only when the expiration date is reached. The next time the user accesses this application, the browser sends the cookie, and the application can greet the user by name. It's even possible to create indexed cookies that contain multiple values, allowing all kinds of information about the user to be stored on the client machine.

Cookies can contain information about a user, such as her name

IIS Basics

Like other Web servers, IIS is designed to accept and process HTTP requests, then send back results. As already described, processing a request might require IIS to simply read an HTML file and send back its contents, or it might require passing the request to some application. IIS is not a small piece of code, so it presents plenty of interesting topics for discussion. Two of them are especially relevant here, however: virtual directories and IIS authentication.

Virtual Directories

When a browser sends a URL as part of a request, IIS must somehow map that URL to the element this URL names. While it would be possible to use complete file pathnames in a URL to do this, the result wouldn't appeal to most users. To allow using simpler URLs, IIS defines the notion of a *virtual directory* (also called a *virtual root*). A virtual directory is just an alias for an actual directory in the file system, and its primary purpose is to make the URLs seen by clients shorter. Internet Services Manager, the IIS snap-in, can be used to designate a particular physical directory as a virtual directory and to assign it a name. Once this is done, a URL passed in from a browser can contain the virtual directory name, and IIS will map it to the actual directory path. Rather than storing this mapping in the registry, as was done in previous releases, IIS 5.0 stores it in the IIS metabase, which is the repository for most IIS configuration information.

For example, suppose QwickBank chooses to store a group of HTML files in the directory c:\inetpub\marketing\information on the machine associated with www.qwickbank.com. Using Internet Services Manager, QwickBank's Web administrator could create a virtual directory called info, and associate it with c:\inetpub\marketing\information. If a client issues a request to this machine with the URL *http://www.qwickbank.com/info/ newcust.htm*, IIS will map the virtual directory name "info" in that URL to the real directory with which it's associated, c:\inetpub\marketing\information, then look in that directory for newcust.htm.

Authentication in IIS

Like any server application that can be accessed remotely, IIS often needs to know who its users are. In other words, it must have some way to authenticate those users. IIS can be configured to do this in several different ways, and can simultaneously use different authentication mechanisms with different clients. The options include:

- *Anonymous authentication*   IIS performs no authentication of its users. Instead, each user is mapped to the same Windows 2000 user account, and so is allowed access to any HTML files, ISAPI DLLs, or ASP pages for which this account has permissions.

- *Basic authentication*   IIS requests a username and password, then transmits them across the network. If requests are made using HTTPS—that is, if SSL is used with HTTP—this information will be encrypted using the normal SSL mechanisms described in Chapter 4. If not, it's sent unencrypted.

- *Digest authentication*   As in Basic authentication, Digest authentication relies on a username and password provided by the client. Unlike Basic authentication, however, this information is not sent in the clear across the network. Instead, the username and password are concatenated together with a timestamp and other information. This information is hashed using the MD5 algorithm, and the resulting hash value is sent to IIS. Since IIS knows the client's password, the timestamp, and everything else the client used to create this hash, it can compute the same hash value. If the client and server have used the same password, the hash value computed by the server will match that sent by the client and authentication will succeed. If they used different passwords, however, the computed hash values won't match, and so authentication will fail. The client still relies on its password to authenticate itself, since the password is part of the information that is hashed, but the password is never sent in the clear across the network. This makes Digest authentication significantly more secure than Basic Authentication.

- *Integrated Windows Authentication*   Typically used in an intranet rather than on the public Internet, this option allows IIS to negotiate with a browser to choose either Kerberos or NTLM as the authentication protocol. This approach can only be used with Internet Explorer, and Kerberos is supported only beginning with Internet Explorer Version 5.0—earlier versions support only NTLM. Note too that using Kerberos allows delegation—the ability to securely authenticate requests passed from IIS to another machine—something that isn't possible with NTLM.

- *SSL*   As described in Chapter 4, IIS relies on the SChannel security service provider (SSP) for its SSL implementation. Recall that SSL uses certificates and digital signatures to prove the server's identity to clients, and that if the client has a private key and certificate, SSL can also be used to authenticate that client. Chapter 4 described how Microsoft Certificate Services can be used to construct a CA hierarchy capable of issuing certificates usable with anyone who trusts that hierarchy. SSL is most commonly used on the public Internet, however, and so typical clients are unwilling to trust certificates issued by any organization's internal CAs (why should they?). As a result, a certificate used by IIS to authenticate itself to clients must usually be acquired from a trusted public CA such as VeriSign, Thawte, or another commercial organization. If IIS is configured to accept client certificates as well, the client's signature sent during the SSL exchange is verified as described in Chapter 4. For example, if the CA that issued the client's certificate or the root CA in the certificate's certification chain has a self-signed certificate in the IIS server machine's Trusted Root CA store and all of the certificates in the chain are valid, the client's certificate will be trusted for signature verification.

Providing good distributed security is never simple. IIS offers several options because different situations have different requirements. In general, it's a good thing to use the strongest authentication mechanism that's practical in your environment, because you might as well have the best security you can. Otherwise, why bother?

Understanding CGI

CGI is both the oldest and the most widely supported mechanism for building Web applications. In the IIS environment, however, it's usually not the best choice for creating new applications. One big reason for this is that, as mentioned earlier, CGI starts a new process for each request from a client, something that is unavoidably slow.

CGI starts a new process for each request

CGI is very simple to understand, however. When IIS receives a request from a client that references a CGI application, it packages the information in that request into a standard format, launches the application as a separate process, then passes the request's information to the new process via standard input and command line arguments. Information that can't be accommodated in this standard format can be placed in environment variables that are also made available to the newly created process. The CGI application performs whatever processing is required to handle this request correctly, then writes its response to standard output. This response is read by IIS, which constructs the appropriate HTML and returns it to the client. Figure 10-4 illustrates the process.

IIS passes client-supplied information to a CGI application, then sends the client information returned by that application

IIS supports CGI, but Microsoft doesn't encourage its use. In fact, it's probably fair to say that CGI support is there primarily to allow IIS to run applications that were originally created for other Web servers. It makes more sense to build new applications using either ISAPI or, most commonly, ASPs.

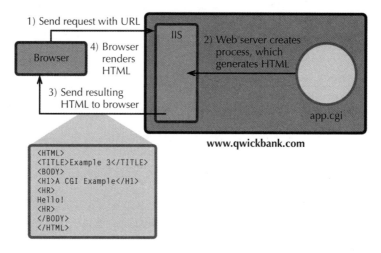

Figure 10-4 *A CGI application is a separate process that accepts parameters, performs some processing, then sends results back to IIS.*

```
<HTML>
<TITLE>Example 3</TITLE>
<BODY>
<H1>A CGI Example</H1>
<HR>
Hello!
<HR>
</BODY>
</HTML>
```

Understanding ISAPI

ISAPI DLLs can be either extensions or filters

An application built using ISAPI can offer the best performance of any option available with IIS. And because the developer is working in a relatively low-level language, typically C++, ISAPI-based code can directly access all the services provided by Windows 2000. For some kinds of problems, then, an ISAPI DLL is just the right solution. Using ISAPI, a developer can create either *extensions* or *filters*. This section first describes extensions, the more commonly used of the two, then looks at filters.

How an extension is typically used is shown in Figure 10-5. A browser sends an HTTP request to IIS, such as a GET, specifying a URL that points to an ISAPI extension. If it's not already loaded, IIS locates this DLL and loads it into memory. IIS then passes the extension any parameters that accompanied the request, and eventually gets a response. This result is sent back to the browser to be displayed to the user.

Figure 10-5 *An ISAPI extension DLL can be loaded when the first request arrives, then remain loaded to handle future requests.*

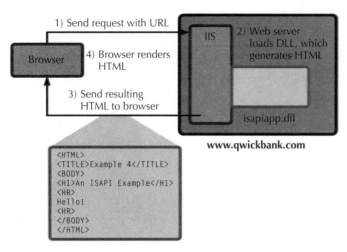

An ISAPI extension can be loaded into the IIS process or into a separate process, depending on how it has been configured. The tradeoff, as usual, is between speed and reliability—loading an ISAPI DLL into IIS allows very fast access, but a bug in that DLL can take down the entire Web server. Once it's loaded, however, whether in the IIS process or a separate process, the ISAPI extension will by default remain loaded until the process it's running in is shut down.

For every request received from a client, IIS creates a data structure called an extension control block, then fills the fields in this data structure with the information received on this HTTP request. This information includes the HTTP method the client specified (such as GET or POST), any query string that appeared on the request (that is, information after the "?" in the URL sent by the browser), and more. Once this is done, IIS passes this data structure to the ISAPI extension by passing it as the sole parameter on its call to the most important function the extension provides, HttpExtensionProc.

The code in the extension examines the extension control block it receives and performs whatever actions it wishes. The extension can do pretty much anything it likes to satisfy this request, including accessing one or more databases, creating and using COM objects, and so on. To send a response back to the client, an ISAPI extension invokes a callback function provided by IIS called WriteClient. Whatever information the extension passes via this call is sent back to the client using HTTP.

A filter is invoked whenever an event occurs for which it has registered

Filters are similar to extensions, but they also have important differences. Like an extension, an ISAPI filter is a DLL that gets loaded into the IIS process. Unlike an extension, however, a filter is loaded when the Web server starts, staying in memory until the process is shut down. When a filter is loaded, it passes IIS a list of the events it wishes to be notified of. There are several possible IIS actions that a filter can hear about, including authorizing a user, sending a response to a user, writing a log record, and more. Whenever an event occurs in which a filter has registered interest, IIS invokes the HttpFilterProc function in that filter, passing it information about the event. The filter can then participate in how this event is handled. A filter can perform specialized authentication, for example, or encryption of data, or it can even add a footer to every page IIS sends. Used excessively, ISAPI filters can hurt performance, since they intervene in many requests, but they're an attractive solution for some kinds of problems.

Writing ISAPI extensions and filters can be hard

Compared to CGI applications or ASPs, writing an ISAPI extension is a difficult task. First of all, working in C++ is significantly more challenging than creating ASP pages in VBScript. Also, ISAPI provides minimal services—as mentioned earlier, for example, there's no built-in support for sessions. Furthermore, an ISAPI extension must handle multiple threads simultaneously, since IIS, which itself contains multiple threads, will not wait for one call to HttpExtensionProc to return before invoking it again to handle another user request. In general, it's probably safe to assume that the majority of IIS applications can be created using ASPs, with ISAPI reserved for those cases that truly demand the highest possible performance.

Understanding ASPs

The basic idea of an ASP page is not hard to understand. As was shown in Figure 10-3 on page 373, a file containing HTML can also contain executable code written in a language such as JavaScript or VBScript. In that earlier example, this code was sent to the client and executed by the browser. An ASP page is based on a very similar notion, consisting of script code embedded in an HTML file. With ASPs, however, the executable code contained in the file is executed on the server rather than on the client machine. The result of that execution, together with any HTML or other information contained in the file, is sent to the client and displayed by the browser. How the process works is shown in Figure 10-6.

An ASP page contains script code executed on the server machine

Figure 10-6 *A request referencing an ASP page causes IIS to execute the script in the named file, then send the result to the client.*

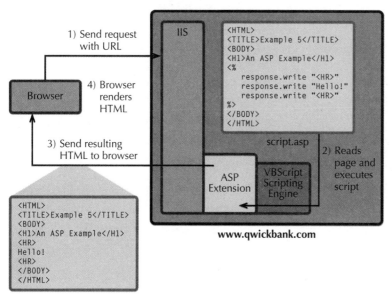

www.qwickbank.com

An ASP page's code is interpreted by a scripting engine

As the example suggests, the ASP functionality can be thought of as two separate parts. One is a scripting engine that actually reads and interprets the script code on the page, and the other is a standard ISAPI extension named asp.dll that actually implements the core ASP functions. Which scripting engine is loaded depends on what language the page contains. In Figure 10-6, the script uses the default ASP language, VBScript, and so the VBScript scripting engine is loaded. For the remainder of this chapter, the scripting engine won't be shown in the diagrams, but it's always present nonetheless.

It's worth pointing out that the sample ASP page shown in Figure 10-6 is unrealistically simple. In fact, it produces essentially the same output as the examples shown in the earlier figures. In a real application, no one would create such a simple page. The goal here, however, is to make clear the fundamental mechanics of how ASPs work, hence this hopelessly simple script.

ASP developers most commonly use VBScript

An ASP file can contain HTML tags, ordinary text, or script statements in some language. To create one, masochists can use an ordinary text editor such as the Windows Notepad. Those with less interest in pain will use a tool with built-in support for writing ASP scripts, such as Microsoft Visual InterDev. However it's done, a scripting engine must be available on the server machine for the language the script statements are written in. Windows 2000 includes engines for VBScript and Microsoft JScript (Microsoft's implementation of JavaScript), and engines for other languages are available from third parties. And while the ASP machinery is language-neutral, VBScript is by far the most commonly used choice for ASP developers.

The names of files containing ASP pages have an .asp extension

Although they're relatively simple languages, both VBScript and JScript allow ASP developers to write code in a familiar way, using variables, conditional statements, loops, and procedures. This chapter won't attempt to teach you either language, but rest assured that writing code for an ASP page is not fundamentally different from writing other kinds of programs. Whatever language it's written in, though, a script is just code wrapped in HTML that's stored in some file. Given this, there must be a way to tell IIS when an HTML file contains code that it should execute—that is, when it contains an ASP script. To do this, the name of any file on the server machine containing ASP script must end in .asp. Originally, putting the .asp extension on a purely HTML file—one containing no server-side script code—was a bad idea, because processing this file would take significantly longer than if it ended in .htm. With Windows 2000, however, this is no longer true, so the .asp extension can be used even for files that don't now but might one day contain ASP scripts.

Within the HTML in an ASP page, server-side scripting commands are typically wrapped with the symbols "<%" and "%>". These commands must be in what's called the *primary scripting language*, which by default is VBScript. It's also possible to wrap script code in the tags <SCRIPT> and </SCRIPT>. If you want to include a chunk of JScript in an ASP page whose default language is VBScript, for example, you can wrap that code with the tags <SCRIPT LANGUAGE=JScript RUNAT=SERVER> and </SCRIPT>. Because the <SCRIPT> tag is also used to wrap client scripts, the RUNAT keyword is required in this case to allow IIS to distinguish this script code from script code that should be passed through and executed in the client's browser.

Code that runs on the server must be wrapped in special symbols

Regardless of what script language is in use, an ASP page can contain language-independent directives as well. One type of ASP directive, called a processing directive, has the form <%@ *keyword=value* %>. Depending on what the keyword is, each one instructs the ASP interpreter to do specific things. The directive <%@ LANGUAGE=JScript %> sets the default scripting language for the page in which it appears to JScript, for example, while the keyword TRANSACTION sets the transactional requirements for this page. (How ASP pages can use transactions is described in more detail later in this chapter).

ASP pages can contain directives

A set of ASP pages can
be configured as an ASP
application

ASP Applications

An ASP application is a group of ASP files stored below a single directory in the file system.[3] Using the IIS snap-in, a Web administrator or application developer can designate a directory as the root for an application, and all .asp files stored in that directory and in all of its subdirectories will be considered part of the same ASP application. This directory might or might not be assigned a virtual directory name—either option is allowed.

Suppose, for example, that QwickBank makes available to its Web customers a retirement calculator, allowing them to estimate how much they must save to avoid working forever, and separately, a way to manage their bank accounts. Suppose further that both of these services are provided by groups of ASP pages. Figure 10-7 shows how those files might be stored on disk. The two ASP pages rc1.asp and rc2.asp, which together implement the retirement calculator, are both stored beneath the retirecalc directory and have been configured to belong to a single ASP application. The ASP pages am1.asp, am2.asp, and am3.asp, implementing the account management application, are stored beneath the acctmgmt directory and have been configured to comprise a second application.

Figure 10-7 *The ASP pages comprising a particular ASP application are stored beneath a designated directory in the server machine's file system.*

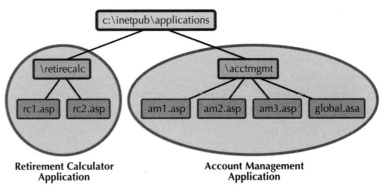

Retirement Calculator Application

Account Management Application

---

3. Don't confuse an ASP application with a COM+ Application—they're separate concepts.

If the root directory for an ASP application contains no sub-directories, as is the case for both applications in Figure 10-7, then the application consists of just the files in that root directory. If the root directory has subdirectories, however, this ASP application will also include all files in all subdirectories and all of their subdirectories. There's one exception to this: if a subdirectory somewhere beneath this root has itself been designated as a root directory for an ASP application, the files beneath it form their own application—they're no longer part of the one defined higher in the directory hierarchy.

All files in a particular ASP application must reside beneath a common root directory

The ASP pages in a single application (or more correctly, the scripting engine that interprets those pages) and any COM components they use might be loaded into processes in various ways. One possibility is that all of them run in the IIS process—that is, in-process with the Web server itself. This will give the best performance, but it's also the riskiest approach, since bugs in components might crash the Web server. Alternatively, it's possible to run the application in a separate process or even to divide the ASP pages and COM components, running each group in a different process. Doing this is safer, since a fault in the application won't bring down the Web server itself. It's also slower, since each client request must now be passed from the main IIS process to another process and back again. Which choice a developer makes depends on the speed and reliability requirements of her application.

ASP pages and COM components can be grouped into processes in various ways

In Figure 10-7, the directory c:\inetpub\applications\acctmgmt contains a file named global.asa. Any ASP application can have a file with this name in its root directory (although it's not required—notice that the other ASP application in Figure 10-7 does not have a global.asa file). If present, this file contains script code that is executed when various events occur. For example, it's sometimes useful to perform some action when an ASP application first starts running and when it shuts down. (By definition, an ASP application begins the first time any client accesses a page in that application, and it ends when IIS itself shuts down.) It might be useful

A global.asa file can contain code that executes at the beginning and end of an application to create a shared COM object when the application begins, for instance, or delete a temporary file when the application ends. To do this, an application's global.asa file can contain scripts that are executed when events called Application OnStart and Application OnEnd occur. As their names suggest, these events happen when this ASP application begins and ends, so any script statements associated with them are executed only once in the lifetime of the application.

A global.asa file can contain code that executes at the beginning and end of a session

For some applications, it can also be useful to execute a standard script at the beginning and/or the end of every session. To allow this, an application's global.asa file can also contain scripts executed when events called Session OnStart and Session OnEnd occur. The Session OnStart event occurs each time a new session begins, and the script associated with this event (if any) is executed before the page a user requested is processed. How a session can end with an ASP application is described later in this section, but however it happens, the Session OnEnd event occurs when it does. A script associated with the Session OnEnd event might, for instance, write a log record recording the results of this session or perform some clean-up function.

Built-In ASP Objects

ASP pages can make use of several built-in objects

The ASP extension provides built-in implementations of several different COM classes. Each class provides a particular set of methods and properties, and objects of each class can be used by ASP pages. The code in an ASP page doesn't need to create an instance of the desired class before using it, however. Instead, the ASP extension creates these objects automatically when required. The objects available for each ASP page to use, shown in Figure 10-8, are Request, Response, Server, Application, Session, ASPError, and ObjectContext (which, as shown in the figure, is actually provided by the COM runtime library). How each one is used is described next.

Figure 10-8 *The ASP extension provides several built-in objects that can be used by ASP pages.*

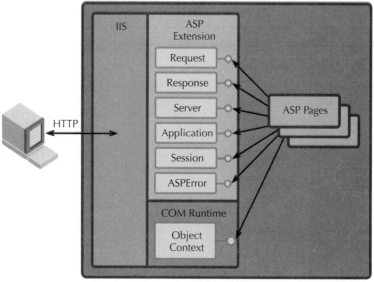

Windows 2000 Server

Request   Recall that an ASP page executes in response to a request from a client, which is usually a request made by a user at a browser. Once it's executing, an ASP page can use the Request object to learn about the client and the information the client passed in on this request. One common scenario begins with IIS sending an HTML page containing one or more FORM tags to a browser. FORM tags are typically used to allow a user to enter information that gets returned to the server, such as a name, a string to search for, or a credit card number. A page containing one or more FORM tags might also include a client-side script that validates the data entered by the user. This script might, for example, check that a telephone number field contains only numbers or that a password is at least of a specified minimum length.

Whether or not a client-side script is used for validation, each FORM tag can contain an ACTION attribute that indicates what

The Request object allows an ASP page to learn about the client's request page should be executed when the user submits that form. One possibility is for that attribute to reference an ASP page, so when the user submits the form the appropriate ASP page will be executed. If the form is sent to IIS using an HTTP GET method, the information the user entered via the FORM tags will be sent following the URL, separated by a "?". Once the ASP page is running, the script code in the page can access the Request object, which will contain the form information, the cookie sent in with the request (if one exists), and more.

The information available through the Request object includes:

- Query String, which is any text appearing after a "?" in the URL sent in by the browser. As just described, the information the user entered using FORM tags might appear here.

- Client certificate, if present. Although it's relatively uncommon for clients to send certificates today, this is likely to change over time, especially as smart cards become more widely used. If a client certificate is sent, however, an ASP page can access the Request object to get detailed information about the certificate's contents, allowing it to make a more intelligent authorization decision.

- Cookies, containing the value of any cookies that were sent with the request. The ASP extension automatically provides session management, so ASP developers don't need to manipulate cookies themselves to do this. If a cookie contains application-specific information, however, such as the name of a user, an ASP page might want to examine its contents.

- Various environment variables, set automatically by IIS and the ASP extension for each request. The available information includes the MIME type of any received information, a description of the browser that made the request, whether this request was made using SSL, the IP address of the client making this request, and many other things.

Response   The Response object allows an ASP page to control what information is sent back to a browser. Anything in an ASP file that's not part of a server-side script, such as HTML tags, client scripts, and ordinary text, is sent through to the browser unchanged. If you need to insert something into the outgoing HTML from within an ASP page, the raison d'etre of ASPs, you can do it using the Response object. The methods this object provides include:

The Response object allows an ASP page to send a response to its client

- *Write*   Allows a script to insert a string or the value of a variable into the stream of information sent back to the browser. The simple script shown in Figure 10-6 (on page 385) uses this method to send a user two HTML tags and the word "Hello".

- *Redirect*   Automatically redirects a client to another page. This method is typically used when the target page is on another machine. If the page the client is redirected to is on the same system, however, it's more efficient to use the Server object's Transfer method, described later.

- *Flush*   Causes any buffered output to be sent immediately. If buffering is on, the entire ASP page is processed before any results are sent to the client—those results are buffered until the processing is completed. Turning buffering off causes results to be sent off as they are created rather than waiting until the entire page has been processed. By default, buffering is turned on in IIS 5.0, which is the opposite of previous releases.

The Response object also exposes several properties. Assigning values to these properties affects what gets sent to the user. These properties include:

- *ContentType*   Allows setting the MIME type of the information being returned.
- *Buffer*   Allows turning on or off result buffering.

- *CacheControl*   Controls whether the results of an ASP page can be cached by a proxy server. A proxy server sits between a Web server and one or more browsers, and can potentially store copies of frequently accessed Web pages. This can greatly speed up access to static Web pages, since a copy can be cached by the proxy server, then used to satisfy future browser requests without bothering the Web server for each one. But for dynamic Web pages, which ASPs typically are, caching and reusing a copy can be problematic. The default is to not allow caching, but that default can be changed using this property.
- *Expires*   Controls how long the results of an ASP page can be cached by a browser, if those results can be cached at all.

The Response object also contains a collection of information called cookies. Using this, an ASP application can set specific cookie values to be returned to the client and set the expiration date on those cookies.

ASPs provide a short-hand for Response.Write

Because calls to Response.Write are so common, a shorthand form exists. Rather than explicitly invoking write, an ASP page can contain an instruction of the form <%= *expression* %>, which means the same thing. For example, the line

```
<%= "Hello" %>
```

in an ASP page has the same effect as

```
<% response.write "Hello" %>
```

Both insert the string "Hello" in the stream of bytes sent back to the browser.

The Server object allows an ASP page to create COM objects

Server   By far the most important thing about the built-in Server object is that it allows creating server-side COM objects via its CreateObject method. For example, to create an instance of the

COM class identified by the ProgID QwickBank.FinCalc, an ASP script could contain the line:

```
<% Obj = Server.CreateObject("QwickBank.FinCalc") %>
```

There are also other ways for an ASP page to create COM objects. For example, a script can contain HTML's <OBJECT> tag, specifying the RUNAT=SERVER attribute. It's also possible to create COM objects from within an ASP page by using the creation function of the scripting language itself—CreateObject in VBScript, and New in JScript—but doing this is generally not a good idea. The ASP extension is not involved in the creation process, so it can't effectively manage objects created in this way.

An ASP page can also create COM objects in other ways

However they're created, COM objects that are accessed from VBScript or JScript, the typical ASP languages, must expose their methods using dual interfaces. Objects whose methods can only be accessed through vtables can't be used from ASP scripts. This limitation is one reason why many, even most, development projects don't create COM objects that exclusively use vtable interfaces—access from ASP pages is too common a requirement to allow this.

COM objects accessed from ASP pages must use dual interfaces

By default, an object created using Server.CreateObject will exist only as long as the ASP page that created it is executing. (This is also the default for objects created using the <OBJECT> tag). Any other script statement in this same .asp file can use the object, but no other .asp files will be able to access this particular instance. This kind of object is said to have *page scope,* which means that when execution of the page completes, the ASP extension calls Release on the object, typically causing the object to destroy itself. It's also possible to give a COM object *application* or *session* scope if desired. How this is accomplished is described later in this section.

A COM object created by an ASP page has page scope by default

ASP pages can also use the Server object to do a few other useful things. By setting the object's ScriptTimeout property, for example, a page can control how long it will run before timing out, while calling its GetLastError method will return an ASPError object that can be examined to learn about an error. One ASP page can also execute another by calling the Server object's Execute method, or transfer a client's request to another page on the same machine by calling the Transfer method. Still, the fact that it offers a key mechanism that an ASP page uses to create COM objects makes this object critically important to ASP developers.

Application   It's sometimes useful for all of the pages in an ASP application to be able to share information—that is, to share state. To make this easy to do, the ASP extension maintains a separate Application object for each running ASP application. Script code on any page in an application can store information in this object, and that information can be retrieved by this or any other page in the application.

The Application object allows all ASP pages in an ASP application to share information

Storing information in the Application object is simple. A script can contain a statement such as:

```
<% Application("StartTime")= Now() %>
```

This calls VBScript's built-in function to return the current time, then stores the function's result in a variable in the Application object called StartTime. To access this value, any page in this ASP application can contain a line such as:

```
Application started at <%= Application("StartTime") %>
```

This would insert into the output stream text such as:

```
Application started at 10/01/00 5:28:00 PM
```

An ASP page can lock the Application object to ensure exclusive access

Application objects also provide a few methods that can be invoked by an ASP page. The most interesting of these are probably Lock, which allows a page to lock all variables stored in the Application object, and Unlock, which releases that lock. Since IIS multi-threads requests to ASP pages, multiple pages from the same application might be executing at the same time. Locking can be used to guarantee that a page has exclusive access to an Application object's variables while changing one or more of them. Holding this lock for longer than absolutely necessary is a bad idea, though, one that's likely to reduce performance.

It's also possible for a page in an ASP application to create a COM object, then store an interface pointer to that object in the Application object. In the jargon of ASPs, this is known as giving an object *application scope*. To do this, a page can contain a statement such as:

Storing a pointer to a COM object in the Application object gives the COM object application scope

```
<% Set Application("FinCalc") =
   Server.CreateObject("QwickBank.FinCalc") %>
```

Once an object has been given application scope, it can be accessed by other pages in the same application. To access the application-scoped object just created, for example, an ASP page executed later as part of the same application could contain the statement

```
<% Set Calc = Application("FinCalc") %>
```

then invoke methods on the Calc object as usual.

Giving a component application scope is relatively rare. There aren't many cases where an entire application needs to share a single instance of a COM object. Also, giving application scope to an object running in a single-threaded apartment (STA) can have a very negative effect on an ASP application's performance. In general, page scope (which as described earlier is the default) and session scope (described in the next section) suffice for most requirements.

Session Simple environments for building Web-based applications, such as CGI, require the developer to manipulate cookies themselves in order to group requests into a session. ASP pages can also access cookies via the Request object, but they're not

The Session object allows all ASP pages accessed in the same session to share information

required to use them. Instead, the ASP extension tracks cookies to maintain a unique instance of a Session object for each active session with a particular browser. Any ASP page in an application can store information in this object, and this same page or a different one accessed on this same session can then retrieve that information. By managing cookies under the covers, IIS and the ASP extension ensure that the information relevant to each session is maintained correctly.

An ASP page can store information in the Session object in the same way that it stores information in the Application object. For example, an ASP page might store a user's login name in a Session object by including the statement:

```
<% Session("LoginName")="Smith" %>
```

That page or another page can then retrieve this information by referencing the same named entry:

```
Account Values for <%= Session("LoginName") %>
```

The same ASP pages can be used for multiple simultaneous sessions—using cookies, the ASP extension determines which Session object should be accessed whenever one is referenced by a page. And if a particular ASP page knows that it will never use a Session object, it can begin with the directive:

```
<%@ EnableSessionState=False %>
```

If present, this line allows the ASP extension to avoid the overhead of managing the Session object, and so can sometimes improve application performance.

Also, just as it's possible to give a created COM object application scope, it's possible to give it session scope by storing a reference to it in a session object. To create an object and give it session scope, an ASP page could contain the statement:

```
<% Set Session("FinCalc") =
   Server.CreateObject("QwickBank.FinCalc") %>
```

Once an object has been given session scope, it can be accessed by any other ASP page in the same session. To access the session-scoped object just created, for example, a page executed as part of the same session could contain the statement

```
<% Set Calc = Session("FinCalc") %>
```

then invoke methods on the Calc object.

Giving a COM object session scope isn't all that unusual a thing to do. For example, think of a page that uses ADO to issue a database query. As described in Chapter 6, the results of that query are returned in a Recordset object. If the data in this Recordset is accessed only by the page that made the query, then leaving this Recordset object at page scope, the default, makes sense. But if this data will be accessed by multiple ASP pages on several future requests, it might make sense to give the Recordset object session scope, allowing all of these pages to access it and the data it contains. As with application scope, however, giving a COM object executing in an STA session scope can hurt performance.

Figure 10-9 shows the relationship among Session objects, Application objects, and ASP applications. As the diagram shows, all pages in a particular ASP application can access the same Application object. Any reference by a page in that application to the Application object will magically refer to the same instance— the ASP extension makes sure of this. Similarly, pages accessed by a particular browser in a single session will access the same Session object, with any references those pages make to this object directed to the correct instance by the ASP extension.

Session objects are created automatically when a new session begins, such as when a request arrives with a new cookie (or with no cookie at all, in which case IIS will create one). A page accessed on that session can destroy the Session object by calling Session.Abandon. But suppose this never happens. When does

Sessions time out automatically after a set number of minutes without a client request the object go away? By default, a session is considered over and the Session object destroyed when there have been no requests made on this session for 20 minutes. Any page accessed in the session can change this, however, by setting the Session object's Timeout property.

Figure 10-9 *All pages in an ASP application share an Application object, while pages accessed in a single browser session share a Session object.*

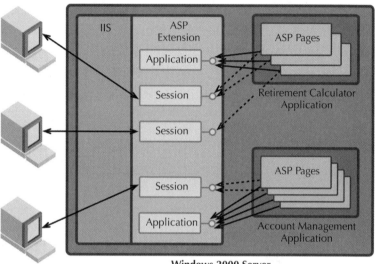

Windows 2000 Server

The ASPError object contains information about the last error that occurred

ASPError   As with any kind of software, debugging an ASP application can be challenging. To make a developer's life simpler, IIS automatically loads a default page when it encounters an error while executing any ASP page. Code on this default ASP page can call the GetLastError method provided by the Server object, which returns an ASPError object. That code can then output information about the error by examining properties in this object. Among those properties are:

- *ASPCode*   Contains an ASP-defined value identifying the error.
- *Description*   Contains a text string describing this error.

- *File*   Contains the name of the ASP file in which the error occurred.

- *Line* and *Column*   Indicate the line in the file and the column position in that line where the error occurred.

ObjectContext   Whenever the ASP extension is loaded, the COM runtime library is loaded, too. This library makes available to every ASP page an ObjectContext object. This is the same ObjectContext object that was described in Chapter 8, so it implements the IObjectContext interface. Only two of this interface's methods are exposed to ASP pages, however: SetComplete and SetAbort. As with transactional COM objects, these methods can be used to vote on the outcome of a transaction. How transactions work with ASP pages is described next.

The ObjectContext object allows an ASP page to vote in a transaction

ASPs and Transactions

As discussed in some detail earlier in this book, grouping operations into a transaction is often a useful thing to do. Like any other COM client, ASP pages are free to create and use transactional COM objects. For example, QwickBank's account management ASP application might rely on the COM object described in Chapter 1 to perform functions such as accessing account balances and transferring money between accounts. As illustrated in steps 1 through 3 of Figure 10-10, a request from a browser can cause an ASP page in this application to create that COM object. The object's transaction attribute is set to Required, so when in step 4 the code in the ASP page invokes a method in the object such as MoveMoney, the COM runtime will instruct DTC to start a transaction, shown in step 5.

An ASP page can create transactional COM objects

This object will perform whatever function was requested, such as transferring money between two accounts, then call SetComplete or SetAbort, as shown in steps 6 and 7 of Figure 10-11. As usual, this tells the COM runtime to end the transaction, shown in step 8. In steps 9 through 11, the method returns a result to the calling ASP page, which sends a response via IIS to the browser.

Figure 10-10 *An ASP page can create a transactional COM object, then invoke a method in that object to begin a new transaction.*

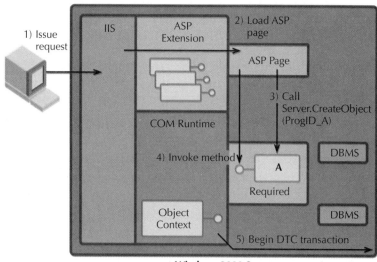

Windows 2000 Server

Figure 10-11 *When the object calls SetComplete, the COM runtime causes the transaction to end, and a result is eventually sent back to the browser.*

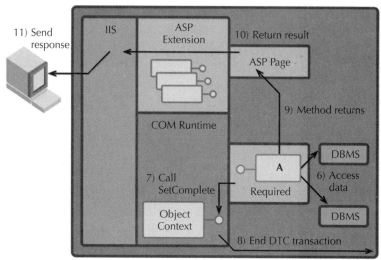

Windows 2000 Server

ASP applications that create and use transactional COM objects are common. Any e-commerce Web site, whether the fictitious QwickBank or a real e-business, will typically have some way to do this. Furthermore, the scalability features provided by the COM runtime are also likely to be useful in this scenario—what situation demands scalability more than an Internet application?

ASP pages can also use transactions directly. An ASP page can even create COM objects while part of a transaction, thus acting as the root of a transaction tree. To do this, an .asp file can begin with the following directive:

```
<%@ TRANSACTION=REQUIRED %>
```

If this is done, all of the operations performed by that ASP page will be grouped into a transaction. If script code on this page creates COM objects, they might also join this transaction, depending on the values of their transaction attributes. If an ASP page begins with this line and no errors occur, SetComplete is automatically called when the page finishes executing. If an error occurs, SetAbort is called. A page can also call either of these methods explicitly, using the ObjectContext object described earlier.

An ASP page can itself be the root of a transaction tree

How this looks, and the small but important ways in which it differs from the previous scenario, is shown in Figures 10-12 and 10-13. The first two steps in Figure 10-12 are just as before: the browser sends in a request and IIS loads the specified ASP page. But because that page contains a directive indicating that it requires a transaction, the ASP extension notifies the COM runtime that a transaction should begin. The runtime therefore tells DTC to start a new transaction, as shown in step 3. The ASP page then creates a transactional COM object, as before, and invokes a method in that object. This time, however, the method call causes the COM object to join the transaction that already exists, with the ASP page at its root, rather than creating a new transaction.

A transaction is started when a transactional ASP page begins executing

Figure 10-12 *A new transaction is started for a transactional ASP page when it begins executing.*

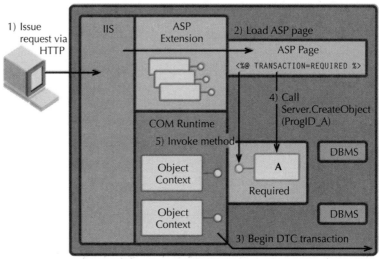

1) Issue request via HTTP

IIS

ASP Extension

2) Load ASP page

ASP Page

`<%@ TRANSACTION=REQUIRED %>`

4) Call Server.CreateObject (ProgID_A)

COM Runtime

5) Invoke method

Object Context

A

Required

DBMS

Object Context

DBMS

3) Begin DTC transaction

Windows 2000 Server

The transaction ends after the ASP page finishes executing

In steps 6 and 7 of Figure 10-13, the object modifies data and calls SetComplete as before. Unlike the previous example, however, this does not cause the transaction to end. The COM object is no longer the root, and so as with any non-root object in a transaction tree, its vote is recorded but not acted upon. Only when the ASP page completes (or when it calls the SetComplete or SetAbort methods in its ObjectContext object) will the COM runtime tell DTC to end this transaction, as shown in step 10 of Figure 10-13. As usual, whether the COM runtime tells DTC to commit or abort depends on what all the participants in the transaction—the ASP page and the COM object—have elected to do. If both voted to commit, the transaction will commit. If either one votes to abort, the COM runtime will tell DTC to abort this transaction.

A transactional ASP page can also contain event handling code that gets called when the transaction commits or aborts. Code associated with the OnTransactionCommit event will execute at commitment time, while code associated with the OnTransaction-Abort event will run if the transaction aborts.

Figure 10-13   *The transaction ends when the ASP page finishes executing.*

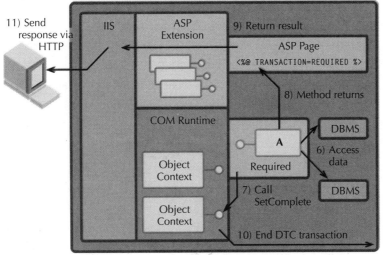

Windows 2000 Server

Recall that each request from a user executes its own ASP page, which can create and use COM objects and perhaps other ASP pages and then return a result to the user. A single transaction can't span more than one user request, however. In other words, when the first ASP page accessed by a user request returns control to the ASP extension, any transaction it began will end. This shouldn't be a surprising limitation, since allowing a transaction to span user requests would also allow returning control to a human being in the middle of the transaction. Yet as described in Chapter 8, transactions should be short and will be aborted by the COM runtime if the transaction timeout value is exceeded. Returning control to a user in the middle of a transaction is not likely to lead to happy users or to an application that performs well. Accordingly, ASPs don't allow one transaction to span multiple requests.

A transaction can't span multiple user requests

Choosing Between Scripts and COM Components

Writing ASP applications is easy. In fact, it can be almost too easy. Drunk with the simplicity of server-side scripting, it's easy for a developer to build large amounts of significant business logic in ASP pages. Doing this is almost always a bad idea, however. While they're very easy to create, substantial ASP applications are not especially simple to maintain. Also, because all ASP code is interpreted, ASP applications that perform much complex business logic in the pages themselves tend not to scale particularly well. A better approach is to build business logic as COM components, then use ASP pages as the glue that connects these components to the user and to each other.

For example, QwickBank's account management application could probably all be written using ASP pages. Scripts can access ADO, use transactions, and do very nearly anything else a Microsoft Visual Basic program can do. Yet packaging the business logic into COM components would probably make more sense. The account management application as described earlier does exactly this, exploiting a COM object to do the actual work of funds transfer, account access, and so on. This approach produces applications that are faster, more maintainable, and more reusable, since the componentized business logic is accessible from any COM client. Resisting the temptation to do too much with ASPs is almost always a good idea.

Installable Components

While every ASP application is different, many of them need to perform some common functions. Rather than require each developer to reinvent these common wheels, Windows 2000 includes a number of prebuilt COM components for use in ASP pages. Among the most interesting of these components are:

- *Ad Rotator*   This component allows the information sent to a browser to include one of a specified group of advertisements, and to rotate which ad is used based on a specified schedule. This component also allows logging how many users click on each ad.

- *Browser Capabilities* If an ASP page can figure out the exact capabilities of the browser it's talking to, that page can potentially tailor what it sends back to best match those capabilities. Each HTTP request from a browser contains an indication of the browser's type and version (such as Internet Explorer 5.0 or Netscape Navigator 4.0). A BrowserType object created using this installable component matches this information with a description of each browser's capabilities stored in a configuration file on the Web server machine, so it can be accessed by an ASP page to get detailed information about the browser that made this request. (The properties in a BrowserType object can also be set from a cookie sent by the client.) Once this object has been created, the application can access properties in it to learn whether the browser supports Java applets, ActiveX controls, JavaScript, VBScript, cookies, and more.

- *File Access* This component allows creating a FileSystem-Object that lets ASP applications access the file system.

- *Page Counter* Every self-respecting Web site wants to let its users know how popular it is. This component lets an ASP application keep track of how many times it has been accessed. The component writes the hit count to disk periodically, allowing totals to be maintained throughout server restarts.

- *Permission Checker* This component allows an ASP page to check whether a user has permission to access a file on the Web server. This object exposes the single method HasAccess, which an ASP page can call, passing in a filename. If the method returns TRUE, the user is allowed access to that file. The permission checker works with several of IIS's authentication choices, including Anonymous, Basic, and Integrated Windows Authentication.

Letting developers create Web applications using server-side scripts is a powerful idea. Providing installable components, built-in objects, and all the rest of the ASP infrastructure makes it even more so. Nothing makes this clearer than the popularity of ASP development in the Microsoft environment.

Using XML

XML has lots of potential

The Extensible Markup Language (XML) has created a storm of hyperbole. Somewhat atypically, this is a case where the hype is justified—XML has a great deal to offer. This short section briefly describes what XML is, then gives an example of how it can be used in building Web-based applications.

Understanding XML

Suppose you're the designer of QwickBank's account management ASP application. This application allows browser-based users to check their account balances, move money between accounts, and perhaps do a few other things. All of these services require sending information to the browser. When a user requests his account balances, for example, the application must send back an account number, a dollar amount, perhaps a list of this customer's deposits and withdrawals within the last week, and maybe even indicate how much the account is overdrawn. How should this information be represented when it's transferred between the application and the browser?

Using a common approach for describing many kinds of information makes sense

One obvious (and very common) answer is, "Any way the application's designer chooses." This approach works, but it also leads to a plethora of data formats, each designed for one particular application. Why not instead define one standard approach for describing all kinds of information? If this were done, many applications could use it, making life simpler for designers, for developers, and for people who must make diverse applications work together.

This is exactly what XML allows. Defined by the World Wide Web Consortium (W3C), XML has become a very popular approach to describing all kinds of information. Whether it's sent across the Web, stored in a DBMS, passed in a message, or used in some other way, XML can provide a lingua franca for data definition.

XML provides a common way to describe data

To get a sense of what this means, suppose QwickBank's account management ASP application chooses to represent the result of customer balance inquiries using XML. The result of a customer's request for two of his account balances might then be represented in an XML document like this:

```
<accountlist>
<account>
  <customer>Gerrit Reitveld</customer>
  <number>4590335317</number>
  <balance>$2,396.54</balance>
  <deposit>$1,000.00</deposit>
  <deposit>$578.39</deposit>
  <withdrawal>$749.00</withdrawal>
</account>
<account>
  <customer>Gerrit Reitveld</customer>
  <number>4590980034</number>
  <balance>$0.00</balance>
  <withdrawal>$9,945.55</withdrawal>
  <overdrawn>$192.13</overdrawn>
</account>
</accountlist>
```

Representing information this way has the potential to make that information more useful. It's now apparent—certainly to people and potentially to software—what each piece of information represents.

An XML document contains information annotated with XML-defined tags

As this simple example shows, XML marks the data using tags with (usually) meaningful names, such as <account> and <customer>. For this to work, there must be some way to define what those tags are for any particular kind of information and how they can be used. Another way to say this is that we need a grammar of

A Document Type Definition defines tags and rules for using those tags some kind defining a legal set of symbols and rules for using those symbols. To allow this, XML's creators gave us a way to create *document type definitions (DTDs)*. Given a DTD, it's possible to determine whether a particular set of XML-defined information corresponds to it. For example, the account information shown previously matches this DTD:

```
<!DOCTYPE accountlist [
<!ELEMENT accountlist (account+)
  <!ELEMENT account(customer, number, balance, deposit*,
  withdrawal*, overdrawn?)>
  <!ELEMENT customer(#PCDATA)>
  <!ELEMENT number(#PCDATA)>
  <!ELEMENT balance(#PCDATA)>
  <!ELEMENT deposit(#PCDATA)>
  <!ELEMENT withdrawal(#PCDATA)>
  <!ELEMENT overdrawn(#PCDATA)>
]>
```

This simple grammar defines an accountlist element as containing one or more accounts. (That's what the "+" means in "account+".) Each account element has a customer, an account number, a balance, zero or more deposits (denoted by the asterisk), zero or more withdrawals, and zero or one (indicated by the question mark) overdrawn indications. Each of those elements consists of parsed character data (PCDATA), which essentially means that it's a character string. If you look back at the account information for Gerrit Reitveld just shown, you'll see that it corresponds to this definition: it's an accountlist describing two of his accounts. The first account includes a customer, an account number, a balance, two deposits, and a withdrawal. The second account also includes elements for customer, account number, and balance—they're required. This one, however, has no deposits, one large withdrawal, and not too surprisingly, an indication of how much the account is overdrawn. This is a very basic example—XML can get more complicated than this. But the fundamental idea is simple, and having a standard way to describe all kinds of information is quite useful.

Having a standard way to access that information programmatically is also useful. Recognizing this, the W3C created the Document Object Model (DOM) standard. The DOM defines a group of object types, with each type exposing an appropriate interface, along with rules for how those object types relate to each other. The goal is to define a standard way to represent the textual information in an XML document as an in-memory data structure that can easily be manipulated by software. For example, a slightly simplified form of how the accountlist document shown earlier can be represented in a tree form is shown in Figure 10-14.

The Document Object Model defines a standard set of objects for representing an XML document as a hierarchical data structure

Figure 10-14 *The Document Object Model defines a standard for representing XML-defined data as a hierarchy.*

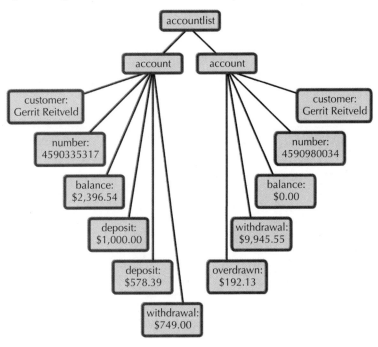

Software capable of reading an XML document, then producing a hierarchical data structure representing the information in that document, is known as an *XML parser*. As described next, Windows 2000 includes an XML parser that can be used in various ways.

An XML parser can transform an XML document into an in-memory data structure

XML in Windows 2000

Microsoft commonly uses the term *schema* rather than *DTD*

Microsoft supports the W3C-defined XML standards, but it has chosen to add to them as well. For example, Microsoft's XML developers believed that DTDs were too simple, and that it made far more sense to use XML itself to define a grammar for documents. As a result, Windows 2000 also supports using a not-yet-finalized standard called XML-Data along with DTDs, and generally refers to a grammar used to describe a type of XML documents as a *schema* rather than a DTD.

MSXML implements an XML parser

Because it can be useful in many contexts, Microsoft provides its XML parser in the form of a COM component. Contained in msxml.dll, this component's official name is XMLDOMDocument (although it's often referred to as just MSXML). As shown in Figure 10-15, a client can create an instance of this object, then instruct it to read an XML document and produce a DOM-conformant tree representation of the information in that document.

Figure 10-15 *The COM component XMLDOMDocument, also called MSXML, implements an XML parser.*

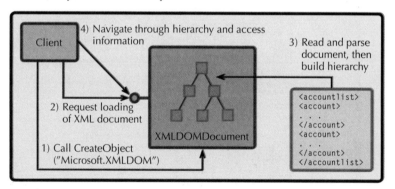

MSXML's methods and properties allow navigating through a hierarchical representation of an XML document

Once this has been done, the client can invoke the object's methods and access its properties to navigate through the tree and access its information. The methods provided by the XMLDOMDocument object include:

- *load*   Reads an XML document from a file.
- *loadXML*   Reads an XML document that's already in memory.

- *save*   Saves an XML document to a file or in some other way.
- *hasChildNodes*   Allows determining whether a node has any nodes below it in the hierarchy.
- *insertBefore*   Inserts a new node in front of the currently referenced node in the hierarchy.

Among the properties this object exposes are:

- *firstChild*   References the first child of the current node.
- *lastChild*   References the last child of the current node.
- *nextSibling*   References the next child below the current node's parent.
- *parentNode*   References the parent of the current node.

Using the methods and properties of the XMLDOMDocument object is straightforward, and so navigating through a parsed XML document is not difficult. But why would anyone want to do this? In what situations is it useful? For one example, think back to QwickBank's account management ASP application. It's entirely possible that the XML format for describing accounts shown earlier can be used to represent account information in many different situations. XML documents that conform to this DTD might be used to send account information between different applications at the bank, to provide a meaningful archive format for the data, and for many other purposes. If a standard format can be used for exchanging information between all kinds of applications, it might also make sense to use that format to send data to a browser.

XML-defined data can be sent to a browser inside an HTML document by embedding it within the <XML> tag. The result, called an *XML island,* can then be parsed and accessed at the client. For example, suppose QwickBank's accounts management ASP application responds to customer queries about their account using the XML-defined format shown earlier. Rather than generating straight HTML, an ASP page can wrap the account data it sends in XML-defined tags, then embed the whole thing in an XML island sent to

An XML island lets XML-defined data appear within an HTML document the browser. The page the browser receives can also contain a VB-Script program capable of using the XMLDOMDocument object[4] to parse the received XML document and display it intelligently to the user. Rather than defining a unique format just for browsers, information could be exchanged using QwickBank's standard format. How this looks is shown in Figure 10-16.

Figure 10-16 *An ASP application can send XML-defined data to a browser in an XML island. A script running in Internet Explorer can then use the XMLDOMDocument object to parse and display this information.*

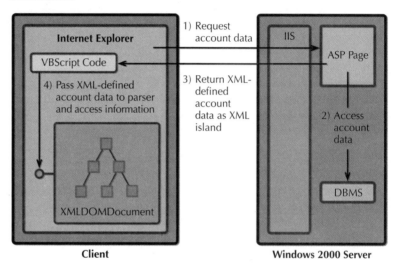

One thing that's not shown in Figure 10-16 is how the ASP page converts information from the DBMS into an XML-defined format. One possibility is that the ASP page, relying on ADO to access the data, reads the account information out of each Recordset and explicitly inserts the appropriate XML tags. Even better, modern DBMS's such as Oracle 8i and Microsoft SQL Server 2000 allow the results of SQL queries to be returned as XML documents, making this process simpler.

---

4. This works only if the browser is Internet Explorer, because it's the only browser that allows loading and running COM components such as XMLDOMDocument.

As its support by DBMS's shows, XML is useful for more than Web-based applications. Yet this technology's roots are in the Web, and XML will certainly be very popular in this environment. Because of the important problem it addresses, XML is also likely to be popular in many other kinds of applications.

XML's impact has just begun

Load Balancing

A busy Web site probably won't be able to handle all customer traffic with a single Windows 2000 server machine. Even if it could, the creators of that site might choose to install two or more machines to allow the site to keep functioning in the event of failures. Using multiple Web server machines intelligently, however, requires some kind of load balancing. To address this problem, Windows 2000 provides Network Load Balancing (NLB).[5]

Network Load Balancing allows spreading client requests across multiple Web servers

As shown in Figure 10-17, up to 32 Windows 2000 servers can be grouped into an NLB cluster. Each of those machines runs the NLB software, and each one typically runs IIS as well. All of the machines in an NLB cluster must share a broadcast domain, and to clients, an NLB cluster looks like a single machine with one IP address. When an HTTP request arrives from a client, the request is broadcast to all machines in the NLB cluster. One machine is chosen to handle the request, while the others ignore it.

Using NLB requires grouping machines into an NLB cluster

Each machine in an NLB cluster is typically configured to handle a specific percentage of the total load received. Each machine also sends a periodic heartbeat packet, allowing other machines in a cluster to detect whether it has failed. If this happens, the percentages handled by each remaining machine are adjusted automatically.

---

5. NLB is included only with the Advanced Server and DataCenter Server versions of Windows 2000.

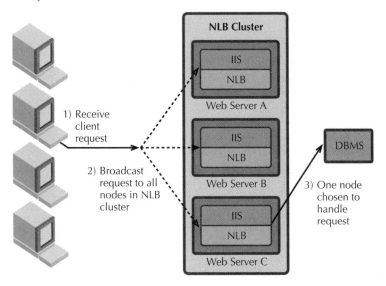

Although this is not shown in Figure 10-17, it's safe to assume that each Web server machine is running the same ASP application. All of those applications are accessing the same database, so the machine that's chosen to handle this request issues a query to that database, then presumably returns some results. As long as this application maintains no state that's specific to a certain client, relying on NLB to load balance each request independently will be effective.

NLB can provide session affinity, allowing applications to maintain per-client state

Yet building Web-accessible applications that maintain no per-client state at all is difficult. By providing built-in support for the Session and Application objects, ASPs make managing state relatively straightforward. But if an ASP page stores any information in, say, its Session object, what happens if the next request from this client is handled by a different machine? Since the information about this client is stored in memory on another machine, it won't be accessible. To address this problem, NLB can provide single-client affinity. This option guarantees that all requests from a particular IP address will be handled by the same server. That ensures that the application handling these requests will be able to store and access state about this client across multiple requests from that client.

The scenario shown in Figure 10-17 assumes that each server machine in the NLB cluster has its own copy of whatever ASP application is being used, and that business logic for each of those applications runs entirely on a single machine. But suppose that business logic is implemented in COM components, as it will be for virtually any significant application. Suppose too that this Web site must handle a very large number of clients and that it must be very resilient to failures. Given the burgeoning world of e-commerce, this is not an uncommon situation. QwickBank, for example, might well have a large number of customers, all of whom expect nonstop access to the bank's services (and perhaps even expect to pay for it). In cases like this, it's possible to divide the application's functionality across two sets of server machines, as shown in Figure 10-18.

Large Web sites might separate Web server machines from those that run business logic

Each machine in the first set runs IIS and the ASP application, with NLB used to load balance HTTP requests across these machines. Each machine in the second set, referred to as object servers in Figure 10-18, runs the COM objects created by the ASP applications on the first set of machines. Each of these objects then accesses the shared database. The Component Load Balancing (CLB) technology described in Chapter 8 can be used to dynamically load balance the ASP pages' creation requests for these objects across all the machines in a CLB cluster. And although it's not shown in the figure, the DBMS might well be running on a two-node cluster created using the Microsoft Cluster Server, providing further reliability. Combining all of these technologies allows creating a Web site with better scalability, better reliability, and ultimately, happier users.

Component Load Balancing can be used to intelligently distribute object creation requests

Figure 10-18 *Combining NLB with CLB allows creating more reliable, more scalable Web sites.*

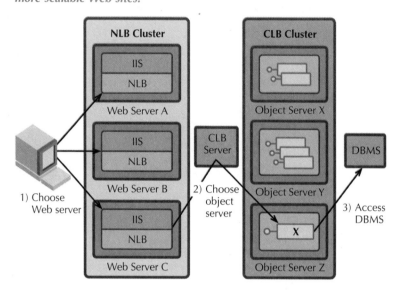

Final Thoughts

Multitier applications
have become the norm

Whether your organization chooses to develop applications on Windows 2000 using the technologies described in this book, or decides instead to use something else, it's a safe bet that the enterprise applications you'll be building will be multitier, component-based, and Web-accessible. Every leading vendor in this area has adopted the same fundamental approach, so no matter which one you pick, the basic architecture will be the same. More important, dividing an application's functions into multiple tiers, building business logic with components, and letting an application's users access it over the Web are all good ideas.

If you don't like change,
get out of the software
business

You can't say that this approach is simple, though. Modern enterprise applications employ a remarkably wide range of technology, and they demand a great deal from their architects, from their developers, and from the people who must manage the effort. As every organization has come to rely on software, so too have those organizations become dependent on the creators of that software. It's incumbent upon all of us who work in this field to understand as much as we can, then make the best choices possible. No matter how much we know today, there's always something new to learn tomorrow.

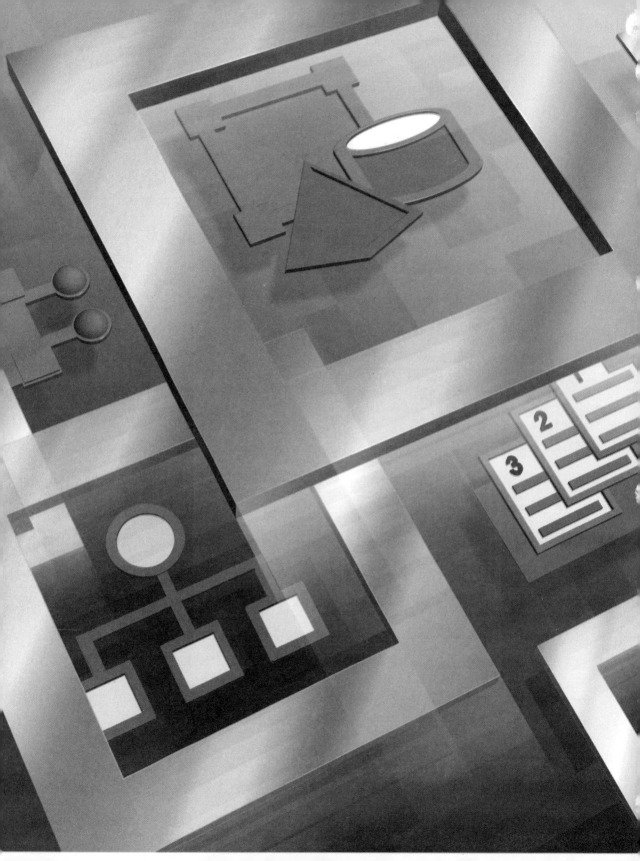

Index

adXactReadUncommitted/adXactBrowse value, IsolationLevel property, 226
adXactRepeatableRead value, IsolationLevel property, 227
adXactSerializable/adXactIsolated value, IsolationLevel property, 227
adXactUnspecified value, IsolationLevel property, 227
A (address) information type, for zone file resource records, 36
Anonymous authentication option, in IIS, 379
Apartment model threading, use of by configured components, 300–301
apartments, making threads more manageable with, 190–93
APIs, for accessing Active Directory databases, 67–69
Application object, use of by ASP pages, 396–97
Application OnEnd event, execution of script code when this occurs, 390
Application OnStart event, execution of script code when this occurs, 390
application program interface (API). *See* APIs, for accessing Active Directory databases
application proxies, 313–317
   configuring, 313–15
   contents of, 313
   copying a remote server name into the client's registry with, 315–16
   effect of Group Policy settings and client-specified flags on, 314–15
   settings that effect downloading, 314–15
application queues, types of, 335–36
applications, adding a browser client to, 29–31
application scope, for COM objects, 395, 397
Application Specific property, for MSMQ messages, 340
application support services, 4, 14–25
Arrived Time property, for MSMQ messages, 340
ASP applications, 388–390
   configuring a set of ASP pages as, 388
   requirement for where files must reside, 389
ASPCode property, for ASPError object, 400
ASPError object
   calling with GetLastError method, 396
   use of by ASP pages, 400–401
ASP extension, built-in objects provided for use by ASP pages, 390–401

.asp filename extension, using for files containing ASP pages, 386–87
ASP objects, built-in, 390–401
ASPs. *See* Active Server Pages (ASPs)
assigned applications
   configuration of application proxies as, 313–15
   controlling access to with Group Policy, 74
asymmetric encryption, 10
asynchronous calls
   limitations of, 190
   optional support for, 189–90
asynchronous methods, division of, 189–90
atomic unit, grouping of sends and receives into, 363–64
attributes
   determining for leaf and container objects, 40
   indexing to speed up searches, 51
   object identifiers assigned to, 41
   types in Active Directory schema, 41–43
auditing
   events for one or more MSMQ queues, 357
   as part of distributed security services, 83–84
audit policy, setting with GPOs, 76
audit trail, of important system events, 83–84
Authenticate property, for MSMQ queues, 337
AuthenticatedEx property, for MSMQ messages, 341
Authenticated property
   for MSMQ messages, 341
   for MSMQ queues, 337
authentication
   between clients and servers in different domains, 106–8
   as part of distributed security services, 9, 83
   services provided by SSL, 13–14, 152
   using secret key encryption for, 92
authentication level, setting automatic security for, 201–2
Authentication Level property, for MSMQ messages, 341
authentication options, supported in IIS, 378–81
authenticators, preventing replay attacks with, 100
Authority Information Access field, in CryptoAPI, 150–51
authorization
   making decisions based on roles, 306
   as part of distributed security services, 9, 83

DTC transaction manager
 accessing, 240–41
 how it communicates with resource managers,
  241–42
 support for TIP, 251
dual interfaces, used by COM objects created in
  Visual Basic, 172
Dynamic DNS, changing information remotely
  with, 37–38

E

e-mail
 gateway to message queuing from, 366–67
 limitations of moving messages to MSMQ from,
  366–67
E-mail-Addresses attribute, User class, 42
e-mail lists, defining with distribution groups,
  64–66
e-mail messages, using Record objects to access
  data in, 232
ENABLE_CODE_DOWNLOAD, side effects of
  using, 316–17
EnableCommit method, setting done bit and
  consistent bit with, 312
encrypted session key. *See* session key
encryption, using as security mechanism, 10
Encryption Algorithm property, for MSMQ
  messages, 341
encryption algorithms, list of proposed contained
  in ClientHello message, 153–55
encryption key, in Kerberos tickets, 93
end-entity cert, for digital signature, 149–50
end time, in Kerberos tickets, 93
Enhanced RSA CSP, function of, 135
enrollment process, creation and storage of a key
  pair and certificate by, 144–46
Enterprise CAs
 automatic issuance of certificates by, 142
 defined, 141–42
Enterprise Root CA, configuring Certificate
  Services as, 143
Enterprise Subordinate CA, configuring Certificate
  Services as, 143
enterprise trust policy, Windows 2000, 148
Enterprise Trust store
 adding CTLs to, 148

Enterprise Trust store, *continued*
 storage of Certificate Trust Lists (CTLs) in, 137
environment variables, available through the
  Request object, 392
Error object, function of, 212
Ethernet, 2
event classes, registering, 320–21
EventClass objects, 320–24
 interfaces and methods for, 321–24
 use of by publisher to send an event, 320
event store, creating subscriptions in, 320
Exchange Connector, as gateway between
  message queuing and e-mail, 366–67
Execute method, for Server object, 396
EXE files, implementation of classes in, 178–79
Expires property, for Response object, 394
Express message delivery vs. Recoverable message
  delivery, 343
Express value, Delivery property, 343
Extensible Markup Language (XML). *See* XML
  (Extensible Markup Language)
extension control block, created by IIS, 383–84
Extension property, for MSMQ messages, 341
extensions, creating with ISAPI, 382–84
external certificates
 generated by external CAs, 354
 registering in the IE personal certificate store,
  355

F

Field objects
 in ADO Recordset object, 211
 in Recordset's Fields collection, 218–19
fields, encrypted in Kerberos ticket, 93–94
Fields collection, in Recordset, 218–19
File Access component, for use in ASP pages, 407
File property, ASPError object, 401
files, using Record objects to access data in, 232
filters, creating with ISAPI, 384–85
firstChild property, XMLDOMDocument object,
  413
First in Transaction property, for MSMQ messages,
  341
Flush method, provided by Response object, 393
folder redirection, using Group Policy, 75

forests
> Active Directory, 54–57
> vs. domain trees, 54–56
> nontransitive trust relationships between domains in, 111
> transitive trust in, 109–10

FORWARDABLE flag, setting, 105–6

frame relay networks, 2

Full Reach Queue value, Acknowledge property, 344

Full Receive value, Acknowledge property, 344

function calls, ODBC, 207

G

Generic Security Service API (GSS-API), 84

GetActivityID method, in IObjectContextInfo interface, 311

GetChildren method, for Record objects, 234

GetContextID method, in IObjectContextInfo interface, 311

GetDeactivateOnReturn method, in IContextState interface, 311

GetLastError method, for Server object, 396

GET method, HTTP (Hypertext Transfer Protocol), 374

GetMyTransactionVote method, in IContextState interface, 311

GetObjectContext, calling to get pointer to IObjectContext, 270

GetRows method, Recordset object, 218

GetTransactionID method, in IObjectContextInfo interface, 311

GetTransaction method, in IObjectContextInfo interface, 310

global.asa file, execution of code in, 389–90

global catalog (GC)
> effect of groups and group scopes on, 64–66
> finding information with, 50–53
> indexing information in multiple domains with, 52
> provided by Active Directory, 51–53
> use of by login process, 53

global catalog server, 52

global groups, effect on global catalog, 65

Globally Unique Identifier (GUID)
> assignment of in Active Directory, 52–53

Globally Unique Identifier (GUID), *continued*
> for COM interface, 173
> creating, 173–174

GPOs. *See* Group Policy objects (GPOs)

group policies
> applying multiple, 77–78
> types of, 71–73

Group Policy
> controlling access to software applications with, 73–74
> controlling security with, 75–76
> defining and enforcing policies with, 70–79
> folder redirection with, 75
> trusted root certificate authority option in, 148
> use of security groups in, 64–66
> using, 78–79
> using for scripting control, 75
> using to place CA certificates in Trusted Root CA store, 148

Group Policy Container, storing policy settings in, 76–77

Group Policy objects (GPOs)
> defining with the Group Policy snap-in, 70–71
> how settings are stored, 76–77
> setting account policies with, 76

Group Policy settings, effect on application proxies, 314–15

Group Policy snap-in, defining a Group Policy object with, 70–71

Group Policy Template, storing GPO information in, 76–77

group scopes, Windows 2000, 64–66

GUID. *See* Globally Unique Identifier (GUID)

H

hasChildNodes method, XMLDOMDocument object, 413

hash algorithm, 91, 122–23

Hash Algorithm property, for MSMQ messages, 341

HEAD method, HTTP (Hypertext Transfer Protocol), 374

host address, in Kerberos tickets, 93

.htm filename extension, 372

HTML files
> execution of embedded scripts in, 372–73

HTML files, *continued*
  referencing on a server machine, 371–72
HTML tags. *See* Hypertext Markup Language
    (HTML), tags
HTTP (Hypertext Transfer Protocol), 374–77
  accessing Web servers with, 369
  protocol basics, 374
  support for sessions in, 375–76
  treatment of method invocations by, 375
HttpExtensionProc function, ISAPI extension,
    383–84
Hypertext Markup Language (HTML)
  tags, 24
  annotating Web server information with, 369

I

IBM's MQSeries, linking of MSMQ to, 366
ICallFactory interface, CreateCall method, 189–90
ICancelMethodCalls::Cancel, invoking to cancel
    an in-progress call, 188
ICancelMethodCalls interface, 188
ICancelIMethodCalls interface, invoking the
    Cancel method in, 190
IClassFactory, implementation of by class factory
    object, 183
IClientSecurity interface, setting client security
    options with, 203
IConnectionPointContainer interface, using, 320
IConnectionPoint interface, using, 320
IContextState interface, methods in, 311
ldap_add, ldap_add_s, issuing an LDAP Add
    request with, 68
ldap_delete, ldap_delete_s, issuing an LDAP
    Delete request with, 68
ldap_modify, ldap_modify_s, issuing an LDAP
    Modify request with, 68
ldap_result, retrieving the result of an
    asynchronous call with, 68
ldap_search, ldap_search_s, issuing an LDAP
    Search request with, 68
ldap_simple_bind_s, establishing an LDAP server
    connection with, 68
ldap_unbind, releasing an LDAP server
    connection with, 68
IDL (Interface Definition Language). *See* Interface
    Definition Language (IDL), defining COM
    interfaces with

IETF RFC 2459, for certificates, 125
IID (Interface Identifier), for COM interfaces, 173
IIS (Internet Information Services). *See* Internet
    Information Services (IIS)
IIS metabase, as repository for IIS configuration
    information, 378
IMarshal interface, implementing custom
    marshaling with, 196
impersonation and delegation vs. role-based
    authorization, 308–9
impersonation level, setting with
    CoInitializeSecurity, 202
independent clients, defined by MSMQ, 333
indexed cookies, multiple values contained in, 377
indexes, finding information with, 50–53
in-doubt transactions
  resolving, 245
  tool for forcing commit or abort, 245–46
infrastructure services, 4–14
in-process server, running a COM class
    implemented in a DLL as, 178–79
insertBefore method, XMLDOMDocument object,
    413
Instance property, for MSMQ queues, 337
Integrated Windows authentication option, in IIS,
    380
interactive login, Kerberos, 94–97
interception, defined, 269
Interface Definition Language (IDL), defining
    COM interfaces with, 174–75
interface inheritance, 175–76
interface names. *See* interfaces, naming
interface pointers
  acquired by clients to invoke methods, 168–69
  acquiring new to COM objects, 185–86
  passing to disconnected Recordsets, 230
  releasing for COM objects, 187
interfaces
  COM definition of in-memory layout for, 170
  configuring to grant access based on roles,
    306–7
  grouping COM object methods into, 167–70
  grouping methods into, 15–17
  human-readable names for, 173
  making callable asynchronously, 189–90
  naming, 172–74
intermediate CAs, certificate signer for, 128

J

secret key encryption, *continued*
> used by SSL, 13
> using destination queue manager's public key, 356
> using for authentication, 92

secret keys
> distributing, 89–90
> using with public key technology, 121–22

secret key security, in Windows 2000, 83–115

secret key technology, speed of vs. public key technology, 121–22

Secure Channel/SChannel, support for Transport Level Security (TLS), 153

Secure Sockets Layer (SSL). *See* SSL (Secure Sockets Layer)

security, controlling with Group Policy, 75–76

security access token, construction of by Local Security Authority (LSA), 87

security blanket, 201

security context, creating for sending authenticated messages, 355

Security Context property, for MSMQ messages, 342

security descriptors, assigned to resources, 87

security groups, using for access control, 64–66

security identifiers (SIDs)
> access control entries (ACEs) in, 87
> as part of authorization data, 87–88

security options, setting with GPOs, 76

security principal, defined, 91

security protocols, supported by Windows 2000, 10–12

Security Service Providers (SSPs), accessed through SSPI, 84–86

security services. *See* distributed security services

Security Support Provider Interface (SSPI), 84–86
> accessing distributed security services through, 85
> compared to CryptoAPI, 133–34
> Security Service Providers accessed through, 84–86

Security Templates snap-in, creating and editing security options with, 76

Sender Certificate property, for MSMQ messages, 342

Sender ID property, for MSMQ messages, 342

Sender ID Type property, for MSMQ messages, 342

Sent Time property, for MSMQ messages, 342

Server Applications. *See* COM+ Server Applications

server applications, storage of passwords for, 104

ServerHelloDone message, sent by server after sending certificate to client, 156

ServerHello message, response to ClientHello message with, 156

server machines, balancing client creation requests across, 324–27

Server object
> setting ScriptTimeout property for, 395–96
> use of by ASP pages, 394–96

server-only vs. mutual authentication protocol exchanges, 158

service tickets
> authenticating a user to a specific service with, 98–99
> decryption of to verify user's identity, 100–101

session concentration, using to reduce network bandwidth, 366

session identifier field
> contained in ClientHello message, 153–55
> increased speed of SSL connection process with, 154–55

session key
> encryption of information by, 100
> providing data privacy with, 103
> sent by KDC for ticket-granting ticket, 96–97

Session object
> destroying, 399–400
> turning off management of, 398
> use of by ASP pages, 397–400

Session OnEnd event, execution of script code when this occurs, 390

Session OnStart event, execution of script code when this occurs, 390

sessions, creating, 376

session scope, for COM objects, 395

SetAbort method
> calling to abort a transaction, 274–75
> ObjectContext object, 401
> setting done bit and consistent bit with, 312

SetComplete method
> calling to commit a transaction, 274–75
> ObjectContext object, 401
> setting done bit and consistent bit with, 312

transactional queues, *continued*
  vs. non-transactional queues, 359
  setting Transaction property for when created,
    358–59
transaction attributes, values for, 276–77
transaction boundaries, coupling with JIT
  activation, 295–96
transaction context object, grouping of objects
  into transactions with, 286–87
transaction deadlocks, 287–88
Transaction Internet Protocol (TIP), function of,
  250–53
Transaction Internet Protocol (TIP) messages,
  performing two-phase commit with, 252–53
transaction managers, other than DTC transaction
  manager, 250–58
Transaction property
  for determining transaction participation of
    queues, 339
  for MSMQ queues, 337
  setting for transactional queues, 358–59
transactions
  ACID properties, 226
  as all-or-nothing sets of events, 223–24
  controlling using ADO's Connection object,
    224
  importance of in applications, 19–20
  importance of not returning control to a user
    during, 288–89
  inability of to span multiple user requests, 405
  invoking Connection object BeginTrans method
    to start, 224–25
  locking of data by, 225
  and MSMQ, 357–64
  using, 223–28
  using activities to protect against concurrent
    access, 304
transaction timeouts, 287–89
Transfer method, for Server object, 396
transient subscriptions, sending events to running
  objects with, 322
transitive trust, between domains without shared
  keys, 109–10
Transmission Control Protocol (TCP). *See* TCP
  (Transmission Control Protocol)
Triple-DES, secret key algorithm, 90

trusted CAs, companies that act as, 131–32
Trusted Root CA store
  deciding which CAs to trust in, 147
  storing certs from trusted root CAs in, 137
trusted root certificate authority, Group Policy
  option, 148
trust relationships, establishing between domains,
  108–11
two-phase commit, 242–46
  potential problems associated with, 244
  querying resource manager, 243
  recovering from failures, 244–45
  resolving in-doubt transactions, 245
  use of by DTC to end a transaction, 243
typelib, 194
type libraries
  use of in standard marshaling, 194
  uses for, 195
Type property
  for MSMQ queues, 337
  using to find a specific kind of queue, 339

U

UDP (User Datagram Protocol), as unreliable
  transport protocol, 3
Unbind operation, LDAP protocol, 47
unconfigured components
  defined, 265
  stored in COM system registry, 181–82
Uniform Resource Locator (URL)
  general format of, 371–72
  referencing an application with, 373–74
  referencing an HTML file with, 371–72
  use of by browser clients, 24
universal groups
  effect on global catalog, 65
  use of, 64–65
universal interface, IUnknown as, 184–88
Universally Unique Identifier (UUID), for COM
  interface, 173
universal marshaler, using, 194
Unlock method, Application object, 396–97
unmarshaling, of call parameters into usable
  object format, 193–96
Update method, calling for Recordset object, 221

Update Sequence Number (USN), use of by Active Directory, 62–64

UPN. *See* User Principal Name (UPN)

URL. *See* Uniform Resource Locator (URL)

User Configuration policies, application of, 72

User Datagram Protocol (UDP). *See* UDP (User Datagram Protocol), as unreliable transport protocol

User object class, attributes defined for, 42

User Principal Name (UPN)
attribute in User class, 42
getting authorization data with, 161–62
using in login process, 53

user rights assignment, setting with GPOs, 76

USN. *See* Update Sequence Number (USN), use of by Active Directory

UUID. *See* Universally Unique Identifier (UUID), for COM interface

V

variants, use of by Visual Basic programmers, 172

VBScript, use of by ASP developers, 386

VeriSign, acting as trusted CA, 131

Version property, for MSMQ messages, 342

virtual directories, using with IIS, 378

virtual root, using with IIS, 378

Visual Basic
defining COM interfaces with, 175
use of properties by, 176–77

Visual Basic clients, creation of COM objects by, 182

Visual Basic new operator, creation of COM objects with, 182

Visual Basic Scripting Edition (VBScript), creating applications with, 25

Visual Studio 7, elimination of thread affinity in, 301

vtable interfaces, in COM, 170–71

W

Web, basics of, 371–77

Web application services, 369–419

Web-based access via HTTP, building distributed applications with, 4

Web browser client
adding to applications, 29–31
example of with DCOM, 29–31
using DNS to locate and SSL to authenticate itself, 29–30

Web browsers. *See* browsers, accessing Web servers with

Web server
sending information to using HTTP POST method, 374
sources of information generated by, 370–71

Web services
for building Web-accessible applications, 15
in Windows 2000, 24–25

wide area networks (WANs), 2

Windows 2000
building a distributed environment with, 2
building Web-accessible applications in, 24–25
clock synchronization, 100
controlling certificate trust in, 147–48
core security protocol in, 88
creating and managing certificates in, 128
CSPs included in, 135–36
directory services, importance in, 5–6
directory services included in, 34–35
distributed security services in, 83–88
distributed services in, 2
distributed transaction services in, 19–20
DNS in, 35–39
enterprise trust policy feature in, 148
group scopes in, 64–66
groups in, 64–66
installable components included in, 406–8
Kerberos as core security in, 162–63
Kerberos vs. SSL in, 152
managing distributed services in, 25–26
managing public key technology in, 133–51
mapping a non-Microsoft ticket into an account in, 114
Microsoft Certificate Services in, 128, 140–44
NTLM (NT LAN Manager) support by, 10
organization of domains in, 6–7
performing authorization in, 86–88
primary data access interfaces in, 205–6
secret key security in, 83–115
security protocols supported by, 10–14
software support for smart card drivers in, 121

David Chappell

David Chappell is Principal of Chappell & Associates (*www.chappellassoc.com*), an education, consulting, and analysis firm focused on enterprise software. David is a regular keynote speaker at conferences and in-house events, and his seminars on enterprise application technologies have been attended by thousands of developers, architects, and technical managers around the world. He has spoken at every major conference in the industry, including COMDEX, Microsoft's TechEd and Professional Developers Conference, Lotusphere, and various Gartner Group events. In his consulting practice, David writes white papers, provides custom research, performs competitive and strategic analysis, and assists end-user organizations in understanding and adopting new technologies. He is a columnist for *Application Development Trends*, and his articles have appeared in *IEEE Software, Microsoft Systems Journal, Business Communications Review,* and many other publications. David holds an M.S. in Computer Science and a B.S. in Economics, both from the University of Wisconsin-Madison.

The manuscript for this book was prepared and submitted to Microsoft Press in electronic form. Text files were prepared using Microsoft Word 2000. Pages were composed by Microsoft Press using Adobe PageMaker 6.52 for Windows, with text in Optima and display type in Optima Bold. Composed pages were delivered to the printer as electronic prepress files.

Cover Graphic Designer
Patrick Lanfear

Cover Illustrator
Todd Daman

Interior Graphic Artist
Rob Nance

Principal Compositor
Paula Gorelick

Indexer
C² Editorial Services

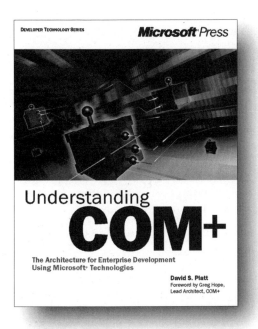